AF555926

CONTEMPORARY ISSUES IN DEVELOPMENT ECONOMICS
Models and Applications

CONTEMPORARY ISSUES IN DEVELOPMENT ECONOMICS

Models and Applications

Edited by

PRANKRISHNA PAL

REGAL PUBLICATIONS
New Delhi - 110 027

CONTEMPORARY ISSUES IN DEVELOPMENT ECONOMICS
Models and Applications

ISBN 978-81-8484-019-3

Typeset by
RAHUL COMPOSERS
358, Pocket-B, Phase-II, Sector-16 B, Dwarka, New Delhi - 110 075

Printed in India at
MAYUR ENTERPRISES
WZ Plot No. 3, Gujjar Market, Tihar Village, New Delhi - 110 018

Published by
REGAL PUBLICATIONS
F-159, Rajouri Garden, New Delhi - 110 027 • Phone : 45546396
E-mail : regalbookspub@yahoo.com

Contents

Introduction

The edited volume *"Contemporary Issues in Development Economics: Models and Applications"* is a product of a UGC sponsored seminar on "Contemporary Issues on Development Economics" held on March 8-9, 2007 at the Department of Economics, Rabindra Bharati University, Kolkata. A large number of delegates participated in the seminar and presented their papers. Out of those papers as good as 11 papers have been finally selected for the book. Another 7 papers have been specially invited from the distinguished scholars. In effect, the book contains a set of 18 papers. Thematically, these papers are arranged into 2 sections: I. Theoretical Issues, and II. Development Issues.

SECTION I

Debendra Narayan Bhattacharyya in his paper "Economic Modeling of Social Interaction: Norms, Networks and Trust" has built up a model in respect of norms, networks and trust and verified it among different groups of agents based on the field survey data in Kolkata. Trust, norms and networks are necessary for organizations to function well. Institutional changes ought to have consequences for network, trusts and norms independent of other factors. Rajendra Narayan Nag and Bhaskar Goswami in their paper "Sectoral Inter-Linkage in a Monetary Framework Under Flexible Exchange Rate Regime: A Post-WTO Perspective" have analysed the issues of intersectoral linkages under flexible exchange rate regime in terms of a model of two sectors, namely, industrial sector and agricultural sector. They have argued that the issue of industrial output expansion and employment generation would be best addressed by the policies that aimed at removing the supply side bottlenecks that a typical emerging transitional economy faces. In their paper "Is the Financial Market Efficient?" Diganta Mukherjee and Sankha Ghosh have built up a theoretical model of market efficiency. They have opined that the market is indeed efficient in the long-run. If the market has evolved in the long time, the price process can be used as a proxy for the value process. In his paper "Incidence of Child Labour and Trade Liberalization: Comments on Chaudhuri and Gupta (2004)" Arnab Ghosh has analyzed the impact of trade liberalization on the incidence of child labour in a two-sector general equilibrium framework. He has modified the theoretical model by Chaudhuri and Gupta and derived the aggregate supply function of child labour in order to establish the opposite result as obtained by Chaudhuri and Gupta. Rajlakshmi Mallick in her paper "Strategic Certification and Performance Related Pay (PRP) in Education" has also formulated a theoretical model to establish why PRP for teachers would show little concern towards rewarding teacher's assessment of student performance. She has made some policy prescriptions. Changes in the design of curriculum and teaching techniques requiring greater student involvement and teacher-student interaction are likely examples of policies belonging to this category. In their paper "Health, Income and Health Expenditure in Indian States: A Search for Causal Explanation", Sushil Kumar Haldar and Debaprasad Sarkar have built up a theoretical relationship between health status and income following the model developed by Hurd and Kapteyn and analysed this relationship in the Indian economy during 1980/81 to 2005-06. The long-run relationship among health status, income and health expenditure holds good for most of the socio-economically backward states like BIMARU States. They argued that more public spending on health is required in most of the BIMARU states in order to get rid of the health poverty trap. Sahana Roy Chowdhury in her paper "Outsourcing in a Model of Occupational Choice" has tried to explain the recently of rising skilled-unskilled wage gap in both North and South. Outsourcing of jobs to South by Northern firms has been modeled in an occupational choice framework. Any technological improvement in North would result in a rise in skilled-unskilled wage-gap in North and then a rise in the same in South *via* trade. In her paper "Immigration *vs.* Outsourcing: A Developing Country's View", Simontini Das has also made a comparative study between the immigration and the outsourcing process in the context developing country by using a simple general equilibrium framework. She has established an inverse relationship between immigration and outsourcing in a two-country framework.

SECTION II

Subrata Majumdar in his paper "Capability Based Approach and India's Poverty" has attempted to estimate the incidence of poverty for the major states in India by using Capability Measures of Poverty and argued that the poverty estimates obtained on the basis of Capability Measures are generally higher than those suggested by both the Planning Commission Expert Group and the NCAER Studies. In her paper "Gender Disparity in India: An Inter-State Analysis", Jaya Mukherjee has tried to highlight the extent of gender disparity in 15 major states in India by focusing on some important dimensions of human life like education, health and participation in economic activity. Gender disparity is found to be highly correlated with female literacy rate but not so strongly correlated with per capita income and female labour force participation rate. Dipa Mukherjee in her paper "Wages and Employment in India: The Post-Reform Dynamics" has analyzed the wage-employment scenario in India in the post-reform period. Embodied human resources like education, age and gender; and structural factors like location, social status, and regional economic condition are important factors in determining daily wages. She has made some policy prescriptions for creating more man-days of work and facilitating capacity building through education and skill information. Indrajit Bairagya in his paper "Sustainable Industrialization: A Case Study of Impact on Income and

Employment" has highlighted the impact of industrialization on income and employment through social cost benefit analysis. He has opined that industrialization is benefiting the local economy through direct employment and income generation and through other demand and supply side linkages on the one hand. On the other hand, because of land conversion and high pollution control these industries are affecting adversely agricultural productivity and hence, creating loss of employment and income in agriculture and across the local economy through linkages. Thus there is a trade-off between employment and income generation. In their paper "River and Government: A Case Study of Narmada" Raj Kumar Sen and Somnath Hazra have highlighted the role of Government, both at the central and the state levels, in the process of monitoring rivers as part of its activities like the use of water for irrigation, supply of drinking water, generation of hydro-power, flood control. They observed that the present policy of overall exploitation of environment including rivers is not sustainable. A basic change in the development paradigm is required to enforce the principle of "live and let live" effectively. Abdul Motin and Hiron Kumar Banerjee in their paper "Role of Micro Finance in Empowering Rural Poor in West-Bengal—A Case Study" have examined the role of the Self-Help Groups (SHGs) in the district of Bankura in West Bengal from the lender's point of view and from the borrower's viewpoint. They have observed that the SHGs have helped the participating rural poor in gaining empowerment. In his paper "Progress, Problems and Impact of Self-Help Groups in West Bengal: A Comparative Study" Subrata Kumar Roy has made a comparative study of Panchayet-led and Non-Governmental Organization (NGO)-led Self-Help Groups for highlighting the progress, problems and impact of SHGs in West Bengal with special reference to Purba and Paschim Midnapore districts. It is observed that the program of micro-finance through SHGs has been making rapid strides in both India and West Bengal. In his paper "Reforms and Growth in India and East Asian Countries: A Comparative Analysis", Prankrishna Pal has made a comparative study of the impact of economic reforms on the growth of output and the growth of merchandise exports and imports in India and East Asian Countries during 1990-2004. Avijit Mandal in his paper "Gravity Analysis of Indo-

ASEAN Trade Flows" has tried to analyze India's trade flows to ASEAN members using gravity analysis during 2000-04. Both export and import gravity equation has explained 90% of the variation in trade flows between India and ASEAN countries. India has tended to have more trade with those ASEAN countries, which were colonies sometime in history. In his paper "FDI in BRIC Economies: How Important?" Suvranshu Pan has discussed the role of FDI in BRIC Economies viz. Brazil, Russia, India and China. BRIC economies would be the leader in the world with their performance in respective fields. Like bricks of a solid wall, BRIC countries would be able to build up a concrete upstairs in the world market very soon.

I hope that the book will be appreciated by the readers and researchers alike interested in development Economics relating to different models and applications. I am thankful to the authors for their scholarly contributions. Without their co-operation, this book would not have come to light. Special thanks are due to Shri R.D.S. Bhatia of Regal Publications, New Delhi for taking personal initiative and interest in publishing this book in an elegant and meticulous manner.

Kolkata PRANKRISHNA PAL

List of Contributors

Abdul Motin, Sr. Gr. Lecturer in Economics, Ghatal R.S. Mahavidyalaya, Paschim Midnapore.

Arnab Ghosh, Lecturer in Economics, K.N. College, Berhampore, Murshidabad.

Avijit Mandal, Lecturer in Economics, A.B.N. Seal College, Cooch Bihar, W.B.

Bhaskar Goswami, Lecturer in Economics, M.U.C. Women's College, Burdwan.

Debaprasad Sarkar, Lecturer in Economics, Barrackpore R.S.N. College, Kolkata.

Debendra Narayan Bhattacharyya (Rtd.), Reader in Economics, D. Andrews College, Garia, Kolkata.

Diganta Mukherjee, Professor, ICFAI Business School, Kolkata.

Dipa Mukherjee, Sr. Lecturer in Economics, Narasinha Dutta College, Howrah.

Hiron Kumar Banerjee (Rtd.), Professor of Economics, Calcutta University.

Indrajit Bairagya, Research Fellow, Deptt. of Economics and Politics, Viswa Bharati University.

Jaya Mukherjee, Lecturer in Economics, St. Paul's C.M. College, Kolkata.

Prankrishna Pal, Reader in Economics, Rabindra Bharati University, Kolkata (Editor).

Raj Kumar Sen, Professor of Economics, Rabindra Bharati University, Kolkata.

Rajendra Narayan Nag, Sr. Lecturer in Economics, St. Xavier's College, Kolkata.

Rajlakshmi Mallick, Asst. Professor, NSHM Knowledge Campus, Kolkata.

Sahana Roy Chowdhury, Economic Research Unit, ISI, Kolkata.

Sankha Ghosh, J.P. Morgan Chase.

Simontini Das, Jr. Research Fellow, Jadavpur University, Kolkata.

Somnath Hazra, Research Associate, ICFAI Research Center, Kolkata.

Subrata Kumar Roy, Sr. Lecturer in Economics, Sabang Sajanikanta Mahavidyalaya, Paschim Midnapore.

Subrata Majumdar, M.Phil. Student, Economics Deptt., Calcutta University.

Sushil Kumar Haldar, Reader in Economics, Jadavpore University, Kolkata.

Suvranshu Pan, Lecturer in Economics, K.M.M. Mahavidyalaya, Purulia, W.B.

SECTION I

THEORETICAL ISSUES

Economic Modeling of Social Interaction : Norms, Networks and Trust

DEBENDRA NARAYAN BHATTACHARYYA

SECTION I

INTRODUCTION

Mainstream economics typically assumes that individual behavior is not directly influenced by the action of others. Every individual of course is only indirectly affected through relative prices and factor rewards. Sociologists and anthropologists repeatedly reminded economists (Granovetter, 1993) about the importance of culture, norms, and social structure in any form of social analysis, since these were essentially outcomes of interactions among social forces and such non-markets outcomes did in fact played dominant role in shaping variety of economic decisions. But economists till recently shied away deeply from viewing them closely and incorporating those social features into economic analysis. Further, social scientists in general, except of course economists, raised questions on whether exclusive reliance on rationality and selfishness were capable of explaining peoples actual economic behavior. They produced evidence (Platteean 1994a, 1994b; Plattner, 1989), that there were important identifiable conditions in which rationality assumption might led to empirically false predictions and generated wrong normative advice. In other words, many predictions that were based on purely selfish behavior appeared systematically wrong.

In an early response, economists reacted sharply and advanced at least two reasons: First, concepts like culture, norms, trust, social structure, etc. were not definable the way economics demanded them to be. All such concepts were found less precise in their meaning and connotations, and at the same time appeared less quantifiable—to be gainfully used by economic analysis to improve analysis, models and prediction of actual behaviors.

However, on the same question the recent staunch of the economists seems appreciably moderate (Bhattacharyya, 2004).[1] Many of them (Khalil *et. al.*, 1994) now convincingly admit the fact that culture, norms, trust, social and economic structure and the likes have had enormous and profound impact in determining social behavior of individuals. Unfortunately economists do not have handy tools to deal with such issues. For example, how well children treat their elderly parents is determined by what other children are doing (interdependence) and by the traditional way of treating parents of past generations (norms). Economics, some say actually lacks powerful techniques to deal adequately with some of the notions and features embedded in interpersonal relationships, as shown by this example (i.e., interdependence, norms reciprocity, etc.).

In fact, it is now widely accepted that a large variety of activities and behavior of many individuals in respect to consumption and others are strongly influenced by their respective peer groups. Examples abound and what transpires is that social influences particularly through the forms of culture, norms, trust, social structure, etc. on behavior are common and even pervasive. What is still seriously lacking in economics is an explicit recognition and admittance of these mutual interactions and relationships between social forces and market behavior in exploring and determining economic performances/outcome (Bhattacharyya, 2004).

SECTION II

OBJECTIVES, LITERATURE REVIEW AND HYPOTHESES

One of the major objectives of our study is to provide a direction to the analysis of the situation where prices, markets and important social institutions are present in an interactive and complex relation. The reason is that, till recently, with few exceptions social forces were either ignored or left to lurk in the background, as a part of general environment. If social forces were found changing, then the typical way used to capture it was to make a shift in the utility function only.

This approach therefore simply dumped social environment outside the purview of economics again by treating it as purely exogenous. Accordingly, economic policies were expected: not to have any direct impact to change the social environment. Now departing from this orthodoxy is not an easy task. In fact little progress has been made so far in economics in this direction except of course some major and pioneering contributions and advancement offered by Becker (1993, 2000), Schelling (1978), Veblen (1934), Coalman (1990) and Sen (2000), and a few others. What differentiate these new approaches from that of the sociologists are that, as economists, we never ignore prices, rather always adhere to the fact that prices are a fundamental part of our analysis which Backer designated as social multiplier on behavior (Backer, 1996).[2]

What is being suggested here at an elementary level, in this paper is that, social environment has to be incorporated as arguments in the utility function along with goods and services, to see, how changes in its value causes change in utility and hence choice. Social environment here is assumed to encapsulate, norms, trust, networks, etc. Following Backer (Backer, *et. al.* 1998) we consider an utility function of the form:

$$U = U(X_1, X_2, E)$$

where X_1, X_2 are goods and services of all kinds and E represents the influences on utility generated through social environment. In conventional method a change in E would simply shifted the U-function. But in this paper we suggest a departure from this tradition. In our approach E being an argument of U-function, implies that a change in its value would affect the level of utility even when there is an exogenous (not policy induced) change in E. The reason is that the effects at change in E are likely to be transmitted through the changes in the marginal utilities of other goods, X_1 and X_2.

However, even in this modified approach changes in E occurs exogenously. Vie further propose to extend the idea that changes in social environment E, does also occur endogenously and economic modeling is capable of capturing that. This means, we advance the idea that social environment and relations could be largely explained and determined within economics by economic reasoning, i.e. some social environments are actually an endogenous outcome of economic process.

In this context two types of attempts have been documented in the literature in making effort to endogenizing social environment.

The first is obviously that of Becker (Becker *et. al.*, 2000), who pioneered in using optimizing approach i.e. rational choice analysis (utility maximization and equilibrium behavior in the groups) in apparently non-economic behavior, such as marriage. But the second approach is highly critical of the orthodoxy, as it views economics mostly pursuing answers in complete abstraction from all human values.[3]

However, there is no denying the fact that justification of ends and means require serious ethical, moral and other social valuations, and this has drawn attention of some economists nowadays (Aron, 1994, Baeker, 1976). The research in this direction has been perceived by many to be quite productive in generating useful answers to a large number of economic questions. Homoeconomicus by virtue of its self-interest and rationality characters preclude the possibility of inducting normative preferences which in fact exist in abundance in social behavior (Etzioni, 1998).

In this study we hypothesize that there are important identifiable conditions in which rationality assumption lead to empirically wrong predictions and generate wrong normative policy advice. Such situations often arise when it is impossible to enforce agreements completely—which means at least one party will not meet its obligations, which induce other parties not to meet their obligations. If all parties violate their respective obligations beforehand (which could be known from an experimental game), it does not mean that the contracts be done not at all (as rationality suggests),—although it involves many efficiency loss. If instead we assume that people do not always fully exploit their opportunities to violate agreements at the expense of others, then it is rational to enter agreement that is not fully enforceable. This is what we believe is the rule rather than exception. Furthermore, we emphasize, and hypothesize that the deviations in actual behavior from the standard predictions of rationality are largely due to the presence of what Backer called social environment E or its current and popular version or nickname "Social Capital". For purpose of illustration and testing of the above hypotheses, three important components of social capital viz., norms, networks and trusts have been considered separately in this paper.

SECTION III

NORMS

Social norms have been conceived and interpreted differently in the literature (Mansbridge, 1988). The most widely accepted interpretation suggests that norms constraints rational behaviors (North, 1990) an individual does not take a particular line of action because a social norm forbids her to do so. In this interpretation therefore, norms are seen as a scapegoat for behavior we cannot explain on the plea that, people be have as they do because they do so. Nothing explains why people observe the moral constraints that are imposed upon them (Basu, 2000).[4]

The Model

Let there of two groups of population A and B. Each group consists a finite number (possibly smaller) number of members. Every individual member of both the groups behaves voluntarily. The distinguishing features of the two groups are that A is richer in terms of income and wealth than B and number of members in A is smaller then that of B. Relative richness of A means that it can spend more resources collectively to promote the interests of its members, while smallness of A enables it to overcome the tendency of its members to free ride on the efforts of other members (it follows from the outcome of a standard game of tight network). It is also assumed that interests of A and B conflicts implying thereby that promotion of interest of A generally harms B's interest.

The community of the two groups A and B also has various institutions (e.g., school, colleges, religious institutions, etc.) which preach various norms and values relating to social behaviors and interactions? However A has the capacity to influence these institutions to promote those norms and values which serve the interests of its members. Affiliation to such institutions by members of the groups is assumed to be completely voluntary. Accordingly whoever joins such institution surely believes that she gains from doing so.

However, B will not volunteer to attend such institution to acquire norms promoted by A as that would lead to a fall in utility levels of B, since interests of A and B are conflicting, except in situations when B would be otherwise over compensated.

Let us now develop conditions under which B will find it attractive to join institution to acquire norms and values promoted by A through such institution. For this, we assume that A subsidizes heavily institutions that promote norms favorable to its members.

Under this condition 13 would acquire norms from their institution although it lowers the utility of B. To demonstrate this behavior, we start with a utility function of B:

$$U^B = U^B(q, N, Z) \quad \ldots\ldots (1)$$

where 'q' represents private goods, received from participating the institutions (e.g. support during crisis, learning to read and write, etc.), N are norms promoted by this institutions, and Z are other goods and services.

By assumption $\delta U^B/\delta N < 0$. But B must absorb N to get the q's produced by the institution. The logic is analogous to the way consumers absorb advertising to get the TV programmers supported by advertisers. Now when A subsidizes the production of 'q', it lowers the cost of q to B say by H (N). Let the monetary equivalent of loss to B due to absorbing N norms equals F (N). In this situation B would not be made worse off by participating institutions that produce N norms if :

$$H(N) - F(N) \geq 0 \qquad \text{..... (2)}$$

The objective of A is to minimize subsidy H for a given value of N such that B participates the institutions. Hence one equilibrium condition would be :

$$H(N) = F(N) \qquad \text{..... (3)}$$

Further, let W (N) be the cost of producing N. Then H (N) + W (N) would be the expenditure of A in order to involve B to accept N. Now, A would be willing to spend this much on N provided it gains at least as much. Therefore, an equilibrium condition for A is :

$$\pi(N) \geq H(N) + W(N) \qquad \text{..... (4)}$$

where π (N) is the gain of A from N. Then equation (3) can be written a :

$$\pi(N) \geq L(N) + W(N) \qquad \text{..... (5)}$$

Equation (5) shows that the gain to A must exceed the loss to B by enough to cover the cost, W of producing norms N favorable to A. In this situation no one is worse-off when these norms become part of both the group's preferences since B voluntarily accepts A as part of these preferences. In this arrangement B receives sufficient compensation for absorbing N to make the acceptance worthwhile, and A would not promote N unless A feels better off or at least no worse-off.

This result is expected since mutual benefit is the property of any voluntary trade and here B voluntarily accepts these norms. This model simply shows that institutions produce those norms that are favorable to A.

This is simply because only A is assumed to be able to act collectively. In this situation institutions do not produce norms those are unfavorable to A but favorable to B, so long as B fails to act collectively as a group.

In so far as the role of habit in the formation of norms is concerned, the literature provides a few formal models explaining the process of how habits lead to the production and sustenance of norms. In essence, habits provide an anchor by strengthening the forces making for persistence in behavior. The reason is that habitual behavior encourages a continuation of past behavior since habits depend on the behavior of past "selves". Backer (1996) developed a framework to show how habitual behavior through habit capital produces different norms of behavior. It took into account a utility function of the following form :

$$U^j = U\ (x^j,\ y^j,\ H^j)$$

Where H^j is habit capital, x and y are goods and services of all kinds consumed by j. If x is habitual; an increase in past consumption of x by j would increase H^j. Whether this would raise the present consumption of x by forward looking individuals depends on the effect of H on both present marginal utilities of x and future stock of H. Norms are also articulated as a habit and carried out without calculations. Habits are hard to identify in empirical analysis. However some norms are more consciously adhered to and are the basis of building personalized trust. In such cases they are based on the need for the social consensus that can enforce sanctions on norms violators and thereby allow agents to trust each other. These sanctions or motivations came in the form of shame and obligation. Individuals are pressured into keeping to norms by those around them.

This can be done by withdrawal of co-operation, disapproval and attaching social stigma to norm-breakers. Although its applicability is limited only to cases in which those involved in proximity or work closely together is admitted. However it seems that there are norms and these can be defined more specifically if the scale of analysis is reduced. Moreover norms vary between localities, between individuals and change as a relationship builds up and friendship involved.

Again, it is an important part of social capital that is drawn on by actors when making decisions on whether to trust an individual. Norms of reciprocity can be seen to be both calculative when part of building a working relationship and also more generalized. There are unanswered questions however, whether there are "pervasive" norms of generalized morality, that shape whole markets or societies, or whether each relationship has to be considered in its own changing context. There is a danger of over socialized or deterministic views that attribute economic success or failure to cultural activities while ignoring the role of agency and the interplay of actors with different power relations.

There are different and opposite views about the relation of incentive based market institutions to values (North, 1990). One version finds capitalism as dependent upon a stock of social capital—trust, norms of co-operation and honesty and other prosocial values—that are cultivated by non-market institutions, such as families, neighborhoods, religious institutions and places, and other communities. Capitalist firms freely make use of the social stock without replenishing it, and undermine the very institutions that are responsible for society's social capital. In this version therefore free markets are responsible for moral decline, anomie and loneliness and eat away at their own foundations. (Schotter, 1981).

The second version argues that capitalism as expanding the scope of co-operation and trust by enabling people to reap gains from trade worldwide, bridging parochial divisions of nationality religion and ethnicity. Capitalism in this view is an engine of cosmopolitanism cooling socially dangerous passions such as religious fanaticism, and overcoming xenophobia. The impersonality anonymity and openness of markets to all corners is favorably contrasted with social orders in which people are tightly constrained by parochial connections and loyalties of families' ethnicity, and neighborhood.[5]

A Scrutiny of the two versions shows that markets cannot function efficiently on the basis of self-interest alone. Moreover, markets are efficient only to the extent that participants accept the rule of the game. Once people extend self-interested reasoning to consider whether they should lie, cheat, and steal, market transactions becomes very costly or breakdown. Herein lies the importance of dependency of market on social norms and values.

SECTION IV

NETWORK

Although most network theories are static, the dynamics of inter-individuals or groups networks are an almost natural object of study for at least two prominent theoretical perspectives: evolutionary and co-evolutionary approaches on the one hand and interventionist approaches subscribing to the idea of Trans-organizational development, on the other. The former contribute to a better understanding of developmental process over time, especially if they acknowledge the importance of the co-evolution of networks and their social context (e.g., NGO, industry, etc.). By contrast, the latter deliver several useful instruments and procedures to purposefully intervene in ongoing network process, for example, by measuring the collaborative climate (as perceived by all network members) and feeding back the data in order to accelerate the development of the network climate.

However, both approaches, though for different reasons, fall short of an adequate conceptualization of the interplay of action and structure. Whereas evolutionary theory lacks an explicit concept of agency, interventionist approaches over emphasize the possibilities of agency while neglecting structures. However, advanced network theories have started attempting to offer a more elaborated understanding of the complex interplay between network action and network structure (Goyal, 1996).

Apart from these two major strands of dynamic network theory, there are quite a few contributions that cannot easily be located within one of these, but nevertheless devote significant attention to the network dynamics. First, Ring and Vande Ven (1994) propose a process model in which network evolution consists of a sequence of negotiations, commitment and execution stages.

Each of the stages comprises a number of interactions, the outcomes of which are assessed in terms of efficiency and equity. Apart from emphasizing the importance of reacting, not only efficient outcomes, but also fair dealings; the model highlights the necessity of balancing formal and informal processes which, in practice, can easily lead to tensions and contradictions hindering smooth network development or even leading to network failure.

Another dynamic model of Doz (1996) emphasized the initial conditions as well as learning process for network development.

Initial conditions also influence a number of critical subsequent learning processes. As partners learn from their interactions in joint or coordinated activities, they re-evaluate the alliance by monitoring it for efficiency, as well as each other for equity and adaptability. The path from re-evaluation to re-adjustment is determined by the partners' willingness to keep committing to the relationship, in itself dependent on the quality of the relationship.

From all these dynamic perspectives the development of interpersonal network is conceived not only as an outcome of intentional action, but also of unintended consequences of this very action. This becomes particularly explicit from interpersonal networks which, above all, emphasizes the recursive interplay between network actions and network payoff in a continuous process of non-linear dynamics and thus raises questions about equilibrium and punctuated equilibrium models of change. Our model is an attempt in that direction.

Jackson and Watts (2002) developed a dynamic model in which individuals were assumed to act myopically which meant that their decisions were guided completely by current payoffs, although the process of network formation takes place over real time. Our model is a departure from these models of network formation in the sense that we instead assume that agents behave in a farsighted manner and take into account the intertemporal repercussions of their own decisions. To formalize this aspect in our model, we just pickup at random a pair of individual who are assumed to be active at the starting period, and each agent has unilateral domains of action. These are the network links that each of the agents has with other agents. Further, the model assumes that agents unilaterally can destroy links and can act together on an equally natural bilateral domains, i.e., link formation must be a joint decision.

The Model

Considers a community of N members each with random endowments of capacity to take decisions and act voluntarily at any given point of time. A set of two players (i, j) are chosen at random from them assigning each with equal probability. Each player has some existing links, i.e., social relationships with other members of the community and each can voluntarily sever such links with other members and also can form new link between them if any such relation did not exists between them initially.

Creation or severance of links bilaterally or unilaterally generates a network or graph 'g' defined over the number of players involved in the game. When this type of graph just shows that i and j are somehow linked and these links are reciprocal, we then get a new undirected graph (g + ij). Further, a component of a network 'g' is a subset c, such that no $i \in C$ is linked outside c and such that every i and j in c are directly or indirectly linked. Thus in our framework, there are two components of a strategy in force: unilateral which involves link severance and bilateral, which involves link creation and will generally be correlated across the relevant actors. Throughout, we will assume that players follow Markov Strategies; i.e., their actions will be presumed to depend only on the existing payoff-relevant state. These actions create a new graph and then one-period payoffs are received according to the given allocation rule—which means the rule that specifies the one-period payoffs to each player i for every conceivable network and value or total worth of players in c. The current period then ends and the whole process being again and repeat continuously for infinite number of times.

Two specific features—the correlation and independent of strategies need careful specifications. Suppose that two individuals 'partially co-operate' in setting a bilateral link, but also take independent actions as they do when link is severed. Then all matters related to the bilateral link between i and j are commonly observed by the two players and can therefore serve as correlation devices: either player can condition his other unilateral actions on the fate of this link. For instance, when a 'bilateral deviation' occurs from some ongoing prescribed strategy, both players will be aware of this and can condition their independent actions on such deviation. In contrast, a unilateral deviation by i that breaks links other than the one with j cannot be used as a conditioning device by j.

This suggests that the situation is formally equivalent to one in which at any date, actions pertaining to ij link are taken 'first' and these are followed by unilateral actions pertaining to all other existing links. Let us make this approach more formal.

Let us define a 'principal state' as a collection s = (g, ij), where g is the historically given graph and ij is the chosen active pair. Further, an intermediate state is defined as a collection s = (g, ij, z), where g and ij are as before, and z is a variable which takes the value 0 if the pair ij is not linked and the value 1 if ij is linked.

An intermediate state does not physically exist; it is a conceptual half way point for defining unilateral actions. In contrast, a principal state physically exists at the start of a period.

When there is no need for a distinction, we shall simply use the same notation 'state' denote either of the two varieties. For any intermediate state s = (g, ij, z) we define D_i (s) ≡ {k≠j | ik €g}, and likewise define D_j (s). These are the sets of existing linkages to i, but never counting j. As already pointed out, a bilateral action to create or maintain the link between an action pair is not undone at the intermediate state. This does not mean that unilateral breaking of an $_i$j link is not permitted; it certainly is but only at the principal state. Put another way, such actions are commonly experienced and can serve as co-relating devises for actions on the "unilateral domains" D_i (s) and D_j (s).

Moreover, note that by assumption, i and j can break links on their unilateral domains; no links other than those pertaining to the active pair can be created during the period.

Formally, then, (mixed) actions may be described as follows. At any principal state s with active pair ij it is simply › probability μ (s) = q of bilateral linkage between i and j. At any ir.'ermediate stage s with active pair ij it is a collection μ (s) Ï {vi, vj }, where for each k = i, j, v_k is a probability measure defined over all subsets (including the empty subsets) of D_k (s). We will let μ stand for the entire profile of μ (s)'s over all states (notice that μ (s) has a different interpretation depending on what sort of state we are looking at), and refer to μ as a strategy profile.

A strategy profile precipitates—for each states s, principal or intermediate—some probability measure λ_s over the feasible set F (s) of future networks starting from s.

In particular, a Markov process is induced on the set S of Principal States: at any state s, λ_s describes the movement to a new network and the given random choice of active players moves the system to a new active pair.

The process creates values for each player. Assuming that the a_k's are vN-M payoffs, we can write—for every state s with active pair ij—the overall payoff to any person k (under the strategy profile μ) as the unique solution to the functional equation

$$V_k(s,\mu) = \sum_{g' \in F(s)} \lambda_s(g')[a_i(g') + \delta_i \sum_{i'j'} \pi(i'j') V_k(s',\mu)]$$

where $\delta_i \in (0, 1)$ is the discount factor of agent is i, λ_s is the probability over *F*(*s*) associated with μ, π (i' j') is the probability that a pair i' j' will be active "tomorrow", and s' stands for the principal state (*g*', *k*' *l*'). (Note that V_k is well-defined on both principal and intermediate states.]

We will also find it convenient to denote $V_k(s, \mu)$ as the (expected) payoff to *k*, at a given network g. This is given by

$$V_k(g',\mu) = \frac{2}{n(n-1)} \sum_{ij \in lxl} V_k((g,ij),\mu)$$

Equilibrium

Loosely speaking, an equilibrium process of network formation is a strategy profile, μ' with the property that there is no active pair at any state s which can benefit either unilaterally or bilaterally—by departing from μ (s). The benefit is evaluated according to the value junction introduced above. The remainder of this section contains a precise formulation of this idea. Before the formalities are introduced, however, note the following points:

1. Profitable deviations are not necessary myopic: individuals take the ongoing process as given and evaluate the entire stream of consequences arising from a single action. One can imitate perfectly myopic behavior by taking the discount factor to zero, and perfect farsightedness by taking the opposite limit.
2. Network formation and payoffs occur together. There is no "waiting" in the model until some "stable" network is formed, following which payoffs are assigned. Indeed, our definition permits cycles and continued flux in the network, and there is no difficulty at all in evaluating overall payoffs.

Now for a precise account. Fix some ongoing strategy profile μ and an intermediate stage s with active pair *ij*.

A *unilateral move for i* at *s* (to be sometimes referred to as an i-unilateral move at s when it's necessary to keep track of th relevant agent) is simply a collection μ' (*s*) = {v'_i, v'_j}, where th *j*th component cannot be altered from that of μ' (*s*). (Likewise for *j*)..Given a principal state (*s*) a bilateral move for the active pair *ij* is a new probability μ' (s) of *ij*-linkage.

A *unilateral* move for *i* at the principal state s is also a new probability of *ij*-linkage, but it "takes effect" only if the *ij*-linkage is 'present in the historically given graph. That is, *i* can unilaterally decide to alter the probability of the *ij*-linkage provided *i* and *j* are already linked together.

In words, unilateral moves for an agent can either destroy *ij*-linkage and/or other existing linkages on that agent's unilateral domain. Of course, an i-unilateral move cannot prescribe changes on j's unilateral domain. A bilateral move can *only* create ij-linkage (everything else belongs to the unilateral domains). Now, in part this compartmentalization is a matter of semantics. For instance, suppose that at some principal state s = (g, ij), ij is unlinked *for sure*, that is, $q(s) = 0$. So the intermediate state s′ = (g, ij, 1) will never happen. Nevertheless, the actions μ (s′)″ = (v_i, v_j) are still specified, even though they don't kick in under μ. Now if a bilateral move or "deviation" links ij, the play will generally change on other fronts as well, as the unilateral action pairs "switch" from m (g, ij, 0) to μ (g, ij, 1). More on these matters below.

Now, fix some profile μ and state s (principal or intermediate). For any μ' (s) and for each player k, define.

$$V_k(s,\mu,\mu'(s)) \equiv \sum_{g'\in F(s)} \lambda_s'(g')[a_k(g')+\delta_i$$

$$\sum_{i'j'}\pi(i'j')V_k(s',\mu\mu'(s))] \qquad \ldots\ldots (3)$$

where s′ is the principal state (g', i' j'). For an intermediate state s with active pair ij, and for some $k = i, j$, say that a k-unilateral move μ' (s) is profitable if

$$V_k(s\ \mu\ \mu'(s)) > V_k(s,\ \mu\ \mu'),\ (s) \qquad \ldots\ldots (4)$$

Likewise, for a principal state s with active pair ij, say that a bilateral move μ' (s) is *profitable* if

$$V_i(s\ \mu\ \mu'(s)) > V_i(s,\ \mu),\ \text{and}\ V_j(s,\ \mu\ \mu'(s)) > V_j(s,\ \mu) \qquad \ldots. (5)$$

A strategy profile μ is and equilibrium if at no s is a unilateral or bilateral move *profitable*.

Notice how our description of equilibrium subsumes a rationality requirement akin to perfection. Equilibrium must be immune to all profitable moves, including those starting from intermediate 'states that may never be reached.

SECTION V

ROLE OF TRUST

Trust, often called a moral resource (Woolcock, 1988) is an integral part of Social Capital (SC). There is no universal definition of the concept 'trust'. It has been defined and understood in different ways in the SC literature (Misztal, 1996).

The literary meaning of trust is "a form of belief in the reliability, truth or strength of a person; a confident expectation, and a reliance on the truth of a statement without examination.

The etymological significance of the term thus implies reliance on or confidence in some events, process or person. Accordingly, it can be stated that a person exhibits trust if he/she believes that another actor (person, group or institution) is willing and able to act in the best interest of this person, even if there is no possibility to monitoring the other actor's intentions or actions, and even if the other actor can use the situation to harm the person.[6]

Jacobsen (1999) identified four characteristics in the above definition of trust: and is used in (i) a situation with imperfect information and therefore uncertainty, (ii) a situation including a risk, for at least one of the actors in the relationship, (iii) the belief that another actor is willing to act on another's behalf, i.e. trust in institutions, and (iv) a belief that another actor is capable of acting on another's behalf, i.e., trust in competence. In literature, the concept however, has been treated mostly as one dimension of interpersonal relationships which precludes opportunistic cheating of the agreement. Another feature of trust is that it suffers from identification problem. Again many SCs are outcomes of motivation and in many instances, they conflict with 'homoeconomicus'—self-interest motive. However, care should be taken in showing such conflicts. In many instances, behavior which appears to be otherwise in one shot game may appear rational in conventional sense in repeated games. Under these circumstances, empirical analysis becomes somewhat doubtful. Finally, trust becomes effective to address situations and solve problems when the nature of social interactions or the goods and services being transacted makes contracting highly incomplete or costly.

Such situations are plenty and more so in LDCs, when dispersed individuals private information becomes unavailable to apply reword or punishment.

As to the sources of trust, the so-called rational approach points out that the accumulation of trust is a result of repeated transactions between actors under conditions of uncertainty (Williamson, 1988). When someone observes that another actor acts to his or her benefit, he/she will increase the probability that this actor will also act in a beneficial way in the future.[7]

Lyon (2000) pointed out that trust could arise from both generalized norms of morality and more personalized sources embedded in social networks. He argues that agents do not always aim to maximize the profit, but may consider the minimizing the risk and maximizing the access through developing personal relationship with other agents. This is especially important in a situation characterized by very imperfect information and a lack of effective legal mechanism and it is central to any market transaction, when agents are not willing to rely on norms or institutional arrangements alone. The risk of other agents being opportunistic cannot be controlled by legal means without prohibitively high transaction cost in terms of monitoring contracts. In fact many transactions are so complex that law cannot possibly cover all contingent circumstances and in many countries there is no formal system of contracts anyway. Trust plays a major role in reducing such transaction costs, especially in situations of complex long distance trade, for example, through reducing the need for monitoring and information.[8]

The employment of trust depends on the probability that other agents will behave in a way that is expected. Granovetter (1993) had pointed out that an action, based on trust, can therefore be described as calculation, although there is a debate over the extent to which agents act under rational choice or calculation and the extent to which their actions are embedded structure of social relations. However, one can see trust as a way of reducing the complexity that comes from freedom of others and trust can make calculations easier or not even necessary. Decisions on whether to trust are not only based on calculations that consider information on other agents and enforceable sanctions. There is non-calculative side as well, in that, habits allow agents to reduce the number of variables by assuming away some of the risk and thereby making calculations possible.

Co-operative and trusting relationships can also be conceptualized as contracts that rely to differing extent on information on reputations, sanctions and moral norms.

The cost of getting information through networks is a major part of the transaction cost in deciding whether to cooperate. This information can be collected through links to networks and through previous interactions, which can allow the parties to know what to expect. Available sanctions in this context include the threat of stopping a contract and loosing future benefits; the threat of damage that can be done to an agent's reputation through bad reports; and social pressure.

Sanctions can also come from more formal institutions, either created by the state or associations/groups of civil society which may create obligations for agents. Obligations toward cooperation and trustfulness can also come through moral and social pressure and are based around common norms most notably, that or reciprocity.

Trust, we therefore mean an inductively derived empirical belief that people have about each others' behavior. For example, in an organization, when workers trust each other, they trust that if they pay their part in high effort level others will as well. Trust then becomes a common shared belief. From this we can speak of two kinds of trusts: The first is believing some thing about others and the second is behaving as if you believed this. On the basis of this empirically viable meaning of trust we develop a very simple model based on trust and report some tentative empirical results in support of our hypotheses below.

The model

Economists and social psychologists have struggled long and hard in an effort to understand the characteristics of situations in which workers will act cooperatively in the working place instead of shirk. Like all public goods problem, the temptation to free ride on the 'efforts of others in many times too tempting for workers and once shirking begins, it snowballs through the organizations. But, such low effort outcomes need not and do not always occur. The puzzle for us to unravel is why, in some organizations, are groups successful in selecting the high effort equilibrium while in others shirking is commonly established norm? The answer probably lies in the match between some norms and the characteristics of the incentive program imposed on the workers.

In other words, the common answer world is the incentive to pay for work. However, but economists are not likely to accept it. They feel that people work well or badly in organization largely for some reason, which is for personal benefits.

In what follows we outline our main arguments in a sketchy manner. We start with an example of labor contract. However, the arguments underlie this example is perfectly general in similar context.

Suppose that a firm stipulates a contract which specifies a wage 'w' and a required effort level 'e'.

The firm can enforce to elicit effort level "e_0" atmost from selfish and rational workers. This means that, when $e>e_0$ a worker who reduces effort level below e can increase his net utility. Therefore, a rational profit maximizing firm who faces a selfish and rational worker cannot enforce $e>e_0$. Our question is, can the existence of trust/reciprocity help the firm to elicit effort levels above e_0. By reciprocity/trust here we mean that people respond to kind acts with kind behavior and if they are treated badly, they try to strike back. Moreover, they are willing to engage in such reciprocal behavior even if it is costly for them. We assume that, kinds and standard of behavior are determined by history or by behavior in other similar relations and institutional environment.

Again, once the firm offers contract (w, e) and workers choose actual effort level e with ($e_0<e$), then a profit maximizing firm may accept the scheme of reword and punishment but if it finds reword and punishment too costly to administer then, the firm will not reword or punish.

But now, say, the firm is motivated by reciprocity/trust consideration. Then it may well reword, when "$e_0> e$" and punish when "$e_0<e$", because of the above reasons. Moreover, contractual agreements usually have some normative force.

Since the worker when provide $e=e_0$, even though $e_0<e$ is in her selfish interest, it is perceived by both parties as a kind of obligation. In worker's perception the obligation is stronger, therefore higher the rent implied higher effort level. Similarly, when some one violates the moralistic obligation the firm may punish him. Similarly, over fulfilment of an obligation may well trigger sympathy and hence a reword.

Empirical Results

At this stage, we cite some data and tentative results, relevant in this context, from the records of one of our field survey on a related research project "Ethics and Economics", to highlight how trust operates among the following group of agents: (1) Services done by maid servants to the households in the city of Calcutta, (2) Vegetable trader's employment of workers for procurement, and (3) Lending and Repayment nature in informal credit market, and the resulting outcomes of trusting behavior.

The survey was conducted in the city of Kolkata in West Bengal, India, in the year 2004. One common point of investigation was to examine the level of Trust, Norms and "Networks" present in the daily transactions of the respondents. For all three categories, the sample size was sixty (60) each. We developed a format in accordance to the spirit of the above model whereby we devised techniques to calculate scores of performance of every respondent in each group with respect to trust and norms and reciprocity.

Our results show that the maid servants engaged by households in Kolkata scored highest points in maintaining trust, norms and network. 66% of the respondents scored between 0.73 to 0.89 in (0, 1) scale, irrespective of their educational and income status. The results for other two groups for the same percentage position i.e., 66% were between 0.51 to 0.68, and 0.38 to 0.53. The results clearly exhibit the ranking of the three categories of respondents across three different activities. Trusting behavior was remarkably found strong among the maid servants employed by many city dwellers. The effects of incentives were also found remarkably higher for this group (and also incentive elasticity of trust found much above unity). From this elementary (also crude at this stage of our analysis) results, we repeat our hypothesis as indicated in the introduction that the performance of workers on the job is influenced not only by the incentive properties of the incentive mechanism they are functioning under, but also by the norms of trust and the net work they have developed with their fellow workers.

Surely a fuller form of analysis of the relationships among these concepts has yet to be carried out and developed and that remains our current research agenda.

SECTION VI

CONCLUSIONS

Trust, norms and networks are necessary for organizations to function well both internally and in their relations with each other. If trust is a good and if we want to promote it, what exactly do we want to promote?

If we want to promote trust in a society or in organizations, either as a belief or as a disposition then we need to know more precisely what kind of trust "believing something about others", or "behaving as if you believed this", we want to promote. Because different kinds of trust corresponds to different beliefs about behavior of others.

Here probably comes the role of institutions. It is said that institutions have an important effect on trust and trustworthiness. Under certain circumstance which we take to be sets of rules may have quite a wide reaching effect; many forms of apparently diffused trust do rely in the end on actors' interest, which may be substantially affected by institutions. Thus institutional change ought to have consequences for network, trust and norms independent of other factors.

NOTES

1. See Bhattacharyya (2004), The three inter-related issues of norms, networks and trust have been dealt with in detail.
2. Actually Backer is the pathfinder in this new direction of research. His contribution "The Economic Approach to Human Behaviour" (1976), paved the way of looking into new areas hitherto neglected by

mainstream economists. Even in dealing with non-conventional areas. Becker clung strongly with optimizing approach.
This however created resentment and clutter that led to the formulation of alternative approaches to treat such issues. For details, see several excellent articles in Avner Ben and L. Puttennan (1988).

3. See Becker and Kalvin's recent book (2004), for discussion.
4. Much of the interest in this area has been fuelled by Robert Putnam's (1993), book 'Making Democracy Work'. Critiques of Putnam, point out that the reasons for differences between north and south Italy can also be ascribed to different explanations based on social relations and the semi colonial status of the south of Italy or the role of the state in the development of civil society. He give the example of ghetto areas in the United States where there is much social capital but no assets attainable through it to allow participants to rise above their poverty.
In this case it is necessary to differentiate between the types of social capital. It is questionable whether the term "capital" can be used if it increases the more it is used.
Harris and Renzio (1997), states that it is capital because it raises incomes; it is also similar to financial capital as it can be invested profitably, but others claim that capital should have an opportunity cost. While this can be the case when people deliberately create social capital, it is not the case when it is an inherited endowment (See Woolcock, 1998, note 21).
5. Here by social norm we mean social convention which are external to the individual actor and do not rest on any perception of justice and injustice, but we believe that moral norms do involve these deeper considerations and is closer to the concept of value which we suppose some kinds of normative commitment which are internal to our actor.
6. The concept of trust has been ignored in most economic research since, under the assumptions of conditions of perfect competition, the issue of trust does not arise since links between agents are not seen to be affected by interpersonal behavioral traits and they do not have the opportunity for dishonest behaviour, Platteau, 1994a, p. 541.
7. Humphrey and Schmitz make the distinction between generalized and selective trust, where generalized trust includes both generalized morality and what Zucker (1986) refers to as institutional-based forms of trust.
Coleman distinguishes between forms of social capital that are used by all members of a group created and destroyed as a by-product of other activities, and also other forms of social capital that are created by agents for their own benefit (Coleman, 1990, p. 317).
8. Axelrod's work on Prisoners' Dilemma shows that it is rational to defect when there is imperfect information about the other player. The optimal strategy is tit-for-tat where the first player co-operates to start with then on subsequent games follows what the other player did on the previous game (Axelrod, 1984).
This adaptive behaviour works when the number of games is indefinite. For this to arise, there is a need or generalised trust (or altruism) in the first move. Prisoner Dilemma however, is based on the assumption that individual action is only for the strict defense of the individuals own

interest. There is also no discussion on how the rules emerge and the process of how individuals learn.

References

Ackerlof, G.A. and Kranton, R.E. (1999): "Economic and Identity", QJE.

Avner Ben-Ner and L. Puttennan (ed.). (1988): *"Economics, Values and Organization"*, Cup .

Backer, G.S. (1976): "The Economic Approach to Human Behaviour," University of Chicago Press.

———, (1994): "A Theory of Social Interactions", IPE, 82, (Nov.-Dec.), 1063-93.

Basu, K. (2000): Prelude to Political Economy. OUP.

Basu, K. (1989): "A Theory of Association: Social Status, Prices and Market". OUP 41, pp. 653-7.

Becker, G. (1993): Nobel Lecture: The Economic Way of Looking Behaviour.

Becker, *et. al.* (2000): Social Economics. HUP. 2000

(1996): "Notes on Evalution to Rationality and Noons", *Journal Institutional and Theoretical Economics*, 152: 739-49.

Behn, M. (1995): "The Big Questions of Public Management", *Public Administration Review*, 55. 313-24.

Bhattacharyya, D. (2004): "Institutions, Social Capital and Economics", Mimeo, Department of Philosophy, Jadavpur University, Calcutta.

Blomquist, K. (1997): "The Many Faces of Trust". *Scandanavian Journal of Management*, 13(2). 271-86.

Bowles, S. and Gintis, H. (1998): "The Moral Economy of Community: Structured Populations and the Evolution of Prosocial Norms", *Evolution and Human Behavior*, Vol. 19(1) (January), pp. 3-25.

Butler, J.K. and Cantrell, R.S. (1984): "A Behavioral Decision Theory Approach to Modeling Dyadic Trust in Superiors and Subordinates". *Psychological Reports*, 55, 19-28.

Coleman, J.S. (1998): "Social Capital in the Creation of Human Capital". *American Journal of Sociology* (supplement) 2, 95-120.

Coleman, J.S. (1990): "Foundations of Social Theory", Cambridge. MA: Harvard University Press.

Deutsch, M. (1958): "Trust and Suspicion", *Journal of Conflict Resolution*, 2, 265-79.

Elster, J. (1989): "Social Norms and Economic Theory", *Jr. of Econ. Perspective*, 3: 99-117.

Fukuyarna, F. (1995): "The Social Virtues and the Creation of Prosperity", New York: Free Press.

Golembiewski, R.T. and McConkie, M. (1975): "The Centrality of Interpersonal Trust in Group Processes", in Theories of Group Processes, (ed). C.L. Cooper, Wiley. London.

Goyal, S. (1996): "Interaction, Structure and Social Change", *Jr. of International and Theoretical Econ.*, 15Z: 472-94.

Granovetter, M. (1985): "Economic Action and Social Structure: The Problem of Embeddedness", *American Journal of Sociology*, 91(3), 481-510.

Granovetter, M. (1993): "The Nature, of Economic Relations", In: R. Swedberg (ed.), *Explorations in Economic Sociology*, pp. 3-14. New York: Sage.

Greif, A., Milgram, P. and Weingast, B.R. (1994): "Coordination, Commitment and Enforcement: The Case of Merchant Guild," *Tr. of Political Economy,* 102: 745-76.

Harriss, J. & De Renzio, P. (1997): "Missing Link' or Analytically Missing? The Concept of Social Capital", *Journal of International Development,* 9 (7).

Humphrey, I. and Schmitz, II. (1996): "Trust and Economic Development", Institute of Development Studies, Discussion Paper 355, IDS, Brighton.

Jackson, M.O and A. Watts (2002): "The Evolution of Social and Economics Networks", *Journal of Economic Theory.*

Jacobsen. D.I. (1996): "The Role of the Public Manager: Loyalty, Autonomy or Advocacy"? *Scandinavian Political Studies,* 19(1), 45-66.

Khalil, E.L. (1994): "Rules", in: G.M. Hodgson, W.J. Samuels, and M.R. Tool (ed.), Elgar Companions to Institutional and Evolutionary Economics (pp. 253-65), Vol. 2. Aldershot: Edward Elgar.

Kramer, R.M. and Tyler, R.M., (eds.). (1996): "Trust in Organizations, Frontiers of Theory and Research", Sage, Thousand Oaks, CA.

Luhmann, N. (1979): "Trust and Power", Chichester: Wiley.

Lyon, F. (1999 : "Understanding Market Relations and Bargaining Power. Farmer-trader Interactions in Agricultural Development in Brong Afro Region, Ghana", In : R. Blench (ed.). *Natural Resource Management in Ghana and its Socio-economic Context,* (pp. 162-77). London: Overseas Development Institute.

Misztal, B.A. (1996) : "Trust", Cambridge : Polity Press.

North, D. (1990): "Institutions, *Institutional Change and Economic Performance".* AUP.

Platteau, J.P. (1994a): "Behind the Market Stage where Real Societies Exist"— Part I.

The Role of Public and Private Order Institutions, *Journal of Development Studies,* 30 (3), 533-77.

Platteau, J.P. (1994b): "Behind the Market Stage where Real Societies Exist"— Part II, the Role of Moral Norms, *Journal of Development Studies,* 30 (4), 753-817.

Plattner, S. (1989): "Economic Behaviour in Markets". In: S. Plattner, *Economic Anthropology,* pp. 209-21, Stanford, CA: Stanford University Press.

Putnam, R. (1993): "Making Democracy Work: Civil Traditions in Modern Italy", Princeton, Princeton University Press.

Schelling, T. (1998). "Micro Motives and Macro Behaviour", Norton, N.Y.

Schotter, A. (1981): "The Economic Theory of Social Institutions", OUP.

Sen, A. (2000): "Development as Freedom", OUP.

Veblen (1934): "The Theory of Leisure Class", Modern Library, N.Y.

Wasserman, S. and K. Faust (1994): *"Social Network Analysis: Methods and Applications",* Cambridge University Press.

Wiliamson, O. (1988): "The Institutions of Governance", AER, 88 (2), pp. 75-79.

Woolcock, M. (1998): "Social Capital and Economic Development: Towards a Theoretical Synthesis and Policy Framework", *Theory and Society,* 27, 151-208.

Zucker, L.G. (1986): "Production of Trust: Institutional Sources of Economic Structure", 1840-1920. Research in Organizational Behaviour, 8, 53-111.

Sectoral Interlinkage in a Monetary Framework Under Flexible Exchange Rate Regime : A Post-WTO Perspective

RAJENDRA NARAYAN NAG AND BHASKAR GOSWAMI

1. INTRODUCTION

There is an urgent need for developing countries to refocus on the agricultural sector in order to take advantage of the comparative advantages that most such countries have in agricultural production. This need for increased emphasis on agricultural sector is not without reasons, particularly in the post-WTO scenario.[1] The different WTO commitments related to agricultural trade liberalization can, in fact, be fruitfully internalize for enhanced overall economic performance. The credibility of such an optimistic view finds a strong support in the aftermath of Uruguay Round Agreement on Agriculture

(URAA).[2] Such a contemporary development in the post-liberalization period revokes the need for macro-model that deals with agriculture-industry interlinkage in open economy setting. This is precisely the motivation behind this present paper. In order to analyse the sectoral interlinkage, we need to specify critically the broad literature on the related issue and by framing our departures from the existing literature. First, the conventional dual economy models frequently used in the mainstream structuralist macro-economics has explored different dimensions of agriculture-industry interlinkage primarily in a closed economy framework.[3] Such dual economy models mainly focus on agricultural sector as provider of wage goods to the industrial sector. The present paper retains this basic feature of the agriculture sector. In addition, the role of agricultural sector as supplier of foreign exchange is adequately highlighted, which can be easily reconciled in terms of potential exportability of agricultural (primary) products as enunciated in various WTO commitments on agricultural trade liberalization. Evidently, the paper can be viewed as study of intersectoral interlinkage in an open economy setting where agricultural sector plays a significant twin role that creates important economic linkages in the production chains.

Secondly, our paper reckons with the stylized fact that the speculative food grain stocks can be considered as one form of asset holding. In this context of financially repressed economy where capital markets are imperfectly developed or simply do not exist, the choice of food grain stocks as one form of asset is of natural consequences.[4] Given this undeniable significance of food grain stocks, very few attempts have been made so far to devise a macro-model so as to study the effects of these stocks. Our contention is to treat food grain stocks as one menu, among others, in the asset structure of a financial repressed economy.

The next departure from the existing literature is the incorporation of monetary factors that plays a crucial role in macroeconomic developments for a dual economy. Moutos and Vines (1992) capture this aspect of monetary macro-model in a close economy framework. Survey of their works in this field proved beneficial on our part. Stated otherwise, our paper can be viewed as an open economy extension of the paper by Moutos and Vines.[5]

Putting together all these departures and contentions as the pretext our analysis, the present paper attempts to bring out the pivotal role that agriculture sector is likely to play in terms of sectoral linkages for a dependent dual economy in the post-WTO regime.

The paper is organized as follows. In section II, we examine the structural features of a dual economy that is relevant to our purpose of study. Section III provides the model for the study of interscetoral interlinkage under flexible exchange rate regime. Section IV offers relevant comparative static analysis in terms of scope and nature of different policies. Section V concludes the paper.

II. STRUCTURAL FEATURES

It is neither easy nor simple to lump together developing countries in a single generic group. Nevertheless, provided the differences between them are acknowledged, we can identify some common features compatible with most developing countries.[6] In fact, the nature of macroeconomic adjustment to changes in any given set of policies will invariably depend on structural features of the economy. In this sense, it becomes pertinent to identify the macroeconomic characteristics of the developing countries that are likely to govern the response of their economies to different policy parameters. Hence, some comments on each of these structural features are in order.

1. The paper considers a dual economy macroeconomic framework. The nature of disaggregation is in terms of two sectors: agriculture and industrial sector. The agricultural sector operates under supply constraint in the sense that marketable surplus of food (wage goods) is fixed. On the other side, industrial sector operates under effective demand.
2. The nature of dependence between the two sectors is addressed in terms of tradability of the sector and hence the possible linkages. The non-traded and protected sector is the industrial sector, which operates under fixed coefficient technology. This sector uses labor and imported intermediate inputs. On the other

hand, agricultural sector produces for domestic market and for sales abroad. Agricultural exports are necessary to finance imports of intermediate goods for industry.[7] In this connection, an agricultural export is the only source of foreign exchange reserves.

3. Nature of openness of the economy is captured in terms of flexible exchange rate[8] and the complete absence of capital account transactions.[9] Any adjustment in foreign exchange market occurs through change in nominal exchange rate. Hence, any current account imbalance causes instantaneous adjustment in the nominal exchange rate such that current account balance is instantaneously guaranteed or always maintained.
4. The present paper acknowledges the portfolio balance approach to the study of determination of food price. To be more precise, we focus on the role of stock of agricultural goods as one form of assets and study the effects of forward-looking food price expectations.[10]

III. THE MODEL

The crux of our model lies in the nature of interlinkage between the two sectors of the economy: the agriculture (traded) sector and the industrial (non-traded) sector. Agricultural sector supplies wage goods to the industry and provides foreign exchange reserves through exports. The market for agricultural product clears through flexibility in food price. The non-traded sector by protection is the industrial sector that uses labor and imported intermediate inputs. Production in this sector is governed by effective demand and its price is 'determined by average variable cost. The economic structure highlights two aspects of static linkages between the sectors—via demand and foreign exchange constraint. The demand linkage contributes to sectoral balance in the sense that higher production in one sector implies higher income and thereby higher demand for the other sector. The other linkage is through the route of availability of foreign exchange (needed for industrial expansion), which we feel is the key extension compared to the existing literature.[11]

Our claim is that the model does not exhaust all possible intersectoral linkages but captures the interactions we think are the most important in the context of the developing countries, particularly in the post-WTO regime.

The model is given by equations 1 to 6:

$$Y = \alpha c\left[\frac{P_f F}{P_Y} + Y\right] + \bar{I} - vr + G \qquad \ldots\ldots (1)$$

$$\frac{M}{P_Y} = a\left[\frac{P_f F}{P_Y} + Y\right] - lr \qquad \ldots\ldots (2)$$

$$r = k + \frac{\dot{P}_f}{P_f} \qquad \ldots\ldots (3)$$

$$P_Y = wh + ea_m \qquad \ldots\ldots (4)$$

$$P_f X\left(\frac{e}{P_f}\right) - ea_m Y = 0 \qquad \ldots\ldots (5)$$

$$\dot{w} = \partial\left(Y - \bar{Y}\right) \qquad \ldots\ldots (6)$$

Industrial output is allocated to domestic private consumption expenditure, investment expenditure and government expenditure as represented by equation (1). Private consumption expenditure on manufactured goods is a constant fraction 'α' of the total consumption expenditure. Total consumption expenditure is equal to $c\left[\frac{P_f F}{P_Y} + Y\right]$, where 'c' is marginal propensity to consume and $\left[\frac{P_f F}{P_Y} + Y\right]$ represent the real income in terms of manufactured goods. A part of investment expenditure is autonomous and the other part is sensitive to nominal interest rate. Government expenditure is exogenous in the model.

Equation (2) represents the conventional money market equilibrium, where 'M' is the nominal money supply that is deflated by industrial price in order to obtain the real money balances is a fraction of real income in terms of manufactured goods and interest rate.

The asset structure of the economy is captured by equation (3). Primary commodities figure out as one form of asset along with money and bond, in a financially repressed economy. Equation (3) states that primary commodities and bond are perfect substitutes and the returns from these two assets are always brought into equality through arbitrage, where 'k' reflects the difference between 'convenience yield' and storage costs of holding primary commodities.[12]

Equation (4) reflects that industrial price is equal to average cost of production, where 'a_m' denotes imported intermediate input per unit of industrial output, 'e' denotes nominal exchange rate; 'h' denotes labor coefficient, that is, labor per unit of industrial output.[13]

Equation (5) specifies the current account balance. The demand for foreign exchange originates from the industrial sector because of its dependence on imported intermediate inputs. On the other hand, supply of foreign exchange comes from agricultural sector through exportability of primary products. The constraint simply suggests that in absence of any capital inflow/outflow, import is to be limited to agricultural export.

Finally, money wages are assumed to evolve in accordance with the conventional Phillips curve phenomenon (equation (6)), where 'Y' denotes output level and $\dot{Y}$ denotes full employment output level.

A. Short Run Analysis

In the short run, we take money wages (w) and price of agricultural commodities (P_f) as given. Equations (1) and (2) determines industrial output (Y) and rate of interest (r).

Equation (5) gives the nominal exchange rate (e), while equation (4) solves for industrial price (P_y).

The basic equations of the model in the hat form can be represented as follows:[14]

(1.1) $\hat{Y} + \beta\hat{P}_y + \frac{mvr}{Y}\hat{\pi} = \beta\hat{P}_f + \beta\hat{F} + \frac{mG}{Y}\hat{G}$,

$$\text{where } \beta = \frac{m\alpha cpF}{Y},\ P = \frac{P_f}{P_y}$$

(1.2) $a\hat{Y} + (\xi - \eta)\hat{P}_Y - \frac{lr}{Y}\hat{r} = -\eta\hat{P}_f - \eta\hat{F} + \xi\hat{M}$,

$$\text{where } \xi = \frac{M}{Y.P_Y},\ \eta = \frac{apF}{Y}$$

(1.4) $\hat{P}_Y - \theta_2\hat{e} = \theta_1\hat{w}$, where $\theta_1 \frac{wh}{wh + ea_m}$, $\theta_2 = \frac{ea_m}{wh + ea_m}$

(1.5) $\hat{Y} - (\alpha - 1)\hat{e} = -(\alpha - 1)\hat{P}_f$, where α is elasticity of export demand

$[\delta X / \delta(e/P_f)](e/P_f)X^{-1}$

Arranging (1.1), (1.2), (1.3) and (1.4) in matrix form, we get

$$\begin{bmatrix} 1 & \beta & \frac{mvr}{Y} & 0 \\ a & (\xi-\eta) & -\frac{lr}{Y} & 0 \\ 0 & 1 & 0 & -\theta_2 \\ 1 & 0 & 0 & -(\alpha-1) \end{bmatrix} \begin{bmatrix} \hat{Y} \\ \hat{P}_Y \\ \hat{r} \\ \hat{e} \end{bmatrix} = \begin{bmatrix} \beta\hat{P}_f + \beta\hat{F} + \frac{mG}{Y}\hat{G} \\ -\eta\hat{P}_f - \mu\hat{F} + \xi\hat{M} \\ \theta_1\hat{w} \\ -(\alpha-1)\hat{P}_f \end{bmatrix}$$

We consider the following determinant:

$$|D| = \begin{vmatrix} 1 & \beta & \frac{mvr}{Y} & 0 \\ a & (\xi-\eta) & -\frac{lr}{Y} & 0 \\ 0 & 1 & 0 & -\theta_2 \\ 1 & 0 & 0 & -(\alpha-1) \end{vmatrix}$$

$$= -\frac{r}{Y}[(\alpha - 1)(l + mva) + \theta_2 \{\beta l + mv(\xi - \eta)\}] \langle 0$$

Now we examine the effects of change in parameters (namely, G, M and F) on the short run variables.

(A.1) Change in Government Expenditure: Rise in government expenditure entails expansion of industrial output, which via money market causes rate of interest to rise. Furthermore, a rise in industrial output results in current account imbalance and hence nominal exchange rate increases for a given food price. The price of industrial output also increases. The effects are given by the following expressions:[15]

$$\left.\frac{\hat{Y}}{\hat{G}}\right|_{SR} = \frac{-mGlr(\alpha - 1)}{Y^2 |D|} \rangle 0 \qquad \text{(A.1.1)}$$

$$\left.\frac{\hat{P}_Y}{\hat{G}}\right|_{SR} = \frac{-mGlr\theta_2}{Y^2 |D|} \rangle 0 \qquad \text{(A.1.2)}$$

$$\left.\frac{\hat{r}}{\hat{G}}\right|_{SR} = \frac{-mG[a(\alpha - 1) + (\xi - \eta)\theta_2]}{Y|D|} \rangle 0 \qquad \text{(A.1.3)}$$

$$\left.\frac{\hat{e}}{\hat{G}}\right|_{SR} = \frac{-mGlr}{Y^2 |D|} \rangle 0 \qquad \text{(A.1.4)}$$

(A.2) Change in Money Supply: An increase in money supply causes interest rate to fall which leads to rise in investment and industrial output. An increase in industrial output requires increased imported intermediate inputs and hence price of industrial goods increases. On the other hand, on account of increase in industrial output, nominal exchange rate has to rise so as to restore the current account balance.

$$\left.\frac{\hat{Y}}{\hat{M}}\right|_{SR} = \frac{-mvr\xi(\alpha - 1)}{Y|D|} \rangle 0 \qquad \text{(A.2.1)}$$

$$\left.\frac{\hat{P}_Y}{\hat{M}}\right|_{SR} = \frac{-mvr\xi\theta_2}{Y|D|} \rangle 0 \qquad \text{(A.2.2)}$$

$$\left.\frac{\hat{r}}{\hat{M}}\right|_{SR} = \frac{\xi[(\alpha-1)+\beta\theta_2]}{|D|} \langle 0 \tag{A.2.3}$$

$$\left.\frac{\hat{e}}{\hat{M}}\right|_{SR} = \frac{-mvr\xi}{Y|D|} \rangle 0 \tag{A.2.4}$$

(A.3) Change in Food Supply: An increase in food supply leads to a rise in real income. Demand for money goes up and interest rate rises to clear money market. However, the effects on industrial output, industrial price and nominal exchange rate are ambiguous.

$$\left.\frac{\hat{Y}}{\hat{F}}\right|_{SR} = \frac{r(\alpha-1)[mv\eta-\beta l]}{Y|D|} ? \tag{A.3.1}$$

$$\left.\frac{\hat{P}}{\hat{F}}\right|_{SR} = \frac{r\theta_2[mv\eta-\beta l]}{Y|D|} ? \tag{A.3.2}$$

$$\left.\frac{\hat{r}}{\hat{F}}\right|_{SR} = \frac{-[\alpha-1)(\eta+\beta a)+\beta\xi\theta_2]}{|D|} \rangle 0 \tag{A.3.3}$$

$$\left.\frac{\hat{e}}{\hat{F}}\right|_{SR} = \frac{r[mv\eta-\beta l]}{Y|D|} ? \tag{A.3.4}$$

B. Steady State

Equations (1) to (6) can be reduced to the following pair of differential equations in 'w' and 'p_r':

$$\begin{bmatrix}\dot{w}\\ \dot{P}_f\end{bmatrix} = \begin{bmatrix}a_{11} & a_{12}\\ a_{21} & a_{22}\end{bmatrix}\begin{bmatrix}\bar{w}-w\\ \bar{P}_f-P_f\end{bmatrix} + \begin{bmatrix}x_1 & x_2 & x_3\\ z_1 & z_2 & z_2\end{bmatrix}\begin{bmatrix}dG\\ dM\\ dF\end{bmatrix}$$

where, $a_{11} = \frac{d\dot{w}}{dw} = \partial\frac{dY}{dw} \langle 0$

$$a_{12} = \frac{d\dot{w}}{dP_f} = \partial\frac{dY}{dP_f} \rangle 0$$

$$a_{21} = \frac{d\dot{P}_f}{dw} = \frac{dr}{dw} \rangle 0$$

$$a_{22} = \frac{d\dot{P}_f}{dP_f} = \frac{dr}{dP_f} \rangle 0$$

$$x_1 = \frac{d\dot{w}}{dG} = \partial \frac{dY}{dG} \rangle 0$$

$$z_1 = \frac{d\dot{P}_f}{dG} = \frac{dr}{dG} \rangle 0$$

$$x_2 = \frac{d\dot{w}}{dM} = \partial \frac{dY}{dM} \rangle 0$$

$$z_2 = \frac{d\dot{P}_f}{dM} = \frac{dr}{dM} \langle 0$$

$$x_3 = \frac{d\dot{w}}{dF} = \partial \frac{dY}{dF} ?$$

$$z_3 = \frac{d\dot{P}_f}{dF} = \frac{dr}{dF} \rangle 0$$

The determinant of the system is:

$\Omega = a_{11} a_{22} - a_{12} a_{21} \langle 0$. Thus, the two characteristic roots of the system are of opposite signs and therefore the system possesses stable saddle path. We assume that food price is the jump variable which adjusts instantaneously so as to place the economy on the stable saddle path. The equation of the saddle path is given by:[16]

$$\left(P_f - P_{f_2}\right) = \left(\frac{\lambda_1 - a_{11}}{a_{12}}\right)(w - w_2)$$

or, equivalently as,

$$\left(P_f - P_{f_2}\right) = \left(\frac{a_{21}}{\lambda_1 - a_{22}}\right)(w - w_2)$$

We note that the slope of the saddle path (SS) is given by:

$$\left.\frac{dP_f}{dw}\right|_{\dot{w}=0} = \left(\frac{a_{21}}{\lambda_1 - a_{22}}\right) = \left(\frac{\lambda_1 - a_{11}}{a_{12}}\right) \langle 0$$

The $\dot{w} = 0$ locus denotes the combination of the wage rate and food price that will maintain full employment. The slope of $\dot{w} = 0$ line is:

$$\left.\frac{dP_f}{dw}\right|_{\dot{w}=0} = \frac{-a_{11}}{a_{12}} \rangle 0$$

Likewise, the $\dot{P}_f = 0$ locus is the combination of wage rate and food price consistent with no change in food price, that is, r = k. The slope of $\dot{P}_f = 0$ line is:

$$\left.\frac{dP_f}{dw}\right|_{\dot{P}_f=0} = \frac{-a_{21}}{a_{22}} \langle 0$$

The formal solutions describing the behaviour of wages and prices can be depicted in terms of the following diagram.

FIG. 2.1
Saddle Path Stability

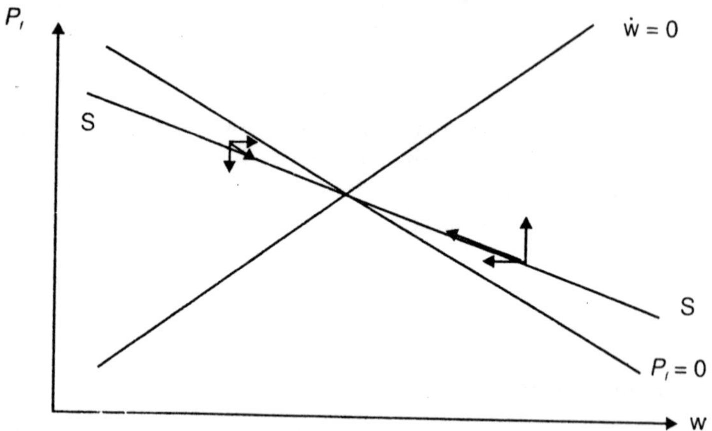

The saddle path is negatively sloped and flatter than $\dot{P}_f = 0$ curve.[17]

IV. COMPARATIVE STATIC ANALYSIS

(1) *Increase in Government Expenditure*: An increase in government expenditure causes industrial output to increase through the conventional demand multiplier effect. This in turn leads to a rise in the interest rate from the money market. Interest rate rises to maintain money market equilibrium, leading to $\dot{P}_f > 0$. Hence, the $\dot{P}_f = 0$ line shifts downward. Output expansion leads to higher wage rate such that $\dot{w} > 0$. Hence, $\dot{w} = 0$ line also shifts downward, as depicted in Figure 2.2.

The initial equilibrium is at point 'E_0' and final equilibrium is at point 'E_1'. Wage rate increases and food price falls and we encounter undershooting of food price.

FIG. 2.2
Undershooting of 'P_f'

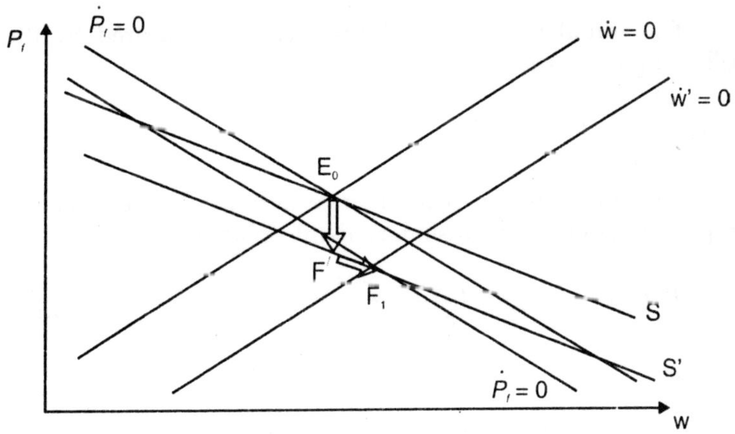

Intuitively the effect of expansionary fiscal policy can be explained as follows: In the short-run, there is a rise in output level which in turn requires additional foreign exchange reserves. Hence, for any given food price nominal exchange rate increases so as to support the initial output expansion. However, in the long run since output level is fixed at $\overline{Y}$, both nominal exchange rate and food price decreases equiproportionately such that current account balance is maintained. Moreover, since in the long run interest rate is fixed at 'k', we encounter a steady state crowding out of private consumption through a fall in food price along with a rise in industrial price.

The effects are given by the following equations.[18]

$$\frac{\hat{w}}{dG} = \frac{apF\theta_1 + \left(M/P_y \right)\theta_2}{\Omega} > 0 \quad \text{(B.1.1)}$$

$$\frac{\hat{P}_f}{dG} = \frac{\left(-\frac{M}{P_y} + apF \right)\theta_1}{\Omega} < 0 \quad \text{(B.1.2)}$$

$$\frac{\hat{P}_f}{dG} = \frac{apF\theta_1}{\Omega} > 0 \quad \text{(B.1.3)}$$

The initial jump in food price can be captured by the following expression:[19]

$$P_f(0) - P_{f1} = \left(\mu - \varphi\left(\frac{\lambda_1 - a_{22}}{a_{21}} \right) \right) dG^{-\lambda_2 T} \quad \text{(B.1.4)}$$

The final change in food price and wage rate after the implementation of expansionary fiscal policy is given by:

$$P_f(T) - P_f(0) = \left(\frac{\lambda_1 - a_{22}}{a_{21}} \right) A'_1 e^{\lambda_1 l} \quad \text{(B.1.5)}$$

$$w(T) - w_2 = A'_1 e^{\lambda_1 l} \quad \text{(B.1.6)}$$

(2) *Increase in Money supply*: In the short run a rise in money supply leads to output expansion. Consequently interest rate decreases to maintain the money market equilibrium. This in turn leads to $\dot{P}_f < 0$ and hence, the $\dot{P}_f < 0$ line shifts in the upward direction. Output expansion leads to higher wage rate such that $\dot{w} > 0$. Hence, $\dot{w} > 0$ line also shifts downward, as

depicted in Figure 2.3. The initial equilibrium is at point 'E_0' and final equilibrium is at point 'E_1'. Both wage rate and food price increases and we encounter overshooting of food price.

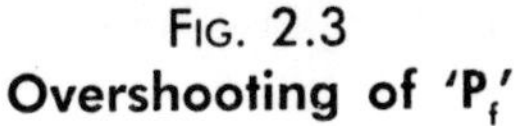

FIG. 2.3
Overshooting of 'P_f'

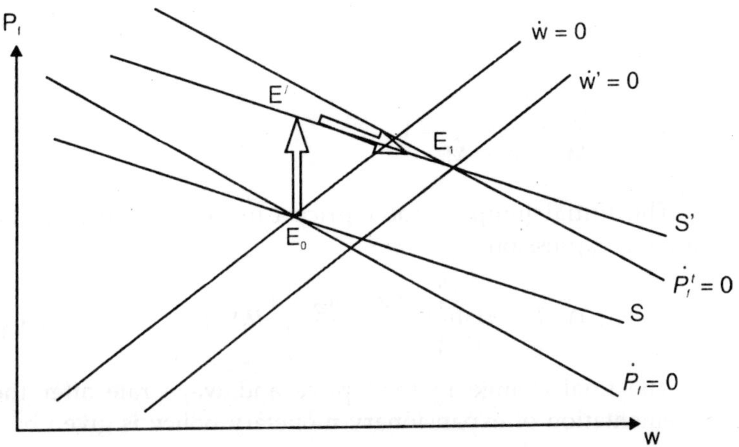

In the long-run expansionary monetary policy is completely ineffective. In fact, a rise in money supply leads to equiproportionate increase in nominal exchange rate, food price and industrial price level. This can be explained as follows: a rise in money supply on impact leads to an increase in food price. This in turn would decrease the real exchange rate for any given value of nominal exchange rate. However, since long run output level is fixed at $\bar{Y}$, to maintain current account balance nominal exchange rate also increases by equal amount such that real exchange rate remains unchanged. Again since in the long run interest rate remains fixed at 'k', a rise in money supply is exactly offset by an equal increase in industrial price such that real money balance in terms of industrial price remains unchanged.

The effects are given by the following equations:[20]

$$\frac{\hat{w}}{dM} = \frac{m\alpha c p F \theta_1}{P_Y \Omega} = \frac{1}{M}$$

$$\Rightarrow \frac{\hat{w}}{\hat{M}} = 1 \qquad \text{(B.2.1)}$$

Similarly, $\frac{\hat{P}_f}{\hat{M}} = 1$ (B.2.2)

and $\frac{\hat{P}_Y}{\hat{M}} = 1$ (B.2.3)

Thus, $\frac{\hat{w}}{\hat{M}} = \frac{\hat{P}_f}{\hat{M}} = \frac{\hat{P}_Y}{\hat{M}} = 1$

The initial jump in food price can be captured by the following expression:[21]

$$\Rightarrow P_f(0) - P_{f1} = \left(\Phi\left\{1 - \left(\frac{\lambda_1 - a_{22}}{a_{21}}\right)\right\}\right) dM^{-\lambda_2 T} \qquad \text{(B.2.4)}$$

The final change in food price and wage rate after the implementation of expansionary monetary policy is given by:

$$P_f(T) - P_f(0) = \left(\frac{\lambda_1 - a_{22}}{a_{21}}\right) A'_1 e^{\lambda_1 l} \qquad \text{(B.2.5)}$$

$$w(T) - w_2 = A'_1 e^{\lambda_1 l} \qquad \text{(B.2.6)}$$

(3) *Increase in Marketable surplus of food*: Rise in food supply on impact may either generate expansionary or contractionary effect. But in the long run the effect on industrial output is unambiguously positive. However, since in the long run industrial output level is fixed at $\overline{Y}$, food price falls equiproportionately in response to rise in marketable surplus of food. In the short run, rate of interest begins to rise in response to rise in food supply, leading to $\dot{P}_f > 0$; hence $\dot{P}_f = 0$ line shifts downward. Output expansion leads to higher wage rate such that $\dot{w} > 0$. Hence, $\dot{w} = 0$ line also shifts downward, as depicted in Figure 2.4. The initial equilibrium is at point 'E_0' and final equilibrium is at point 'E_1'. Wage rate increases and food price falls and we encounter undershooting of food price.

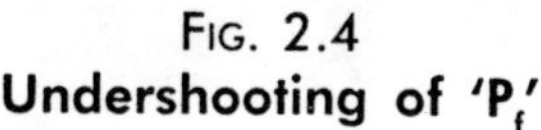

FIG. 2.4
Undershooting of 'P_f'

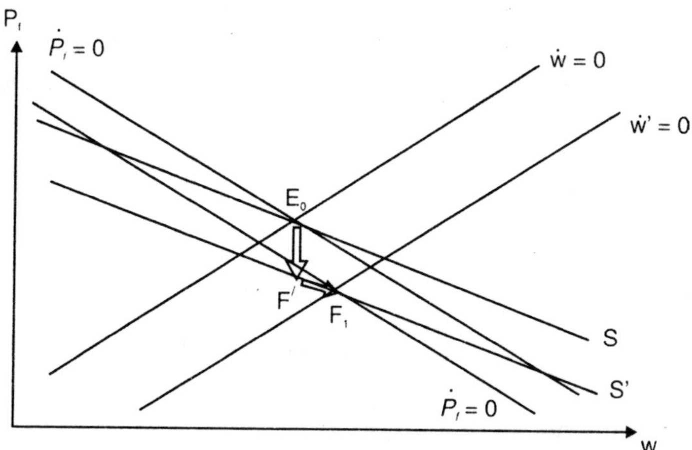

The result is amenable to easy economic interpretation. Rise in food supply leads to an increase in the real income in terms of manufactured goods, that is, $\left[\frac{P_f F}{P_Y} + Y\right]$. This would tend to put an upward pressure on industrial output level, at least in the short run. However, in the long run, output level is fixed at $\bar{Y}$ and hence any upward pressure on output level is completely absorbed by an equiproportionate fall in the food price such that real income in terms of manufactured goods remains unchanged. Moreover, this fall in food price necessitates an equal fall in nominal exchange rate such that the real exchange rate remains unchanged and the current account balance is always restored.

Thus on account of fall in nominal exchange rate and rise in wage rate, industrial price remains unchanged.

The effects are given by the following equations:[22]

$$\frac{\hat{w}}{\hat{F}} = \frac{\theta_2}{\theta_1} > 0 \qquad \text{(B.3.1)}$$

$$\frac{\hat{P}_f}{\hat{F}} = -1 < 0 \tag{B.3.2}$$

$$\frac{\hat{P}_Y}{\hat{F}} = 0 \tag{B.3.3}$$

The initial jump in food price can be captured by the following expression:[23]

$$P_f\,(0) - P_{f\,1} = \left(\Psi - \Lambda \left(\frac{\lambda_1 - a_{22}}{a_{21}} \right) \right) dF^{-\lambda_2 T} \tag{B.3.4}$$

V. CONCLUSION

The crux of the paper lies in the treatment of the agricultural sector as a provider of wage goods and foreign exchange reserves for the dual economy. The paper adequately highlights the agricultural sector's contribution to foreign exchange, which in the context of ongoing reforms in the post-WTO period is a pertinent issue. Given this significance of the agriculture sector, our paper studies the sectoral interlinkage in a dependent monetary economy setting under flexible exchange rate regime. The paper acknowledges the stylized fact of the structural macroeconomics in the sense that the relevant balance of payment issues are addressed along with the food constraint, thereby emphasizing typical features of a transitional or emerging market economy. In the context of the paper, the agricultural sector being a traded sector operates under supply-side constraint specified in terms of a given marketable surplus of food. On the other hand, the non-traded industrial sector operates under demand constraint in the sense that its output is demand determined. However, the availability of foreign exchange reserves throws up another constraint for the industrial sector as the performance of this sector depends on the availability of imported intermediate inputs. It is at this juncture the role of agricultural sector as potential provider of foreign exchange reserves comes into play and thereby defining the specific nature of sectoral linkage.

This paper has developed a long run dependent economy macromodel with a clear focus on sectoral interlinkage in a dual economy. The paper is actually based on a monetary dual economy model by Moutos and Vines. We have extended their model by incorporating specific details of international trade. In the long run, the steady state variables are food price and wage rate. Food price adjusts instantaneously to clear asset market while wage rate changes continuously in response to gap between actual and full employment output level. The model in this paper offers saddle path stability of the system.

The different comparative static exercises attempted in this paper indicate that short-run and long run effects of different policy prescription are significantly different. The long run expansionary effect of rise in government expenditure is less compared to its short-run effect due to crowding out through fall in food price. Identical conclusion holds for rise in the marketable surplus of food. Again, short run expansionary effect of rise in money supply becomes completely neutral in the long run through a equiproportionate rise in food price, nominal exchange rate and industrial price level. Hence, the clear policy message is that short run effect is not a reliable guide to design of macroeconomic policy.

The paper can be extended in different direction. The long run issues of capital accumulation in the traded agricultural sector and export dynamics through J-curve effect can be easily accommodated. In the short run capital stock in the agricultural sector is fixed, but over time it could change in response to terms of trade movement.[24] Capital accumulation in the agricultural sector responds positively to terms of trade movement in favour of the agricultural sector. This extension will significantly change long run effects of shocks. In particular, we note that increase in government expenditure on industrial product would reduce agricultural production in the long run, since it causes terms of trade movement against the agricultural sector. Moreover, the model in our paper is based on sticky wage. In a more complicated model than ours, wage dynamics can be accommodated.

Notes

1. See Raed Safadi and Sam Laird, 1996, "The Uruguay Round Agreements: Impact on Developing Countries", *World Development*, Vol. 24, No. 7, pp. 1223-42 for a survey of the various estimates of the likely increases in world trade due to the Uruguay Round and the effects of the round on developing countries.
2. The potential gains from liberalization of agricultural markets (US $ 248 billion) are estimated to be substantially higher than the potential benefits from manufacturing (US $ 111 billion), even though agriculture accounts for a much smaller share of total world merchandise trade. For the most part, this is due to the high level of agricultural protection in high-income countries. Considering that agriculture and processed food products in high-income countries contribute only 4 percent of global GDP and only 6 percent of world trade, a disproportionately large share of the global welfare gains would come from abolishing protection and trade barriers in these countries. [*Source*: World Bank, 2002a].
3. See Rakshit (1982), Taylor (1983, 1991), Dutta (1990). Open economy dimensions of sectoral interlinkage have been explored by Nag and Ghosh (2003), Nag and Goswami (2005).
4. The most important reproducible asset in such economies is the stock of foodgrains and agricultural raw-materials, the money prices of which are subject to intertemporal fluctuations. The traders seck (almost literally) to make capital out of these fluctuations and thus their behaviour assumes great significance in governing the level of money prices (at least in the short run). [Rakshit (1982, p. 86)]
5. It is pertinent to construct open economy macromodel that can be related to the contemporary developments in the post-liberalization period.
6. The model specific developing countries that we are focusing are the Sub-Saharan African countries and the South-East Asian developing countries.
7. This is essentially very important from the developing countries perspective to avail the opportunities that are thrown up by Agricultural Trade liberalization in the light of various WTO commitments.
8. Analysts agree that "getting the exchange rate right" is essential for economic stability and growth in developing countries. Over the past two decades, many developing countries have shifted away from fixed exchange rates and moved toward more flexible exchange rates. During a period of rapid economic growth, driven by twin forces of globalization and liberalization of markets and trade, this shift seems to have served a number of countries well. (Francesco Caramazza, Jahangir Aziz, 1998).
9. Many developing countries prohibit destabilizing capital inflows/outflows by imposing variety of capital controls. (Agenor and Montiel, 1999)
10. This is similar to portfolio balance approach to exchange rate determination in an open economy framework with capital account transactions.
11. See Jorn Rattso and Ragnar Torvik (2003).

12. See Kaldor (1939), Gilbert (1985), Frankel (1986), Moutous and Vines (1992).
13. Under perfect competition price is equal to average cost. If we introduce market imperfection, price is determined by typical Kaleckian markup formula, which is however, inconsequential in the context of our paper.
14. See mathematical appendix.
15. *Ibid.*
16. See mathematical appendix for the derivation of saddle path equation.
17. Note that $\left.\frac{dP_f}{dw}\right|_{ss} = \left|\left(\frac{a_{21}}{\lambda_1 - a_{22}}\right)\right| < \left.\frac{dP_f}{dw}\right|_{\dot{P}_f = 0} = \left|\frac{a_{21}}{a_{22}}\right|$
18. See mathematical appendix.
19. *Ibid.*
20. *Ibid.*
21. *Ibid.*
22. *Ibid.*
23. *Ibid.*
24. See Ratts Φ (1989).

REFERENCES

Badao, A. and Martin, W. (1993) : Implications of Agriculture Trade Liberalization for the Developing Countries, *Agricultural Economics*, 8, pp. 313-43.

Baland, J.M. (1991): Foodgrain stocks and macrodynamic adjustment mechanisms in a dual semi-industrialized economy. *Journal of Development Economics*, 40, 171-85, 1991.

Bhaduri, A. and Skarstein, R. (2001) : Effective Demand and the Terms of Trade: A Kaldorian Perspective (mimeo), Indian Institute of Management, Kolkata.

Bose, A. (1989) : Short Period Equilibrium in a Less Developed Economy, in Mihir Rakshit (ed.), Studies in the Macroeconomics of Developing Countries, Delhi, Oxford University Press.

Buffie, E. (1986) : Devaluation, Investment and Growth in LDCs, *Journal of Development Economics*, 20, pp. 361-79.

Caramazza, F. and Aziz, J. (1998) : Fixed or Flexible? Getting the Exchange Rate Right in the 1990s. *International Monetary Fund*, 1998.

Cardoso, E.A. (1980): Food Supply and Inflation, *Journal of Development Economics*, 8, 269-84, 1981.

Desai, B.M. (2002) : Terms of Trade, Trade and Technical Change: Strategies for Agricultural Growth in EPW, February 23, 2002, pp. 801-04.

DuH, A.X. (1990) : Growth, Distribution and Uneven Development, Cambridge: Cambridge University Press.

Frankel, J.A. (1986) : "Expectations and Commodity Price Dynamics: The Overshooting Model." *American Journal of Agricultural Economics*, 344-8.

Gill, S.S. and Brar, J.S. (1996): Global Market and Competitiveness of Indian Agriculture, Some Issues. *Economic and Political Weekly*, Vol. XXXI, No. 32, Aug. (1996).

Gilbert, C. (1985) : "Optimal and Competitive Storage Rules, the Gustafson Problem Revisited." Department of Economics, Queen's University, Kingston (mimeo).

Haug, Rand Oygard, R. (1999) : Trade Liberalization in Agriculture: Consequences for Growth, Poverty Reduction and Environment in Developing countries, Center for International Environment and Development Studies, Agricultural University of Norway.

Hertel, T.; Anderson, K.; Francois, J. and Martin, W. (2000) : Agriculture and Non-Agricultural Liberalization in the Millennium Round Centre For International Economic Studies, Policy Discussion Paper, No. 0016.

Kaldor, N. (1939) : "Speculation and Economic Stability." *Review of Economic Studies*, 7, 1-27.

Martin, Wand Winters, L.A. ed. (1995) : The Uruguay Round and The Developing Economics, World Bank *Discussion Paper* 307, World Bank, Washington, DC.

Moutos, T. and Vines, D. (1992) : "Output, Inflation and Commodity Prices", *Oxford Economic Papers*, 44, pp. 355-72.

Nag, N.R. and Ghosh, P.P. (2003) : Industry-Agriculture Interlinkage, Agricultural Trade liberalization and Supply constraints: A Post-WTO Perspective. *Indian Economic Review*, Vol. XXXVIII, No. 2, 2003, pp. 235-51.

Nag, N.R. and Goswami, B. (2005): Dual Economy Interlinkage in a Monetary Framework: A Post-WTO Perspective, *Journal of Economic Integration*, Vol. 20, No. 3, September 2005.

Rakshit, M. (1982) : The Labour Surplus Economy, Delhi: Macmillan.

Ratts Φ , J. (1989) : Macrodynamic Adjustment Mechanisms in a Dual Semi-Industrialized Economy, *Journal of Development Economics*, 30, pp. 47-69.

Ratts Φ , J. and Torvik, R. (2003): Interactions between Agriculture and Industry: Theoretical Analysis of the Consequences of Discriminating Agriculture In Sub-Saharan Africa. *Review of Development Economics*, 7(1), 138-51, 2003.

Schuknecht, L. (1998) : Fiscal Policy Cycles and the Exchange Regime in Developing Countries, Working Paper WTO (1998).

Taylor, L. (1983) : Structuralist Macroeconomics: Applicable Models for the Third World, New York, Basic Books.

Taylor, L. (1985) : A Stagnationist Model of Economic Growth. Cambridge *Journal of Economics*, 9, 383-405, 1985.

———, (1991), Income Distribution, Growth and Inflation. Lectures of Structuralist Macro-economic Theory, Cambridge, MMA : MIT Press.

——— and Krugman, P. (1978) : Contractionary Effects of Devaluation, *Journal of International Economics*, 8, pp. 445-56.

Turnovsky, S.J. (1977): Macroeconomic Analysis and Stabilization Policies, Cambridge University Press, Cambridge.

Wijnbergen, S. (1986) : Exchange Rate Management and Stabilization Policies in Developing Countries, *Journal of Development Economics*, 23, pp. 227-47.

MATHEMATICAL APPENDIX

The basic equations in hat form are derived as follows:

(1) $Y = \alpha c\left[\frac{P_f F}{P_F} + Y\right] + \bar{I} - vr + G$

$\Rightarrow Y = m\alpha cpF + m\left(\bar{I} - vr\right) + mG$, where $p = \frac{P_f}{P_Y}$ and $m = \frac{1}{1-\alpha c}$

Differentiating and dividing by Y, we get

$$\hat{Y} = \frac{m\alpha cpF}{Y}\hat{p} + \frac{m\alpha cpF}{Y}\hat{F} - \frac{mvr}{Y}\hat{r} + \frac{mG}{Y}\hat{G}$$

$$\Rightarrow \hat{Y} = \beta\left(\hat{P}_f - \hat{P}_Y\right)_{-}\beta\hat{F} - \frac{mvr}{Y}\hat{r} + \frac{mG}{Y}\hat{G}, \text{ where } \beta = \frac{m\alpha cpF}{Y}$$

$$\Rightarrow \hat{Y} = \beta\hat{P}_y + \frac{mvr}{Y}\hat{r} = \beta\hat{P}_f + \beta\hat{F} + \frac{mG}{Y}\hat{G},$$

as given by equation (1.1)

By similar approach equations (1.2), (1.4) and (1.5) are derived.

Short-run Comparative Static Analysis

A.1. Increase in Government expenditure :

$$\hat{Y} = \frac{\begin{vmatrix} \frac{mG}{Y}\hat{G} & \beta & \frac{mvr}{Y} & 0 \\ 0 & (\xi - \eta) & -\frac{lr}{Y} & 0 \\ 0 & 1 & 0 & -\theta_2 \\ 0 & 0 & 0 & -(\alpha - 1) \end{vmatrix}}{|D|}$$

$$\Rightarrow \frac{\hat{Y}}{\hat{G}} = \frac{\frac{mG}{Y}\begin{vmatrix} (\xi - \eta) & -\frac{lr}{Y} & 0 \\ 1 & 0 & -\theta_2 \\ 0 & 1 & -(\alpha - 1) \end{vmatrix}}{|D|}$$

$$\Rightarrow \frac{\hat{Y}}{\hat{G}}\bigg|_{SR} = \frac{-mGlr(\alpha-1)}{Y^2|D|} \rangle 0,$$ as given by expression (A.1.1).

Similarly, the other expressions for all the short run comparative static results are obtained.

Derivation of Saddle Path

The initial steady-state equilibrium solutions for w, P_f, denoted by w_1, P_{f_1}, say are obtained by solving

$$\begin{bmatrix} \dot{w} \\ \dot{P}_f \end{bmatrix} = \begin{bmatrix} a_{11} & a_{12} \\ a_{21} & a_{22} \end{bmatrix} \begin{bmatrix} \overline{w} - w_1 \\ \overline{P}_f - P_{f_1} \end{bmatrix} \qquad \ldots\ldots (1)$$

Now suppose that at time 0 it is announced that a parameter (For example, G, or F or M) are to increase, at time T ≥ 0. The new steady states after the shifts have occurred are specified by

$$\begin{bmatrix} \dot{w} \\ \dot{P}_f \end{bmatrix} = \begin{bmatrix} a_{11} & a_{12} \\ a_{21} & a_{22} \end{bmatrix} \begin{bmatrix} \overline{w} - w_2 \\ \overline{P}_f - P_{f_2} \end{bmatrix} \qquad \ldots\ldots (2)$$

As long as the shifts are additive, so that the coefficients a_{ij} remain unchanged between the two regimes, the eigen values λ_1, λ_2 say of (1) and (2) are identical. For simplicity and without loss of generality, we shall assume that they are real. The fact that the dynamics are described by a saddle point means that the product

$$\lambda_1 \lambda_2 = a_{11} a_{22} - a_{12} a_{21} < 0.$$

We shall assume $\lambda_1 < 0$, $\lambda_2 > 0$. In order to ensure stability, one of variables say P_f, must be a jump variable, while the other w, is assumed to evolve continuously at all times.

Over the period $0 < t \leq T$, before the shifts have occurred, the solutions for w, P_f are of the form

$$w = w_1 + A_1 e^{\lambda_1 t} + A_2 e^{\lambda_2 t} \qquad \ldots\ldots (3.1)$$

$$P_f = P_{f_1} + \left(\frac{\lambda_1 - a_{11}}{a_{12}}\right) A_1 e^{\lambda_1 t} + \left(\frac{\lambda_2 - a_{11}}{a_{12}}\right) A_2 e^{\lambda_2 t} \qquad \ldots\ldots (3.2)$$

Note that because λ_i are eigen values

$$\frac{\lambda_1 - a_{11}}{a_{12}} = \frac{a_{21}}{\lambda_i - a_{22}}, \, i = 1, 2$$

in which case (3.2) can be rewritten equivalently as:

$$P_f = P_{f_1} + \left(\frac{a_{21}}{\lambda_1 - a_{22}}\right) A_1 e^{\lambda_1 t} + \left(\frac{a_{21}}{\lambda_2 - a_{22}}\right) A_2 e^{\lambda_2 t}$$

Likewise, for the period $t \geq T$, after the shifts have occurred, the solutions for w, P_f is

$$w = w_2 + A_1' e^{\lambda_1 t} + A_2' \, e^{\lambda_2 t} \qquad \ldots\ldots (4.1)$$

$$P_f = P_{f_2} + \left(\frac{\lambda_1 - a_{11}}{a_{12}}\right) A_1' e^{\lambda_1 t} + \left(\frac{\lambda_2 - a_{11}}{a_{12}}\right) A_2' e^{\lambda_2 t} \qquad \ldots\ldots (4.2)$$

Now convergence required that as $t \to \infty$. $A_?' = 0$, so that

$$w = w_2 + A_1' e^{\lambda_1 t} \qquad \ldots\ldots (5.1)$$

$$P_f = P_{f_2} + \left(\frac{\lambda_1 - a_{11}}{a_{12}}\right) A_1' e^{\lambda_1 t} \qquad \ldots\ldots (5.2)$$

The remaining constant A_1 , A_2 , A_1' are obtained by solving the equations

$$A_1 + A_2 = 0 \qquad \ldots\ldots (6)$$

$$\left(A_1 - A_1'\right) e^{\lambda_1 T} + A_2 e^{\lambda_2 T} = dw \qquad \ldots\ldots (7)$$

$$\left(\frac{\lambda_1 - a_{11}}{a_{12}}\right)\left(A_1 - A_1'\right) e^{\lambda_1 T} + \left(\frac{\lambda_1 - a_{11}}{a_{12}}\right) A_2 e^{\lambda_2 T} = dP_f \qquad \ldots\ldots (8)$$

where dw and dP_f are shifts of steady state in w and P_f respectively.

Now the stable saddle paths after time T are described by equation (4.1) and (4.2).

Eliminating $A_1^{/} e^{\lambda_1 T}$ from these equations we get,

$$\left(P_f - P_{f_2}\right) = \left(\frac{\lambda_1 - a_{11}}{a_{12}}\right)(w - w_2) \quad \ldots\ldots (9.1)$$

or, equivalently as

$$\left(P_f - P_{f_2}\right) = \left(\frac{a_{21}}{\lambda_1 - a_{22}}\right)(w - w_2) \quad \ldots\ldots (9.2)$$

Equation (9.1) or (9.2) describes the equation of saddle path.

Long-run Comparative Static Analysis

In the long-run $Y = \bar{Y}$ and $r = k$. Hence, the basic equations in the long-run becomes :

(1) $\bar{Y} = m\left[\alpha cpF + \bar{I} - vk + G\right]$, where $m = \dfrac{1}{1-\alpha c}$ and $p = \dfrac{P_f}{P_Y}$

(2) $\dfrac{M}{P_Y} = a\left[pF + \bar{Y}\right] - lk$

(3) $P_Y = wh + ea_m$

(4) $P_f X\left(\dfrac{e}{P_f}\right) = ea_m \bar{Y}$

Differentiating equations (1) to (4), we get,

(1.1) $m\alpha cpF\hat{P}_f - m\alpha cpF\hat{P}_Y = dG - m\alpha cpF\hat{F}$

(1.2) $apF\hat{P}_f + \left(\dfrac{M}{P_Y} - apF\right)\hat{P}_Y = \dfrac{dM}{P_Y} - apF\hat{F}$

(1.3) $\hat{P}_Y = \theta_1 \hat{w} + \theta_2 \hat{e}$, where $\theta_1 = \dfrac{wh}{wh + ea_m}$

and $\theta_2 = \dfrac{ea_m}{wh + ea_m}$; $\theta_1 + \theta_2 = 1$

(1.4) $\hat{P}_f = \hat{e}$

Substituting equations (1.3) and (1.4) in equation (1.1), we get

(A) $macpF\theta_1 \hat{w} - macpF\theta_1 \hat{P}_f = dG - macpF\hat{F}$

(B) $\left(\dfrac{M}{P_Y} - apF\right)\theta_1 \hat{w} + \left(apF\theta_1 + \dfrac{M}{P_Y}\theta_2\right)\hat{P}_f = \dfrac{dM}{P_Y} - apF\hat{F}$

Arranging (A) and (B) in matrix form we get,

$$\begin{bmatrix} macpF\theta_1 & -macpF\theta_1 \\ \left(\dfrac{M}{P_Y} - apF\right)\theta_1 & \left(apF\theta_1 + \dfrac{M}{P_Y}\theta_2\right) \end{bmatrix} \begin{bmatrix} \hat{w} \\ \hat{P}_f \end{bmatrix} = \begin{bmatrix} dG - macpF\hat{F} \\ \dfrac{dM}{P_Y} - apF\hat{F} \end{bmatrix}$$

The sign of the above determinant is:

$$\Omega = \begin{vmatrix} macpF\theta_1 & -macpF\theta_1 \\ \left(\dfrac{M}{P_Y} - apF\right)\theta_1 & \left(apF\theta_1 + \dfrac{M}{P_Y}\theta_2\right) \end{vmatrix}$$

$$\Omega = macpF\theta_1 \left(\frac{M}{P_Y}\right) > 0$$

Increase in Government Expenditure

Setting $\hat{F} = \dfrac{dM}{P_Y} = 0$ in expression (C), we get

$$\frac{\hat{w}}{dG} = \frac{apF\theta_1 + \left(M/P_y\right)\theta_2}{\Omega} > 0$$, as given by result (B.1.1)

$\Rightarrow dw = \mu dG$ . . . . . (10)

$$\text{where } \mu = \frac{\left\{apF\theta_1 + \left(M/P_y\right)\theta_2\right\}w}{\Omega} > 0$$

$$\frac{\hat{P}_f}{dG} = \frac{\left(-\frac{M}{P_y} + apF\right)\theta_1}{\Omega} < 0, \text{ as given by result (B.1.2)}$$

$$\Rightarrow dP_f = \varphi dG \qquad \ldots\ldots (11)$$

$$\text{where } \varphi = \frac{\left\{\left(-\frac{M}{P_y} + apF\right)\theta_1\right\}P_f}{\Omega} < 0$$

$$\frac{\hat{P}_Y}{dG} = \frac{apF\theta_1}{\Omega} > 0, \text{ as given by result (B.1.3)}$$

Transitional Details

To obtain the initial jump in P_f after increase in G, we set t = 0 and using $A_1 = -A_2$ in equation (3.2) we get,

$$P_f(0) = P_{f_1} + \left(\frac{\lambda_2 - \lambda_1}{a_{21}}\right)A_2 \qquad \ldots\ldots (12)$$

Solving equation (7) and (8) and using expression (10) and (11), we get

$$A_2 = \frac{\left(\mu - \varphi\left(\frac{\lambda_1 - a_{22}}{a_{21}}\right)\right)}{\frac{\lambda_2 - \lambda_1}{a_{21}}} dGe^{-\lambda_2 T} \qquad \ldots\ldots (13)$$

Substituting the value of A_2 in equation (12) we get,

$$P_f(0) = P_{f_1} + \left(\mu - \varphi\left(\frac{\lambda_1 - a_{22}}{a_{21}}\right)\right)dG^{-\lambda_2 T}$$

Therefore, the initial jump in food price is:

$\Rightarrow P_f(0)-P_{f1}=\left(\mu-\varphi\left(\frac{\lambda_1-a_{22}}{a_{21}}\right)\right)dG^{-\lambda_2 T}$, as given in the text by result (B.1.4)

Again at time T, we get from equation (5.1)

$$w(T)=w_2+A_1^{\prime}e^{\lambda_1 t}$$

$$\Rightarrow w(T)-w_2=A_1^{\prime}e^{\lambda_1 t} \qquad \ldots\ldots (14)$$

Now, substituting value of $A_1=-A_2$ in equation (7) we get the value of $A_1^{\prime}$ as

$$A_1^{\prime}=\left[\left(\frac{\mu-\varphi\left(\frac{\lambda_1-a_{22}}{a_{21}}\right)}{\frac{\lambda_2-\lambda_1}{a_{21}}}\right)\left(e^{\lambda_2 T}-e^{\lambda_1 T}\right)\left(e^{-\lambda_2 T}\right)-\mu\right]e^{-\lambda_2 T}dG \qquad (15)$$

$$=(\gamma-\mu)e^{-\lambda_1 T}dG \qquad (16)$$

where $\gamma=\left(\frac{\mu-\varphi\left(\frac{\lambda_1-a_{22}}{a_{21}}\right)}{\frac{\lambda_2-\lambda_1}{a_{21}}}\right)\left(e^{\lambda_2 T}-e^{\lambda_1 T}\right)\left(e^{-\lambda_2 T}\right)$

From equation (14) it is seen that w increases in the long-run if $A_1^{\prime}>0$.

Again in period T, we get from equation (5.2)

$$P_f(T)-P_{f_2}=\left(\frac{\lambda_1-a_{22}}{a_{21}}\right)A_1^{\prime}e^{\lambda_1 t}$$

$$\Rightarrow P_f(T)-P_f(0)=\left(\frac{\lambda_1-a_{22}}{a_{21}}\right)A_1^{\prime}e^{\lambda_1 t} \qquad (17)$$

Since $a_{22}>0,\ a_{21}>0,\lambda_1<0,A_1^{\prime}>0$, it is evident from equation (17) that P_f decreases in the long-run.

Equations (17) and (14) determines the final change in food price and wage rate respectively.

Increase in Money Supply

Setting $dG = \hat{F} = 0$ in expression (C) we get,

$$\frac{\hat{w}}{dM} = \frac{m\alpha cpF\theta_1}{P_Y.\Omega} = \frac{1}{M}$$

$\Rightarrow \frac{\hat{w}}{\hat{M}} = 1$, as given by result (B.2.1)

$$\Rightarrow dw = \Phi dM \tag{18}$$

where $\Phi = \frac{w}{M} > 0$

And $\frac{\hat{P}_f}{\hat{M}} = 1$, as given by result (B.2.2)

$$\Rightarrow dP_f = \Phi dM \tag{19}$$

Transitional Details

To obtain the initial jump in P_f after increase in M, we set t = 0 and using $A_1 = -A_2$ in equation (3.2) we get,

$$P_f(0) = P_{f_1} + \left(\frac{\lambda_2 - \lambda_1}{a_{21}}\right)A_2 \tag{20}$$

Solving equations (7) and (8) and using expressions (18) and (19), we get

$$A_2 = \frac{\left(\Phi - \Phi\left(\frac{\lambda_2 - a_{22}}{a_{21}}\right)\right)}{\frac{\lambda_2 - \lambda_1}{a_{21}}} dMe^{-\lambda_2 T} \tag{21}$$

Substituting the value of A_2 in equation (20) we get,

$$P_f(0) = P_{f_1} + \left(\Phi - \Phi\left(\frac{\lambda_1 - a_{22}}{a_{21}}\right)\right) dM^{-\lambda_2 T}$$

Therefore, the initial jump in food price is:

$\Rightarrow P_f(0) - P_{f_1} + \left(\Phi\left\{1 - \left(\frac{\lambda_1 - a_{22}}{a_{21}}\right)\right\}\right) dM^{-\lambda_2 T}$, as given by the result (B.2.4).

Again at time T, we get from equation (5.1)

$$w(T) = w_2 + A_1' e^{\lambda_1 t}$$

$$\Rightarrow w(T) - w_2 = A_1' e^{\lambda_1 t} \qquad (22)$$

Now, substituting value of $A_1 = -A_2$ in equation (7) we get the value of A_1' as.

$$A_1' = \left[\left(\frac{\left\{1 - \left(\frac{\lambda_1 - a_{22}}{a_{21}}\right)\right\}}{\frac{\lambda_2 - \lambda_1}{a_{21}}}\right)\left(e^{\lambda_2 T} - e^{\lambda_1 T}\right)\left(e^{\lambda_2 T}\right) - 1\right] \Phi e^{-\lambda_2 T} dM \qquad (23)$$

$$= (\Delta - 1)\Phi e^{-\lambda_2 T} dM \qquad (24)$$

$$\text{where } \Delta = \left(\frac{\left\{1 - \left(\frac{\lambda_1 - a_{22}}{a_{21}}\right)\right\}}{\frac{\lambda_2 - \lambda_1}{a_{21}}}\right)\left(e^{\lambda_2 T} - e^{\lambda_1 T}\right)\left(e^{-\lambda_2 T}\right)$$

From equation (22) it is seen that w increases in the long-run if $A_1' > 0$.

Again in period T, we get from equation (5.2)

$$P_f(T) - P_{f_2} = \left(\frac{\lambda_1 - a_{22}}{a_{21}}\right) A_1' e^{\lambda_1 t}$$

$$=> P_f(T) - P_f(0) = \left(\frac{\lambda_1 - a_{22}}{a_{21}}\right) A_1' e^{\lambda_1 t} \qquad (25)$$

Since $a_{22} > 0, a_{21} > 0, \lambda_1 < 0, A_1' > 0$, it is evident from equation (25) that P_f increases in the long-run.

Equations (25) and (22) determines the final change in food price and wage rate respectively.

Increase in Marketable Surplus of Food

Setting $dG = \frac{dM}{P_Y} = 0$ in expression (C), we get

$\frac{\hat{w}}{\hat{F}} = \frac{\theta_2}{\theta_1} > 0$, as given by result the (B.3.1)

$$\Rightarrow dw = \left(\frac{\theta_2}{\theta_1 F}\right) dF$$

$$\Rightarrow dw = \Psi dF \qquad (26)$$

where $\Psi = \frac{\theta_2}{\theta_1 F} > 0$

$\frac{\hat{P}_f}{\hat{F}} = -1 < 0$, as given by the result (B.3.2)

$$\Rightarrow dP_f = -\frac{P_f}{F} dF$$

$$\Rightarrow dP_f = -\Lambda dF \qquad (27)$$

where $\Lambda = \frac{P_f}{F} > 0$

Transitional Details

To obtain the initial jump in P_f after increase in F, we set t= 0 and using $A_1 = -A_2$ in equation (3.2) we get,

$$P_f(0) - P_{f1} + \left(\frac{\lambda_2 - \lambda_1}{a_{21}}\right) A_2 \qquad (28)$$

Solving equations (7) and (8) and using expressions (26) and (27), we get

$$A_2 = \frac{\left(\Psi - \Lambda\left(\frac{\lambda_2 - a_{22}}{a_{21}}\right)\right)}{\frac{\lambda_2 - \lambda_1}{a_{21}}} dFe^{-\lambda_2 T} \tag{29}$$

Substituting the value of A_2 in equation (28) we get,

$$P_f\,(0) = P_{f_1} + \left(\Psi - \Lambda\left(\frac{\lambda_1 - a_{22}}{a_{21}}\right)\right) dF^{-\lambda_2 T}$$

Therefore, the initial jump in food price is:

$$\Rightarrow P_f\,(0) - P_{f_1} = \left(\Psi - \Lambda\left(\frac{\lambda_1 - a_{22}}{a_{21}}\right)\right) dF^{-\lambda_2 T},$$

as given by the result (B.3.4)

Again at time T, we get from equation (5.1)

$$w(T) = w_2 + A_1' e^{\lambda_1 t}$$

$$\Rightarrow w(T) - w_2 + A_1' e^{\lambda_1 t} \tag{30}$$

Now, substituting value of $A_1 = -A_2$ in equation (7) we get the value of A_1' as

$$A_1' = \left[\left(\frac{\Psi - \Lambda\left(\frac{\lambda_2 - a_{22}}{a_{21}}\right)}{\frac{\lambda_2 - \lambda_1}{a_{21}}}\right)\left(e^{\lambda_2 T} - e^{\lambda_1 T}\right)\left(e^{-\lambda_2 T}\right) \quad \Psi\right] c^{-\lambda_1 T} d\Gamma \tag{31}$$

$$= (\Pi - \Psi) e^{-\lambda_1 T} dF \tag{32}$$

$$\text{where } \Pi = \left(\frac{\Psi - \Lambda\left(\frac{\lambda_2 - a_{22}}{a_{21}}\right)}{\frac{\lambda_2 - \lambda_1}{a_{21}}}\right)\left(e^{\lambda_2 T} - e^{\lambda_1 T}\right)\left(e^{-\lambda_2 T}\right)$$

From equation (30) it is seen that w increases in the long-run if $A_1^{/} > 0$.

Again in period T, we get from equation (5.2)

$$P_f(T) - P_{f_2} = \left(\frac{\lambda_1 - a_{22}}{a_{21}}\right) A_1^{/} e^{\lambda_1 t}$$

$$\Rightarrow P_f(T) - P_f(0) = \left(\frac{\lambda_1 - a_{22}}{a_{21}}\right) A_1^{/} e^{\lambda_1 t} \quad (33)$$

Since $a_{22} > 0, a_{21} > 0, \lambda_1 < 0, A_1^{/} > 0$, it is evident from equation (33) that P_f decreases in the long-run.

Equations (33) and (30) determines the final change in food price and wage rate respectively.

Is the Financial Market Efficient?

DIGANTA MUKHERJEE AND SANKHA GHOSH

1. INTRODUCTION

One of the problems that has drawn the interest of all the market forces involved in trading and which has a very high impact potential in the body of academic thinking on investments is the problem of market efficiency. The issue of efficiency is a very fundamental one and it is something which most market players would like to settle once and for all so that they can make long-term decisions based on the notion of market efficiency. Unless they are doing reckless speculation and trading momentum, almost everybody believes that the market is efficient in the long run whereas short term inefficiencies still remain. The problem is giving a concrete shape to the understanding to validate the existing beliefs about short and long-term efficiency or to disprove the conjecture.

Although the problem of market efficiency is a burning one and a lot of econometric and empirical research has been done on this topic [see *Campbell, Lo and Mackinlay (1997), Fama (1965),*

Fama and French (1993)], surprisingly there is very little theoretical literature on it and no one has ever attempted to formulate the problem mathematically or attack it analytically. In this paper our aim is to define market efficiency rigorously and do an analytical and numerical study of a simple model of trading in the light of this definition. In particular we ask questions like what is an optimal model for R&D in the financial market, what are the structural specifications of the stock market that help in gaining efficiency and whether traders can gain in efficiency with trading.

The formulation of the model, including the traders' trading and R&D activities, the trading rules in the market are discussed in several sub-sections of section 2. The discussion here borrows from the material in *Hull (2004) and Reilly and Brown (2003)*. The basic analytical derivations are presented in section 3. Section 4 takes up the issue of defining market efficiency in a formal way and we propose alternative definitions to this purpose. The results are verified through simulation studies which are outlined in section 5 along with the results.

An additional issue of interest in this area is whether the market participants gain in efficiency through repeated participation in trading. This phenomenon of learning by doing is modelled and analysed in our set-up in section 6. Finally we try to match the results of our model with the results from the standard econometrics literature in section 7. Finally section 8 concludes.

2. FORMULATING THE PROBLEM

We will attempt a very simplistic formulation of the stock market trading problem to make ideas clear.

1. The Traders and the Market

Suppose there is a security or an asset such as a stock to be traded. Suppose there is a previously determined 'fundamental real value' function which for our purposes can be modeled as a Brownian motion. Nobody knows the function or the drift and volatility parameters of the Brownian motion.

Let us start with discrete time, $t \in \mathbb{N}$ to fix ideas. Suppose the fundamental value is a stochastic process $\{v_t\}_{t \in \mathbb{N}}$ where $v_t = v(et, e_{t-1}, \ldots)$ and $\{e_i : i \leq t\}$ is the history of fundamental economic variables.

Suppose there are many players in the market, which could be large investment banks, financial institutions or individual investors. Each market player possesses a market prediction, a function of public information on previous trades, prices and economic variables and a private unknown called 'processing capacity.' The processing capacity could be thought of as the intrinsic capacity of a firm to do high end research so as to maximize its profit by improving prediction accuracy or to take advantage of arbitrage opportunities in the market as and when they arise. Assume that there is no borrowing or short selling to start with and all commitments are honored so that there is no risk of non-compliance in a deal.

There is another variable called market price which changes only through trade. The market price is a stochastic process $\{p_t\}_{t \in \mathbb{N}}$ whose value is governed by the demand supply law of economics, i.e. if more traders put a 'buy' on the asset or the stock then the market price increases whereas if more traders put a 'sell' on the asset then it's market price decreases. Assume that the market price is determined on a first come first serve basis, i.e. if the first trader to trade that asset in a particular instant of time quotes the market price to be higher or lower than the price in the previous of time then his quoted price is taken to be the market price for that instant of time.

2. R & D by Traders

To process the information and decide on trading (buy/sell) the trader engages in research. Trader i at time t starts with initial wealth w_t^i or shareholding q_t^i (he would always have one or the other as he always uses all his wealth). Each trader has his own prediction for the fundamental real value function. The outcome of the prediction process for person i is a valuation,

$$\hat{v}_t^i = v_t + \sigma_t^i \in_t^i$$

where $\sigma_t^i = \sigma(c_t^i, \rho^i)$ such that $\frac{\partial(\sigma_t^2)^i}{\partial c_t^i} < 0, \frac{\partial(\sigma_t^2)^i}{\partial \rho^i} < 0, (\sigma_t^2)^i (0,0) < \infty$ and $\epsilon_t^i \overset{i.i.d}{\sim} N(0,1)$

Here ρ^i is the processing capacity of the ith trader and c_t^i is the amount of money invested in R&D by the ith trader during the tth instant of time.

For obvious reasons the accuracy of the ith trader's prediction, $(\sigma_t^2)^i$ is a non-increasing function of ρ^i and c_t^i. Let us assume $v_t \sim N(at, t)$ where a is known. Therefore, the prediction is a noisy estimate of the fundamental value.

The vital question that crops up now is that: When holding share, how is c_t^i funded? To circumvent this problem we make the following assumption:

Let c be the minimal amount of money that a trader always wants to keep aside for doing R&D.

Suppose that the bank pays an interest at the rate of r percent per annum on the amount deposited by a trader in the bank. We make the assumption that initially each trader deposits the amount $\frac{100c}{r}$ *in the bank so that he is always assured of the amount c for pursuing his research even when he is holding shares and has no cash in hand.*

An almost immediate question that follows is: Does the trader always spend the amount c on R&D or does he spend a fraction of it and if so what fraction does he spend? We will come back to this question later. Suppose for the moment we have an optimum amount c_t^i for the ith trader to spend on R&D at the tth instant of time. Suppose q_t^i is the number of stocks owned by the ith trader at time t.

3. The Trading Rule

A simple trading rule follows:

Whenever a person's prediction is above the current market price he buys the asset using all his wealth at a price marginally above the current price. Similarly, whenever a person's prediction is below the current market price he sells the asset. This price differential which is assumed to be a constant but small amount is the market impact of his trade.

In essence what we are saying is:

If at time instant t, the market price is p_t and the first trader to make a trade puts a buy on the asset then $p_{t+1} = p_t + \delta$ where 0 is a known constant. Similarly if the first trader to make a trade puts a sell on the asset then $p_{t+1} = p_t - \delta$.

At the instant of time t, the following variables are known to us:

w_t^i = The amount of wealth the ith trader has at time t.
q_t^i = Number of stocks owned by the ith trader at time t.
p_{t+1} = The market price that will prevail at time $t + 1$.

Now we analyze the three cases that may arise.

Case I: $(\hat{v}_t^i > p_t + \delta)$ and $p_{t+1} = p_t + \delta$

If the prediction of the ith trader is assumed to be approximately correct, then the market has undervalued the shares and the price is expected to rise further. The trader should buy more shares now so that he can sell them off later when the prices have peaked so as to earn a profit.

Therefore, $q_{t+1}^i = q_t^i + \dfrac{(w_t^i + c) - c_{t+1}^i}{(p_t + \delta)}$ and $w_{t+1}^i = 0$

Case II: $(\hat{v}_t^i < p_t + \delta)$ and $p_{t+1} = p_t + \delta$

Again assuming the prediction of the ith trader to be correct, the market has overvalued the shares and the price is expected to fall further. The trader should sell off all his shares to take advantage of the overvaluation.

Therefore, $q_{t+1}^i = 0$ and $w_{t+1}^i = w_t^i + q_t^i\,(p_t - \delta)$

In this case we will always use the amount c earned as interest to do R&D since q^i_{t+1} or w^i_{t+1} (and hence the expected utility as we will see later) is not a function of c^i_{t+1} and therefore there is no question of obtaining an optimum c^i_{t+1} by maximizing utility.

Case III: $(p_t - \delta \leq \hat{v}^i_t \leq p_t + \delta)$

In this case the market prediction p_t and the trader's prediction $\hat{v}^i_t$ are incompatible with trade. $p_{t+1} = p_t + \delta$, implies that more traders are interested in buying rather than selling and hence prices will increase whereas $v^i_t \leq p_t + \delta$ implies that the market has over valued the share and prices will fall. Similarly when $(v^i_t \geq p_t - \delta)$ and $p_{t+1} = p_t - \delta$. Hence in this case the trader does not take a stand and neither buys nor sells shares. So, $q^i_{t+1} = q^i_t$ and $w^i_{t+1} = w^i_t$.

In this case also we will again allocate the amount c for doing R&D for the same reasons as in case II.

4. The Optimization Problem

Now we get back to the question of trying to find an optimum amount for doing R&D so as to maximize the returns. We try to maximize the expected utility of the trades. The utility is a function of the amount of tangible wealth a trader has. Suppose we want to find an optimum value c^i_{t+1}, i.e. the amount of money to be spent on R&D by the ith trader at the $(t + 1)^{th}$ unit of time. The total amount of tangible wealth the ith trader has at the $(t + 1)^{th}$ unit of time is $w^i_{t+1} + q^i_{t+1} v^i_{t+1}$.

Since v_{t+1} is unknown we will use $\widehat{v^i_{t+1}}$ as a proxy for v_{t+1} for the ith trader. Hence the utility is a function of $w^i_{t+1} + q^i_{t+1}\widehat{v^i_{t+1}}$.

$$U = U(w^i_{t+1} + q^i_{t+1}\widehat{v^i_{t+1}})$$

A natural question is what should be the functional form of the utility function? Intuition tells us that it should be such that $U(x)$ should have slope decreasing in x, i.e. as x increases the rate of change of the utility should not increase rapidly.

Therefore, $u(x) = 1 - e^{-x}$ is a reasonable form of the utility function. For this section for the sake of convenience in notation, let us drop the suffix i. Then expected Utility = $EU(w_{t+1} + q_{t+1}\hat{v}_{t+1})$. Now,

$$w_{t+1} + q_{t+1}\hat{v}_{t+1} = \left\{\left(q_t + \frac{(w_t + c) - c_{t+1}}{p_t + \delta}\right)\hat{v}_{t+1}\right\}$$

$$|| (p_{t+1} = p_t + \delta, \hat{v}_t > p_t + \delta)$$

$$+ \{(w_t + q_t (p_t - \delta))\} || (p_{t+1} = p_t - \delta, \hat{v}_t < p_t - \delta)$$

$$+ \{(w_t + q_t \hat{v}_{t+1})\} || (p_{t+1} = p_t + \delta, \hat{v}_t \le p_t + \delta)$$

$$+ \{(w_t + q_t \hat{v}_{t+1})\} || (p_{t+1} = p_t - \delta, \hat{v}_t \ge p_t + \delta)$$

Since only the first term involves c_{t+1} with respect to which we want to maximize the expected utility we define the modified utility as :

$$U^* = U^*\left\{\left(q_t + \frac{(w_t + c) - c_{t+1}}{p_t + \delta}\right)\hat{v}_{t+1}\right\}$$

We have assumed,

1. $v_{t+1} \sim N(a(l+1),(l+1))$.
2. $\hat{v}_{t+1} = v_{t+1} + \delta_{t+1} \in_t +1$ where $\in_{t+1} \sim N(0,1)$ and $\in_{t+1}$ is independent of $v_{t+1.}$
3. σ^2_{t+1} is a function of σ and c_{l+1}.

3. THE ANALYSIS

From the above discussion we observe that:

$$v_{t+1} \sim N(a(t+1), (t+1) + \sigma^2_{t+1})$$

As the utility function is $u(x) = 1 - e^{-x}$ we have

$$EU^* = E\left(U^*\left\{\left(q_t + \frac{(w_t + c) - c_{t+1}}{p_t + \delta}\right)\hat{v}_{t+1}\right\}\right),$$

$$\text{Or, } EU^* = \int\left\{1-\exp\left[\left(-q_t - \frac{w_t + c}{p_t + \sigma} + \frac{c_{t+1}}{p_{t+\delta}}\right)x\right]\right\}$$

$$\frac{1}{\sqrt{2\pi(t+1+\sigma_{t+1}^2)}}\exp\left(-\frac{(x-a(t+1))^2}{2(t+1+\sigma_{t+1}^2)}\right)dx$$

Substituting $\dfrac{x-a(t+1)}{\sqrt{(t+1+\sigma_{t+1}^2)}} = y$, we have

$$x = y\sqrt{(t+1+\sigma_{t+1}^2)} + a(t+1).$$

Hence $\dfrac{dx}{\sqrt{(t+1+\sigma_{t+1}^2)}} = dy.$

Let $k = -qt - \dfrac{w_{t+C}}{p_{t+\delta}}$, then

$$EU^* = \frac{1}{\sqrt{2\pi}}\int\left(1-\exp\left\{\left(k+\frac{c_{t+1}}{p_t+\sigma}\right)\left(y\sqrt{(t+1+\sigma_{t+1}^2)} + a(t+1)\right)\right\}\right)e^{-\frac{y^2}{2}dy}$$

$$= 1 - \frac{1}{\sqrt{2\pi}}\int\exp\left\{\left(k+\frac{c_{t+1}}{p_t+\sigma}\right)\left(y\sqrt{(t+1+\sigma_{t+1}^2)} + a(t+1)\right)\right\}e^{-\frac{y^2}{2}dy}$$

$$= 1 - \frac{1}{\sqrt{2\pi}}\exp\left\{\left(k+\frac{c_{t+1}}{p_t+\delta}\right)a(t+1)\right\}\int\exp\left\{\left(k+\frac{c_{t+1}}{p_t+\sigma}\right)\sqrt{(t+1+\sigma_{t+1}^2}\,y - \frac{y^2}{2}\right\}dy$$

The index of e inside the integral is

$$= -\frac{1}{2}\left(y^2 - 2\left(k+\frac{c_{t+1}}{p_t+\delta}\right)\sqrt{t+1+\sigma_{t+1}^2\,y}\right)$$

$$= -\frac{1}{2}\left\{y - \left(k+\frac{c_{t+1}}{p_t+\delta}\right)\sqrt{t+1+\sigma_{t+1}^2}\right\}^2 + \frac{1}{2}\left(k+\frac{c_{t+1}}{p_t+\delta}\right)^2 (t+1+\sigma_{t+1}^2)$$

Therefore,

$$EU^* = 1 - \exp\left\{\left(k + \frac{c_{t+1}}{p_t + \delta}\right)a(t+1) + \frac{1}{2}\left(k + \frac{c_{t+1}}{p_t + \delta}\right)^2 (t+1+\sigma_{t+1}^2)\right\}$$

To maximize the expected utility we have to minimize the following function

$$f(c_{t+1}) = \left(k + \frac{c_{t+1}}{p_t + \delta}\right)a(t+1) + \frac{1}{2}\left(k + \frac{c_{t+1}}{p_t + \delta}\right)^2 (t+1+\sigma_{t+1}^2)$$

Let

$$g(c_{t+1}) = \frac{\partial f}{\partial c_{t+1}} = \frac{a(t+1)}{p_t + \delta} + \left(k + \frac{c_{t+1}}{p_t + \delta}\right)\frac{(t+1+\sigma_{t+1}^2)}{(p_t + \delta)}$$

$$+ \frac{1}{2}\left(k^2 + \frac{c_{t+1}}{p_t + \delta}\right)^2 \frac{\partial \sigma_{t+1}^2}{\partial c_{t+1}}$$

Case I: Consider an additive form for the variance function, $\sigma_{t+1}^2 = \alpha + \beta c_{t+1} + \gamma \rho$

Here,

$$g(c_{t+1}) = \frac{a(t+1)}{p_t + \delta} + \left(k + \frac{c_{t+1}}{p_t + \delta}\right)\frac{(t+1+\alpha + \beta c_{t+1} + \gamma\rho)}{(p_t + \delta)}$$

$$+ \frac{1}{2}\left(k^2 + \frac{c_{t+1}^2}{(p_t + \delta)^2} + \frac{2kc_{t+1}}{p_t + \delta}\right)\beta$$

Elementary calculation shows the function g can be represented as a quadratic polynomial in c_{t+1}. To be precise,

$$g(c_{t+1}) = Ac_{t+1}^2 + Bc_{t+1} + C \tag{1}$$

where $A = \frac{3\beta}{2(p_t + \delta)^2}$, $B = \frac{2k\beta}{(p_t + \delta)} + \frac{t+1+\alpha+\gamma\rho}{(p_t + \delta)^2}$

and $C = \frac{a(t+1)}{(p_t + \delta)} + \frac{k(t+1+\alpha+\gamma\rho)}{(p_t + \delta)} + \frac{1}{2}k^2\beta$

Case II: Now consider a multiplicative form,

$$\sigma_{t+1}^2 = \eta + \gamma c_{t+1}\beta$$

In this case the same calculation as done before will work if we replace $\alpha+\gamma\rho$ by η and β by $\gamma\rho$. Thus we have the same quadratic (1) where now $A=\frac{3\gamma\rho}{2(p_t+\delta)^2}$, and $B=\frac{2k\gamma\rho}{(p_t+\delta)}+\frac{t+1+\eta}{(p_t+\delta)^2}$ and $C=\frac{a(t+1)}{(p_t+\delta)}+\frac{k(t+1+\eta)}{(p_t+\delta)}+\frac{1}{2}k^2\gamma\rho$.

In both cases we have to solve for the quadratic (1) to get the optimum value of c_{t+1}. We are going to call it $\hat{c}_{t+1}$. If the quadratic has no real solution then $f(c_{t+1})$ is unbounded below and hence we take $\hat{c}_{t+1}=c$ where c is the money received as interest from the bank. Otherwise, let x_1 and x_2 be two solutions of (1) and if $f(x_1) \leq f(x_2)$ and $x_1 \geq 0$ then $\hat{c}_{t+1} = \min(x_1, c)$, Likewise if $f(x_1) > f(x_2)$ and $x_2 \geq 0$ then $\hat{c}_{t+1} = \min(x_2, c)$. On the other hand if both x_1 and x_2 are negative then $\hat{c}_{t+1} = 0$. Therefore, we have arrived at an optimum amount $\hat{c}_{t+1}$ which we will use for doing R&D.

4. DEFINING MARKET EFFICIENCY

We now come to the crucial question of this paper: What is Market Efficiency? Or What should be a reasonable definition of market efficiency? One definition could be as follows:

Definition 1. *We will say a market is inefficient if* $\exists \in > 0$ *such that the set where the absolute difference of the market price and the fundamental value function exceeds* $\in$ *has positive Lebesgue measure. Mathematically writing, a market is inefficient if* $\exists \in > 0$ *such that* $\lambda(\{s : |v(s)-p(s)| > \in\}) > 0$ *where* λ *denotes the Lebesgue measure on* $\mathbb{R}$.

A market is efficient if it is not inefficient.

But there seems to be a problem with this definition. As the market evolves the order of magnitude of $v(t)$ and hence $p(t)$ increases with time since the expected value *at* is a increasing function of t. Hence no fixed $\in$ can be used as a measure of the absolute difference of the market price and the fundamental value at all time points unless the difference is suitably scaled.

An alternative and more workable definition of market efficiency is as follows:

Definition 2. A market is inefficient if $\exists \in > 0$ *such that the set where the absolute relative difference of the market price and the fundamental value function exceeds* $\in$ *has positive Lebesgue measure, i.e., a market is inefficient if* $\exists \in > 0$ *such that*

$$\lambda\left(\left\{s : \left|\frac{v(s)-p(s)}{v(s)}\right| > \in\right\}\right) > 0$$ *where* λ *denotes the Lebesgue measure on* $\mathbb{R}$.

A market is efficient if it is not inefficient.

We define a measure of market efficiency by,

$$\chi_{\in} \overset{def}{=} \lambda\left(\left\{s : \left|\frac{v(s)-p(s)}{v(s)}\right| > \in\right\}\right) \tag{2}$$

Since we only restrict ourself to discrete time case, we will use counting measure on time space instead of Lebesgue measure.

Let N be the number of times the stock has been traded. Then we can redefine the above measure for our purpose as follows :

$$\chi_{\in} \overset{def}{=} \frac{\#\left\{n : \left|\frac{v(n)-p(n)}{v(n)}\right| > \in\right\}}{N} \tag{3}$$

Since we must allow the market to evolve for the price process to correct and match the fundamental value process we start counting after $n > 200$.

Then market is efficient in our sense if

$$\chi_{\in} \to 0 \text{ as } N \to \infty \ \forall_{\in} > 0$$

5. SIMULATION STUDIES

We have assumed that there are $m = 100$ traders in the exchange. Let N represent total number of rounds of trade in the stock. To simulate $v_1, v_2 \ldots, v_N$ we simulate N i.i.d. $N(a, 1)$

random variables, say, $X_1, X_2, \ldots, X_N$. Then $v_i = \max\left(\sum_{j=1}^{i} X_i, 0\right)$. We have chosen $a = 0.25$. To simulate the processing capacities of the m traders we generate m independent $U(0, 1)$ numbers and allocate them to be the processing capacity of the m traders.

A subtle point here is how do we choose p_1, the initial market price, because the rate of convergence of the market price process to the fundamental value process will depend on the proximity of p_1 to v_1. We take $p_1 = I^+$ where $I \sim N(a, 10)$, independent of $\{X_i\}_{i\geq 1}$ for our simulation.

Now increments or decrements for the price process occurs in the steps of δ. Should δ be equal to a, the mean of valuation process? Notice that if δ is very large compared to a it could lead to an incorrect decision during the next trade even when the price process and the fundamental value process are at the same level during the present round of trading.

On the other hand suppose an incorrect decision is made at the ith round of trading. For the price process to catch up with the value process within shortest possible time of trading, δ must be approximately equal to $3a$. Similarly, to make up for two consecutive wrong decisions in minimum amount of time, δ has to be approximately equal to $5a$. Hence there is a tradeoff involved here regarding the magnitude of δ as compared to that of a. Simulation studies give us the best result when $\delta = 4a$, which is shown in details later. Therefore, we have chosen $\delta = 1$.

We have chosen the two functional forms of σ^2 as follows:

$$\left(\sigma_t^2\right)^i = 0.25 - 0.6\,c_t^i - 0.005\,\rho^i \tag{4}$$

$$\left(\sigma_t^2\right)^i = 0.25 - 0.6\,c_t^i\,\rho^i \tag{5}$$

Now we simulate the values of χ for $N = 1000$, $N = 5000$ and $N = 10000$. We have chosen $a = 0.25$ and $\delta = 1$, a choice which will be justified later. We plot $\left|\dfrac{v(i)-p(i)}{v(i)}\right|$ versus i. The plots are as shown in Figures 3.1, 3.2 and 3.3 where the (a) panels show the results for the additive form of σ^2 and the (b) panels are for the multiplicative form.

FIG. 3.1(a)

The Plot of χ with

$\sigma_t^2 = 0.25 - 0.06\, c_t - 0.005\, \rho$ and $N = 1000$

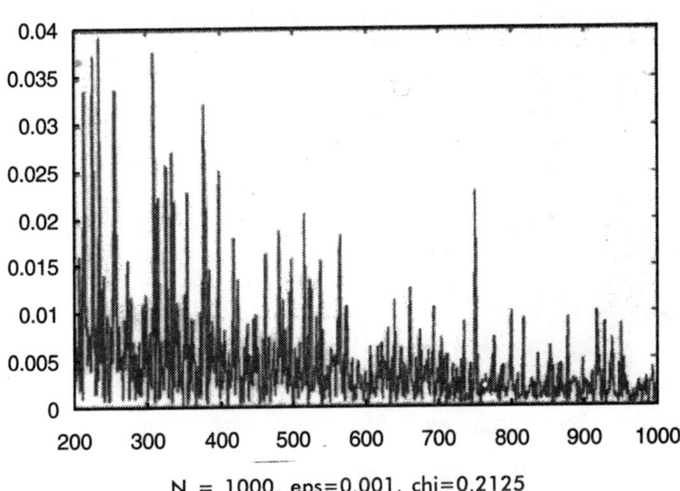

N = 1000, eps=0.001, chi=0.2125

FIG. 3.1(b)

The Plot of χ with

$\sigma_t^2 = 0.25 - 0.06\, c_t\, \rho$ and $N = 1000$

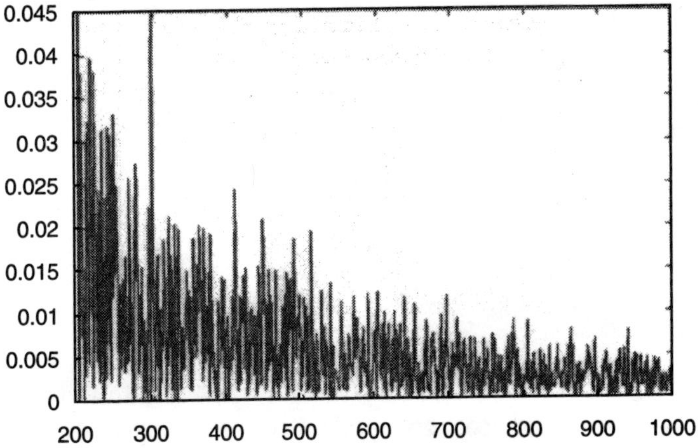

N = 1000, eps=0.001, chi=0.1825

FIG. 3.2(a)

The Plot of χ with

$\sigma_t^2 = 0.25 - 0.06\,c_t - 0.005\,\rho$ and $N = 5000$

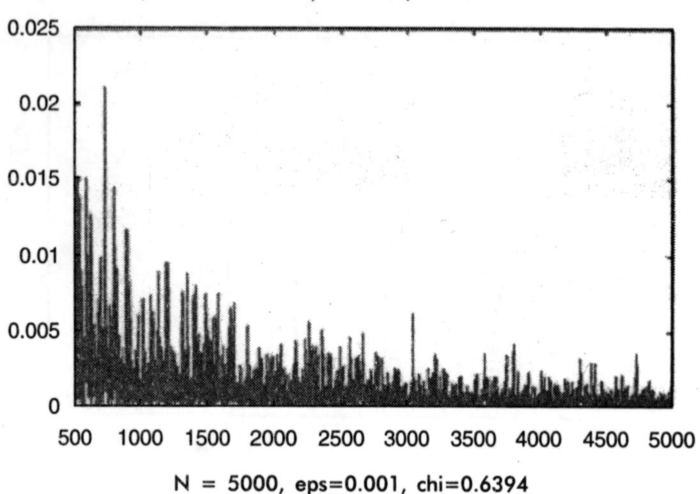

FIG. 3.2(b)

The Plot of χ with

$\sigma_t^2 = 0.25 - 0.06\,c_t\,\rho$ and $N = 5000$

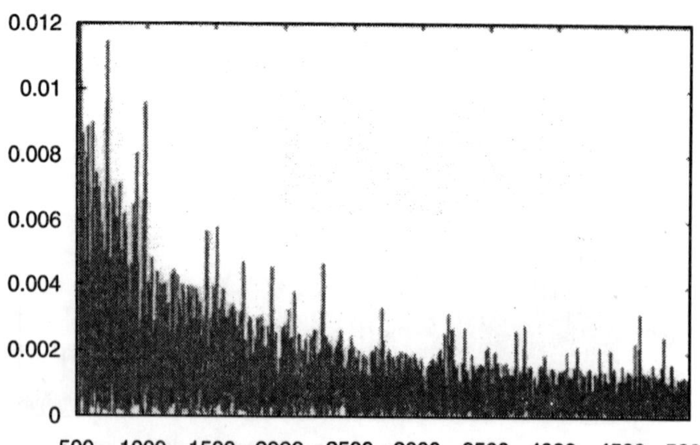

N = 5000, eps=0.001, chi=0.5773

FIG. 3.3(a)

The Plot of χ with

$\sigma_t^2 = 0.25 - 0.06\,c_t - 0.005\,\rho$ and $N = 10000$

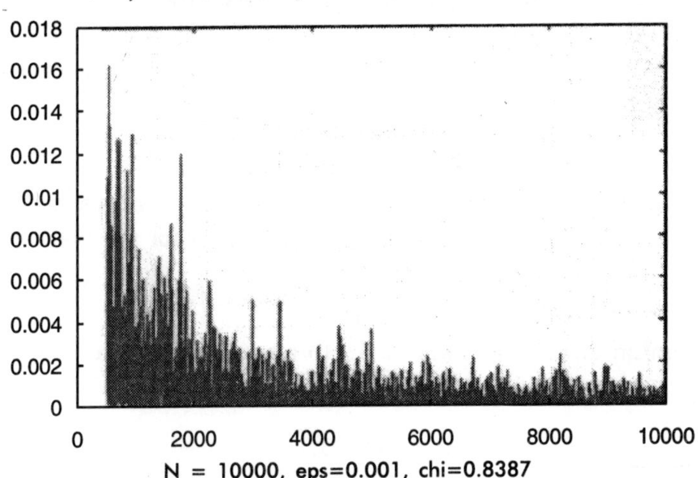

FIG. 3.3(b)

The Plot of χ with

$\sigma_t^2 = 0.25 - 0.06\,c_t\,\rho$ and $N = 10000$

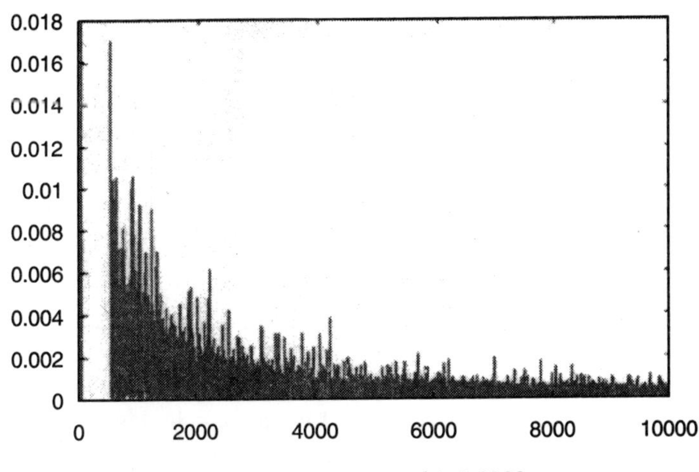

N = 10000, eps=0.001, chi=0.8103

The plots clearly show the decreasing nature of $\left|\frac{v(i)-p(i)}{v(i)}\right|$ in i and hence the convergence of the price process towards the fundamental value process as $N \to \infty$ in the sense of χ is clear.

What are the factors on which the rate of convergence of the market price process to the fundamental value process depends? Clearly the convergence rate depends on the market differential δ and a, the mean increment of the value process at each step. We have already argued earlier that there is a tradeoff involved in the magnitude of δ relative to a for the market to be efficient. What should be the value of the ratio $\frac{\delta}{a}$ so that optimum efficiency is attained? To answer the above question we produce the Tables 3.1 and 3.2 below.

TABLE 3.1

$\sigma_t^2 = 0.25 - 0.06\, c_t - 0.005\, \rho$, N = 500

$\in -\delta / a$	1	2	3	4	5	6
0.01	0.1629	0.9113	0.9773	0.9865	0.9798	0.9608
0.005	0.0650	0.8187	0.9113	0.9598	0.9706	0.9533
0.001	0	0.4054	0.5496	0.6819	0.6669	0.6590

TABLE 3.2

$\sigma_t^2 = 0.25 - 0.06\, c_t\, \rho$, N = 500

$\in -\delta / a$	1	2	3	4	5	6
0.01	0.2291	0.8998	0.9719	0.9810	0.9731	0.9748
0.005	0.0233	0.8227	0.9327	0.9504	0.9535	0.9319
0.001	0.0062	0.3908	0.5406	0.5910	0.5804	0.5375

The above tables show that in both the cases the price discovery process is most efficient when δ = 4a. Hence we have chosen a = 0.25 and δ = 1 in all the later simulations unless specifically mentioned otherwise.

We now attempt a more comprehensive analysis of the convergence of the price process to the value process and provide even more substantial evidence of the long-term efficiency of the market. We take N = 5000 and $\in$ = 0.001 and find the proportion of times $\left|\frac{v(i)-p(i)}{v(i)}\right| < \in$ in the intervals [1, 200], [201, 1000], [1001, 2000], [2001, 3000], [3001, 4000] and [4001, 5000]. If the market is efficient in the long-run then the proportions must increase as we move to the intervals on the right. We also plot $\left|\frac{v(i)-p(i)}{v(i)}\right|$ versus i on these intervals. The plots are given in Figures 3.4 and 3.5, again for the two functional forms of σ^2 separately.

Both the above plots and values of χ obtained over the different intervals substantiate the claim about the long-term efficiency of the market.

Our definition of market efficiency says that the market is efficient if $\frac{\#\left\{n : \left|\frac{v(n)-p(n)}{v(n)}\right| < \in\right\}}{N} \to 1$ as $N \to \infty \ \forall_{\in} > 0$. We have worked with $\in$ upto as small as 0.001. What happens for still smaller values of $\in$? To provide a suitable answer to this question we have taken $\in$ = 0.0001, N = 50000 and calculated the χ value for blocks of 1000. Then we have plotted these values so as to obtain a graphical verification as $\frac{\#\left\{n : \left|\frac{v(n)-p(n)}{v(n)}\right| < \in\right\}}{N} \to 1$ as $N \to \infty$ even for $\in$ as small as 0.0001. The plots for the two functional forms of δ^2 are shown in Figure 3.6.

In both the cases we get an almost increasing curve except for the inherent randomness in the process. The rate of increase of the curve decreases with the intervals moving to the right

FIG. 3.4

Improvement of χ with $\sigma_t^2 = 0.25 - 0.06\,c_t - 0.005\,\rho$

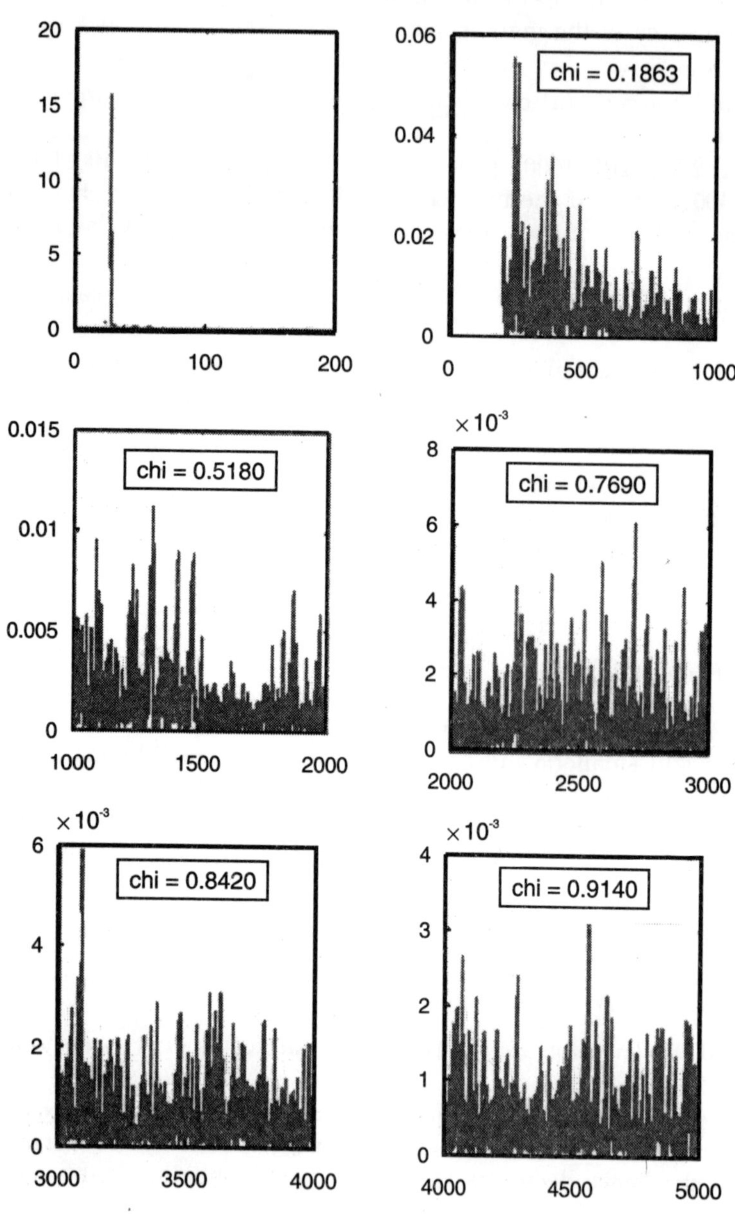

FIG. 3.5

Improvement of χ with $\sigma_t^2 = 0.25 - 0.06\,c_t - 0.006\,\rho$

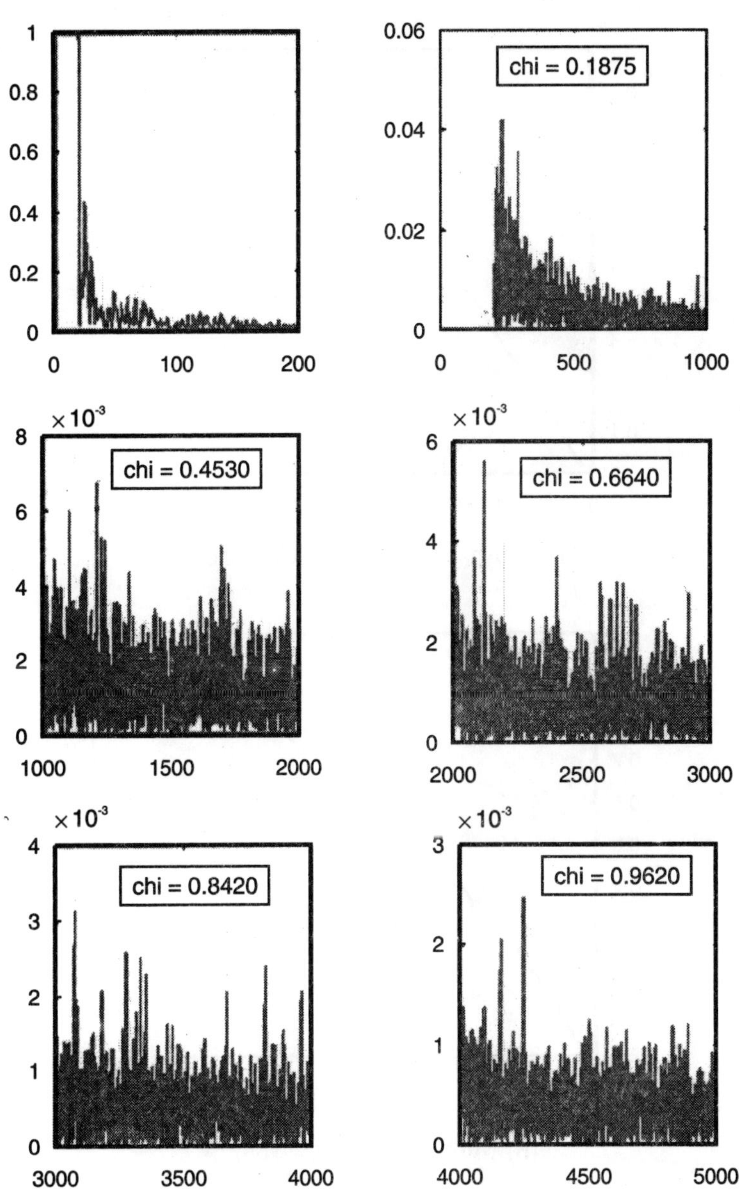

FIG. 3.6
Graphical Verification of Improvement of χ, ε = 0.0001 and N=50,000

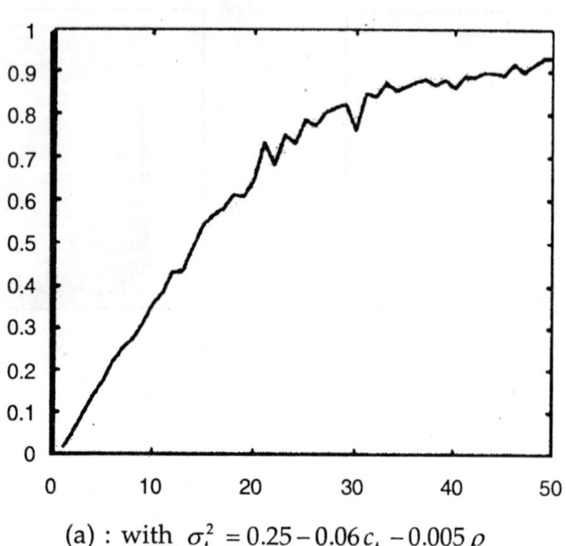

(a) : with $\sigma_t^2 = 0.25 - 0.06\,c_t - 0.005\,\rho$

(b) : with $\sigma_t^2 = 0.25 - 0.06\,c_t\,\rho$

which is to be expected. Thus we conclude that the market is indeed efficient in the long run according to our definition of efficiency.

6. LEARNING BY DOING

Learning by doing means augmentation of one's research potential with experience. As a trader does more and more trades his processing capacity increases with each trade. To model this in a simple fashion, we have assumed that if ρ_n is the processing capacity of a particular trader after n trades, then

$$\rho_n = 1-(1-\rho)c^{-n}$$

where ρ is the trader's initial processing capacity. Therefore as $n \to \infty$, $\rho_n \to 1$. We implemented this learning in our program and again plotted the χ values for blocks of 1000 taking N = 50000 and $\in$ = 0.0001 as in section 5. The plots for the two functional forms of σ_t^2 are given in Figure 3.7.

FIG. 3.7
Graphical Verification of Improvement of χ Under "Learning by Doing", ε = 0.0001 and N=50,000

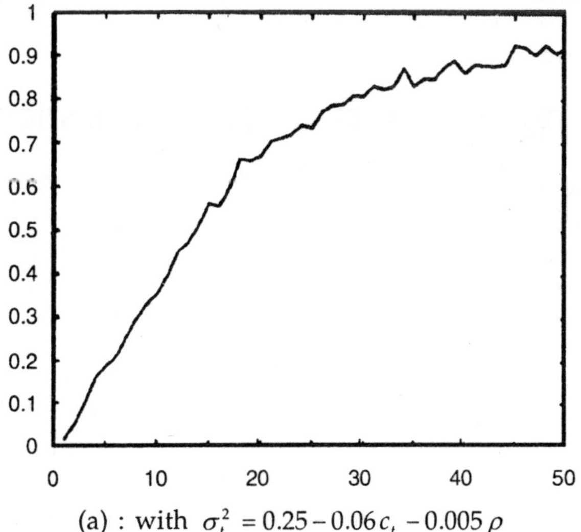

(a) : with $\sigma_t^2 = 0.25 - 0.06c_t - 0.005\rho$

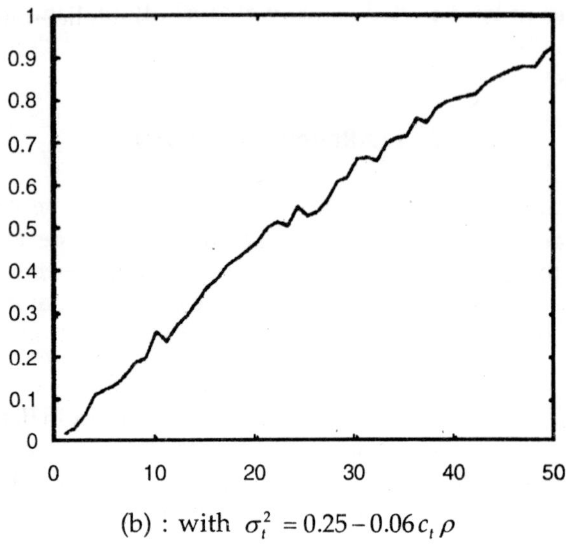

(b) : with $\sigma_t^2 = 0.25 - 0.06 c_t \rho$

From the above plots and comparing with the plots in Figure 3.6 we see that there is no considerable improvement in the convergence rate of the price process to the value process even after implementation of learning by doing. Hence experienced traders enjoy no distinct competitive advantage *vis-a-vis* inexperienced traders as far as trading capacity is concerned.

7. TESTING MARKET EFFICIENCY STATISTICALLY

We have talked about market efficiency and have tried to measure it directly through the closeness of the price with the underlying value process. But in the conventional financial econometrics literature one of the most popular tests for efficiency of the stock market is the one proposed by *Fama (1965)*. Given that the underlying value function is unobservable in real life, the indirect efficiency tests popularised by Fama and others are pervasive in this literature. (For a survey, see *Campbell, Lo and Mckinlay, 1997*.) To complete our discussion, we now attempt to link our methodology with the existing literature by testing the efficiency of the market with the price series generated by our algorithm. We test the following model and hypothesis.

$$\Delta p_t = \alpha + \sum_{i=1}^{12} \beta_i p_{t-i} + \epsilon_t \tag{6}$$

$$H_0 : \beta_1 - \beta_2 = ... = \beta_{12} = 0 \tag{7}$$

That is, we are testing for the significance of the first 12 lags of the price process as a predictor of the price change, $\Delta p_t = p_t - p_{t-1.}$

The estimation is done separately for the data sets of length 1000 generated from models with variance functions (4) and (5). The results of the regression exercises are shown in Tables 3.3 and 3.4 below.

TABLE 3.3
Estimation Results for Model I
Dependent Variable: Δ (price)
Method: Least Squares, Included observations: 988 after adjusting endpoints

Variable	*Coefficient*	*Std. Error*	*t-Statistic*	*Prob.*
PRICE(-I)	0.023327	0.031980	0.729439	0.4659
PRICE(-2)	-0.001519	0.045775	-0.033181	0.9735
PRICE(-3)	-0.007910	0.045781	-0.172775	0.8629
PRICE(-4)	0.031342	0.045779	0.684627	0.4937
PRICE(-5)	-0.003603	0.045901	-0.078490	0.9375
PRICE(-6)	-0.019369	0.045924	-0.421755	0.6733
PRICE(-7)	-0.026839	0.045925	-0.584401	0.5591
PRICE(-8)	0.002031	0.045960	0.044184	0.9648
PRICE(-9)	-0.010576	0.045979	-0.230019	0.8181
PRICE(-10)	0.047313	0.046007	1.028387	0.3040
PRICE(-11)	-0.016446	0.046032	-0.357279	0.7210
PRICE(-12)	-0.016605	0.031968	-0.519422	0.6036
R^2	-0.007627	Log likelihood	-1358.885	
Durbin-Watson stat	2.002270			

TABLE 3.4
Estimation Results for Model II
Dependent Variable: Δ (price)
Method: Least Squares, Included observations: 988 after adjusting endpoints

Variable	*Coefficient*	*Std. Error*	*t-Statistic*	*Prob.*
PRICE(-I)	0.015427	0.031903	0.483569	0.6288
PRICE(-2)	0.016074	0.045560	0.352816	0.7243
PRICE(-3)	-0.016623	0.045479	-0.365504	0.7148
PRICE(-4)	-0.021571	0.045351	-0.475650	0.6344
PRICE(-5)	0.097557	0.045350	2.151178	0.0317
PRICE(-6)	-0.072941	0.045452	-1.604793	0.1089
PRICE(-7)	-0.024904	0.045537	-0.546891	0.5846
PRICE(-8)	-0.032228	0.045477	-0.708668	0.4787
PRICE(-9)	0.012222	0.045483	0.268724	0.7882
PRICE(-10)	0.088798	0.045479	1.952486	0.0512
PRICE(-11)	0.004171	0.045594	0.091481	0.9271
PRICE(-12)	-0.064843	0.031841	-2.036458	0.0420
R^2	-0.003032	Log likelihood	-1315.919	
Durbin-Watson stat	2.009324			

Note that we have the expected efficiency results in terms of the goodness of fit (R^2 measure having values almost equal to zero) but in case of model II (multiplicative variance model) the coefficients of p_{t-5} and p_{t-12} turns out to be statistically significant in explaining Δp_t. There is thus some evidence in favour of market inefficiency in terms of the second model. All the coefficients turn out to be insignificant for model I. So overall we may say that our modelling and methodology for studying market efficiency is consistent with the usual statistical approach.

8. CONCLUSION

To sum up, in this paper we attempted to simulate the

trading scenario in a stock exchange using a set of heuristically justified assumptions. We also arrived at a reasonable and workable definition of market efficiency which is the χ measure (3). The convergence of the price process to the fundamental value process was subjected to a battery of diagnostic and graphical tests. The optimum ratio between the differential impact of the trade and the mean increment of the fundamental value process is obtained so as to achieve maximum market efficiency. Learning by doing concept is also incorporated to check the dependence of trading prowess on experience.

We conclude that the market is indeed efficient in the long run. Therefore, after the market has evolved for a significant amount of time the price process can be used as a proxy for the value process. The amount of time depends on how closely we want to approximate the value process by the price process. From our discussion on learning by doing (section 6) it seems that in general the amount of experience is not a criterion on which trading capability depends.

References

Hull, John, C. (2004). Option, Futures and Other Derivatives. Sixth edition. Prentice Hall.

Frank K. Reilly and Keith C. Brown. (2003). Investment Analysis and Portfolio Management, 7th edition. South-Western.

Campbell, J.Y., A.W. Lo, and A.C. MacKinlay (1997). The Econometrics of Financial Markets. Princeton, New Jersey: Princeton University Press.

Fama, Eugene F. (1965). The Behavior of Stock Market Prices, *Journal of Business*, 38, 34-105.

Fama, Eugene F. and Kenneth R. French (1993). Common risk factors in the returns on stocks and bonds, *Journal of Financial Economics*, 33, 3-56.

Incidence of Child Labour and Trade Liberalization : Comments on Chaudhuri and Gupta (2004)

Arnab Ghosh

INTRODUCTION

Presently one of the most distressing problems in the transitional societies of developing economies is the incidence of child labour. According to ILO (2002), one in every six children aged between 5 and 17 – or 246 million children are involved in child labour.[1] If the "invisible" workers who perform unpaid and household jobs are included, it is likely that the estimates would shoot up significantly further.

The supply of child labour has been attributed to factors such as poverty, lack of educational facilities and poor quality of schooling, capital market imperfection, parental attitudes including the objectives to maximize present income, reflecting cultural norms and social values, etc. However, poverty is considered to be the single largest factor behind the child labour incidence. To eradicate the problem of child labour, *World Development Report*, 1995 called for a multifaceted approach with programs that increase income security, reduce education costs, and improve the quality of schooling. It is believed that betterment of educational opportunities and a policy of compulsory education designed to human capital formation instead of poverty alleviation programs can more effectively remove children from work.

The developing countries have chosen free trade as their development strategy and been vigorously implementing liberalized trade and investment policies for the last two decades or so. It was believed that growth with foreign capital and reduction of tariff and non-tariff barriers would take the developing countries into higher growth orbits, the benefits of which would definitely percolate down to the bottom of the society, thereby leading to reduction of poverty and poverty-driven child labour incidence. Cigno *et. al.* (2002), Edmond and Pavcnik (2005) and Neumayer and Soysa (2005) have analyzed the impact of liberalized trade and investment policies on child work using cross-country data and found that countries with more liberalized trade regime and greater penetration by foreign direct investment are associated with lower child labour incidence. On the contrary there are studies like Swaminathan (1998) that have found that the child labour problem has been on the rise even in some high growth-prone areas. Therefore, why economic reforms have produced dissimilar results under different situations is quite perplexing.

Unfortunately, the existing theoretical literature on child labour does not deal adequately with issues like economic reforms and the supply of child labour in a multi-sector general equilibrium framework,[2] which is crucial when child labour and adult labour are substitutes.[3] However, an important piece of work in this area is that of Chaudhuri and Gupta (2004) who have theoretically examined the implications of trade reform on the incidence of child labour in a developing economy in terms of a two-sector general equilibrium model. In both the sectors child labour is used and adult labour and child labour are perfect substitutes. The import-competing sector is protected by an import tariff. In their model the supply function of child labour has been derived from the utility-maximizing behavior of the working families. They have assumed that workers are the owners of capital and receive the tariff revenue from the government as transfer payments. They have found that the effect of trade liberalization on the incidence of child labour crucially hinges on the relative factor intensities of the two sectors and that removal of the protectionist policy may have an adverse effect on child labour if the tariff protected import-competing sector is less capital-intensive than the export sector and *vice versa*.

However, Chaudhuri and Gupta (2004) have assumed a specific algebraic nature of the utility function of the households. A slight modification of the function may lead to different results. This is exactly what is done in the present note. Here we assume that the workers derive utility from the consumption of final goods and children's leisure. We will show that this simple modification would give just the opposite result as found in Chaudhuri and Gupta (2004).

2. THE MODEL

We consider a two-sector model where a small open less-developed economy consists of two sectors. Sector 1 produces exportable commodities *(X)* using labour and capital. Sector 2 produces importable *(Z)* using labour and capital. There are two types of labour available in the economy: adult labour and child labour. Both the sectors use child labour as well as adult labour. Following Basu and Von (1998),[3] it is assumed here that child labour is perfect substitute for adult labour. We assume here that an adult worker is equivalent to β number of child workers, where $\beta > 1$. Each adult worker earns a wage of *W*. Therefore, the child wage rate should be $(W/\beta) = W_c$.

We assume that both types of labour and capital are completely mobile between the two sectors. Rentals on capital are assumed to be same across the two sectors. Production functions in sector 1 and sector 2 satisfy constant returns to scale with positive but diminishing returns to each factor. Markets are perfectly competitive and all factors of production are fully employed. Each firm maximizes profit. Owing to small open economy assumption, commodity prices are given internationally. Sector 2 is the tariff protected import-competing sector. For the moment we do not make any assumption regarding the relative factor intensities of the two sectors.

The following symbols will be used in the model:

a_{Li} : Labour-output ratio in the *i*th sector, i = X, Z.
a_{Ki} : Capital-output ratio in the *i*th sector, i = X, Z.
θ_{ji} : Distributive share of the *j*th input in the *i*th industry, j = L, K and i = X, Z.
λ_{ji} : Proportion of the *j*th input employed in the *i*th sector, j = L, K and i = X, Z.
P_i : World price of the *i*th good, i = X, Z.
t : Ad-valorem tariff rate on the import of commodity Z.
T : Total tariff revenue of the government.
M : Volume of imports of commodity Z.
W : Adult wage rate.
W_c $(= W/\beta)$: Child wage rate.
R : Rate of return to capital.
C_x : Consumption of commodity X by each working family.
C_z : Consumption of commodity Z by each working family.
L : Adult labour endowment.
L_c : Aggregate supply of child labour.
K : Domestic capital stock of the economy.
'$\wedge$' : Proportional change.

1. Supply Function of Child Labour

In this section we derive the supply function of child labour from the utility-maximizing behavior of the representative adult worker who sends his children to work. There are L number of working families each having n number of children. The family derives utility from the consumption of final goods (C_x and C_z) and from children's leisure ($n-l_c$) where l_c number of workers are sent out to work. The utility function of the representative adult worker is given by,

$$U = W(C_x, C_z) + V(n-l_c)$$

For the analytical simplicity let us consider the following specific algebraic form of the utility function:

$$U = (C_x)^{\alpha} + (C_z)^{\alpha} + (n - l_c)^{\alpha} \text{ With } 0 < \alpha < 1 \tag{1}$$

This satisfies all the standard properties. Also it is additive and symmetric. It is homogeneous of degree α and has constant elasticity of substitution between any two arguments.

The worker maximizes this utility function subject to the budget constraint.

$$P_x C_x + P_z (l + t) C_z = \{(W / \beta) l_c + (Y / L)\} \tag{2}$$

where the own income of the adult worker is

$$(Y/L) = (WL + RK + T)/L \tag{3}$$

Here it is assumed that the workers are the owners of capital. So the income from capital is distributed equally among the workers. Besides, each worker receives a fraction of the tariff revenue as income transfer from the government.

The following first-order conditions are required to satisfy in order to maximize each adult worker's utility:

$$(C_x / C_z)^{(\alpha-1)} = [P_x / P_z (1+t)] \tag{4}$$

$$(C_x / (n - l_c))^{(\alpha-1)} = [P_x / (W / \beta)] \tag{5}$$

$$(C_z / (n - l_c))^{(\alpha-1)} = [(P_z (1+t)) / (W / \beta)] \tag{6}$$

Using (4)–(6) the aggregate child labour function in the economy is obtained as follows :

$$L_c = \frac{[\{P_x^{(\alpha/(\alpha-1))} + (P_z (1+t))^{(\alpha/(\alpha-1))}\}\{\beta^{(1/(\alpha-1))} / W^{(\alpha/(\alpha-1))}\}) N - (L + (R/W)K + (T/W))\}]}{[\{P_x^{(\alpha/(\alpha-1))} + (P_z (1+t))^{(\alpha/(\alpha-1))}\}(\beta^{(1/(\alpha-1))} / W^{(\alpha/(\alpha-1))}) + (1/\beta)]} \tag{7}$$

where L_c (= Ll_c) = Aggregate supply of labour; and, $N(=nL)$=aggregate potential child worker.

We now analyze the properties of the aggregate supply function of child labour. First, the supply of child labour varies inversely with rental rate on capital stock, *K* and the labour endowment, *L*. L_c also varies inversely with the tariff revenue, *T*; *T* in turn varies positively with the tariff rate, *t*, if the import demand is inelastic. Here income effect on child labour supply is negative. Second, L_c varies negatively with the adult wage rate, *W*. A rise in *W* produces a positive income effect so that the adult worker sends a larger number of children to school and therefore decides to send a lower number of children to the workplace. An increase in W_c, on the other hand, produces a negative price effect, which increases the supply of child labour from the family.

In this case, the negative price effect of an increase in the adult wage rate, *W*, taking place through an increase in the effective child wage rate outweighs the positive income effect so that the net effect would be an increase in the supply of child labour. Consequently, an increase in the adult wage, *W*, leads to an increase in the supply of child labour by each working family when the two types of labour are perfect substitute. Thus the aggregate supply of child labour in the economy is given by,

$$L_c = f(W, R, t, L, K, T) \tag{8}$$
$$\quad (+)(-)(-)(-)(-)(-)$$

2. The General Equilibrium Analysis

Given the assumption of perfectly competitive markets, the usual price-unit cost equality conditions relating to the two sectors of the economy are given by the following two equations:

$$a_{LX}W + a_{KX}R = P_x \tag{9}$$

$$a_{LZ}W + a_{KZ}R = P(1+t) \tag{10}$$

The capital endowment equation, which shows capital market equilibrium, is given by,

$$a_{KX}X + a_{KZ}Z = K \tag{11}$$

The aggregate supply function of child labour in general form is that given above in (8). The effective labour endowment of the economy consists of both adult and child labour. The labour market equilibrium is given by,

$$a_{LX}X + a_{LZ}\,Z = L+(L_c/\beta \tag{12}$$

In this model there are five endogenous variables W, R, X, Z, L_c and five independent equations. The parameters in this system are P_x, P_z, β, L, K and t. Equations (9) and (10) constitute the price system, and (8), (11) and (12) form the output system. It should be noted that the system possesses the decomposition property since the two unknown input prices, W and R, can be determined from the price system alone, independently of the output system. Once the factor prices are known, the factor coefficients, a_{ji} are known too. Also the amount of child labour L_c, is obtained from (8). Finally, X and Z are solved from (11) and (12).

3. Comparative Static Exercises

The conventional wisdom suggests that liberalized trade and investment policies would lead to an overall economic expansion in the developing countries. There will be trickle down of these benefits to the lowest stratum of the population, thereby lowering the extent of poverty. Thus these policies were expected to exert downward pressure on the incidence of poverty induced child labour. In this section of the paper we shall examine the impact of trade liberalization on the incidence of child labour. In the present setup, trade liberalization means a reduction in the import tariff on commodity Z .

Totally differentiating (9) and (10) and solving by Cramer's rule, the following expressions can be obtained:

$$\hat{W} = (-)(1/|\theta|)\theta_{KX}\,S\hat{t} \tag{13}$$

$$\hat{R} = (1/|\theta|)\theta_{LX}\,S\hat{t} \tag{14}$$

where $|\theta| = \theta_{Lx}\theta_{KZ} - \theta_{KX}\theta_{lZ}$ and $S = t/(1+t) > 0$

Differentiating (8) with respect to t, the following expressions are obtained:

$$(dL_c/dt) = (\partial L_c/\partial W)\,(dW/dt) + (\partial L_c/\partial R)\,(dR/dt) + (\partial L_c/\partial t) + (\partial L_c/\partial T)(dT/dt) \qquad (15)$$

$$\qquad (+) \qquad\qquad (-) \qquad\qquad (-) \qquad\qquad (-)$$

Here $(\partial L_c/\partial t)$ represents the price effect of the change in the tariff rate that is taking place via the change in the relative price of the importable. However, a change in the tariff rate causes change in the tariff revenue and $(\partial L_c/\partial T)\ (dT/dt)$ represents the effect resulting from the change in the tariff revenue. The combined effect is negative if $(dT/dt) \geq 0$, i.e. if the import demand is not elastic.

Depending on the relative factor intensities between the sectors, the following two cases arise.

Case 1: $|\theta| = \theta_{LX}\theta_{KZ} - \theta_{KX}\theta_{LZ} > 0$

This means that the import-competing sector is more capital intensive than the export sector. From (13) and (14), it follows that $(dW/dt) < 0$ and $(dR/dt) > 0$. Therefore, from (15) it follows that $(dL_c/dt) < 0$ if $(dT/dt) \geq 0$.[4]

Case 2: $|\theta| = \theta_{LX}\theta_{KZ} - \theta_{KX}\theta_{LZ} < 0$

This means that import-competing sector is more labour intensive than the export sector. This may be the trade pattern for a newly industrialized economy. From (13) and (14) it follows that $(dW/dt) > 0$ and $(dR/dt) < 0$. Therefore from (15) it follows that (dL_c/dt) can be positive if the direct effect of a reduction in t is outweighed by indirect effects via change in W and R and by the tariff revenue effect.

Combining the above two cases, we arrive at the following proposition which gives just the opposite result as found in Chaudhuri and Gupta (2004).

Proposition 1: A reduction in import tariff may have an adverse effect on the incidence of child labour if the tariff-protected import-competing sector is more capital intensive than the export sector. However, it may reduce the pervasiveness of child labour when the import-competing sector is less capital intensive than the export sector.

Trade liberalization, in the form of reduction of tariff rates, has two types of effect on the supply of child labour. One is the price effect, which lowers the effective price of the importable. The other is the income effect, which takes place through changes in factor prices (and hence through changes in factor income of the household) and through a change in tariff revenue, which is transferred to the household by the government. A reduction in tariff rate leads to a rise in W and fall in R following the Stolper-Samuelson effect if import-competing sector is more capital intensive than the export sector. A rise in W produces a positive income effect so that the adult worker sends a larger number of children to school and therefore decides to send a lower number of children to workplace. An increase in W_c, on the other hand, produces a negative price effect, which increases the supply of child labour from the family. In this case, the negative price effect of an increase in the adult wage, W, taking place through an increase in the effective child wage rate outweighs the positive income effect so that the net effect would be an increase in the supply of child labour. Consequently, an increase in the adult wage, W, leads to an increase in the supply of child labour by each working family when the two types of labour are perfectly substitute. The residual part of the aggregate income of each household decreases if $(dT/dt) \geq 0$. This results in increase in the supply of child labour. Hence the tariff reduction results in increase in the supply of child labour if the import-competing sector is more capital intensive. The clue to the difference in results between the present analysis and Chaudhuri and Gupta (2004) lies in the nature of the utility function of the working households. In Chaudhuri and Gupta (2004) the households derive disutility from child labour while in the present analysis they derive utility from children's leisure.

3. CONCLUDING REMARKS

It is evident that, in developing countries, parents send their children to workplace out of utter poverty. Trade and investment liberalization programs are supposed to reduce poverty through an overall economic expansion, benefits of which will percolate down to the lowest stratum of the population. This will in turn put a brake on the incidence of poverty-induced child labour. Although the incidence of child labour in general has decreased in the developing countries with economic growth in relative terms, in some high growth-prone areas, the incidence has been on the rise. The question therefore arises why liberalized trade and investment policies have produced contradictory results in different cases. Chaudhuri and Gupta (2004) have shown that the effect of trade liberalization on the incidence of child labour depends crucially on the relative factor intensities of the two sectors of the economy. They found that if the tariff-protected import competing sector is capital intensive, a reduction of import tariff may lower the supply of child labour. The present paper makes a simple modification in the utility function of the representative adult worker as used by Chaudhuri and Gupta (2004). Here we assume that the worker derives utility from the consumption of the final goods and also children's leisure. Interestingly, this modification gives just the opposite result. We have shown that a reduction in import tariff may have an adverse effect on the incidence of child labour if the tariff-protected import-competing sector is more capital intensive than the export sector and *vice versa*.

Notes

1. Out of 246 million about 170 million child workers were found in different hazardous works. Some 8.4 million children were caught in the worst forms of child labour including slavery, trafficking, debt bondage and other forms of forced labour, forced recruitment for armed conflict, prostitution, pornography and other illicit activities (ILO, June 2002).
2. The Basu and Van (1998) model, of course, can be easily embedded in a general equilibrium framework. Besides, Jafarey and Lahiri (2002) and Gupta (2002) have examined the efficacy of imposition of trade sanctions on export items of the developing countries produced by child labour as a policy in curbing the incidence of child labour in terms of general equilibrium models.
3. In the developing economies child workers are mostly found in the production of carpets, glass, bangles, leather bags, shoes, garments, matchbox and fireworks and cattle feeding. It is sensible to assume that

adults can perform all these tasks. First, all these industries exist in countries where there is no child labour. Second, not all the firms producing these goods in countries where child labour exists actually use child labour—after all, this is the justification for 'social labelling'. The 'nimble fingers' argument, which once has been put forward, especially to carpet weaving, is an excuse given by employers and fails to convince researchers (see Burra (1995) and Weiner (1991)). Even if present technologies required the use of child labour and not adult labour in certain production activities, major changes in economic conditions coupled with the mobility of capital across sectors, would certainly result in the adoption of different technologies allowing the substitution of adult for child labour.

4. See Appendices I and II.

References

Basu, K. and Van, P.H. (1998): 'The Economics of Child Labour', *American Economic Review,* 88(3), 412-27.

Burra, N. (1995): *Born to Work: Child Labour in India,* Delhi: Oxford University Press.

Chaudhuri, S. and Gupta, M.R. (2004): 'Child labour and trade liberalization', *The Japanese Economic Review,* 55(2), pp. 201-11.

Cigno, A., Rosati, F.E. and Guarcello, L. (2002): 'Does Globalization Increase Child Labor? *World Development,* 30, 1579-89.

Edmonds, E. and Pavcnik, N. (2005): 'The Effect of Trade Liberalization on Child Labour', *Journal of International Economics,* 65(2), pp. 401-19.

Gupta, M.R. (2002): 'Trade Sanctions, Adult Unemployment and the Supply of Child Labour: A Theoretical Analysis', *Development Policy Review,* 20(3), 317-32.

ILO (2002): 'A Future Without Child Labour?', International Labour Conference, 90th Session, June 2002, International Labour Office, Geneva.

Jafarey, S. and Lahiri, S. (2002): 'Will Trade Sanctions Reduce Child Labour? The Role of Credit Markets', *Journal of Development Economics,* 68, pp. 137-56.

Neumayer, E. and Soysa, I. (2005): 'Trade Openness, Foreign Direct Investment and Child Labour', *World Development,* 33(1), 43-63.

Swaminathan, M. (1998): 'Economic Growth and the Persistence of Child Labor: Evidence from an Indian City', *World Development,* 26 (8), 1513-28.

Weiner, M. (1991): *The Child and the State in India: Child Labor and Education Policy in Comparative Perspective,* Oxford University Press, Delhi.

World Development Report (1995), published by Oxford University Press for The World Bank.

APPENDIX I

The aggregate tariff revenue of the government is given by

$T = tP_zM = tP_z(C_zL - Z) = tP_zL(C_z - Z/L)$

From (4) and (6), we get respectively,

$$C_x = C_z\,[P_x/P_z(1+t)]^{1/(\alpha-1)} \quad \text{(A1)}$$

$$l_c = n-[(W/\beta)/P_z(1+t)]^{1/(\alpha-1)}\,C_z \quad \text{(A2)}$$

Now the budget constraint of each working family is given by,

$P_xC_x + P_z(1+t)C_z = (1/L)[(w/\beta)Ll_c + WL + RK + T]$

Now using (A1) and (A2) we get

$P_xC_z[P_x/P_z(1+t)]^{1/(\alpha-1)} + P_z(1+t)C_z = (W/\beta)l_c + W + R(K/L)$
$+tP_z(C_z - Z/L) = (W/\beta)[n-\{(W/\beta)/P_z(1+t)\}^{1/(\alpha-1)}C_z] + W$
$+ R(K/L) + tP_z(C_z - Z/L)$

or

$$C_z = \frac{(W/\beta)n + W + R(K/L) - tP_zZ/L}{P_x[P_x/P_z(1+t)]^{1/(\alpha-1)} + P_zC_z + (W/\beta)[(W/\beta)/P_z(1+t)]^{1/(\alpha-1)}} \quad \text{(A3)}$$

Now, $T = tP_zL(C_z - Z/L)$. Using (A3), this becomes

$$T = tP_zC_zL - tP_zZ$$

$$= \frac{tP_zL(W/\beta)n + W + R(K/L) - tP_zZ/L}{P_x[P_x/P_z(1+t)]^{1/(\alpha-1)} + P_z + (W/\beta)[(W/\beta)/P_z(1+t)]^{1/(\alpha-1)}} - tP_zZ$$

$$\frac{dT}{dt} = \left[\frac{P_z}{B}\left\{(W/\beta)N + WL + RK - tP_zZ + (((N/\beta)+L)\frac{dW}{dt} + \right\}\right]$$

$$K\frac{dR}{dt} - P_z(Z + t\frac{dZ}{dt})))\Big\} - P_z(Z + t\frac{dZ}{dt} - \left(\frac{tP_z}{(1-\alpha)B^2}\right)$$

$$\left(W\left(\frac{N}{\beta}+L\right)+RK-tP_zZ\right)(1+t)^{\alpha/(\alpha-1)}\{P_x(P_x/P_z)\}^{1/\alpha-1}-\left(\frac{1}{\beta}\right)$$

$$(\beta P_z)^{1/(\alpha-1)}(W)^{\alpha/(\alpha-1)}+\frac{\alpha}{\beta}(\beta P_z)^{1/(\alpha-1)}(1+t)W^{1/(\alpha-1)}\left(\frac{dW}{dt}\right)\}\Bigg] \tag{A4}$$

where:

$$B=[P_x(P_x/P_z)^{1/(\alpha-1)}(1+t)^{1/(\alpha-1)}+P_z-(1/\beta)(\beta P_z)^{1/(1-\alpha)}$$
$$(W)^{\alpha/(\alpha-1)}(1+t)^{1/(1-\alpha)}].$$

The expression for *(dZ/dt) is* obtained after totally differentiating (11) and (12) and solving by Cramer's rule. As t decreases, the domestic price of Z , i.e. $P_z(1+t)$, decreases, which in turn causes the factor prices to change. The input-output coefficients will also change, as these are the functions of the factor price ratios. Given the product mix, there will be a shortage of capital (labour) if sector Z is more capital (labour) intensive than sector X. In both cases, sector Z contracts following Rybczynski-type effects. However, the sign of *(dT/dt) is* ambiguous, depending on the values of parameters such as α, L, P_x, P_z, t and β.

APPENDIX II

We can express equation (7) as,

$$L_c = \frac{VN - (L + (R/W)K + (T/W))}{V + (1/\beta)}$$

where $V = [P_x^{(\alpha/(\alpha-1))} + (P_z(1+t))^{(\alpha/\alpha-1))}](\beta^{(1/\alpha-1)} / W^{(\alpha/\alpha-1))})]$

$$(\partial V/\partial W) = (-)[P_X^{(\alpha/(\alpha-1))} + (P_Z(1+t))^{(\alpha/\alpha-1))}]\beta^{(1/\alpha-1))}$$

$$(\alpha/(\alpha-1))W^{(1-2\alpha)/(\alpha-1))} > 0$$

(Note that $(\alpha-1)<0$)

Taking partial differential of equation (7) we obtain,

$$\frac{\partial L_c}{\partial W} = \frac{(\partial V/\partial W)N + (RK/W^2) + (T/W^2) - (\partial V/\partial W)}{(V + (1/\beta))^2}$$

$$= \frac{(\partial V/\partial W)(N-1) + (RK/W^2) + (T/W^2)}{(V + (1/\beta))^2} > 0$$

Similarly we obtain,

$$(\partial V/\partial t) = (\beta^{(1/\alpha-1))} / W^{(\alpha/(\alpha-1))})P_Z^{(\alpha/\alpha-1))}\left(\frac{\alpha}{\alpha-1}\right)$$

$$(1+t)^{(1/(\alpha-1))} < 0$$

Taking partial differentials of equation (7) with respect to t, R and T we obtain respectively,

$$\frac{\partial L_c}{\partial t} = \frac{(\partial V/\partial t)(N-1) - (1/W)(\partial T/\partial t)}{(V + (1/\beta))^2} < 0$$

(Provided that $(\partial T/\partial t) \geq 0$);

$$\frac{\partial L_c}{\partial R} = -\frac{(K/W)}{(V + (1/\beta))} < 0; \text{ and, } \frac{\partial L_c}{\partial T} = -\frac{(1/W)}{(V + (1/\beta))^2} < 0$$

5

Strategic Certification and Performance Related Pay in Education

RAJLAKSHMI MALLICK

1. INTRODUCTION

More and more countries have come to recognize the importance of human capital for economic growth. Both highly skilled graduate labour and semi-skilled (high school) labour constitute one of the most important factors of production for enterprises that are pivotal to economic growth. Educational generates this human capital by enhancing all individual's embodied skills above their raw labour ability (*Belfield and Levin, 2003*). Empirical research have found evidence of a strong positive relationship between eąrnings and education indicating the quality enhancing role of the educational process (*Cohn and Addison, 1998*). It is this economic benefit of education that explains why students enroll with educational institutions and government funding of both secondary and higher education is substantial (*Goldin and Katz, 1998*) although the funding for higher education is larger.

Given its importance, question arises as to what are the characteristics of the production that takes place in educational institutions. *Rothschild and White (1995)* and *Dolan et. al.* (1985) stress on the joint role played by students (willing to invest their time and effort to learn skills) and teachers (who have the skill and are able to impart the training) in the generation of human capital. More importantly they stress on students' effort and participation as the main input in production function for higher education. Findings based on school level data on the other hand (*Hanushek et. al., 1999*) reveal that teachers dominate student achievement differences associated with schools, compared to other school resources and characteristics (e.g. student mix class size, technology, organisation and leadership, etc.) including peer groups. The latter as mentioned above, is considered to be one of the most important distinguishing features of higher education.

The studies indicate that relative importance of teacher and student effort as inputs in the educational production function varies across the type and level of the educational institution. Among the other inputs, one that is less frequently mentioned is the role of university managers who influence the technical efficiency of the universities by allocating resources within the institution and acting as principals in structuring incentives for the agents (*Johnes*, 1999).

The realisation about the importance of education has led to the urgency being given to educational reforms in many countries. Among the various policy reforms one that has attracted a lot of interest pertains to the policy of performance related pay (PRP) for teachers both at school level and in higher education. Infact a large number of empirical studies find evidence for a positive impact of teacher salary levels on students outcomes at the school level (*Loeb and Page, 1999, Dewey et. al., 2000*). Evidence also reveals that teacher pay affects teacher performance by influencing the recruitment and retention of more able teachers (*Jacobson, 1995, Dolton* and *Van der Klaauw, 1996, 99*) but more importantly by inducing better performance by continuing teachers (*Hanuhek et. al., 1999*).

Using this evidence and from the proceeding discussion on the characteristics of educational production function we find that the empirical basis for developing a principal-agent model of education for analysing the impact of PRP for teachers in education is significant.

That the reward for teacher assessment of student performance has always occupied a back seat, is common knowledge. While educational reforms have shown substantial concern with PRP for teachers (at the school level as well as in higher education) the major concern of PRP has been promotion of quality teaching. Teaching is a multifaceted occupation. It involves not only teaching (imparting training to students leading to generation of human capital) but also certification of student effort by teachers. In this paper we develop a model of an academic institution involving a teacher, a student and the governing body (GB) of the institution.

We consider a principal-agent framework in which the principal, that is the Governing Body (GB) is faced with an exogenously given award or funding scheme. Given the exogenous award scheme, the GB wants the agents to perform two activities resulting in two observable outputs—realised output as an indicator of skill formation and certificates of student effort. The first activity, skill formation, involves : Government by both the teacher and the student who must incur effort in teaching and learning respectively. We assume that the student chooses his effort after observing teacher's effort choice. Thus we have a principal-agent set up with joint production by multiple agents where agents' efforts can not be distinguished. The other activity, namely certification of student effort is done by the teacher who can observe the student's effort in learning. This introduces an element of multi-tasking into our principal-agent framework with multiple agents.

In the context of our model we show why PRP for teacher may show little concern towards rewarding teacher's assessment of student effort. For alternative structural assumptions on relative teacher-student productivity we try to locate the kind of equilibria that would prevail under different award schemes. Specifically we address the question when are we likely to observe equilibria with either high or low effort by both agents or high effort by only one of the agents. On the basis of these observations we draw some policy inferences regarding the type of incentive structure that might, promote socially dissemble equilibria.

The principal-agent model-choice variables, cost and pay functions of the agents along with the GB's objective are described in the next section. The principal agent interaction in this paper is modelled as a sequential move game, which is described at the end of section 2. We proceed by backward induction. Given the GB's choice of pay schedule for the teacher, section 3 identifies the equilibrium strategies for the agents under different structural assumptions regarding teacher-student productivity. Section 4 then looks at the GB's optimisation and implementation problem and identifies the optimal pay schedules corresponding to the different productivity restrictions. On the basis of the analysis in sections 3 and 4, section 5 makes some observations on the design of educational grant schemes and policy alternatives to PRP. Concluding remarks are made in section 6.

2. DEVELOPING THE MODEL

We now make a formal statement of the model described in the introduction. We consider a set-up with three participants, the GB of an educational institution faced with a grant, a teacher and a student. The academic institution we consider is an institution of basic or higher education. The GB and the teacher are directly tied in a principal-agent relationship. The GB recruits the teacher to perform some activities which may involve effort on part of the teacher. The GB's payoff also depends on the action of the student which involves effort as well. The GB however does not directly interact with the student. The incentive for student participation is there as the student is a potential recruit of the industry.[1] The pay that the student receives as an employee of a firm serves as the incentive. Thus in our model, the student's choice of action is influenced by the wage schedule offered by the firm and the teacher's actions. The GB does not monitor the student directly but only indirectly. Moreover, we assume that the wage schedule faced by the student is exogenously given.[2] Thus although the student receives pay from a firm, the firm plays a passive role in this model. In other words, this model does not consider any principal-agent interaction between the firm and the student.

The following sub-sections describe the activities, cost and pay functions for the teacher and the student.

1. Choice Variables or Actions

The teacher performs two activities. First the teacher trains the student, who learns to produce an output (good or service) q. Secondly, the teacher issues certificates of student effort. The student finds employment and produces output in return for a wage.

We consider two levels for teacher's effort in teaching, t, and student's effort in learnings. Without loss of generality we normalise the lower effort levels to zero and denote the higher levels by 1. Thus $t, s \in \{0, 1\}$. Certification however does not involve any effort on part of the teacher as he can observe student's effort. Denoting certificates by c, the teacher must choose $c \in \{0, 1\}$ where 0 and 1 correspond to low and high effort certificates respectively. Thus in this set-up the teacher may issue false or correct certificate of student effort.

Production is uncertain. We consider a two point production function with $q \in \{0.1\}$. We assume that the teacher and student effort levels jointly determine the probability of $q = 0$ (low) or $q = 1$ (high) output being realised. Let $p_{ts} = P(q=1 \mid t, s)$. Thus, $1 - p_{ts} = P(q = 0 \mid t, s)$. We assume that

$$p_{00} < \frac{1}{2} < p_{11}, \tag{1a}$$

$$p_{0s} < p_{1s}, p_{t0} < p_{t1}, \tag{1b}$$

$$p_{00} + p_{10} > 1, \text{ if } p_{10} > \frac{1}{2} \tag{1c}$$

We need not explain 1(a). 1(b) states that higher effort *by* either teacher or student keeping the other's effort constant increases the probability of high output being realised. Assumption 1(c) imposes certain lower bounds on p_{00}. Its implications are discussed in section 3. Here we have considered only the student's effort in learning which along with the teacher's effort in teaching jointly determine the probabilities of high or low (quality) output being realised when the student participates in the production process. We have **not** considered the student's effort in production. Thus we rule out any decision problem or moral hazard for the student when he actually participates in production.

2. Cost and Wage Functions

Teaching and learning efforts are costly to the agents. d_t and d_s denote the disutilities from effort in teaching and learning respectively. $d_t \in \{0, D\}$, $d_s \in \{0, d\}$ with $d = D$ if $t = 1$ and $d_s = d$ if $s = 1$. We do not consider any student or teacher types so that the cost functions for the teacher and student are both unique.

The teacher and student's efforts are non-observable to the CB. Only the realised output q and the student's effort signalled by the teacher, c, are observable to all, including the GB and the firms.

The GB pays the teacher a composite salary consisting of a basic salary, a performance based remuneration for teaching and another for certification. Teacher's basic salary is F. If $q = 1$ is realised he gets an additional amount T; and if output matches certificate, i.e. $q = c$, he gets an additional amount C. Thus in our model the teacher's pay depends on realised output (which is an indicator of teaching effort) and on whether the output matches certificate (which is an indicator of authenticity of certification). Let us denote the composite salary by $R(q, c)$, depending on q and c. We assume that $C \geq \in > 0$ where f is the smallest unit of payment. Unlike in case of teaching where the teacher would always choose $t = 0$ if $T = 0$, the teacher's behaviour is not predictable when $C = 0$. Since certification does not involve effort, therefore issue of certificate will be dictated by the incentive to tell truth or to lie, neither of which exist in case $C = 0$.[3] Considering student's pay when he joins the firm, the student earns W_0 (or W_1 if the certificate issued by the teacher is 0 (or 1). W_0, W_1 are exogenously given with $W_\delta < W_1$.

3. Payoff for Teacher and Student

Given the wage and cost functions for the teacher and student the expected payoff to the teacher when t, sand c are chosen may be expressed as follows:

$$U_{ts,c} = (F+C-d_t)P(q=0|t,s,c=0)+(F-d_t)P(q=0|t,s,c=1)$$

$$+(F+T-d_t)P(q=1|t,s,c=0)+(F+T+C-d_t)P(q=1|t,s,c=1)$$

Further simplification yields

$$U_{ts,0} = F+p_{ts}T+(1-p_{ts})C-d_t \qquad \text{(2a)}$$

$$U_{ts,1} = F+p_{ts}(T+C)-d_t. \qquad \text{(2b)}$$

The corresponding payoff to student is $V_{ts,c}$ where

$$V_{ts,c} = W-d_s \qquad \text{(2)}$$

with $W = W_0$ (or W_1) if $c = 0$ (or 1) is certified.

4. The Governing Body's Objective

We assume that the GB is faced with a grant which has two components x and y. The values of x and y, i.e. the amount of grant, depend on the quality of realised output and on whether realised output, matches certificate issued by teacher, respectively. Given the exogenous funding scheme, the GB's objective is to achieve excellence in skill formation (teaching and learning) and promote credible certification by choosing an appropriate pay function for teachers.[4]

The GB benefits in terms of funding when either high quality output is realised or when the realised output matches the certificate, i.e., $q = 1$ (or 0) output is realised by a student with $c = 1$ (or 0). The GB's payoff when the teacher chooses (t, c), the student chooses s and q output is realised is given by,

$$x+y-R(q, c) \qquad \text{(3)}$$

where $x = A > 0$ if $q = 1$ and $y = B > 0$ if $q = c$. Thus the expected payoff to the GB when t, s and c are chosen may be expressed as follows:

$$\Pi_{ts,c} = AP(q=1|t, s, c) + BP(q=c|t, s, c) - [F + TP(q=1 |t, s, c) + CP(q=c|t, s, c)].$$

Further simplification yields :

$$\Pi_{ts,0} = Ap_{ts} + B(1-p_{ts}) - [F + p_{ts}T + (1-p_{ts})C] \quad (4a)$$

$$\Pi_{ts,0} = (A+B)p_{ts} - [F - p_{ts}(T+C)] \quad (4b)$$

5. Description of the Game

The above principal-agent problem may be formulated as a sequential move game with three players—the GB, teacher and student—and four stages. The sequencing of the moves is as follows.

The GB, faced with a government grant scheme, moves first in stage 1 and declares the teacher's pay function *R(q, c)*. The wage schedule offered by firms to its employees is exogenously given and observable to all. In stage 2, the teacher observes the pay function declared by the GB and the prevailing labour market wage schedule and chooses effort in teaching *t*. The pay functions are also observed by the student who chooses his effort in learning *s* in stage 3 after observing the *t* chosen by the teacher. In stage 4, the teacher issues certificates of student effort, *c* after observing *s* chosen by the student. The student finds a job and produces output in return for a wage based on the effort certified by the teacher.

3. IDENTIFYING THE EQUILIBRIUM STRATEGIES FOR TEACHER AND STUDENT

In order to obtain the solution (SPNE) of the above game we first locate the equilibrium of the sub-game between the teacher and student. For ease of presentation we enumerate and number all the pure strategy vectors as shown on next page.

student effort		$s = 0$	$s = 1$
teacher teaching effort	certificates		
$t = 0$	$c = 0$	I	III
	$c = 1$	II	IV
$t = 1$	$c = 0$	V	VII
c	$c = 1$	VI	VIII

We solve the sub-game for alternative assumptions regarding the relationship between teacher and student effort and their relative productivity. These are summarised in equation (5).

Weak Complementarity : $\frac{1}{2} < p_{10} < p_{01}$ (5ai)

$\frac{1}{2} < p_{01} < p_{10}$ (5aii)

Strong Complementarity : $p_{10} < p_{01} < \frac{1}{2}$ (5bi)

$p_{01} < p_{10} < \frac{1}{2}$ (5bii)

Teacher's effort significantly more important than that of student : $p_{01} < \frac{1}{2} < p_{10}$ (5c)

Student's effort significantly more important than that of teacher : $p_{10} < \frac{1}{2} < p_{01}$ (5d)

Assumption (5a) states that high effort by anyone agent is enough to make the probability of high output greater than $\frac{1}{2}$ implying weak complementarity between teacher and student effort. (5b) corresponds to a situation where there is strong complementarity between the two so that low effort by either one of the agents will lower the probability to less than $\frac{1}{2}$ Assumption (5c) depicts a scenario where high effort by teacher is both necessary and sufficient to make the probability greater than $\frac{1}{2}$. High effort by student alone is not enough. Assumption (5d) reflects just the reverse scenario. The different scenarios described above may be linked with the type and level of the educational institution. For example in higher education, which is more research, oriented, or in technical educational institutions (engineering, managerial, professional or vocational), involving laboratory, project and field survey-based subjects, we will expect student's effort to play a more significant role so that assumptions (5a) and (5d) will be more relevant; while (5b) and (5c) will better approximate the picture in social sciences or lower levels of education.

Stage 4

Given the payoff functions for the teacher and student (equations (2) and (3) respectively) we solve the game by backward induction. So we start by analysing the teacher's certification problem in *stage 4*. When making his choice in stage 4, the teacher knows the pay schedule declared by the GB, his own effort in teaching t and can observe student's effort choice s. Given these the teacher will choose a certificate that will maximise the probability of match between certificate and realised output. Hence teacher will optimally issue high (or low) effort certificates if and only if the probability of high (or low) output is greater than $\frac{1}{2}$.

Thus, for example, with weak complementarity high effort certificates will be issued, as $p_{ts} > \frac{1}{2}$, except in the case where both t and s equal 0. This will rule out strategy vectors that involve low effort certificates along with high effort by at least one of the agents (III, V, VII) or high effort certificate with low effort by both agents (II) as Nash equilibria of the game. Hence, given (1a) teacher's choice in stage 4 (comparison of $U_{ts,\,c}$'s) will yield {I, IV, VI, VIII} as the possible equilibria of the game between teacher and student under productivity assumption (5a).

Similar analysis reveals that, with strong complementarity low effort certificate will be issued except in the case where both *t* and *s* equal 1. While for productivity assumptions 5(c) and (d) teacher will find it optimal to certify according to his effort and student's effort respectively. Hence comparison of $U_{ts,\ c}$'s will yield only { I, III, V, VIII}, { I, III, VI, VIII }, { I, IV, V, VIII} as the possible equilibria of the game between teacher and student, under productivity assumptions (5b) to (5d) respectively.[5]

Stage 3

We now consider the student's choice problem in stage 3. For our analysis we assume that student's marginal wage compensation is greater than his marginal disutility from effort. This is ensured if $W_1 - W_0 > d$. Otherwise the student will always choose low effort and that leads to absence of strategic interaction between the teacher and student.

Now when choosing his effort in learning *s*, the student can observe the teacher's effort in teaching *t;* and knows that he will get a higher wage if and only if he chooses an *s* such that the probability of high output is $> \frac{1}{2}$. Thus if the teacher chooses $t = 0$, then the student is better off choosing $s = 1$ iff $p_{01} > \frac{1}{2}$. And if teacher chooses $t = 1$ then the student is better off choosing $s = 1$ iff $p_{10} < \frac{1}{2}$. Following the above argument, with weak complementarity student is better off choosing an effort level opposite to that of teacher as both p_{01} and p_{10} are $> \frac{1}{2}$. Such a strategy is only rational as high effort by either one of the agents is enough to get him W_1. This will rule out equilibria involving similar effort choices by teacher and student (i.e. I and VIII) out of the four possible equilibria. Thus comparison of student payoffs will yield only IV and VI as the possible equilibria.

With strong complementarity, the student will match teacher's effort as high effort by both is necessary to get W_1. When teacher's effort is significantly more important, student will not have the incentive to choose $s = 1$ as certificates will reflect teacher's effort only. Finally, if student's effort is significantly more important, then given (6), he will always choose $s = 1$ as his effort alone is going to be reflected in the certificate. Hence comparison of student payoffs leaves us with {I, VIII}, {I, VI} and {IV, VIII} as the pairs of possible equilibrium strategy vectors under assumptions (5b) to (5d) respectively.

Stage 2

In stage 2, when choosing between $t = 0$ and $t = 1$, the teacher knows what the subsequent optimal plays would be. Thus he will compare his payoffs only for the pairs of strategy vectors that are admissible as equilibrium under the different productivity assumptions. As a general rule, the teacher will choose t to maximise the probability of realisation of high output along with the probability of match and also lower his effort cost. The resulting equilibrium strategy vectors for the sub-game between teacher and student for different productivity configurations and incentive compatibility conditions (6a-d) are summarised in Table 5.1.

TABLE 5.1

Complementarity	*Weak:* $(p_{01}, p_{10} > \frac{1}{2})$	*Strong:* $(p_{01}, p_{10} < \frac{1}{2})$
Relative importance of teacher and student		
Student important: $p_{01} > p_{10}$	only IV	I or VIII
Teacher important: $p_{01} < p_{10}$	IV or VI	according as (6b)
	according as (6a) or reverse inequality holds	or reverse inequality holds
Teacher significantly more important : $p_{01} < \frac{1}{2} < p_{10}$	I or VI according as (6c) or reverse inequality holds	
Student significantly more important: $p_{10} < \frac{1}{2} < p_{01}$	IV or VIII according as (6d) or reverse inequality holds	

$$(T + C)(p_{01} - p_{10}) + D > 0 \tag{6a}$$

$$T(p_{11} - p_{00}) + C(p_{11} + p_{00} - 1) < D \tag{6b}$$

$$T(p_{10} - p_{00}) + C(p_{10} + p_{00} - 1) < D \tag{6c}$$

$$(T + C)(p_{11} - p_{01}) < D \tag{6d}$$

As continuation of our discussion we first focus on weak complementarity. When there is weak complementarity (5a holds), the teacher knows that the student will choose $s = 0$ ($s = 1$) if he chose $t = 1$ ($t = 0$) and it is optimal to certify $c = 1$ in either case. Thus the teacher needs to compare only two values of p_{ts} viz. p_{01} and p_{10}. This corroborates our observation that with weak complementarity teacher's and student's choices of teaching and learning effort respectively leave us with only two admissible equilibria {IV and VI}. Moreover, given that the teacher issues high certificates only, a choice of t that maximises probability of high output will also maximise the probability of match in this case; and thus maximise the expected pay for both teaching and certification. Hence when there is weak complementarity and student's productivity is greater, i.e. (5ai) holds, then teacher is better off choosing $t = 0$ which induces the student to choose $s = 1$ and result in $p_{ts} = p_{01} > p_{10}$. Also $t = 0$ involves less effort cost. Thus with $p_{01} > p_{10} > \frac{1}{2}$, IV is the only equilibrium strategy vector. If however (5aii) holds, i.e. $p_{10} > p_{01} > \frac{1}{2}$ then p_{ts} is higher if teacher chooses $t = 1$ and induce $s = 0$ by student; but higher teaching effort is costlier as well. Hence either IV or VI could be the equilibrium strategy vector. Also in case VI turns out to be the equilibrium vector, it will involve lying about student effort by teacher. Such certification however will correctly perfect student productivity.

With strong complementarity (see condition 5b) teacher knows that student will choose $t = 1$ ($t = 0$) if he close $t = 1$ ($t = 0$) and that he should optimally certify $c = 1$ ($c = 0$) respectively. The two probabilities that the teacher will compare are thus p_{11} and p_{00}. Since ($t = 1, s = 0$) or ($t = 0, s = 1$) will never be realised in equilibrium, the relative importance of teacher and student in productivity will not matter in this case. Further as $p_{11} > p_{00}$ by (1a) and $(1 - p_{00}) < p_{11}$ by (1c), therefore choosing $t = 1$ will maximise both the expected pay for teaching and probability of match, although teaching effort cost will be higher. Therefore, the equilibrium strategy vector could be either I or VIII.

Again if (5c) holds then the two relevant probabilities will be p_{10} and p_{00}. Teacher will certify $c = 1$ and $c = 0$ in the two cases $(t = 1, s = 0)$, $(t = 0, s = 0)$ respectively. Thus arguing as before $t = 1$ will maximise expected earning from both teaching and certification as $p_{10} > p_{00}$ and $p_{10} > (i - p_{00})$ (given l(b) and (c)) but involve higher effort cost. Thus either I or VI could constitute equilibrium. As mentioned earlier this will involve false certification of student effort but correct reflection of student productivity.

Finally if (5d) holds, then arguing as above we can show that either IV or VIII will constitute an equilibrium in this case.

On the basis of the preceding discussion we state the following propositions:

Proposition 1(a): Rewarding the match between certificates of student effort and realised output will indeed maximise the probability of match. It will also lead to correct certification of student effort in most cases. However in situations where teacher's effort is more significant, it will involve false certification of student effort. Such certification however would correctly reflect student's productivity which depends on both teacher and student effort.

(b): In equilibrium low effort certificate will be observed only if there is low effort in both teaching and learning. Otherwise high effort certificates will be observed irrespective of productivity assumptions. This could explain the high incidence of good certificates or marks inflation.

Proposition 2 (a): An equilibrium involving high effort by both teacher and student will be implemented only if $p_{10} < \frac{1}{2}$; i.e. either there is strong complementarity in production or the student's effort is significantly more important.

(b): An equilibrium involving low effort by both teacher and student will result only if $p_{01} < \frac{1}{2}$; i.e. either the teacher's effort is significantly more important or there is strong complementarity in production. Under other productivity conditions such an outcome will never occur.

(c): An equilibrium involving high effort by only one of the agents will result if there is weak complementarity. Such outcomes are not possible under strong complementarity. Under other productivity conditions the equilibrium outcome may or may not be of this type.

Clearly student will have the incentive to choose high (or low) effort along with the teacher only if higher student effort is necessary (or not sufficient) for making $p_{ts} > \frac{1}{2}$. This could be alternatively stated as follows. For both high equilibrium it is necessary that low student effort be sufficient for making $p_{ts} < \frac{1}{2}$; thus student will never choose low effort when teacher chooses high (as this will fetch him a low wage). For both low equilibrium it is necessary that low teacher effort be sufficient for making $p_{ts} < \frac{1}{2}$. Hence student will never choose high when teacher chooses low (as he can not get a high wage by doing so). The first two parts of the above proposition highlight the possibility that "both high" or "both low" outcomes may not occur or be achievable under certain productivity assumptions.

4. GOVERNING BODY'S OPTIMISATION PROBLEM IN STAGE 1

In section 3 we identified the equilibrium strategy vectors for the sub-game between teacher and student under alternative assumptions regarding productivity. We now discuss the GB's implementation problem and choice of optimal pay schedule for teacher *(F, T, C)*, in *stage I*.

Now, given the conditions on productivity the equilibrium strategy for the sub-game between teacher and student may or may not be unique, as Table 5.1 shows. If the equilibrium is unique, as in case of weak complementarity with student's productivity being greater, then the GB does not really face any choice. The GB has to implement IV. This emphasises the fact that the GB may not necessarily be effective in affecting changes in teaching effort through optimal design of performance-related pay for teachers. Hence we have the following remark.

Remark 1: When there is weak complementarity between teacher and student effort and the student's productivity is greater, the only possible equilibrium outcome will involve low teaching effort by teacher, high learning effort by student and issue of high effort certificate by teacher. This will be irrespective of the pay function offered to the teacher.

If on the other hand there exist multiple equilibria for the sub-game, then for each equilibrium the GB must first solve for the teacher's pay function that will maximise the GB's payoff, subject to inducing the teacher and student to choose that particular equilibrium strategy vector. Inequalities (6a) to (6d) stated what these conditions are for the different productivity assumptions. In other words given any productivity condition (5) and *(t, s,* c) as possible equilibrium, the GB must choose a pay schedule for teacher that will maximise $\Pi^{*}_{ts,c}$ (equation (4)) such that the corresponding condition (6) is satisfied along with the teacher's and student's participation constraints, $U_{ts,c} > 0$ and $V_{ts,c} > 0$ (equations (2) and (3)). Denoting by $\Pi^{*}_{ts,c}$ the value of $\Pi^{*}_{ts,c}$ evaluated at $T*$, $C*$, i.e. the optimal value of the teacher's pay function, which particular equilibrium the GB implements will he determined by the strategy vector that yields the highest $\Pi^{*}_{ts,c}$.

Given the productivity conditions, the outcome of GB's maximisation exercise, viz. the optimal pay function for the teacher and the GB's optimal payoff for the different possible equilibria are summarised in Table 5.2 and proposition 3.

TABLE 5.2

Complementarity	*Weak:* $(p_{01}, p_{10} > \frac{1}{2})$	*Strong:* $(p_{01}, p_{10} < \frac{1}{2})$
Relative importance of teacher and student		
Student important: $(p_{01} > p_{10})$	IV: $T^* = 0$. $C^* = \in$	I: $T^* = 0$, $C^* = \in$ VIII: $T^* = \dfrac{D}{p_{11} - p_{00}}$, $C^* = \in$
Teacher important: $(p_{01} > p_{10})$	IV: $T^* = 0$, $C^* = \in$ VI: $T^* \geq 0$, $C^* \geq \in$ such that $T^* + C^* = \dfrac{D}{p_{11} - p_{00}} + \delta$ VI or IV according as $\Pi^*_{21.2} > \Pi^*_{12.2}$ or not i.e. (8a) or reverse holds.	VIII or I according as $\Pi^*_{22.2} > \Pi^*_{11.1}$ or not i.e. (8b) or reverse holds.
Teacher significantly more Important: $p_{01} < \frac{1}{2} < p_{10}$	I: $T^* = 0$, $C^* = \in$ IV: $T^* = \dfrac{D}{p_{10} - p_{00}}$ $C^* = \in$ VI or I according as $\Pi^*_{21.2} > \Pi^*_{11.1}$ or not i.e. (8c) or reverse holds.	
Student significantly more Important: $p_{01} > \frac{1}{2} > p_{10}$	IV: $T^* = 0$, $C^* = \in$ VIII: $T^* \geq 0$, $C^* \geq \in$ such that $T^* + C^* = \dfrac{D}{p_{11} - p_{01}} + b$ VIII or IV according as $\Pi^*_{22.2} > \Pi^*_{12.2}$ or not i.e. (8d) or reverse holds.	

where $\in, \delta, b$ are arbitrarily small positive constraints and inequalities (8a) to (8d) are as follows :

$$A + B > \theta_1 \tag{8a}$$

$$B > \theta_2 - A\frac{p_{11} - p_{00}}{p_{11} + p_{00} - 1} \tag{8b}$$

$$B > \theta_3 - A\frac{p_{10} - p_{00}}{p_{10} + p_{00} - 1} \tag{8c}$$

$$A + B > \theta_2 \tag{8d}$$

where θ_1, θ_2, θ_3, θ_4 are positive and function of p_{ts}'s and D.

From Table 5.2 we observe that in equilibrium teacher's pay function will assume anyone of following three forms (irrespective of productivity conditions): (i) $T^* = 0$, $C^* = \in$, (ii) $T^* > 0$, $C^* = \in$, and (iii) $T^* \geq 0$, $C^* \geq \in$ such that $T^* + C^*$ = constant. Thus given any strategy vector that the GB wants to implement there are just two possibilities. One, GB has the incentive not to offer an C that is larger than $\in$ (cases (i) and (ii) mentioned above). Two, offering C larger than $\in$ is optimal (case (iii) above) but so is offering $C = \in$. The same equilibrium outcome can be achieved by offering the extra reward for certification i.e. $(C - \in)$ not as C but as part of the reward for teaching, i.e. T^* and choosing $C = \in$. This is because any $T^* \geq 0$, $C^* \geq \in$ which satisfies $T^* + C^*$ = constant, will achieve the same outcome. The teacher's pay packet is not unique in this case. In fact $C^* = \in$ and T^* = (constant $- \in$) would be an admissible solution. This leads us to the following proposition:

Proposition 3: In equilibrium GB will not have the incentive to offer any significantly large C.

This may explain why we observe such poor returns for the assessment and certification done by teachers; and why PRP for teachers always stresses on quality teaching and ignore certification.

5. DESIGN OF GRANT SCHEME : VALUE *vs.* COMPOSITION

We now make some observations about the design of the grant scheme. Inequalities (8a) to (8d) enable us to draw inferences regarding the value and composition of the total grant. The absolute slope of the level contours corresponding to different values of total grant in *A, B* space is one. Thus depending on whether the absolute value of the slope coefficient (coefficient of *A)* in the equations corresponding to the inequalities (8a) to (8d) is greater or less than one, we may state the following proposition.

Proposition 4(a): If there is weak complementarity or if student effort is significantly more important then changing equilibrium outcomes will involve change in total amount of grant.

(b): If there is strong complementarity or teacher is significantly more important then changing equilibrium outcomes does not necessarily require changes in total amount of grant. It could be achieved through a change in the allocation of grant between reward for teaching and certification.

Part (b) of the above proposition is of significance since an equilibrium involving low effort by both teacher and student may be realised only under the productivity conditions mentioned therein. The upshot is that suppose the observed productivity relationship between teacher and student are such; then the GB may be induced to implement high effort by at least one of the agents simply by increasing A (the reward for high output as a proxy for teaching effort) and reducing B (the reward for correct certification) while keeping the total amount of grant (A+B) constant. Thus increasing the share of reward for teaching in total grant without any increase in the value of total grant will enable us to avoid "both low" outcome. If on the other hand the observed productivity relationships are as in proposition 2(a) then changing the allocation of grant between teaching and certification will be ineffective. The total amount of grant will have to be increased. This however will not necessarily lead to high effort by both teacher and student. It may also result in an equilibrium involving high teaching and low student effort if there is weak complementarity and teacher's effort is more important, i.e. (5aii) holds.

6. CONCLUSION

Poor returns for the assessment and certification done by

teachers and its consequences on human capital formation has caught the attention of academic researchers for some time. This paper develops a model of joint moral hazard in a principal agent framework to study the interaction between the governing body faced with a grant scheme the teacher and the student of an academic institution. Given the grant scheme the choices of unobservable effort levels by the teacher and the student for the relevant activities can be manipulated by the governing body by choosing appropriate incentive mechanisms for the teacher. In a sequential move game, we solve for all possible such mechanisms by the method of backward induction and establish necessary and sufficient conditions for these mechanisms to be equilibrium behaviour.

Our analysis enables us to present a possible explanation for why we observe such poor returns for certification done by teacher. It also leads to policy inferences about the design of grant scheme. The effect of changes in the amount and composition of grant will vary with the nature of the relationship between teacher and student effort. One needs to consider this while designing policies for inducing certain kind of outcomes. Also some kind of equilibria are not achievable under certain productivity conditions. Therefore, simply increasing the amount of grant will not necessarily achieve the objective. In some cases equilibrium may be unique. Under the circumstances, PRP may be ineffective in affecting changes in teacher's effort. Finally, educational reform policies should not aim simply at design of performance related pay for teachers. But should include policies that impact on the relationship between teacher and student effort; that is policies that affect the educational production function. Changes in the design of curriculum and teaching techniques requiring greater student involvement and teacher-student interaction are likely examples of policies belonging to this category.

Notes

1. We have deliberately kept firm's training out of the picture to delineate the teacher's effect on productivity. This is a departure from Spence (1974). In this model we assume that the probability of finding a job is one for those with training and zero for others.

2. We can think of the prevailing labour market wage schedule as the exogenously given wage schedule.
3. It can be worked out from subsequent analysis that even if we postulate any tie breaking assumption on teacher's hehaviour when $C = 0$. offering $C = 0$ is a dominated strategy for the GB. GB will not be able to maximise probability of match in this situation. See proposition 2.
4. The GB receives its funding from outside sources like central planning body rather than from student fees. For literature which model students as customers and pay a fee or price for acquiring education see Winston (1999) and Rothschild and White (1995).
5. Indeed, due to (1a), II and VII gets ruled out as nash equilibrium under any productivity assumption.

References

Belfield, C.R. and H.M. Levin (Editor) (2003): The Economics of Higher Education, The International Library of Critical Writings in Economics, Edward Elgar.

Cohn, E. and J.T. Addison (1998): The Economic Returns to Lifelong Learning in OECD Countries, *Education Economics*, 6 (3), 253-307.

Dewey, J., T. Husted and L. Kenny (2000): The Ineffectiveness of School Inputs: A Product of Misspecification? *Economics of Education Review*, 19(1).

Dolan, R.C., C.R. Jung and R.M. Schmidt (1985): Evaluating Educational Inputs in Undergraduate Education, *Review of Economics and Statistics*, LXVII (3): 514-20.

Dolton, P.J. and W. van der Klaauw (1996): Teacher Salaries and Teacher Retention, Assessing Educational Practices: The Contribution of Economics, MIT Press, Baumol and Becker (eds.).

Dolton, P.J. and W. van der Klaauw (1999): The Turnover of Teachers: A Competing Risks Explanation, *Review of Economics and Statistics*.

Goldin, C. and L.F. Katz (1998): The Origins of State-Level Difference in the Public Provision of Higher Education: 1890-1940, *American Economic Review*, Papers and Proceedings, 88 (2), 303-8.

Hanushek E., J. Kain and S. Rivkin (1999): Do Higher Salaries Buy Better Teachers? *NBER Working Paper 7082*.

Jacobson S.L. (1995): Monetary Incentives and the Reform of Teacher Compensation: A Persistent Organizational Dilemma, *International Journal of Educational Reform*, 4, 29-35.

Johnes, G. (1999): The Management of Universities: President's Lecture Delivered at Annual General Meeting of the Scottish Economics Society, 6-8th April 1999, *Scottish Journal of Political Economy*, 46 (5): 505-22.

Loeb, S. and M. Page (1999): Examining the Link between Teacher Wages and Student Outcomes: The Importance of Alternative Labor Market Opportunities and Non-Pecuniary Variation, Stanford University mimeo.

Rothschild M. and L.J. White (1995): Some Simple Analytics of the Pricing of Higher Education, *Journal of Political Economy*, Volume 103 (III), pp. 573-86.

Winston, G.C. (1999): Subsidies, Hierarchy, and Peers: The Awkward Economics of Higher Education, *Journal of Economic Perspectives*.

Health, Income and Health Expenditure in Indian States : A Search for Causal Explanation

SUSHIL KR. HALDAR AND DEBAPRASAD SARKAR

INTRODUCTION

From the early 1990s, various studies have attempted to identify the determinants of economic growth. The role of human capital (comprising health, education and skill) is now almost universally regarded as being indispensable in this regard. Sustained economic growth depends on levels of human capital whose stocks increase as a result of higher levels of health status, better education and new learning and training procedures. Without a labour force with some minimum levels of education and health status, a country is incapable of maintaining a state of continuous growth [*Lopez-Casasnovas et. al. 2005*].

It is commonly believed that economic growth leads populations to live better, longer lives and good health. Firstly, economic growth means rising per capita income and part of this increased income is translated into the consumption of higher quantity and better quality nutrients. Through nutrition, health as measured by life expectancy responds to increases in income [*Fogel, 1997*]. Secondly, economic growth is fueled by technological progress and part of this progress is reflected in improvements in medical science [*Rosen, 1993, Morand, 2005*]. The state of health in a country affects its economic growth through various channels.[1] When health improves the country can produce more output with any given combination of skills, physical capital and technological knowledge. One way to think about this effect is to treat health as another component of human capitat[2] incorporated in formulating the endogenous growth models [*Barro, 1991, Mankiw et. al. 1992, Thomas et. al. 1997, Bloom et. al. 2001*]. Central to these long-term growth models is the idea that technology is endogenous to the growth process [*Romer, 1986, Lucas 1988*]. The effects of human capital variables (namely, health and education) imply that the investment rate tends to increase as levels of education and socio-economic status of health rise. Higher educational level and better health status evolve systematically in accordance with the economic development of an economy. The provision of public resources for better health can assist the poor to release resources for other investments, such as in education, as a means to escape poverty.

The relationship between socio-economic status and health is one of the most robust findings in health economics. A positive relationship between socio-economic status[3] and health has been observed across the countries in the world at different time periods [*Berkman, 1988, Marmot et. al. 1991, Feinstein, 1993, Deaton et. al. 2001, Deaton, 2003*]. A prominent view in the literature is that higher socio-economic status leads to reductions in psycho-social and environmental risk factors. For example, education could induce better health behaviors or income could be used to purchase housing in clean or to visit doctors for regular health checkups. Similarly, studies of the effects of health on income or its growth divide the whole literature into two broad heads. The first comprises cross-national data over the long time period to assess the impact of measures of health at the national level on income or its growth. These quantitative studies certainly have some strong micro-foundations. The second comprises studies at the individual level that include one or more measures of health status along with extensive other information. Healthier populations tend to have higher labor productivity, because workers are physically more energetic, mentally more robust and suffer fewer lost workdays from illness of their own or family members.

A BRIEF REVIEW OF LITERATURE

The long-term relationship between income growth and health is examined by *Arora [1999]* considering the developed countries in the world and has observed the hypotheses that health of the population has influenced economic growth and that it should be an integral component of the productivity of economies and supporting the endogenous growth models. A similar study made by *Arora [2001]* provides that in the cointegrated relation between health and income, innovations in health lead to economic growth and not the vice versa. Arora's findings is found to be similar to those reported by *Fogel [1994, 1997]* who has carried out a study on Western Economies over the past two centuries, from 1780 to 1979. In analyzing cross-country data over the past 25 years, Bloom and Sachs [1998] have obtained empirical evidence that health and demographic variables play an extremely important role in determining economic growth rates. More recent studies have examined the effects of life expectancy (as a measure of health) on economic growth in the subsequent 15 to 25 years which have consistently found strong positive direct effects as well as indirect ones operating through rates of investment in physical capital or demographic profiles of the populations *[Barro, 1997; Sachs and Warner, 1997; Bloom and Williamson, 1998]*. *Bhargava et. al. [2001]* have assessed the effects of initial health status on growth over a shorter period of 5 years in a panel of countries and likewise found strong effects, but only in low income countries. A series of macro-economic cross-country studies also have found evidence for a significant impact of health (measured by life expectancy) on economic growth *[Mayer-Foulkes, 2001; Caselli, et. al. 1996, Gallup and Sachs, 2000].* The impact of health on income is an important policy issues that has motivated research at the *World Health [2001].* Mayer Foulkes *et. al.* [2001] has observed in the Mexican states that there has been a significant long-term impact (25-30 years) of life expectancy on economic growth. Considering longitudinal data from two countries (with different institutional environments), USA and Netherlands, Hurd and Kapteyn [2003] have arrived at the conclusion that income and wealth inequality is closely connected with health inequality. Deaton [2003] has argued that it is not true that income inequality itself is a major determinant of population health. He does not find a high (significant) correlation between life expectancy and income inequality among the rich countries; infant and child mortality in developing countries is primarily a consequences of poverty so that, conditional on average income, income inequality is important only because it is effectively a measure of poverty.

Very few studies, however, are designed to distinguish whether there are qualitative differences in how health affects growth and *vice versa* (i.e., both way causality) across the countries. Bhargava's (2001) and Adams *et. al.* (2003) studies are really exceptional in this direction. Bhargava finds that adult survival rate leads to growth in low-income countries. This is more or less consistent with a recent study by Archand (2001) on the role of nutrition in growth. By studying the productivity growth associated with stature rises in Korea and Norway, Weil (2001) arrives at similar magnitudes for the contribution of health to economic growth. Adams *et. al.* (2003) have tested Granger causality between income and health based on data from three waves of the AHEAD. They use 19 health conditions to explain wealth change; and wealth, income and education to explain mortality and incidence of the 19 health conditions. Their results suggest a causal link from health to changes in SES (as measured by wealth change).

A majority of the studies, analyzing the relationship between income and health belong to the OECD countries. Since India is the second largest populous country in the world, with a wide range of health and socio-economic diversity (across the states), the health income association is of paramount importance.

A SIMPLE THEORETICAL MODEL

Following the basic model developed by Hurd and Kapteyn (2003), we reformulate the following three basic equation model explaining the relationship between health status, income earning and health spending. The model is derived from an individual's point of view, later on it would be extended with a view to examine the relationship at the aggregate data sets. The basic assumptions of this model are: The evolution of health depends on the amount of spending for health care.[4] Income growth depends on health status. Healthier person tends to have higher labor productivity, because workers are more physically energetic and suffer fewer lost workdays from illness of his own and can avoid DALYs. It is plausible that healthier person who lives longer has stronger incentives to invest in enhancing his/her skills.

Case I

For person who is having with a normal health, assuming his/her health disturbance does not affect his earning but health expenditure is required for maintaining his/her efficiency in productivity.

In symbolic terms, $Y_t \rightarrow S_t \rightarrow H_t \rightarrow Y_{t+1}$

Basic Equations:

$$Y_{t+1} - Y_t = y(H_t) = a + bH_t \tag{1}$$

$$H_t - H_{t-1} = h(S_t) = \alpha + \beta S_t \tag{2}$$

$$S_t = s(Y_t) = c + \tau Y_t \tag{3}$$

where, Y_t = Income of the individual at time period t, H_t = Health status at time period t, S_t= Spending on health; a, b, α, β, c and τ all are positive parameters.

Equation (2) has some interesting feature. In a less developed economy, people's health expenditure is assumed to be negligible, tending towards zero. This means that $H_t - H_{t-1} = H_{t-1} - H_{t-2} = \ldots\ldots = \alpha$. This implies that health status is invariant over time and the economy is characterized by 'Health Poverty Trap'. This concept of health poverty trap is especially useful when it comes to trying to understand the growth dynamics in Sub-Saharan Africa when compared to the parts of East Asia. At the beginning of the 1960's, the two areas had similar level of PCGDP but the costs of illness and disease in Africa have been much greater; as a result African Countries have been suffering from poverty trap caused by poor health status.

From eqn. (2) and (3), we have:

$H_t - H_{t-1} = d + \gamma Y_t$ [Here, $d = c\beta + \alpha$ and $y = \beta\tau$]

$$\rightarrow Y_t = -d/\gamma + 1/\gamma(H_t - H_{t-1}) \rightarrow Y_{t+1} = d/\gamma + 1/\gamma(H_{t+1} - H_t) \quad \ldots. (4)$$

Introducing eq. (4) into eq. (l), we get:

$$H_{t+2} - (2 + b\gamma)H_{t+1} + H_t = a\gamma \quad \ldots. (5)$$

This is a 2nd order non homogeneous difference equation, the solution of this equation provides divergent and non-oscillatory time path of health provided $0 < b, \gamma < 1$ and $0 < b\gamma < 1$.

Case II (Person Suffering from Ill Health)

(a) For person who is having with an ill health, assuming his/her health disturbance does affect the earning and health expenditure is required for recovery his/her efficiency level. The person needs longer treatment to recover his/her normal health status. Therefore, income responds to improve at the same period of health recovery on the basis of last period health expenditure.

In symbolic terms, $Y_{t+1} \rightarrow S_{t-1} \rightarrow H_t \rightarrow Y_t$

Basic Equations:

$$Y_t - Y_{t-1} = y(H_t) = a + bH_t \quad (6)$$

$$H_t - H_{t-1} = h(S_t) = \alpha + \beta S_t \quad (2)$$

$$S_t = s(Y_t) = c + \tau Y_t \quad (3)$$

The relevant difference equation from eqs. (6), (2) and (3) is:

$$H_{t+2} - (2 + b\gamma) H_{t+1} + H_t = a\gamma \qquad \ldots\ldots (7)$$

This is identical to eq. (5) and hence the same solution follows.

(b) For person who is having with an ill health, assuming his/her health disturbance does affect the earning and health expenditure is required for recovery his/her efficiency level. The person needs longer treatment to recover his/her normal health status. Therefore, income responds to improve at the next period on the basis of last period health expenditure.

In symbolic terms,

$Y_{t+1} \rightarrow S_{t-1} \rightarrow H_t \rightarrow Y_{t+1}$

Basic Equations:

$$Y_{t+1} - Y_t = y(H_t) = a + bH_t \qquad (8)$$

$$H_t - H_{t-1} = h(S_t) = \alpha + \beta S_t \qquad (2)$$

$$S_t = s(Y_t) = c + \tau Y_t \qquad (3)$$

The relevant difference equation from eqs. (8), (2) and (3) is:

$$H_{t+2} - 2H_{t+1} + (1 - b\gamma) H_t = a\gamma \qquad \ldots\ldots (9)$$

This is a 2nd order non homogeneous difference equation, the solution of this equation provides divergent and non-oscillatory time path of health provided $0 < b, g < 1$ and $0 < b$ $g < 1$.

OBJECTIVE OF THE STUDY

The objective of our study is to examine the relationship between (a) health status and income, and (b) health status and health expenditure across the large fifteen states in India from 1981 to 2006. Since the variables like health status[5] (measured by IMR), income (measured by PCGDP) and health expenditure (measured by Per Capita Health Expenditure) are time dependent, therefore, simple regression of health status on income (or income on health status) or regression of health expenditure on health status (or health status on health expenditure) may generate spurious regression (or correlation). In order to get rid off this problem in time series econometrics, we have considered different tools as discussed in the methodology.

LIMITATION OF THE DATA

The majority of our population depends on the public health care services. However, privately run health care system has been running in India. The poor people do not have the capability to go for treatment at the privately run institutions. Since data on private health expenditure is unavailable, we just consider the per capita public health expenditure as a proxy for total health expenditure. The socio-economic status of health (which is an unobservable variable) of the common mass is generally measured by life expectancy at birth but due to non-availability of yearly data, we consider only the IMR as a proxy for health status. (we assumed that a positive relationship do exists between PCGDP and PCHE, there are a lot of literature investigate this).

The Data

The data on infant mortality rate was drawn from Sample Registration System—Registrar General, Government of India. The Per Capita Gross Domestic Product of the state and Per Capita Health Expenditure (as percentage of GDP) were collected from Reserve Bank of India Bulletin, various issues. In some of the cases, Govt. of India's website (www.indiastat.com) was visited. The health care expenditure as well as SDP is measured in real (at 1980-81 price) per capita terms. The variables are measured in natural logarithm. The notations used in the analysis is given as:

g=Log(PCGDP), i=Log(IMR) and e=Log(PCHE)

METHODOLOGY

For estimating the relationship of those variables (viz.

PCGDP, IMR, PCHE) the present study employs Granger's (1981) Test for causality that proposed first in testing the direction of causality in time series econometrics between two variables in each phase. The application of standard Granger causality test requires that the series of variables to be stationary and their linear combination are non-stationary. The Dickey-Fuller (DF) and Augmented Dickey Fuller (ADF) tests are applied to the three series to examine the unit root and stationary properties of the variables. In a bivariate framework, the first variable used to cause the second variable in the Granger sense if the forecast for the second variable improves when lagged values of the first variable are taken into account.

To test for Granger causality between (1) PCGDP & IMR, (2) IMR & HE, 4-bivariate models are specified as (arrows implies cause):

$$\text{PCGDP} \rightarrow \text{IMR and IMR} \rightarrow \text{PCGDP}$$
$$\text{IMR} \rightarrow \text{HE and HE} \rightarrow \text{IMR.}$$

The process in which the models are tested is in following two sections.

First—The Stationarity Test

Unit root test are important in examining the stationarity of time series.

Suppose we have a series $\{Y_t\}$ with AR(1) process such that

$$Y_t = \Phi Y_{t-1} + \varepsilon_t \qquad \text{(i)}$$

where $|\Phi| < 1$ and $\varepsilon \sim \text{iid } N(0, \sigma_t^2)$

We can estimate the parameters in (i) by OLS. Our estimator is efficient and the series is stationary since $|\Phi| < 1$. We could use a test statistic to test the hypothesis.

$H_0 : \Phi = 0$ against $H_A : \Phi = 0$

This is a legitimate test since the null-hypothesis, is a refutable hypothesis, even though the power against a local alternate is negligible.

Now suppose the data set reveals $|\Phi| = 1$ then it is non-stationary, under this circumstance spurious regression with high R-square but near zero D-W statistic is found in time series analysis as the usual test fails the stationarity properties.

Unit root test: Let us consider the data generating process

$$Y_t = \Phi\, Y_{t-1} + \varepsilon_t$$

The association question is whether—$\Phi = 1$. Subtracting Y_{t-1} from both sides we get,

$$\begin{aligned} \Delta\, Y_t &= (\Phi - 1)\, Y_{t-1} + \varepsilon_t \\ &= \gamma Y_{t-1} + \varepsilon_t \end{aligned}$$

$\gamma = 0$ implies that $\Phi = 1$ which indicates the presence of unit root in $\{Y_t\}$.

The unit root theory has been examined with an emphasis on testing principle.* The summary of the findings is given below:

Estimate:

$\Delta Y_t = \alpha_0 + \gamma Y_{t-1} + \alpha_2 t + \Sigma \beta_i Y_{t-i} + \varepsilon_t$ (No) → No unit root.

Is $\gamma = 0$?

(Yes)

↓ (No) ↑

Test for presence of trend. Is $\alpha_2 = 1$, given $\gamma = 0$? (No) → Is $\gamma = 0$? using normal distribution → (Yes) has unit root.

(Yes)

↓

Estimate:

$\Delta Y_t = \alpha_0 + \gamma Y_{t-1} + \alpha_2 t + \Sigma \beta_i \Delta Y_{t-i} + \varepsilon_t$ (No) → No unit root.

Is $\gamma = 0$?

(Yes)

↓

Test for Presence of Drift

↓ (No) ↑

Test for presence of trend. Is α_0=0, given $\gamma = 0$? (No) → Is $\gamma = 0$? → (Yes) using normal distribution has unit root.

(Yes)

↓

Estimate: $\Delta Y_t = \gamma Y_{t-1} + \alpha_2 t + \Sigma \beta_i \Delta Y_{t-i} + \varepsilon_t$

Is $\gamma = 0$? → No? → No Unit Root,

→ Yes? → Has Unit Root.

Findings :If the estimated *F* statistic (F*) is less than the critical value of *F* for *n* number of observations the Dicky-Fuller results is signifant at 5% level.

Second—The Granger Causality Test

The granger causality test follows the following procedure for different set of bivariate series separately. A time series (X) is said to be Granger cause to another time series (Y) if the prediction error (FPE-final prediction error) of current Y declines by using the past values of X in addition to past values of Y. The Granger causality test can only be applied if a linear combination of two non-stationary variables is stationary. The standard Granger's causality test can only be specified as :

$$\Delta X_1 = \alpha_1 + \sum_{i-1}^{m} \beta_{li} \Delta X_{t-1} + \varepsilon_{lt} \qquad 1'$$

$$\Delta X_1 = \alpha_2 + \sum_{i>1}^{m} \beta_{1i} \Delta X_{t-I} + \sum_{j=1}^{n} \beta_{2j} \Delta Y_{t-j} + \varepsilon_{2t} \qquad 2'$$

$$\Delta Y_t = \alpha_3 + \sum_{i=1}^{n} \beta_{3j} \Delta X_{t-i} + \varepsilon_{3t} \qquad 3'$$

$$\Delta Y_t = \alpha_4 + \sum_{j=1}^{n} \beta_{3j} \Delta X_{t-i} + \sum_{i=1}^{m} \beta_{4j} \Delta X_{t-i} + \varepsilon_{4t} \qquad 4'$$

where Δ refers to the difference operator; *n* is the number of lags; αs and βs are the parameters to be estimated and ε_t is the error terms. Equation 1′ and *i* are made as a pair to detect whether the coefficients of the past lags Y can be zero as a whole. Similarly, equations 3′ and 4′ are made a pair to detect whether the coefficients of the past lags of X can be zero as a whole. If the estimated lagged values of Y variable in equation *i* is significant, then Y is said to be Granger cause X. Further if the estimated F-statistics for lagged values of X variable in equation 4′ is statistically significant, then X is said to be Granger cause Y. This setting forms the basic framework for Granger Causality. It is important to note that the results of the causality test depends on critically on the choice of the lag length. More often the choice of the lag length is done in an *ad hoc* manner. More specifically, too short the lag length results in estimation bias, while too long the lag length causes a loss of degree of freedom and estimation efficiency. To solve the problem, Hsiao's approach (1982) can be applied. Hsiao's (1982) procedure combines Akaike's final prediction error (FPE) criterion with Granger causality and is employed to guide the selection of the appropriate lag length of the independent variables. The estimation of FPE is a two step procedure. The first step is to estimate equation 1′ by varying its order of lags from 1 to m. Next we calculate the residual sum squares (RSS) and final prediction error (FPE) defined by Akaike (1973) at each lag length of the independent variables. The lag that minimizes the following FPE value is considered as appropriate. The FPE at m lag is estimated by the following equation,

$$FPE(m, 0) = (T + m + 1)/(T - m - 1). RSS(m, 0)/T \qquad 5'$$

where RSS (m , 0) is the residual sum of square, T denotes the number of observations, m is the order of lags varying from 1 to m for variable X and RSS is the residual sum of square. The optimal lag m is determined by the smallest value of FPE. In the next step, we estimate equation 2′ where Y is treated as control variable holding the optimal lag of m and the additional variables X, treated as manipulated variable varying its order of lags from n to N and calculate the corresponding two dimensional FPEs.

$$FPE(m, n) = (T+m+n+1)/(T-m-n-1). RSS(m, n)/T \qquad 6'$$

Here also minimum FPE determines the optimal lag (n). After the determination of optimal lag we can test for the direction of causality by comparing with the smallest FPEs. If the minimum FPE calculated from equation 6′ is smaller than FPE in equation 5′ then we can say that X causes Y. The same procedure is applied in order to find the subsequent causality from Y to X by using equation 3′ and 4′.

THE RESULTS

TABLE 6.1
Unit Root Test without Trend

State	*Variable*	*Level*		*First Difference*	
		DF	*ADF(1)*	*DF*	*ADF(1)*
(1)	*(2)*	*(3)*	*(4)*	*(5)*	*(6)*
	g	0.870 #	0.998 #	-4.922	-3.056
Andhra Pradesh	i	-0.074158 #	-0.0630 #	-5.390	-5.676
	e	-1.9838 #	-1.8345 #	-5.3128	-5.4758
	g	1.1811 #	1.2968 #	-5.049	-4.299
Assam	i	-0.54331 #	0.42357 #	-5.875	-2.891 #
	e	-5.0820	-2.9922 #	-3.2458	-3.9874
	g	-2.3085 #	0.80428 #	-9.1419	-3.4792
Bihar	i	-1.6028 #	-1.5630 #	-4.5947	-4.0939
	e	-2.0747 #	-2.2717 #	-7.6217	-4.7227
	g	-1.2720 #	-2.7243 #	-8.7041	-6.1080
Orissa	i	0.83313 #	0.86905 #	-4.5149	-2.9542 #
	e	-2.0736 #	-1.3444 #	-3.4616	-3.2350
	g	-0.5467 #	-0.4969 #	-5.1427	-5.1203
Maharashtra	i	0.59715 #	1.0165 #	-5.7022	-5.4264
	e	-5.9971	-4.6819	-5.2836	-3.9418
	g	-0.86266 #	-2.2556 #	-8.7148	-4.2977
Madhya Pradesh	i	-0.17080 #	-0.11417 #	-8.5584	-4.4914
	e	-3.6453	-2.3879 #	-4.1960	-3.3983
	g	-0.39258 #	-0.57859 #	-5.8976	-5.7457

(*Contd.*)

TABLE 6.1 (Contd.)

(1)	(2)	(3)	(4)	(5)	(6)
Punjab	i	-0.76371 #	-0.42992 #	-7.8014	-5.2175
	e	-4.5350	-3.7135	-3.9903	-3.0084 #
	g	-1.0958 #	-0.58733 #	-9.5148	-3.6638
Rajasthan	i	-0.34710 #	0.043311 #	-5.7630	-4.5519
	e	-7.9526	-2.7756 #	-4.4939	-4.1981
	g	-0.38032 #	-0.12061 #	-7.2452	-5.8726
Haryana	i	-0.99137 #	-0.73942 #	-6.3408	-5.5419
	e	-3.5974	-3.9308	-6.1815	-3.9466
	g	-0.64945 #	-0.12802 #	-7.7062	-3.8053
Gujarat	i	-1.5012 #	-1.4342 #	-5.3619	-3.9158
	e	-3.0429	-2.2482 #	-3.3481	-3.1059 #
	g	1.1721 #	1.2923 #	-4.7870	-3.5984
Kerala	i	-1.2197 #	-1.2038 #	-5.7968	-3.7278
	e	-3.4094	-2.9393 #	-3.1737	-1.7975 #
Karnataka	g	2.5552 #	0.65910 #	-6.9409	-3.7327
	i	-0.33176 #	-0.35815 #	-5.5265	-3.9625
	e	-3.8429	-2.1840 #	-2.4761 #	-2.2182 #
Tamilnadu	g	0.62418 #	0.69888 #	-5.5209	-5.8274
	i	-0.17253 #	0.11582 #	-4.7519	-3.2202 #
	e	-3.9169	-3.2752	-4.8604	-4.1095
	g	-1.1537 #	-1.1167 #	-4.7870	-3.7278
Uttar Pradesh	i	-0.85909 #	-0.85244 #	-5.2352	-4.7179
	e	-2.1374 #	-1.8117 #	-2.4761 #	-2.2381 #
	g	3.3453	3.1127	-3.8312	-3.6521
West Bengal	i	0.024778 #	0.77674 #	-3.9908	-3.3126
	e	-4.1953	-4.3542	-3.9113	-4.2176
India	g	1.0581 #	1.5756 #	-5.6568	-2.6206 #
	i	0.09961 #	0.12793 #	-5.2357	-4.7179
	e	-2.7398 #-	-1.6018 #	-3.7218	-3.7377

Note : 95% critical value for the augmented Dickey-Fuller statistic -2.9907 (for level), and -3.6291 (for 1st difference) where, g=log (PCGDP), i=log (IMR) and e=log (PCHE), # means Non-Stationary.

TABLE 6.2
Unit Root Test without Trend

Industry	*Variable*	*Level*		*First Difference*	
		DF	*ADF(1)*	*DF*	*ADF(1)*
(1)	*(2)*	*(3)*	*(4)*	*(5)*	*(6)*
	g	-2.795 #	-2.707 #	-5.132	-3.289 #
Andhra Pradesh	i	-2.743 #	-2.736 #	-4.0806	-5.680
	e	-3.1257 #	-3.1568#	-4.4762	-3.9874
	g	-0.971 #	-0.601 #	-4.11	-4.229
Assam	i	-2.768 #	-2.832 #	-6.744	-3.528
	e	-2.9922 #	-2.9907 #	-5.897	-4.5231
	g	-2.8666 #	-1.2296 #	-8.9582	-3.3865
Bihar	i	-2.0279 #	-2.2943 #	-4.4783	-4.0188
	e	-3.8104	-2.8470 #	-7.6820	-4.9645
	g	-4.5234	-2.9360 #	-8.4885	-5.9607
Orissa	i	-1.6639 #	-1.6104 #	-5.0265	-3.5224 #
	e	-4.2171	-2.6365 #	-3.8518	-3.8633
	g	-2.044 #	-2.0015 #	-5.0518	-4.9833
Maharashtra	i	-2.3789 #	-1.8802 #	-5.7311	-5.7500
	e	-8.0669	-8.0015	-5.1282	-3.0219#
	g	-4.1779	-2.5207 #	-8.5241	-4.2015
Madhya Pradesh	i	-3.5467 #	-2.1347 #	-8.9805	-4.5460
	e	-4.1582	-3.5017 #	-4.1387	-2.7848 #
	g	-2.7963 #	-2.2539 #	-5.7996	-5.8845
Punjab	i	-3.2268 #	-2.0355 #	7.6225	-5.1256
	e	-2.3227 #	-2.3458 #	-5.2774	-4.2695
	g	-4.3884	-2.3235 #-	-9.2966	-3.5794 #
Rajasthan	i	-3.1317 #	-2.7173 #	-5.6496	-4.5435
	e	-4.9681	-2.3441 #	-4.6225	-4.4722
	g	-4.0698	-3.0079 #-	-7.0733	-5.7198
Haryana	i	-3.3014 #	-2.7452 #	-6.1915	-5.3952
	e	-4.5715	-5.0460	-6.8875	-3.8773
	g	-3.8751	-2.5993 #	-7.5309	-3.7121

(*Contd.*)

TABLE 6.2 (Contd.)

(1)	(2)	(3)	(4)	(5)	(6)
Gujarat	i	-1.7090 #	-1.4653 #	-5.3576	-4.0472
	e	-3.0656 #	-3.2238 #	-3.4235 #	-3.3133 #
	g	-3.1479 #	-3.0401 #	-5.3235	-4.4823
Kerala	i	-2.4486 #	-1.8501 #	-5.8078	-3.8120
	e	-1.0767 #	-1.0614 #	-4.5111	-2.6937 #
Karnataka	g	-3.1556	-2.4826 #	-6.8457	-3.6687
	i	-3.0628 #	-2.7057 #	-5.5933	-4.1681
	e	-0.81352 #	-2.1840 #	-3.1507 #	-3.0988 #
Tamilnadu	g	-1.7475 #	-1.6615 #	-5.3718	-5.8208
	i	-2.9902 #	-2.9317 #	-4.7339	-3.2386 #
	e	-2.2135 #	-2.2892 #-	-6.4532	-4.5152
	g	-2.2903 #	-2.2089 #	-5.3809	-5.6850
Uttar Pradesh	i	-1.2959 #	-1.7450 #	-4.4728	-4.0936
	e	-2.7948 #	-2.7176 #	-7.3163	-4.9648
West Bengal	g	0.14804 #	0.16664 #	-4.7921	-4.8236
	i	-2.6022 #	-1.2367 #	-4.7332	-3.5291 #
	e	-2.8874 #	-3.3920 #	-4.5156	-4.5218
	g	-2.1837 #	-1.7977 #	-5.9312	-2.6888 #
India	i	-2.4009 #	-2.1935 #	-5.1141	-4.6072
	e	-2.2168 #	-1.7818 #	-3.8815	-3.6158

Note : 95% critical value for the augmented Dickey-Fuller statistic -3.6119 (for level), and 3.6291 (for 1st difference), g=log (PCGDP), i=log(IMR) and e=Log (PCHE) # — Non-Stationary.

The Analysis of the Result

The study of Dickey-Fuller method of testing unit root with or without trend with respect to our data set (PCGDP, IMR & HE) reveals the following:

(a) The data series of PCGDP & IMR of all states (except PCGDP of West Bengal) and India itself are non-stationary with or without trend.

(b) The HE series are also non-stationary for all (except Maharashtra, Punjab, Haryana, Tamilnadu and West Bengal) without trend and are non stationary (except Maharashtra, Haryana) with trend.

Therefore we have to go to the process of making data series stationary.

To avoid the spurious regression problem that may arise from regression of a non-stationary time series on another non-stationary time series, we have to transform the non-stationary time series to stationary time series that is we have to set regression of a unit root time series on another unit root time series. If the linear combination of two stochastic gives the residual with drift is stationary (having no unit root) then only we can go to the causal relation between variables. In our analysis as log (PCGDP), log (IMR) and log (PCHE) are non-stationary individually and the first difference of all three variables attain stationarity, the linear combination of any two will be economically meaningful (not spurious) of the residual (u_t) has no unit root that is the regression will be meaningful and they contain Long-term equilibrium relationship between them in each combination.

TABLE 6.3
Results of Unit Root Tests of Residuals

Industry	*Regression Equation*	*DF*	*ADF*
(1)	*(?)*	*(3)*	*(4)*
	g on i	-3.146 #	-2.724 #
Andhra Pradesh	i on g	-3.365 #	-3.018 #
	e on i	-2.7685 #	-3.1059 #
	i on e	-3.575	-3.383 #
	g on i	-2.4688 #	-2.3812 #
Assam	i on g	-2.6606 #	-2.5204 #
	e on i	-2.8518 #	-2.8684 #
	i on e	-1.9010 #	-1.8869 #
	g on i	-2.7685 #	-1.1098 #

(*Contd.*)

TABLE 6.3 (Contd.)

(1)	(2)	(3)	(4)
Bihar	i on g	-1.9532 #	-1.4285 #
	e on i	-3.9635	-3.1665 #
	i on e	-3.4710 #	-2.7757 #
Orissa	g on i	-4.3709	-3.1032 #
	i on g	-3.6084	-2.4824 #
	e on i	-3.4886 #	-2.2472 #
	i on e	-2.2482 #	-1.1881 #
	g on i	-1.7063 #	-1.3582 #
Maharashtra	i on g	-1.3895 #	-0.98366 #
	e on i	-3.9100	-3.9257
	i on e	-1.4627 #	-1.4518 #
	g on i	-4.2612	-2.2635 #
Madhya Pradesh	i on g	-4.4632	-2.4477 #
	e on i	-2.3231 #	-2.2326 #
	i on e	-1.3496 #	-0.96195 #
	g on i	-3.5617 #	-2.3906 #
Punjab	i on g	-3.8435	-2.6250 #
	e on i	-3.3507 #	-2.4052 #
	i on e	-3.1158 #	-2.0205 #
	g on i	-3.6067	-2.7793 #
Rajasthan	i on g	-3.1773 #	-2.5018 #
	e on i	-3.8073	-3.7345
	i on e	-1.5470 #	-1.7321 #
	g on i	- 4.4620	-2.7864 #
Haryana	i on g	-4.7793	-3.1763 #
	e on i	-4.1891	-3.7313
	i on e	-3.0765 #	-2.4887 #
	g on i	-1.9584 #	-1.4193 #
Gujarat	i on g	-2.3041 #-	-1.9313 #
	e on i	-2.0418 #	-2.4338 #
	i on e	-1.8718 #	-2.1812 #
	g on i	-1.7601 #	-1.0167 #

(Contd.)

TABLE 6.3 (Contd.)

(1)	*(2)*	*(3)*	*(4)*
Kerala	i on g	-2.4680 #	-1.8497 #
	e on i	-3.0042 #	-2.5504 #
	i on e	-3.0292 #	-2.5362 #
	g on i	-3.0148 #	-2.9489 #
Karnataka	i on g	-2.7738 #	-2.7009 #
	e on i	-3.4612 #	-3.3824 #
	i on e	-2.1891 #	-2.0589 #
Tamilnadu	g on i	-1.6738 #	-1.8588 #
	i on g	-1.5165 #	-1.7380 #
	e on i	-2.0419 #	-2.3074 #
	i on e	-1.0218 #	-1.5891 #
	g on i	-4.0191	-4.0650
Uttar Pradesh	i on g	-3.6813 #	-3.5559 #
	e on i	-2.8814 #	-3.5282 #
	i on e	-2.2967 #	-2.9749 #
	g on i	-3.4863 #	-2.4277 #
West Bengal	i on g	-1.3216 #	
	e on i	-2.4752 #	
	i on e	-1.6407 #	-0.94277 #
	g on i	-1.8185 #	-1.1611 #
India	i on g	-1.9537 #	-1.6371#
	e on i	-1.6938 #	-1.9385 #
	i on e	-0.89474 #	-1.3389 #

Notes : 95% critical value for the Dickey-Fuller statistic = -3,6018, g=log (PCGDP), i=log(IMR) and e=Log (PCHE), # — Non-Stationary.

The non-stationarity of g, i and e explain the stationarity upon the first difference that means the co-integration between variables do exist. The result of unit root test of residuals and Akaike's FPE explains the dependency level of one individual non-stationary variable on other non-stationary variable with optimum lags. The lagged changes in g, i and e continue to extract significant at 5% level for India and her some states as shown in the following Tables 6.4, 6.5, 6.6 and 6.7.

TABLE 6.4
Granger Causality Test between PCGDP and IMR: PCGDP as Dependent Variable

State	*FPE: Regress Δg at t on Δg at t-k*	*FPE: Regress Δg at t on Δg at t-k and Δi at t-j*	*Optimal lag of g*	*Optimal lag of i*	*F-Value*
Andhra Pradesh	0.00266	0.00285	1	1	0.32267
Assam	0.005406	0.00594	3	1	2.007
Bihar	.0005348	.0005519	1	1	6.7633
Orissa	0.005917	0.0.006371	2	1	4.4775
Maharashtra	0.00234	0.00248	2	1	1.5506
Madhya Pradesh	0.004061	0.004415	1	1	4.9648
Punjab	0.000317	0.000345	2	1	2.0460
Rajasthan	0.00859	0.007905	1	2	7.6968 *
Haryana	0.002495	0.002130	2	1	5.8577 *
Gujarat	0.010715	0.01068	1	1	4.2983*
Kerala	0.0018864	0.0018905	1	1	0.89866
Karnataka	0.001426	0.001182	1	1	6.2077 *
Tamilnadu	0.00122	0.00123	2	1	1.9326
Uttar Pradesh	0.0009122	0.0008823	1	1	0.59495 *
West Bengal	0.000756	0.00038	1	4	4.9012 *
India	0.00066208	0.00060315	3	2	2.4015 *

Note : g=log (PCGDP), i=log(IMR) and e=log (PCHE); k=Optimal lag period of Dependent variable, j=Optimum lag period of Independent Variable.

† FPE represents Akaike's final prediction error.

* Significant at 5% level.

TABLE 6.5
Granger Causality Test between PCGDP and IMR: IMR as Dependent Variable

State	*FPE: Regress Δi at t on Δi at t-k*	*FPE: Regress Δi at t on Δi at t-k and Δi at t-j*	*Optimal lag of i*	*Optimal lag of g*	*F-Value*
Andhra Pradesh	0.002532	0.002188	2	2	3.453*
Assam	0.00721	0.00784	1	1	0.26063
Bihar	0.004905	0.005151	2	1	0.64560
Orissa	0.002036	0.002115	1	1	0.50099
Maharashtra	0.0059	0.005805	2	2	2.2725*
Madhya Pradesh	0.001331	0.0013656	2	1	3.6357
Panjab	0.003343	0.003349	3	1	2.1215
Rajasthan	0.006108	0.006495	1	1	0.86112
Haryana	0.0051117	0.005265	3	1	1.8075
Gujarat	0.0070697	0.007586	1	1	0.44558
Kerala	0.02541	0.031004	1	2	0.48291
Karnataka	0.0051025	0.0048106	1	1	0.73191 *
Tamilnadu	0.00410	0.004206	1	1	0.57059
Uttar Pradesh	0.001576	0.001214	2	1	4.1318 *
West Bengal	0.004737	0.004413	1	1	4.5561 *
India	0.0001213	0.001214	3	1	1.3603

Note : g=log (PCGDP), i=log(IMR) and e=log (PCHE); k=Optimal lag period of Dependent variable, j=Optimum lag period of Independent Variable, g=log (PCGDP), i=log(IMR) and e=log (PCHE).

† FPE represents Akaike's final prediction error.

* Significant at 5% level.

Table 6.6
Granger Causality Test between HE and IMR: IMR as Dependent Variable

State	*FPE: Regress Δi at t on Δi at t-k*	*FPE: Regress Δi at t on Δi at t-k and Δe at t-j*	*Optimal lag of i*	*Optimal lag of e*	*F-Value*
Andhra Pradesh	0.002532	0.002742	2	1	1.1975
Assam	0.00721	0.00761	1	2	1.2027
Bihar	0.004905	0.004724	2	2	1.4190*
Orissa	0.002036	0.002172	1	3	0.91050
Maharashtra	0.0059	0.00644	2	1	1.5149
Madhya Pradesh	0.001331	0.00108	2	2	5.3000*
Punjab	0.003343	0.003668	3	1	1.5664
Rajasthan	0.006108	0.005505	1	1	2.9034 *
Haryana	0.0051117	0.0046356	3	1	2.6309 *
Gujarat	0.0070697	0.0074003	I	1	0.72037
Kerala	0.02541	0.02763	1	1	0.89456
Karnataka	0.0051025	0.005099	1	1	1.2977 *
Tamilnadu	0.00410	0.004171	1	1	0.83907
Uttar Pradesh	0.001576	0.001337	2	1	3.7381* *
West Bengal	0.004737	0.005152	1	1	2.6142
India	0.0001213	0.001313	3	1	0.93833

Note : g=log (PCGDP), i=log(IMR) and e=log (PCHE); k=Optimal lag period of Dependent variable, j=Optimum lag period of Independent Variable, g=log (PCGDP), i=log(IMR) and e=log (PCHE), g=log (PCGDP), i=log(IMR) and e=log (PCHE).

† FPE represents Akaike's final prediction error.

* Significant at 5% level.

TABLE 6.7

Granger Causality Test between HE and IMR: HE as Dependent Variable

State	*FPE: Regress Δe at t on Δe at t-k*	*FPE: Regress Δe at t on Δe at t-k and Δi at t-j*	*Optimal lag of e*	*Optimal lag of i*	*F-Value*
Andhra Pradesh	0.0111	0.001189	1	1	0.26274
Assam	0.00398	0.00432	3	1	3.6544
Bihar	0.05937	0.05663	1	3	3.4426*
Orissa	0.001523	0.001164	3	2	5.1401 *
Maharashtra	0.003318	0.00238	2	2	8.0851 *
Madhya Pradesh	0.007253	0.007452	2	1	1.5590
Punjab	0.00491	0.004994	2	1	1.2482
Rajasthan	0.002898	0.003157	1	1	22.558
Haryana	0.011104	0.008681	2	2	3.7460*
Gujarat	0.008784	0.009301	1	1	2.5710
Kerala	0.002303	0.002433	2	2	2.1000
Karnataka	0.003494	0.0037129	1	1	6.4148
Tamilnadu	0.00469	0.004805	2	1	2.2502
Uttar Pradesh	0.006095	0.006287	1	1	1.0700
West Bengal	0.001286	0.0008856	3	3	4.7523 *
India	0.0032028	0.003438	1	1	3.4093

Note : g=log (PCGDP), i=log(IMR) and e=log (PCHE); k=Optimal lag period of Dependent variable, j=Optimum lag period of Independent Variable, g=log (PCGDP), i=log(IMR) and e=log (PCHE) g=log (PCGDP), i=log(IMR) and e=log (PCHE).

† FPE represents Akaike's final prediction error.

* Significant at 5% level.

The Causality

The study of co-integration indicates only a long run equilibrium relation between variables in each set of variable but it does not mean the direction of causality. Co-integration results just rules out the possibility of "no causation" between variables. So, further we have to use the Granger causality test to establish the direction of causality. The Granger causal relations for different cases are the following.

TABLE 6.8
Granger Causality between NSDP and IMR

State	*Direction of Causality*
Andhra Pradesh	PCGDP→IMR
Assam	NO CAUSAL RELATION
Bihar	IMR→HE, HE→IMR
Orissa	IMR→HE
Maharashtra	PCGDP→IMR, IMR→HE
Madhya Pradesh	HE→IMR
Punjab	NO CAUSAL RELATION
Rajasthan	IMR→PCGDP, HE→IMR
Haryana	IMR→PCGDP, HE→IMR, IMR→HE
Gujarat	IMR→PCGDP
Kerala	NO CAUSAL RELATION
Karnataka	PCGDP→IMR, IMR→PCGDP, HE→IMR
Tamilnadu	NO CAUSAL RELATION
Uttar Pradesh	PCGDP→IMR, IMR→PCGDP, HE→IMR
West Bengal	PCGDP→IMR, IMR→PCGDP, IMR→HE
India	IMR→PCGDP

Following the theoretical model as discussed earlier, we have attempted here to examine the role of per capita health expenditure (public) on the health status of the people (measured by IMR) and the role of improvement of health status (measured by declining IMR) on the improvement of per capita gross domestic product in India and her 15 large states.

From Table 6.8, in analyzing the long run relationship among the variables (g, i and e), we can conclude the following:

(a) The both way causality do exist between PCHE and

IMR in Bihar and Haryana and one way causality do exist in Orissa, MP, Rajasthan, Karnataka, UP and WB.

(b) The both way causality do exist between PCGDP and IMR in Karnataka, UP and WB. and one way causality do exist in Orissa, AP, Rajasthan, Haryana, Gujarat and India.

(c) No causal relationship is found among all the variables in Assam, Punjab, Kerala and Tamil Nadu.

CONCLUDING OBSERVATIONS

The long run relationship (both way) between health status, income and health expenditure do hold good in most of the states which are socio-economically backward. One plausible explanation is that people in the BIMARU states largely depend on publicly provided health facility. The result could be different if the private spending on health care is incorporated in our analysis. More public spending on health is required in most of the BIMARU states in order to get rid of the health poverty trap.

NOTES

1. Good health and nutrition enhance worker productivity. Healthier people who live longer have stronger incentives to invest in developing their skills, because they expect to reap the benefits of such investments over longer periods. Better health increases workforce productivity by reducing incapacity, debility, number of days lost to sick leave. Moreover, good health helps to forge improved levels of education by increasing levels of schooling and scholastic performance [Schultz 1997]. Health affects economic growth through its impact on demographic factors. Shorter life expectancies inhibit investment in education and other forms of human capital, since there is greater risk that each individual will not survive long enough to benefit from investment. In addition, a larger proportion of the population which is dependent has a detrimental effect on rates of savings and capital investment and hence on subsequent growth [Kelly and Schmidt, 1996]. Healthier workers are more productive for a variety of reasons—increased vigor, strength, attentiveness, stamina, creativity and so forth. Ill-health and malnutrition reduce the physical capacity of the laborer, leading to lower productivity and resulting in lower wages (Zimmer *et. al.* 2000).
2. Adriaan *v.* Zon and J. Muysken (2005) have argued that economic growth is driven by knowledge accumulation in the traditional Lucas Model (1988) and as such is based on labour services supplied by healthy

people. The health state of the population at the aggregate level (the share of healthy people in the population) determines the extent to which potential labor services embodied in the population can be used effectively. Moreover, knowledge accumulation requires the spending of 'healthy hours', wherein the embodiment of knowledge can take hold in individual people.

3. Socio-economic status can be measured in many ways including occupation, social class, education, income and wealth, etc. Adams *et. al.* (2003) have used 19 health conditions such as cancer, heart attack, and self rated health to explain wealth change; and wealth, income and education to explain mortality and incidence of 19 health conditions. Their findings did not reject the null hypotheses of no causal link from socio-economic status to mortality. They observed some statistical evidence for a causal link from health to changes in socio-economic status as measured by wealth change.
4. Spending should be thought of broadly as spending on nutrition, housing in an area with good air and water quality, peaceful area free from negative externalities and other socio-cultural factors that are thought to influence health [Hurd and Kapteyn, 2003].
5. Health status is an unobservable variable but it can be assessed by the reduction of mortality, morbidity and sickness. Progress of health at the macro-level can be measured by the improvement of life expectancy, reduction of infant or child mortality, etc. [Santerre and Neun, 2000].

References

Adams, Peter, Michael D. Hurd, Daniel McFadden, Angela Merrill., and Tiago Ribeiro. (2003): 'Healthy, Wealthy, and Wise? Tests for Direct Causal Paths between Health and Socio-economic Status', *Journal of Econometrics,* 112, pp. 3-56.

Adriaan van Zon, and Joan, Muysken (2005): 'Health as a Principal Determinant of Economic Growth' in *Health and Economic Growth: Findings and Policy Implications*, edited by Guillem Lopez-Casasnovas, Berta Rivera, and Luis Currais, The MIT Press, pp. 41-65.

Akaike, H. (1973): 'Information Theory and an extension of the Maximum Likelihood Principle' in *Proceedings of the 2nd International Symposium on Information Theory,* edited by R.N. Petrov and F. Csaki, pp. 267-81, Budapest, Akademiai Kiado.

Archand, J.L. (2001): 'Undernourishment and Economic Growth', in *The State of Food and Agriculture, 2001,* Rome: Food and Agriculture Organization of the United Nations.

Arora, Suchit (1999): Health and Long-Term Economic Growth: A Multi-Country Study, Ph.D. Dissertation, Ohio State University, USA.

———, (2001): 'Health Human Productivity and Long-Term Economic Growth', *Journal of Economic History,* 61(3), pp. 699-749.

Barro, R.J. (1991): 'Economic Growth in a Cross Section of Countries', *Quarterly Journal of Economics*, 196, 2nd May, pp. 407-43.

———, (1997): Determinants of Economic Growth, Cambridge, Mass : MIT Press.

Berkman, Lisa F. (1988): 'The Changing and Heterogeneous Nature of Aging and Longevity: A Social and Biochemical Perspective', in *Annual Review of Gerontology and Geriatrics*, 8, ed. George L. Maddox and M. Powell Lawton, pp. 37-68.

Bhargava, A., D.T. Jamison, L., J. Lau, and C.J.L. Murray (2001): 'Modelling the Effects of Health on Economic Growth', *Journal of Health Economics*, 20(3), pp. 423-440.

Bloom, D.E., Canning, D. and E. Sevilla, J. (2001): The Effect of Health on Economic Growth: Theory and Evidence, Cambridge: National Bureau of Economic Research, Working Paper 8587, p. 26

Bloom, D.E., and J. Williamson (1998): Demographic Transitions and Economic Miracles in Emerging Asia, *World Bank Economic Review*, 12: pp. 419-55.

Bloom, D.E., Sachs, J.D. (1998): Geography, Demography and Economic Growth in Africa, *Brookings Papers on Economic Activity*, 2, pp. 207-95.

Caselli, F., G. Esquivel, and F. Lefort (1996): Reopening the Convergence Debate: A New Look at the Cross-Country Growth Empirics, *Journal of Economic Growth*, 1, pp. 363-89.

Deaton, Angus (2003): 'Health, Inequality and Economic Development', *Journal of Economic Literature*, Vol. XLI, March, pp. 113-58.

Deaton, Angus and Christina Paxon (2001): 'Mortality, Education, Income, and Inequality among American Cohorts', in *Themes in the Economics of Aging*, David Wise (ed.), Chicago University Press for NBER, Paper 7140.

Feinstein, Jonathan (1993): 'The Relationship between Socio-economic Status and Health: A Review of Literature', *Milbank Quarterly*, 71(2), pp. 279-322.

Fogel, R.W. (1994): The Relevance of Malthus for the Study of Mortality Today: Long Run Influences on Health, Mortality, Labor Force Participation and Population Growth, *Historical Paper No. 54*, National Bureau of Economic Research, March, pp. 36.

———, (1997): 'New Findings on Secular Trends in Nutrition and Mortality: Some Implications for Population Theory', in *The Handbook of Population and Family Economics*, Vol. 1A, edited by M. Rosenzweig and O. Stark, Amsterdam, North Holland.

Gallup, I. and J. Sachs (2000): 'The Economic Burden of Malaria', *Working Paper No. 52*, Centre for International Development, Harvard University, Cambridge, Mass.

Granger, C. (1981): 'Some Properties of Time Series Data and their use in Econometric Model Specification', *Journal of Econometrics*, 16, pp. 121-30.

Hsiao, C. (1982): 'Auto-regressive Modelling and Causal Ordering of Economic Variables', *Jr. of Economic Dynamics and Controlling*, 4, pp. 243-59.

Hurd, Michael, and Arie Kapteyn (2003): 'Health, Wealth, and the Role of Institutions', *The Journal of Human Resources*, 38(2), pp. 387-415.

Kelly, Allen C., and Robert M. Schmidt (1996): 'Savings, Dependency and Development', *Journal of Population Economics*, 9(4), pp. 365-86.

Lopez-Casasnovas, G., Berta Rivera and Luis Currais (2005): 'The Role Health Plays in Economic Growth' in *Health and Economic Growth: Findings and Policy Implications,* edited by Lopez-Casasnovas, G., Berta Rivera, MIT Press, MIT Cambridge, Massachusetts.

Lucas, R.E. (1988): 'On the Mechanics of Economic Development', *Journal of Monetary Economics,* 22: pp. 3-42.

Mankiw, N.G., Romer, D. and Weil, D. (1992): 'A Contribution to the Empirics of Economic Growth', *Quarterly Journal of Economics,* May, pp. A07-37.

Mayer-Foulkes, D. (2001): 'The Long-term Impact of Health on Economic Growth in Mexico, 1950-95, *Journal of International Development,* 13(1), pp. 123-26.

Mayer-Foulkes, D., H. Mora, R. Cermeno, A.B. Barona, and S. Duryea (2001): 'Health, Growth and Income Distribution in Latin America and the Caribbean: A Study of Determinants and Regional and Local Behavior', in *Investment in Health, Social and Economic Returns,* PAHO Scientific and Technical Publication, 582, Washington D.C.

Marmot, Michael G., George Davey Smith., Stephen Stansfeld, C. Patel, Fiona N., J. Head., I. White., E. Brunner and Ananda Feeny (1991): 'Health Inequalities among British Civil Servants: The Whitehall II Study', Lancet, June 8, pp. 1387-93.

Morand, Oliver F. (2005): 'Economic Growth, Health, and Longevity in the Very Long Term: Facts and Mechanisms', in *Health and Economic Growth: Findings and Policy Implications,* edited by Guillem Lopez-Casasnovas, Berta Rivera, and Luis Currais, The MIT Press, pp. 239-54.

Romer, P. (1986): Increasing Returns and Long-Run Growth, *Journal of Political Economy,* 94 (5), pp. 1002-37.

Sachs, J., and A. Warner (1997): Fundamental Sources of Long-Run Growth, *American Economic Review,* (Papers and Proceedings) 87:184-88.

Santerre, R.E., and S.P. Neun (2000): Health Economics: Theories, Insights and Industry Studies, ++, pp. 51-59.

Schultz, T.P. (1997): 'Assessing the Productive Benefits of Nutrition and Health: An Integrated Human Capital Approach', *Journal of Econometrics,* 77(1), pp. 141-58.

Thomas, D. and J. Strauss (1997): 'Health and Wages: Evidence on Men and Women in Urban Brazil', *Journal of Econometrics,* 77.

Weil, D.N. (2001): Accounting for the Effect of Health on Economic Growth, Unpublished Paper.

World Health Organization (2001): Macro-economics and Health: Investing in Health for Economic Development, *Report of the Commission on Macro-Economics and Health,* Geneva: WHO, pp. 1-213.

Zimmer, Z., Natividad, J., H.S. Lin and N. Chayovan (2000): 'A Cross National Examination of the Determinants of Self-assessed Health', *Journal of Health and Social Behaviour,* 41 (December), pp. 465-81.

Outsourcing in a Model of Occupational Choice

SAHANA ROY CHOWDHURY

1. INTRODUCTION

Casual as well as rigorous empirical investigations show that in the recent phase of globalization there has been a substantial rise in skilled-unskilled wage gap in both the developed and developing countries. This rise in wage inequality being a great concern for economists, several attempts have been made to provide ex-post justifications. While, for the developed countries, who export mostly skilled intensive commodities, simple trade theory can explain such a rise in wage inequality as an impact of opening up of economies but such theories contradict the rise in wage inequality in the developing countries that primarily export unskilled labour intensive commodities. The arguments for such an observation relate mainly to technology bias towards skilled labour (*Lawrence and Slaughter, 1993*), increased trade (*Leamer, 1993;*

Borjas and Ramey, 1995) or, outsourcing activities of Northern firms to South, with cheaper labour cost as well as large market for their products in South. Feenstra and Hanson (1999) attribute 15% of the rise in wage-gap in US to outsourcing by US MNFs. Feenstra and Hanson (1997) construct a factor endowment model where one good is produced by continuum of goods ranked with skill intensity. North outsources relatively unskilled intensive products to South, where these are relatively skilled intensive. This causes a relative demand rise for skilled labour in both the countries. Gao (2002) presents a two-country model where outsourcing and skilled-unskilled wage are endogenously determined. Globalization, in terms of reduction in trade costs, leads to a rise in both outsourcing and skilled-unskilled wage in both the countries. Glazer and Ranjan (2003) provide another interesting explanation. In a two-country framework, if skilled people consume relatively skilled intensive goods compared to the unskilled people, an increase in supply of skilled in either country, might result in an increase in demand for skilled labour and raise skilled-unskilled wage-gap in both countries.

The present paper builds up a simple model of outsourcing and shows that neither technology nor trade alone but both taken together are responsible for this recently observed and empirically tested phenomenon. Zeira (1999) too has emphasized that the widening of the wage gap between skilled and unskilled workers cannot be attributed to one single factor, neither to trade liberalization nor to skill-biased technical progress. According to his model trade liberalization increases the wage gap in developed countries, but reduces it in less developed countries. Since in recent decades an increase in the wage gap in less developed countries is also observed, he concludes that it cannot be the result of trade liberalization only and one needs to add the effect of skill biased technical progress, which according to his model increases the wage gap both in developed and in less developed countries. But such technical progress can not be the only factor that explains the rise in the wage gap for the following reason. His model shows that skill-biased technical progress does not increase trade in all countries, and we know that in recent decades trade increased

(Zeira, 1999) in all groups of countries. Hence, in order to account for the stylized facts of the recent decades, he concludes, both technical progress and trade liberalization have to act together. Beaulieu *et. al.* (2004) argue, a reduction in trade barrier in hi-tech sectors might lead to such a rise in both gap in both developed and developing countries.

Outsourcing being a very recent phenomenon, so far it has hardly been explored theoretically. The paper formally models outsourcing activity of Northern firms to South in a simple model of occupational choice. In the model economy with imperfect credit market, an indivisible education cost is there for becoming skilled and a fixed set-up cost, higher than the education cost, has to be incurred to become entrepreneur. Now, depending upon the inheritance and opportunity cost of investment, people decide over their occupational choice. Entrepreneurs in North take the outsourcing decision in addition. In equilibrium, skilled wages offered and profits enjoyed by Northern firms operating in North and outsourcing in South are equalized. Suppose now there is a technological upgradation in North. This will increase the productivity of skilled workers and Northern entrepreneurs will provide higher skilled wage both in North and in South where they outsource jobs. This will induce some workers to move from domestic skilled sector in South to the outsourcing Northern firms till the domestic skilled wage increases to the level of the skilled wage offered by the outsourcing Northern firms. Skilled wage increases in South purely because of outsourcing or trade reason. Therefore, it is neither technology nor trade alone but both that resulted in such a simultaneous rise in skilled-unskilled wage-gap in North and South.

A small number of papers on outsourcing exist in the trade literature but with different contexts. The paper by Feenstra and Hanson (1995) is the pioneering one in providing a theoretical structure to outsourcing and explaining the rising skilled-unskilled wage gap as described above. Egger and Falinger (2006) show negative effect of national public infrastructure investment on outsourcing where final goods producers outsource intermediate goods. Grossman and Helpman (2004) examine implication of falling trade costs for the relevant prevalence of outsourcing and FDI. Glass and Saggi (2001) investigate the effect of increased outsourcing of production on a low wage country. Outsourcing lowers marginal cost of production and raises profit thus creating greater incentives for innovation. Chen *et. al.* (2004) show trade liberalization may create multi-market interdependence and cause strategic outsourcing. Unlike outsourcing motivated by cost saving, strategic outsourcing has a collusive effect and raises prices in the intermediate goods and final goods market. Zhao (2001), in a model of unionization and outsourcing of multinationals, demonstrates that negotiated wage decreases and firm profits increase with outsourcing. The present paper deviates from these theoretical models of outsourcing by formally modelling outsourcing in an occupational choice framework. The paper in addition examines the impact of outsourcing on the national income of the destination country or South relating it to the inequality level of the outsourcing country.

In Section 2 the model economy is presented with the results and finally the concluding remarks of the paper is presented in Section 3.

2. THE MODEL

The model has two-period overlapping generations (OLG) framework. There are two countries, North and South. Entrepreneurs in the North can outsource skilled jobs to the South. In each country, there are infinitely many altruistic people with population normalized to unity.

Assuming international capital mobility, rate of interest is fixed at the international level. Credit market is imperfect with a gap between lending and borrowing interest rate. There is full employment in both the labour markets.

There is only one good, the numeraire, can be both consumed and invested. The good can be produced in two sectors one with only unskilled labour (home production type) and in the other sector by entrepreneurs with skilled workers.

In each country, people make following decisions in the two periods:

Period 1

(a) Each individual receives inheritance and decides over occupational choice. If he decides neither to take education nor to become entrepreneur, he invests the wealth in capital market and works as unskilled in the first period.

(b) Otherwise, borrows for educational investment (if he chooses to become a skilled worker) or, to incur the set-up cost (if he chooses to become entrepreneur). Else, makes the desired investment and lends the rest of inheritance in capital market.

Period 2

Earns according to investment made in first period, consumes and keeps bequest from net wealth (i.e., wealth after paying back loans, if he was a borrower and wealth after getting back the returns, if he was a lender) and then dies.

In addition to the above decisions the entrepreneurs in North decide whether to outsource jobs to South or start production in their own country.

1. Preferences and Investment Decisions

The utility function is given by:

$$U = \ln u = \delta \ln c + (1-\delta)\ln b;\ 0 < \delta < 1$$

Her problem is: *max* U subject to, $b + c \leq Z$, where, b: bequest, c: consumption, Z: net wealth defined as:

$$Z = \begin{cases} (x + w)(1 + r) + w; & \text{if doesn't invest in education or as entrepreneur,} \\ (x - h)(1 + i) + v; & \text{if invests in education and is borrower,} \\ (x - h)(1 + r) + v; & \text{if invests in education and is lender,} \\ (x - g)(1 + i) + \pi; & \text{if invests in set-up cost and is borrower,} \\ (x - g)(1 + r) + \pi; & \text{if invests in set-up cost and is lender,} \end{cases}$$

Since utility function is linear in net-wealth, for every

individual, maximization of utility by occupational choice is same as maximization of net-wealth by the same.

2. Occupational Choice of the Agents

A person receiving x inheritance borrows and invests in education if:

$$\left.\begin{aligned}&(x+w)(1+r)+w\le(x-h)(1+i)+v\\ &\text{or, } x\ge s=\frac{w(2+r)+h(1+i)-v}{i-r}\end{aligned}\right\}\text{ if } x<h \tag{1}$$

$$\left.\begin{aligned}&(x+w)(1+r)+w\le(x-h)(1+r)+v\\ &\text{or, } v\ge[w(2+r)+h(1+r)]\end{aligned}\right\}\text{ if } x\ge h \tag{2}$$

A person will borrow and invest in set-up cost if:

$$\left.\begin{aligned}&(x+h)(1+r)+v\le(x+g)(1+i)+\pi\\ &\text{or, } x\ge e=\frac{v-h(1+r)+g(1+i)-\pi}{i-r}\end{aligned}\right\}\text{ if } h\le x<g \tag{3}$$

$$\left.\begin{aligned}&(x+g)(1+r)+\pi\ge(x-h)(1+r)+v\\ &\text{or, } \pi\ge[v+(g-h)(1+r)]\end{aligned}\right\}\text{ if } x\ge g \tag{4}$$

Endogenous Variables : v and π.

x denotes the inheritance, w is unskilled wage, v is skilled wage, h is indivisible education cost, and g is indivisible set-up cost.

Assume, $g > h$. From the capital market imperfection assumption; $i > r$ where, i is the borrowing rate and the lender enjoys r.[1]

3. Production Technology

The sector using unskilled labour is a home production sector producing under CRS with production function:

$Y = wL \qquad w > 0$[2]

where, L is the fraction of unskilled.

The good is produced by each entrepreneur, j, with skilled labour by the following production function[4]:

$$Y_j = A_k H_j^\gamma \; ; \qquad A_k > 1 \forall k = f,\ d\,;\ \pi\, 0 < \gamma < 1$$

f: foreign firm, d: domestic firm; A_k: technology parameter; H_j skilled labour employed by each entrepreneur j.

Profit of each entrepreneur is given by, $\pi_j = Y_j - H_j v$
From profit maximization,

$$v = A_k \gamma H_j^{\gamma-1} \qquad \forall k = f\,,\, d\,;\left(\frac{\partial v}{\partial H_j} < 0\right) \tag{5}$$

By the assumption of full employment of skilled labour and assuming all entrepreneurs are identical in their profit maximizing behavior,

$$\pi_j = A_k\,(1-\gamma)H_j^\gamma \qquad \forall k = f\,,\, d\,;\left(\frac{\partial v}{\partial H_j} > 0\right) \tag{6}$$

Note that decreasing returns to scale ($\gamma < 1$) ensures positive profit.

As a result of global integration, Northern firms with higher skilled wage outsource jobs to South where skilled wage are relatively cheaper and profit higher. Suppose, North (country A) has skilled wage $v_A > v_B$ and $\pi_A < \pi_B$ at equilibrium. Now, A starts outsourcing jobs to South (country B) and ultimately in equilibrium both the skilled wage and the profit are equalized.

Let 'E' be the number of firms outsourcing jobs in B. This is endogenously determined. v^f is the skilled wage offered by the foreign firm in country B and π^f is the profit earned by them in B. v^d is the skilled wage offered by domestic firms. $\tilde{\pi}$ is the profit earned by firms operating in A, $\tilde{v}$ is the skilled wage in country A and $\tilde{H}_{if}$ is the skilled-entrepreneur ratio in North. Equilibrium in the skilled labour market in B must satisfy:

$$v^f = v^d$$

$$\Rightarrow A_f \gamma H_{if}^{(\gamma-1)} = A_d \gamma H_{jd}^{(\gamma-1)}$$

$$or\,,\ H_{if} = \left(\frac{A_f}{A_d}\right)^{\frac{1}{1-\gamma}} H_{jd}$$

Equilibrium in the world market (outsourcing equilibrium) must satisfy—

$$\pi^{f} = \tilde{\pi}$$

$$\Rightarrow A_f (1-\gamma) H_{if}^{\gamma} = A_f (1-\gamma) \tilde{H}_{if}^{\gamma}$$

$$or, H_{if} = \tilde{H}_{if}$$

4. Determination of Equilibrium H_{jd}: A Self-fulfilling Expectation Equilibrium

$$H_{jd} = \frac{F(e) - F(s) - {}_E H_{jf}}{1 - F(e)}$$

$$\text{or, } H_{jd} = \frac{F(e) - F(s)}{1 - F(e) + \left(\frac{A_f}{A_d}\right)^{\frac{1}{1-\gamma}} E} \tag{7}$$

(substituting skilled labour market equilibrium condition)

RHS is decreasing in $H_{jd}\left(\text{since}, \frac{de}{dH_j} < 0, \frac{ds}{dH_j} > 0\right)$ and LHS is increasing in H_{jd} for all E. As shown in Figure 7.1. LHS is a 45° line passing through the origin and the RHS is a

FIG. 7.1
Equilibrium Skilled-Entrepreneur Ratio of Southern Skilled Sector

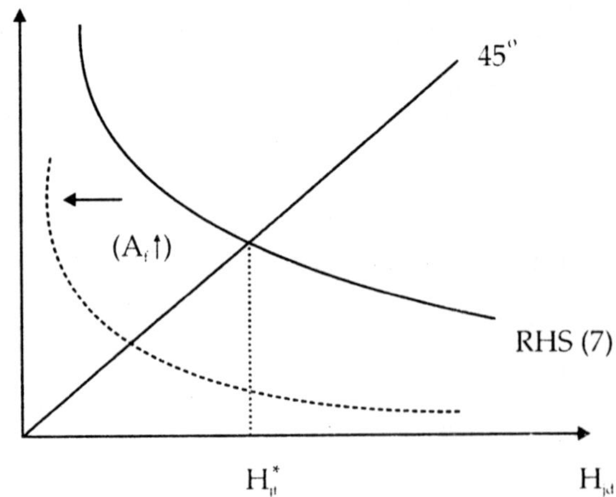

downward sloping curve. The point of intersection gives equilibrium H_{jd}. It is obvious that the equilibrium H_{jd} obtained above is unique.

Observation 1 : $H^*_{jd} = H^*_{jd}(E), \frac{dH^*_{jd}}{dE} < 0$

As E rises RHS(7) shifts down and cuts the 45° line at a lower value of H_{jd}. Therefore, H^*_{jd} falls.

5. Determination of Equilibrium E

$$\tilde{H}_{if} = H_{if} = \frac{\tilde{F}(e) - \tilde{F}(s)}{1 - \tilde{F}(e) - E} \tag{8}$$

(from the equilibrium condition derived earlier)

RHS(8) is decreasing in H_{if} $\left(\text{since}, \frac{de}{dH_{if}} < 0, \frac{ds}{dH_{if}} > 0 \right)$ and LHS is increasing in H_{if} for all E. This is shown in Figure 7.2. We find, the equilibrium H_{if} , H^*_{if} obtained above is unique.

FIG. 7.2
Equilibrium Skilled-Entrepreneur Ratio of Skilled Sector in North

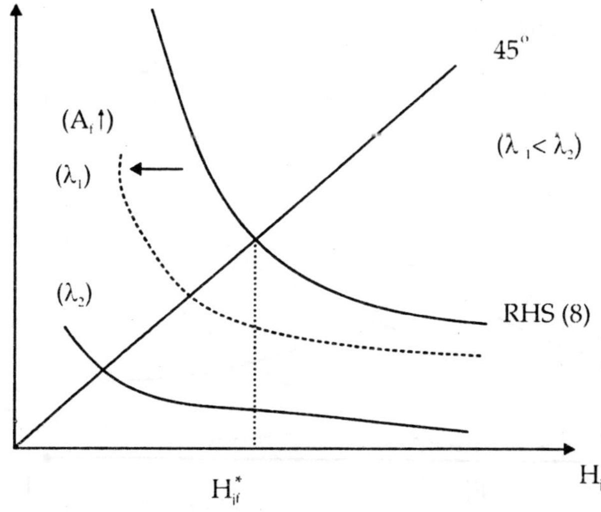

Observation 2 : $H^*_{if}\ ,\ H^*_{if}\,(E), \dfrac{dH^*_{if}}{dE} > 0$

As E rises RHS(8) shifts up and cuts the 45° line at a higher value of H_{if}. Therefore, H^*_{if} rises.

Now, from the skilled labour market equilibrium condition of country B,

$$\left(\frac{A_d}{A_f}\right)^{\frac{1}{1-\gamma}} H^*_{if}\,(E) = H^*_{jd}\,(E) \tag{9}$$

RHS of the above equation is decreasing and LHS is increasing in E (from Observation-1 and Observation-2 respectively). Hence we get unique equilibrium E, say E^*. This can be plotted in a diagram, as shown in Figure 7.3, where DD plots H^*_{jd} which is downward sloping and FF plots $\left(\frac{A_d}{A_f}\right)^{\frac{1}{1-\gamma}} H^*_{if}\,(E)$ which is upward sloping in E. The point of intersection gives equilibrium E, E^*.

FIG. 7.3
Determination of Equilibrium Outsourcing

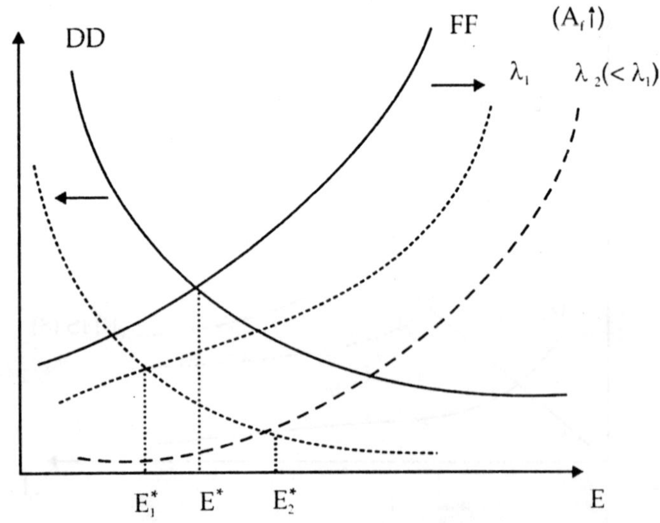

Let us suppose wealth follows Pareto distribution. The density function is:

$$f(x)=\frac{\lambda m^{\lambda}}{x^{\lambda+1}};\ x\geq m>0$$

where, λ : Pareto inequality parameter, λ>1 ensures finite variance.

$$F(x)=\int_{m}^{x}\frac{\lambda m^{\lambda^{\lambda+1}}}{X}dX$$
$$=m^{\lambda}\left[m^{-\lambda}-x^{-\lambda}\right]$$
$$=1-\left(\frac{m}{x}\right)^{\lambda}$$

$$\text{Hence, } \tilde{H}^{*}_{jd}=\frac{F(e)-F(s)}{1-F(e)+\left(\frac{A_f}{A_d}\right)^{\frac{1}{1-\lambda}}E}=\frac{\left(\frac{e}{s}\right)^{\lambda}-1}{1+\left(\frac{A_f}{A_d}\right)^{\frac{1}{1-\lambda}}\left(\frac{e}{m}\right)^{\lambda}E} \tag{10}$$

$$\tilde{H}^{*}_{jd}=\frac{\tilde{F}(e)-\tilde{F}(s)}{1-\tilde{F}(e)-E}=\frac{\left(\frac{m}{s}\right)^{\bar{\lambda}}-\left(\frac{m}{e}\right)^{\bar{\lambda}}}{\left(\frac{m}{e}\right)^{\bar{\lambda}}-E}=\frac{\left(\frac{e}{s}\right)^{\bar{\lambda}}-1}{1-E\left(\frac{e}{m}\right)^{\bar{\lambda}}} \tag{11}$$

where, $\bar{\lambda}$ is the inequality parameter of wealth distribution and $\tilde{F}(x)$ is the density function of wealth derived at x wealth level for country A.

Proposition 1 (a) Any technological improvement in the outsourcing country (A), given by a rise in A_f, will cause a rise in the skilled-unskilled wage gap in both the countries.

(b) With sufficient wealth inequality in A, equilibrium outsourcing will increase, *i.e.*, there exists $\bar{\lambda}^{*}$ such that if $\bar{\lambda}>(<)\bar{\lambda}^{*}$, equilibrium E will increase (decrease) as a result of technological upgradation in A.

Proof 1(a): From (10), it is clear that, as A_f increases, *RHS*(10) decreases for all H_{jd}. Therefore, equilibrium H_{jd}, H^{4}_{jd}, falls for all E. This can be shown in Figure 7.1, the downward sloping curve shifts down as A_f increases leading to a fall in H_{jd}^4, the point of intersection of the 45° line and the curve.

From (11), given the assumptions of the model, it can be shown that, as A_f increases, $RHS(11)$ decreases for all H_{if}^4. Therefore, equilibrium H_{if}, H_{if}^*, falls for all E. Similarly, it can be shown from Figure 7.2, the downward sloping curve shifts down as A_f increases leading to a fall in H_{if}, the point of intersection of the 45° line and the curve.

From above we find, both $H_{jd}^*(E)$ and $H_{if}^*(E)$ fall for all E. Therefore, both the curves, DD, plotting $H_{jd}^*(E)$, and FF, plotting $H_{if}^*(E)$ shift down. Therefore, both equilibrium $H_{jd}^*(E^*)$ and $\left(\frac{A_d}{A_f}\right)^{\frac{1}{1-\lambda}} H_{if}^*(E^*)$ fall. However, E^* may fall, rise or remain constant.

Now, a fall in $H_{jd}(E^*)$ indicates a rise in $v_d^* = \gamma A_d H_{jd}^{*\gamma-1}(E^*)$. Similarly, a fall in $\left(\frac{A_d}{A_f}\right)^{\frac{1}{1-\lambda}} H_{if}^*(E^*)$ implies a rise in $\frac{1}{\left(\frac{1}{A_f}^{\frac{1}{1-\gamma}} H_{if}^*(E^*)\right)}$ i.e., a rise in $\frac{\gamma}{\left(\frac{1}{A_f}^{\frac{1-\gamma}{1-\gamma}} H_{if}^{*1-\gamma}(E^*)\right)} = \gamma A_f H_{if}^{*1-\gamma}$ $(E^*) = v_f^*$ (since, A_d has not changed).

Economic reason: With a technological improvement (rise in A_f) in North, the outsourcing country (A), the productivity of skilled workers employed by foreign firms rises. This leads to an increase in skilled wage in the firms with this improved technology, both in country A and country B. Therefore, technology explains the rise in skilled wage, hence the rise in skilled-unskilled wage gap in the outsourcing country. Now, in the destination country (B), with a higher skilled wage offered by the foreign firms, some workers move away from the domestic skilled sector. This goes on till equilibrium skilled wage in the domestic skilled sector increases and catches up the increased skilled wage offered by the outsourcing firms. Therefore, trade (outsourcing) explains the rise in the skilled wage in the destination country or the South. Thus the simultaneous rise in skilled-unskilled wage-gap in North and South is a combined effect of both technology and trade.

Proof of 1 (*b*): We have seen in the proof of Proposition 1 (*a*) with the help of Figure 7.3 that the two curves DD and F F shift down as a result of a rise in A_f. Now, from the proof of fall in H_{if} for all E (done in Appendix), we find, the higher the inequality parameter of the outsourcing country ($\bar{\lambda}$), the higher is the fall in H_{if} for all E. Diagrammatically, the larger the λ is, the larger the downward shift in *FF* is. Therefore, given the downward shift in *DD* (depending upon A, inequality parameter of *B*), there exists a $\bar{\lambda}$ say $\bar{\lambda}^*$, such that *FF* shifts down to the extent that there is no change in equilibrium E. Hence, for any $\tilde{\lambda} > (<) \tilde{\lambda}^*$, the downward shift of *FF* will be such that the rise in equilibrium *E*, E^*, will be strictly positive (negative).

Economic Reason: The higher the wealth inequality level ($\bar{\lambda}^*$), the larger the fraction of people concentrated at the lower wealth level and the lower the number of entrepreneurs. Now, as A_f increases, both skilled wage and profit of entrepreneurs in *A* increases. This lowers the wealth threshold for both entrepreneurship and skill acquisition in *A* and both the number of entrepreneurs and the skilled people increase. We have seen in the proof of Proposition 1 that the ratio H_{if} falls for all E, for all economy. Since the number of entrepreneurs was not so large for this economy compared to a more equal one, the relative rise of entrepreneurs will be more than that of skilled such that the fall in the ratio $H_{if}(E)$ will be more for all E (i.e., downward shift in *FF* will be more for all E). From the expression of profit in (6), a rise in A_f raises profit but a fall in H_{jf} causes it to decline. Therefore, given a rise in A_f, the higher the fall in H_{if}, the lower will be the profit of a firm operating in country *A*. This will obviously result in increased outsourcing till profit levels of the firm operating in *A* and the firm outsourcing jobs to B are equalized. Suppose, for $\bar{\lambda} = \bar{\lambda}^*$, the fall in H_{if} is such that the profit of a firm operating in *A* is just equal to the firm outsourcing in *B*. Here no increase in outsourcing will be resulted. For all $\bar{\lambda} > (<) \bar{\lambda}^*$, the fall in H_{if} will be larger (smaller) than the above case and the profit of a firm operating in A will be lower (higher) than that of a firm outsourcing in B resulting in increased (decreased) outsourcing.

Proposition 2: If the outsourcing country (A) is too much equal $(\bar{\lambda} > (<) \bar{\lambda}^*)$, any technological upgradation in the outsourcing country will lead to a definite fall in the national income of the destination economy (B) with the sufficient condition $|\in_{cE}| \geq 1$; where, $c = A_f^{\frac{1}{1-\gamma}}$ and $\in_{cE} = \dfrac{dE}{dc}\dfrac{c}{E}$.

Proof : The National Income (NI) of B is given by :

$$NI_d = nA_d H_{jd}^{\gamma} +_E H_{jf} v_f$$

$$= nA_d H_{jd}^{\gamma} + \gamma_E A_f H_{jf}^{\gamma} \text{ (putting the value of } v_f)$$

$$= nA_d H_{jd}^{\gamma} + \gamma_E A_f \left(\frac{A_f}{A_d}\right)^{\frac{\gamma}{1-\gamma}} H_{jd}^{\gamma} \text{ (substituting } H_{jf} \text{ by } H_{jd} \text{ from (9))}$$

$$= nA_d H_{jd}^{\gamma} + \gamma_E A_f^{\frac{1}{1-\gamma}} \left(\frac{1}{A_d}\right)^{\frac{\gamma}{1-\gamma}} H_{jd}^{\gamma}$$

$$= nA_d H_{jd}^{\gamma} + \gamma EC \left(\frac{1}{A_d}\right)^{\frac{\gamma}{1-\gamma}} H_{jd}^{\gamma}$$

From the proof of Proposition 2 it is clear that H_{jd} falls as a result of a technological upgradation in A (rise in A_f) which implies, n falls (since, $H_{jd} \downarrow \Rightarrow e \downarrow \Rightarrow n \downarrow$). Therefore, NI_d will have a definite fall with the sufficient condition that EC falls or remains constant. Frorn Proposition 1 we find, as A_f increases $\Rightarrow c = A_f^{\frac{1}{1-\gamma}}$ increases, E falls (or remains constant) in case of a very equal outsourcing country $(\bar{\lambda} \leq \bar{\lambda}^*)$. Now, the product Ee will fall (will remain constant) only if $|\in_{cE}| \geq 1$. Hence, NI_d will fall for a too much equal outsourcing country with the sufficient condition $|\in_{cE}| \geq 1$.

Observation 3: The share of the domestic sector in the National Income of B will shrink if the outsourcing country is too much unequal ($\bar{\lambda} \leq \bar{\lambda}^*$).

Proof: This is very obvious and intuitive. Share of Domestic Sector in National Income of B (α).

$$= \frac{nA_d H_{jd}^{\gamma}}{nA_d H_{jd}^{\gamma} +_E H_{if} v_f}$$

$$= \frac{nA_d H_{jd}^{\gamma}}{nA_d H_{jd}^{\gamma} +_E A_f^{\frac{1}{1-\gamma}} \left(\frac{1}{A_d}\right)^{\frac{\gamma}{1-\gamma}} H_{jd}^{\gamma}}$$

$$= \frac{1}{1 + \dfrac{E\left(\dfrac{A_f}{A_d}\right)^{\frac{1}{1-\gamma}}}{n}} \qquad \text{(rearranging terms)}$$

From Proposition 1 we find that for $\bar{\lambda} \succ \bar{\lambda}^*$ (too much unequal outsourcing country), E increases as a result of a technological upgradation (rise in A_f). And we know that H_{jd} falls implying a fall in n. Therefore, from the above expression, it is obvious that the term $\left(\frac{E}{n}\right)\left(\frac{A_f}{A_d}\right)^{\frac{1}{1-\gamma}}$ rises resulting in a rise in the denominator of α, hence a fall in α.

3. CONCLUSION

The paper tries to explain the recent observation of rising skilled-unskilled wage gap in both North and South. There are some papers that state, it is the skilled biased technology shift that resulted in such a rise and others explain that it is purely an effect of trade. The present paper focuses that it is the combined effect of both by a simple model of occupational choice where Northern firms have a choice of outsourcing jobs to South. Any technological improvement by Northern firms will increase the productivity of skilled workers and Northern entrepreneurs will provide higher skilled wage both in North and in South where they outsource jobs. This will induce some workers to move from domestic skilled sector in South to the outsourcing Northern firms till the domestic skilled wage increases to the level of the skilled wage offered by the outsourcing Northern firms. Skilled wage increases in South purely because of trade reason. Therefore, it is neither technology nor trade alone but both that resulted in such a simultaneous rise in skilled-unskilled wage-gap in North and South.

The paper focuses on the condition when there will be a fall in national income in South as a result of such a technological improvement in North. The condition for such a fall is derived in case the outsourcing country is very much equal (defined by the parameter of the wealth distribution). In this case the equilibrium outsourcing is found to fall as a result of technological improvement by North. For a very unequal outsourcing country, an intuitive and obvious observation of shrinking domestic skilled sector of South has been obtained via a rise in equilibrium outsourcing.

NOTES

1. This difference might be due to the cost the lender bears to keep track of the borrower.
2. Assume, $w \geq w_{\min} = \frac{1}{2+r}\left[\frac{g(1+i)-h(1+r)}{\left(\frac{1-\gamma}{\gamma}\right)} - h(2+i)\right]$.
3. Capital could be taken as another input but the results would remain same. For simplicity, skilled labour has been taken as the sole input of production in this sector..
4. Proof done in the Appendix.

REFERENCES

Beaulieu, E., Benarroch, M., Gaisford, J. 2004. Trade barriers and wage inequality in a North-South model with technology-driven intra-industry trade. *Journal of Development Economics*, 75 (1), 113-36.

Borjas, G.J., Ramey, V.A., 1995. Foreign Competition, Market Power and Wage Inequality: Theory and Evidence. *Quarterly Journal of Economics*, 110, 1075-10.

Chen, Y., Ishikawa, J., Yu, Z., 2004. Trade Liberalization and Strategic Outsourcing. *Journal of International Economics*, 63 (2), 419-36.

Egger, H., Falkinger, J., 2005. The Role of Public Infrastructure and Subsidies for Firm Location and International Outsourcing, *European Economic Review*, December 2005.

Feenstra, R.C., Hanson, G.H., 1996. Globalization, Outsourcing, and Wage Inequality. *American Economic Review*, 86(2), 240-45.

Feenstra, R.C., Hanson, G.H., 1997. Foreign Direct Investment and Relative Wages: Evidence from Mexico's Maquiladoras. *Journal of International Economics*, 42(3-4), 371-93.

Feenstra, R.C., Hanson, G.H., 1999. The Impact of Outsourcing and High-Technology Capital on Wages: Estimates for the United States, 1979-90. *Quarterly Journal of Economics*, 114(3), 907-40.

Galor, O., Zeira, J., 1993. Income Distribution and Macro-economics. *Review of Economic Studies*, 60(1), 35-52.

Gao, T., 2002. Outsourcing and Wage Inequality in a Simple Economic Geography Model, *Research Paper*, University of Missouri, USA, Department of Economics.

Glass, A.J., Saggi, K., 2001. Innovation and wage effects of international outsourcing. *European Economic Review*, 45 (1), 67-86.

Glazer, A., Ranjan, P., 2003. Preference heterogeneity, wage inequality, and trade. *Journal of International Economics*, 60(2), 455-69.

Grossman, G.M., Helpman, E., 2004. Managerial Incentives and the International Organization of Production. *Journal of International Economics*, 63, 237-62.

Lawrence, R.Z., Slaughter, M.J., 1993. Trade and US Wages: Great Sucking Sound or Small Hiccup? *Brookings Papers on Economic Activity*, 2, 161-226.

Leamer, E.E., 1993. Wage Effects of a US-Mexican Free Trade Agreement, in Peter M. Garber, ed., *The Mexico-U.S. Free Trade Agreement*, Cambridge, Mass: MIT Press, pp. 57-162.

Zeira, J., 1999. Wage Inequality, Technology and Trade. Unpublished Manuscript.

Zhao, L., 2001. Unionization, Vertical Markets, and the Outsourcing of Multinationals. *Journal of International Economics*, 55 (1), 187-202.

APPENDIX

Claim: As A_f increases, $H_{if}(E)$ falls for all E.
Proof: We know,

$$e = \frac{v - h(1+r) + g(1+i) - \pi}{i = r.}$$

$$de = \frac{dv - d\pi}{i-r} - \frac{dA_f\left[\gamma H_{if}^{\gamma-1} - (1-\gamma)H_{if}^{\gamma}\right]}{i-r}$$

$$= \frac{\frac{dA_f}{A_f}\left[\gamma A_f H_{if}^{\gamma-1} - (1-\gamma)A_f H_{if}^{\gamma}\right]}{i=r} = \frac{\frac{dA_f}{A_f}[v-\pi]}{i-r}$$

< 0 for $dA_f > 0$ (since $\pi > v$)

From the expression of H_{if} in (11) it is clear that if $\left(\frac{e}{s}\right)$ falls, it will fall for all E. Now,

$$\left(\frac{e}{s}\right) = \frac{g(1+i) - h(1+r) + v - \pi}{w(2+r) + h(1+i) - v} = \frac{A + v - \pi}{B - v}$$

$$\frac{d\left(\frac{e}{s}\right)}{dA_f}\Big| H_{if} = \frac{(B-v)(dv - d\pi) + (A + v - \pi)dv}{(B-v)^2}$$

$$= \frac{dv(B+A) + vd\pi - \pi dv - Bd\pi}{(B-v)^2}$$

Now, $dv = dA_{f\gamma} H_{if}^{\gamma-1}$; $d\pi = dA_f\,(1-\gamma)H_{if}^{\gamma}$

$$vd\pi = (\gamma A_{if}^{\gamma-1})(dA_f\,(1-\gamma)H_{if}^{\gamma}) = A_f dA_{f\gamma}\,(1-\gamma)H_{if}^{2\gamma-1}$$

$$\pi dv = ((1-\gamma)A_f H_{if}^{\gamma})(dA_{f\gamma} H_{if}^{\gamma-1}) = A_f dA_{f\gamma}\,(1-\gamma)H_{if}^{2\gamma-1}$$

$$\Rightarrow vd\pi = \pi dv$$

$$\text{Therefore}, \frac{d\left(\frac{e}{s}\right)}{dA_f}\Big| H_{if} = \frac{dv(B+A) - Bd\pi}{(B-v)^2} \leq 0 \text{ if} [dv(B+A) - Bd\pi] \leq 0$$

$$\Rightarrow (A+B)dA_{f\gamma}H_{if}^{\gamma-1} - BdA_f(1-\gamma)H_{if}^{\gamma} \le 0$$

$$\text{or}, \left(\frac{\gamma}{1-\gamma}\right)\left(\frac{A}{B}+1\right) \le H_{if}$$

H_{if}: skilled labour employed by each entrepreneur. Therefore, $H_{if} \ge 1$.

If $\left(\frac{\gamma}{1-\gamma}\right)\left(\frac{A}{B}+1\right) \le 1$, then $H_{if} \ge \left(\frac{\gamma}{1-\gamma}\right)\left(\frac{A}{B}+1\right)$ holds. This implies,

$$\frac{d\left(\frac{e}{s}\right)}{dA_f}\Bigg|H_{if} \le 0 \text{ if } \left(\frac{\gamma}{1-\gamma}\right)\left(\frac{A}{B}+1\right) \le 1.$$

Now, from the assumption,

$$w \ge w_{\min} = \frac{1}{(2+r)}\left[\frac{g(1+i)-h(1+r)}{\left(\frac{1-\gamma}{\gamma}-1\right)} - h(2+i)\right],$$

We get, $$w \ge \frac{1}{(2+r)}\left[\frac{g(1+i)-h(1+r)}{\left(\frac{1-\gamma}{\gamma}-1\right)} - h(2+i)\right]$$

$$\Rightarrow \left(\frac{\gamma}{1-\gamma}\right)\left(\frac{g(1+i)-h(1+r)}{w(2+r)+h(1+i)}+1\right) \le 1 \Rightarrow \left(\frac{\gamma}{1-\gamma}\right)\left(\frac{A}{B}+1\right) \le 1.$$

Therefore, given the parametric assumptions of the model, we find, $\frac{d\left(\frac{e}{s}\right)}{dA_f}\Bigg|H_{if} \le 0.$

Immigration vs. Outsourcing : A Developing Country's View

SIMONTINI DAS

1. INTRODUCTION

Differences in factor endowment encourage the international trade. Following the conventional literature, a developed country is well endowed with capital and a developing country with labour. In fact low-cost labour supply and unemployment (open and disguised) are two important characteristics of a developing country. International trade helps to utilise this excess supply of labour. Though prime focus of the international trade literature is on goods trade, but recently trade in service, especially trade in factor inputs becomes more and more important.

The developed countries always try to innovate new channels to utilise the cheap labour force of the developing countries. Immigration and outsourcing are two such avenues. Immigration is an age old process. In recent days, outsourcing has emerged as another process to take the advantage of cost differences between developing and developed countries. Often the developed countries outsource labour intensive component of the production process to the labour abundant developing countries. This outfarming method helps to reduce overall cost of production and increases the competitiveness of the host country in the international market.

Though both processes, immigration and outsourcing, serve more or less the same purposes from the broader perspective, still there are some basic differences. While immigration involves physical movement of labour, outsourcing involves only the exportation of labour service to the developed countries.

The developed countries, involved in outsourcing contracts, are benefiting due to cost minimisation, technical improvement and specialisation. On the other hand, the developing countries, involved in outsourcing, are benefiting due to employment generation, profit maximisation, quality upgradation, capacity utilisation and skill improvisation.

Labour abundant developing countries are also benefited from the immigration process. Immigration helps to reduce the size of work force by transferring a part of it to developed countries. Immigration process also reduces many other liabilities (like health care, education, etc.), since the immigrants are dwelling in the developed countries. But immigration only generates labour demand, while outsourcing generates demand for labour as well as for other factor inputs. So outsourcing is more helpful than immigration for optimal utilisation of resources in the developing countries.

Turing towards reality, a huge empirical support can easily be found in favour of growing outsourcing activity and immigration activity. Over the period 1996 to 2005 total number of immigrants of U.S.A. from the different parts of the world amounts to 87,54,458. In the fiscal year 2005, the size of immigrants in U.S.A. was 11,22,273. Over the same period, total 5,37,275 Indian had migrated to the U.S.A. India, being a developing country, tells the other part of the story. In recent years, the migration trend from India to U.S.A. is increasing, since 1999, though there is a downward fall in 2003. In 2005, 84,681 people had migrated from India. Side by side, a growing outsourcing demand is directed to India from the different countries. Most of the outsourcing venture has taken place in manufacturing sector, textile sector, chemical industry, software service sector, BPO (Business Process Outsourcing) sector, etc. Confederation of Indian Industry (CII) has estimated that India can receive $10 billion outsourcing order in manufacturing sector by 2007. This amount will increase by $50 billion to $60 billion (which is equivalent to India's present export earning) by 2015. Software industry, in India, is another industry, which faces a huge outsourcing demand. Indian software industry supplies parts or entire IT infrastructural support to multinational corporations. Software export has increased from US $9.2 billion in 2003-04 to US $12 billion 2004-05, indicating growth of 30.4 percent for the year. The number of companies, who are accustomed with off-shore adoption, has increased from 400 companies in 2004 to 500 companies in 2005. This figure is actually indicator of the growing outsourcing activity of software industry in India.

The current discussion has focussed on the economic impact of immigration and outsourcing on the welfare level of the developing country as well as of the developed country. Various social issues, related to immigration and outsourcing, may have an influence on the welfare level of both the developed and the developing countries. But for the time being, those effects are ignored. The paper focuses on:

- The inter-relation between immigration and outsourcing.
- The impact of an increase in immigration quota on the national income level of a developing country.
- The impact of an increase in immigration quota on the national income level of a developed country.
- The impact of an increase in immigration quota on the world welfare level.

The second part of the paper presents a brief literature review. Third part of the paper contains the general equilibrium model. The last part of the paper concludes.

II. LITERATURE REVIEW

Often the existing trade literature have discussed the immigration and outsourcing issue separately. But the number of literatures, which have discussed these two topics together, is few. Ronald, W. Jones (2004) and Subhayu Bandyopadhyay and Howard J. Wall (2005) have done this work by doing a comparative study between immigration and outsourcing.

In this respect, Ramaswami (1968) has done an important work. He has discussed about two strategic options of a capital abundant country. The main question is whether exportation of capital or importation of labour would be the optimal for a capital rich country. According to him importation of foreign labour would be the optimal for increasing the national income of the host country. Present paper tries to analyse the same fact but for the labour market and from the point of view of a labour abundant country.

Ronald W. Jones (2004) has analysed the effects of immigration and outsourcing on the labour market of the developed countries. He showed that immigration and outsourcing of labour intensive part of the product might raise the wage rate of domestic workers of the developed countries. Though these two effects differed from each other. In the presence of quality differences between immigrants and domestic labour, two groups might be complement to each other, and here immigration might lead the productivity gain of the domestic workers also. Similarly, if the workers engaged in outsourcing were complements to the domestic workers, then outsourcing also led to an increase in wage of domestic workers. According to Jones, outsourcing would be a better option than immigration, while immigrants received higher local wage and labour engaged in outsourcing received lower foreign wage, though there is the higher coordinating cost allied to outsourcing.

Another important work, in this respect, has been done by Subhayu Bandyopadhyay and Howard, J. Wall in 2005. In a general equilibrium framework, they did a comparative study from the point of view of a developed country. In this paper, they showed that outsourcing and immigration were substitute to each other. Relaxation of immigration quota increased the national income of the developed countries. Increase in immigration quota reallocated the income in favour of the domestic capitalists. They said that immigration was more harmful for domestic workers than outsourcing. According to them, under certain circumstances (especially in the presence of immigration target and wage target) an outsourcing subsidy would be encouraged.

Most of the works have analysed this issue from the point of view of developed countries. The present paper has made an attempt to investigate the 'immigration *vs.* outsourcing' issue from the point of view of developing countries. The main concerning fact of this paper is which one . . . outsourcing or immigration . . . is good for a developing country?

III. GENERAL EQUILIBRIUM MODEL

General equilibrium framework is a very useful tool to study the different international trade theories. Here we adopt this general equilibrium framework to analyse the immigration *vs.* outsourcing issue in a two-country model. The general equilibrium model gives us the broader scope to analyse the welfare aspects of the economy, since it considers the demand-supply equilibrium mechanism for all tile factor inputs as well as the final output markets. In this paper, the impact of the immigration policy on the welfare level will be studied from the aggregative (total world output level) and distributive (allocation of the total world output between the developed and the developing countries) perspectives.

Model

We start with a very simple two-country model, where skill variation and the technological differences (across the countries) are not considered. There are two countries: a developed country and a developing country. In this paper, the developed country is known as the foreign country and the developing country is known as the domestic country, since the whole analysis is done from the point of view of the developing country.

The foreign country produces a final output (Q) with the help of two inputs—foreign labour (N) and an intermediate input (I). This intermediate input (I) can be produced in two ways. The foreign country can herself produce the part or the whole requirement of the intermediate input with the help of foreign capital (K_I) and immigrant workers (n). I_F denotes the intermediate input, produced by the foreign country. Or the foreign country can outsource the part or the whole of her intermediate input demand (I_D) to the domestic country. Domestic country can produce this outsourcing product with the help of domestic capital (K_O) and domestic labour (L_O). Here $I = I_F + 1_D$.

There is full employment in all the factor input markets. All the markets are assumed to be competitive, that means the prices of the factor inputs are decided by the joint interaction between demand and supply of the factors, and the return (price) to the factor is equal with the value of the marginal product of the factor in the production system.

In this model, we are interested with the welfare aspect of the economy. So we are concerning about the real or actual consumption level of the economy, which is a good proxy measurement of the welfare level. In our model, we have only one final consumption good (Q), which is totally consumed by the factor inputs of the both countries. Here, saving is not considered.

Though there is no technical differences in producing I_D and I_F across the countries, but the existence of wage differences between the immigrant workers (n) and the workers employed in the domestic outsourcing sector is required to ensure the migration process across the countries.

In this model, all the production functions are assumed as the neoclassical type. Therefore, all the production functions have three properties given below:

(a) For any positive amount of each factor input, marginal product is positive and diminishing.
(b) Production technology exhibits constant returns to scale.
(c) The marginal product of each factor input approaches infinity as the use of that input goes to zero and

approaches zero as the use of that input goes to infinity.

Foreign Country

The production function of the final output (Q) is given by,

$Q = Q\ (I, N)$

where $I = I_D + I_F$

The production function of the intermediate input (I_F) is,

$I_F = F\ (K_I, n)$

Joint profit function of the foreign country is given by,

$\Pi_F = Q\ (I_D + F\ (K_I, n), N) - r_k\ K_I - P_I I_D - W_N N - W_I n$

where, P_I = Price of outsourcing product
W_N = Wage of the foreign worker
r_k = Rent of the foreign capital
W_I = Wage of the immigrants

Here, the final output is treated as the numeriar. So the prices of the factor inputs are actually denoting the payment to the factor inputs in terms of the final consumption good (Q). In this respect, one important thing has to mention that the welfare level of the individual country and the world are also measured in terms of the final consumption good.

Final Consumption Good Market

Optimisation problem:

Maximise $\Pi_F = P_Q.Q\ (I_D + F\ (K_I, n), N) - r_k\ K_I - P_I I_D - W_N N - W_I n\ \ I_D, N, K_I, n > 0$

First Order Conditions for Profit Maximisation

$\partial \Pi_F / \partial I_D = Q_I - P_I = 0 \Rightarrow Q_I = P_I$ (1)
$\partial \Pi_F / \partial K_I = Q_I .\ F_{KI} - r_k = 0 \Rightarrow Q_I\ F_{K1} = r_k$ (2)

$$\partial\Pi_F/\partial n = Q_I \cdot F_N - W_I = 0 \Rightarrow Q_I F_n = W_I \qquad (3)$$
$$\partial\Pi_F/\partial N = Q_N - W_N = 0 \Rightarrow Q_N = W_N \qquad (4)$$

From (1) and (4) we obtain the optimum demand for the intermediate input (I^d) and the foreign labour (N^d).

$$I^d = I^d (P_I, W_N)$$
$$N^d = N^d (P_I, W_N)$$

From (2) and (3) we obtain the optimum demand for the immigrant workers (n^d) and the foreign capital (K_I^d).

$$n^d = n^d (P_I, W_I, r_k)$$
$$K_I^d = K_I^d (P_I, W_I, r_k)$$

Factor Input Market

Foreign labour market equilibrium is,

$N_F = N^d (P_I, W_N)$
N_F = fixed labour supply to the foreign country

Foreign capital market equilibrium is,

$K_F = K_I^d (P_I, W_I, r_k)$
K_F = fixed capital supply to the foreign country

Many social and political factors usually determine the immigration policy. There are many allied costs, related to immigration; those have to be borne by the foreign country. So the number of immigrants is often restricted within a limit and this limit is decided by several social and political factors. This restricted number is often referred as immigration quota. Suppose the immigration quota has already been decided by the foreign government at n* level. Therefore, the supply of the immigrants is given fixed at n* level.

Immigration market equilibrium is,

$$n^* = n^d (P_I, W_I, r_k)$$

Solving these three factor market equilibrium and first order conditions, we obtain equilibrium value of the W_N, W_I, and r_k in terms of N_F, K_F, n^*, and P_I.

$$W_N = W_N(N_F, K_F, n^*, P_I) \quad (5)$$
$$W_I = W_I(N_F, K_F, n^*, P_I) \quad (6)$$
$$r_k = r_k(N_F, K_F, n^*, P_I) \quad (7)$$

Putting the optimum value of W_N in the demand function for the intermediate input demand (I) can be written as,

$$I^d = I^d (P_I, N_F, K_F, n^*) \quad (A)$$

For obtaining equilibrium price of the intermediate input, we need demand-supply side interaction. The demand side equation is given by (A). The supply part of the intermediate input constitutes two components: supply of the intermediate input by the foreign country and the supply of the outsourcing intermediate input by the domestic country.

Supply of the intermediate input by the foreign country

$$= I_F^S = F (K_F, n^*) \quad (B)$$

Domestic Country

The domestic country is assumed to produce the intermediate input only. All available factor inputs of the domestic country are involved to produce the outsourcing demand (I_D).

Outsourcing Market

Production function of the outsourcing intermediate input demand can be written as,

$I_D = F (K_O, L_O)$
K_O = domestic capital used in the outsourcing sector
L_O = domestic labour used in the outsourcing sector

Suppose, K_D is the total capital endowment to the domestic country and L_D is the total labour supply to the domestic country. The foreign government has already decided about the level of immigrants at n*. Now if there is a wage difference between the immigrants and the domestic workers employed in the outsourcing sector (necessary condition for ensuring labour migration from the domestic country to the foreign country), n* number of the domestic workers migrate to the foreign country. Then (L_D – n*) number of the workers is available to the domestic outsourcing sector. We have already assumed that there is no unemployment. Therefore, total K_D and (L_D – n*) factor inputs will be engaged in the domestic outsourcing sector. Total possible supply of the domestic outsourcing sector is,

$$I_D^S = F(K_D, L_D - n^*) \qquad \text{(C)}$$

Combining (B) and (C) we obtain the total supply of the intermediate input (I^S).

$$I^S = I_F^S + I_D^S$$

$$\Rightarrow I^S = I^S(K_F, n^*, K_D, L_D) \qquad \text{(D)}$$

Here one important observation is that the supply of the intermediate input is independent of the price of the intermediate input (P_I). The supply is mainly determined by the capital endowment of the both countries and the labour allocation of the domestic country (since we are ruling out the possibility that the foreign workers can produce the intermediate input).

The market clearing condition for the intermediate input can be written as,

$$I^d = I^S$$

From equation (A) and equation (D) we obtain,

$$I^d(P_I, N_F, K_F, n^*) = I^S(K_F, n^*, K_D, L_D)$$

Solving this equation we obtain the market clearing equilibrium price of the intermediate input.

$$P_I^* = P_I^*(L_D, K_D, n^*, K_F, N_F)$$

The equilibrium intermediate input quantity is,

$$I^* = I^*(L_D, K_D, n^*, K_F, N_F)$$

Once the price of the outsourcing product has been decided, the domestic wage level (w) and the domestic capital rental (r) will be decided automatically through the profit maximising conditions of the domestic country.

The profit function of the domestic country is

$$\Pi_D = P_I^* I_D - w.L_O - r.K_O$$
$$\Rightarrow \Pi_D = P_I^* F(K_O, L_O) - w.L_O - r.K_O$$

First Order Conditions for Profit Maximisation

$$\partial\Pi_F/\partial L_O = P_I^* \, \partial(F(K_O, L_O))/\partial L_O - w = 0$$
$$\Rightarrow P_1^* F_{KO} = W \quad (8)$$
$$\partial\Pi_D/\partial K_O = P_I^* \partial(F(K_O, L_O))/\partial K_O - r = 0$$
$$\Rightarrow P_I^* F_{KO} = r \quad (9)$$

Solving (8) and (9) we obtain the optimum demand for the domestic capital and the domestic labour.

$$L_O^* = L_O^*(r, w, P_I^*)$$
$$K_O^* = K_O^*(r, w, P_I^*)$$

Putting the value of the market clearing P_1^* in the above expression we obtain,

$$L_O^* = L_O^*(r, w, L_D, K_D, n^*, K_F, N_F)$$
$$K_O^* = K_O^*(r, w, L_D, K_D, n^*, K_F, N_F)$$

Solving two market clearing equations we obtain the equilibrium value of the domestic wage (w*) and the domestic rental (r*),

$$w^* = w^*(L_D, K_D, n^*, K_F, N_F)$$
$$r^* = r^*(L_D, K_D, n^*, K_F, N_F)$$

Welfare Measurement

Following traditional literature, it can be said that the national income (in real terms) of any country can be a good proxy measure of the welfare level of that country. The national income of any country is the sum of the income of that country's factor inputs.

National Income Accounting of the Foreign Country

Let, Y_F^*= National income identity of the foreign country

Let $Y_F^* = W_N^*. N_F + r_k^* K_F$

where $W_N^* = W_N^*(L_D, K_D, n^*, K_F, N_F)$

(Obtained from substituting P_1^* in equation (5))

$r_k^* = r_k^*(L_D, K_D, n^*, K_F, N_F)$

(Obtained from substituting P_1^* in equation (7))

Under the competitive market, when the production function follows CRS, then we have, $P_I^* I_F^* = r_k^* K_F + W_I^* n^*$

where $W_I^* = W_I^*(L_D, K_D, n^*, K_F, N_F)$

(Obtained from substituting P_I^* in equation (6))

$\Rightarrow r_k^* K_F = P_I^* I_F^* - W_I^* n^*$

$$\text{Therefore, } Y_F^* = W_N^*. N_F + P_I^* I_F^* - W_I^* n^* \qquad (10)$$

This national income of the foreign country is actually measured in terms of the final consumption good, since all the payments are made in terms of Q. Here if we do not consider any saving or tax, then the national income level can also indicate the real consumption level of the factor inputs.

National Income Accounting of the Domestic Country

Let, Y_D^*= National income identity of the domestic country

$Y_D^* = r^*. K_D + w^*. (L_D - n^*) + W_I^*.n^*$

Here one thing has to mention that the national income of the domestic country should includes the income of the emigrants also, since the domestic labours are either employed in the domestic outsourcing sector or in the foreign intermediate input producing sector. Same as before, this Y_D^* shows the actual consumption level of the domestic factor inputs, if there be no saving or tax.

Under the competitive market, when the production function follows CRS, then we have,

$P_I^* I_D^* = r^*. K_D + w^*. (L_D - n^*)$

$$\text{Therefore, } Y_D^* = P_I^* I_D^* + W_I^*.n^* \qquad (11)$$

Final Consumption Good Market

Total supply of the final consumption good is given by,

$Q^* = Q^* (I^*, N_F)$

Now, $I^* = I^*(L_D, K_D, n^*, K_F, N_F)$

$\Rightarrow Q^* = Q^* (I^*(L_D, K_D, n^*, K_F, N_F), N_F)$

This total produced final consumption good is consumed by the factor inputs of both the countries. That means, this Q^* is distributed between the foreign country and the domestic country as their national income.

Therefore, $Q^* = Y_F^* + Y_D^*$ (12)

This can be interpreted in another way. The total world welfare is actually the sum of the welfare level of two individual countries in a simple two-country model.

Solution set:

$Q^* = Q^*(L_D, K_D, n^*, K_F, N_F)$
$Y_F^* = Y_F^*(L_D, K_D, n^*, K_F, N_F)$
$Y_D^* = Y_D^*(L_D, K_D, n^*, K_F, N_F)$
$I^* = I^*(L_D, K_D, n^*, K_F, N_F)$
$P_I^* = P_I^*(L_D, K_D, n^*, K_F, N_F)$
$I_D^* = I_D^* (L_D^*, K_D, n^*)$ (since $I_D = F (K_D, L_D - n)$; $n = n^*$)
$I_F = I_F (n^*, K_F$ (since $I_F = F (K_I, n)$; $n = n^*$, $K_I = K_F$)
$W_I^* = W_I^* (L_D, K_D, n^*, K_F, N_F)$
$W_N^* = W_N^* (L_D, K_D, n^*, K_F, N_F)$
$r_k^* = r_k^* (L_D, K_D, n^*, K_F, N_F)$
$w^* = w^*(L_D, K_D, n^*, K_F, N_F)$
$r^* = r^*(L_D, K_D, n^*, K_F, N_F)$

Impact of an Increase in Immigration Quota on Different Variables

In this two-country general equilibrium model, immigration policy of the foreign government has crucial influence on the welfare level of the whole economy. Suppose there is a stable equilibrium with a particular immigration policy of the foreign government (that means for a particular value of n). All the factor inputs of both the countries are employed in the competitive environment, and they are receiving the value of the marginal productivity as their return.

In this situation, suppose the foreign government decides to relax their immigration policy and they increase the immigration quota. This change in the immigration policy affects all the factor input and final consumption good markets. Now we will do the market-wise analysis.

Immigration Market

When immigration quota increases, then the supply of the immigrant workers increases. Given the demand curve of the immigrant workers, the increase in the supply of the immigrant reduces the equilibrium wage of the immigrant.

From equation (3) in equilibrium we have,

$$Q_I\,(I_D{}^*(n^*) + F\,(K_F, n^*), N_F)\, F_n\,(K_F, n^*) = W_I\,(n^*)$$

Differentiating both sides with respect to n* and after some manipulation we obtain,

$$\Rightarrow d\, W_I{}^*/dn^* = Q_{II}\,\{-F_{LO} + F_n\}\,F_n + Q_I\,F_{nn}$$

In the region $(F_n - F_{LO}) > 0$, $dW_1{}^*/dn^* < 0$

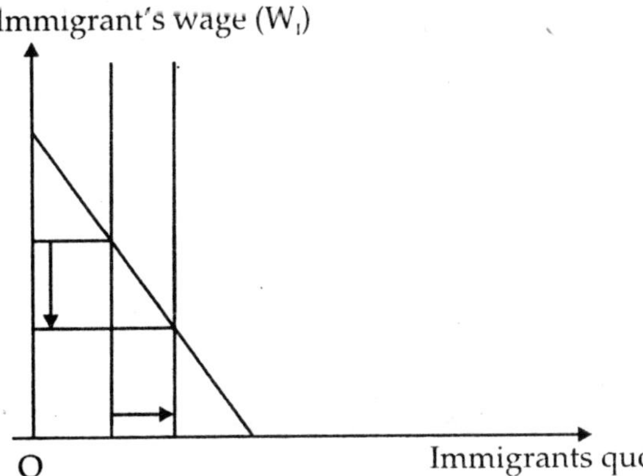

The Intermediate Input Market

An increase in the immigration quota reduces the labour availability to the domestic outsourcing sector. As a result the production of the outsourcing sector is reduced by F_{LO} amount. This reduces the total supply of the total intermediate input.

On the other hand, an increase in the immigration quota increases the labour availability to the foreign intermediate input production. As a result, the production of the intermediate input in the foreign country is increased by F_n amount. This again increases the supply of the intermediate input.

Now, $F_n > F_{LO}$, since the people migrate from the domestic country to the foreign country. Therefore, the total supply of the intermediate input is increased by $(F_n - F_{LO})$ amount.

But the demand curve of the intermediate input remains same. As a result, the equilibrium price of the intermediate input demand falls.

From equation (1) in equilibrium we have,

$$Q_I(I_D^*(n^*) + F(K_F, n^*), \dot{N}_F) = P_I(n^*)$$

Differentiating both sides with respect to n* and after some manipulation we obtain,

$$\Rightarrow dP_I^*/dn^* = Q_{II}\ (F_n - F_{LO})$$

In the region $(F_n - F_{LO}) > 0$, $dP_I^*/dn^* > 0$.

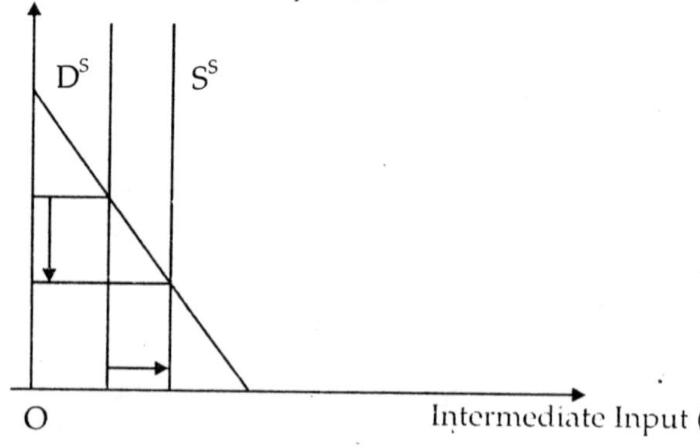

Foreign Capital Mark I^D

By our model specification, foreign capital is only employed in the foreign intermediate input production. An increase in the immigration quota has two opposite effects on the foreign capital demand. The productivity of the foreign capital increases due to an increase in n* (that means, $F_{Kin}>0$). This will try to shift the value of the marginal product curve of the foreign capital (vMP_{KF}) (which can be interpreted as the demand curve in the competitive environment) to right. But on the other hand, the price of the intermediate input falls. This will shift the vMP_{KF} Curve to the left. So ultimately the new demand curve of the foreign capital may lie to the right or left or on the previous demand curve. Given the fixed supply of the foreign capital, an increase in immigration quota may increase, decrease or not change the equilibrium rental of the foreign capital.

From equation (2) in equilibrium we have,

$$Q_I(I_D^*(n^*) + F(K_F, n^*), N_F).F_{KI}(K_F. n^*) = r_k{}^*(n^*)$$

Differentiating both sides with respect to n* and after some manipulation we obtain,

$$d\, r_k^*/dn^* = Q_I\, F_{Kin} + Q_{II}\,(F_n - F_{LO})\, F_{KI}$$

Therefore in the region $(F_n - F_{LO}) > 0$, $d\, r_k{}^*/dn^* \gtrless 0$.

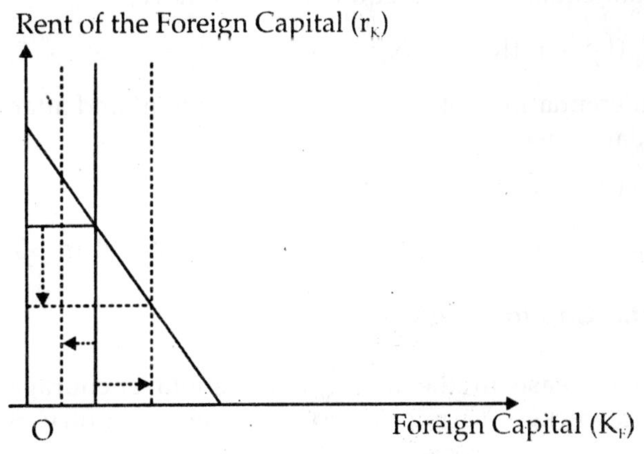

Rent of the Foreign Capital (r_K)

O

Foreign Capital (K_F)

Foreign Labour Market

An increase in the immigration quota increases the equilibrium use of the intermediate input. So this will increase the demand for the foreign labour, since we have assumed that the foreign labour and the intermediate input are complement to each other in the final consumption good production. As a result, the demand curve of the foreign labour shifts rightward.

Given the fixed supply of the foreign labour at N_F level, an increase in the immigration quota increases the equilibrium wage of the foreign labour.

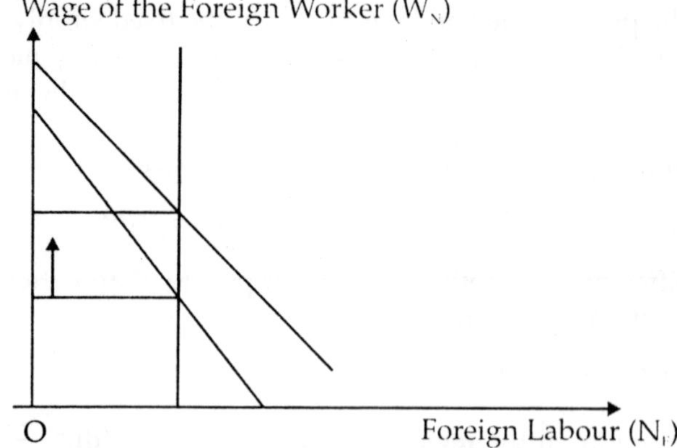

From equation (4) in equilibrium we have,

$$Q_N (I_D^* + F(K_F, n^*), N_F) = W_N$$

Differentiating both sides with respect to n* and after some manipulation we obtain,

$$\Rightarrow dW_N/d\,n^* = Q_{NI}\,[F_n - F_{LO}]$$

Therefore in the region $(F_n - F_{LO}) > 0$, $dW_N/d\,n^* > 0$.

Domestic Capital Market

An increase in the immigration quota encourages the domestic workers to migrate to the foreign country. So the labour available to the domestic outsourcing sector decreases. Therefore, the productivity of the domestic capital decreases, since we have assumed that the domestic capital and domestic workers are complement to each other in the outsourcing production. This will shift the value of the marginal product curve of the domestic capital (VMP_{KD}) towards left. On the other hand, an increase in the immigration quota reduces the price of the outsourcing product. This will also shifts the VMP_{KD} curve to the left. Given the fixed supply of the domestic capital, an increase in the immigration quota decreases the equilibrium rent of the domestic capital.

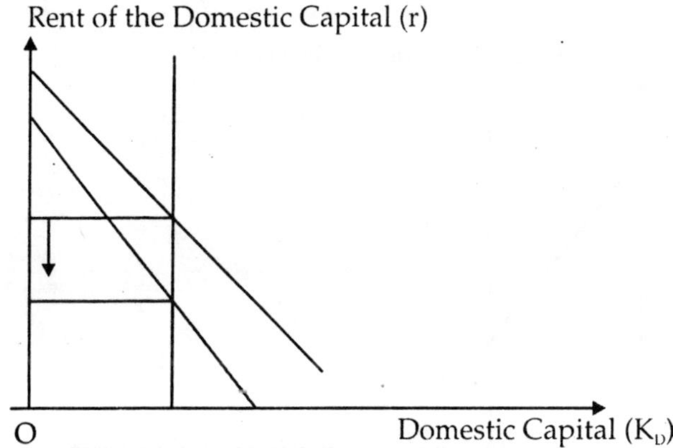

From equation (9) in equilibrium we have,

$P_I^* F_{KO} (K_D, L_D - n^*) = r^*$

Differentiating both sides with respect to n* and after some manipulation we obtain,

$\Rightarrow d(r^*)/dn^* = F_{KO} Q_{II} [F_n - F_{LO}] - P_1^* F_{KOLO}$

Therefore in the region $(F_n - F_{LO}) > 0$, $d(r^*)/dn^* < 0$.

Domestic Labour Market

Total labour demand (DL) of the domestic country has two components: demand for emigrants and the demand for labour by the domestic outsourcing sector.

An increase in immigration quota directly increases the domestic labour demand (since immigration is a component of total domestic country's labour demand). On the other hand, there is an inverse relation between immigration quota and outsourcing demand. So an increase in immigration quota leads to a decline in outsourcing demand. This automatically reduces the demand for labour in domestic outsourcing sector. In this way, immigration quota indirectly reduces the total domestic labour demand. But mathematically we have d (DL)/dn* = 0. As a result, given the fixed labour supply of the domestic country, the market clearing domestic wage level (w*) does not change.

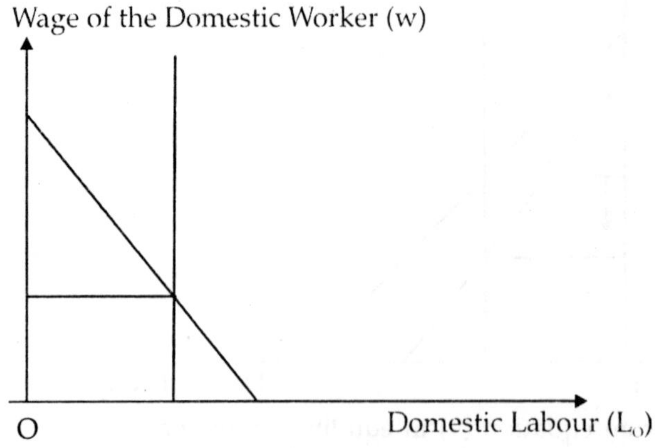

Total labour demand (DL) of the domestic country has two components: demand for emigrants and the demand for labour by the domestic outsourcing sector.

$$DL = L_o^* (I_D^*(n^*)) + n^*$$

Differentiating both sides with respect to n* we obtain,

$$d\,(DL)/dn^* = (\partial L_O^*/\partial I_D^*).(d\,I_D^*/dn^*) + I$$

After manipulating we obtain,

$$\Rightarrow d\,(DL)/dn^* = 0$$

Therefore, the total domestic labour demand does not change due to an increase in the immigration quota. As a result, given the fixed labour supply of the domestic country, the market clearing domestic wage level (w*) does not change.

Impact of all Increase in the Immigration Quota on the Welfare Level (measured in terms of the national income)

Final Consumption Good Production

An increase in the immigration quota increases the total production of the intermediate input (I). Since in this model, unemployment is not considered in any factor input market, so the total produced intermediated input will be used in the production of the final consumption good; as a result, the production of the final consumption good increases.

In this respect, one thing has to be mentioned that in the region where $F_n > F_{LO}$, an increase in the immigration quota increases the production of the final consumption good, by increasing the total production of the intermediate input (I). In the region $F_n < F_{LO}$, no further migration from the domestic country to the foreign country takes place, since the wage difference disappears at $F_n = F_{LO}$ stage. So, the production of the final consumption good is maximised at $F_n = F_{LO}$.

$$Q^* = Q(I^*, N_F)$$

Differentiating both sides with respect to n* we obtain,

$$d\,Q^*/dn^* - Q_I[F_n\ F_{LO}]$$

Differentiating both sides with respect to n* we obtain,

$$d^2\,Q^*/d\,n^{*2} = Q_{II}[F_n - F_{LO}]^2 + Q_I[F_{nn} + F_{LOLO}]$$

Therefore in the region $(F_n - F_{LO}) > 0$, $d\,Q^*/d\,n^* > 0$ and $d^2\,Q^*/d\,n^{*2} < 0$. Q* curve is a positively sloped concave to the origin.

OA of Q* curve shows total production of the final consumption good at zero level of immigration (that means, the migration is completely restricted by the government of the foreign country). $OA = P_I{}^*I_A + W_N{}^*.\ N_F$.

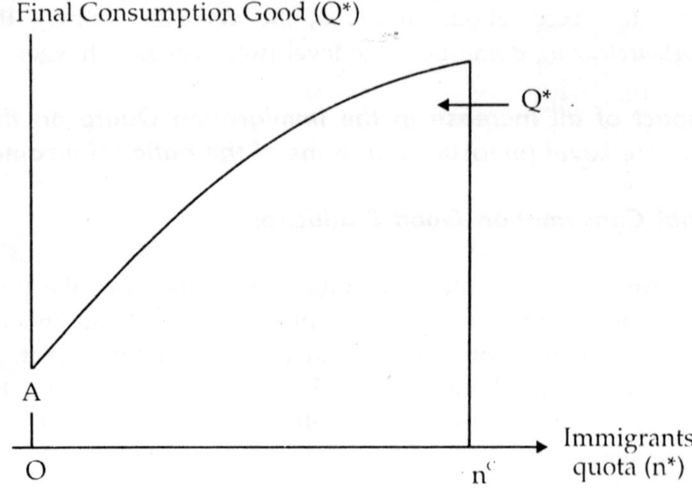

(Whole I_A is produced in the domestic country, when migration is completely restricted by the foreign government).

Domestic National Income (measured in terms of the final consumption good)

Domestic national income identity can be written as,

$$Y_D^* = P_I^* I_D^* + W_I^*.n^*$$

(Using equation (11))

The domestic national income has two components—value of the total outsourcing product ($P_I^* I_D^*$) produced in the domestic country and total wage earning by the immigrants in the foreign country ($W_I^*.n^*$).

When immigration quota increases, then I_D^* as well as P_I^* decrease, so their product (that means the value of the total outsourcing product = $P_I^* I_D^*$) decreases. On the other hand, market clearing wage of the immigrants (W_I^*) decreases due to an increase in the immigration quota (n^*). But ultimately total wage earning by the immigrants ($W_I^*.n^*$) in the foreign country may increase, decrease or remain same, due to an increase in the immigration quota.

Therefore, the sum of $P_I^*I_D^*$ and $W_I^*.n^*$ may increase, decrease or remain same due to an increase in the immigration quota. In the region $F_n > F_{LO}$, the domestic national income may increase, decrease or remain same due to an increase in the immigration quota.

$$Y_D^* = P_I^* I_D^* + W_I^*.n^*$$

Differentiating both sides with respect to n* and after some manipulation we obtain,

$$dY_D^*/dn^* = [F_n - F_{LO}]\,[I_D^*\,Q_{II} + P_I^* + n^*\,Q_{II}\,F_n] + n^*\,Q_I\,F_{nn}$$

In the region $F_n > F_{LO}$, $dY_D^*/dn^* \gtreqless 0$.

Differentiating both sides with respect to n* we obtain,

$$d^2\,Y_D^*/d\,n^{*2} = 2Q_{II}\,[F_n - F_{LO}]^2 + 2n^*Q_{II}\,F_{nn}\,[F_n - F_{LO}] + [F_{nn} + F_{LOLO}]\,[I_D^*\,Q_{II} + P_I^* + n^*\,Q_{II}\,F_n] + n^*\,Q_I\,F_{nn}$$

In the region $F_n > F_{LO}$, $d^2\,Y_D^*/d\,n^{*2} \gtreqless 0$.

At $F_n = F_{LO}$, $dY_D^*/dn^* = n^*\,Q_I\,F_{nn}$ and $d^2\,Y_D^*/d\,n^{*2} = n^*\,Q_I F_{nn}$

That means, $dY_D^*/dn^* < 0$, and $d^2\,Y_D^*/d\,n^{*2} < 0$.

Therefore, Y_D^* curve is an inverse 'U' shaped curve.

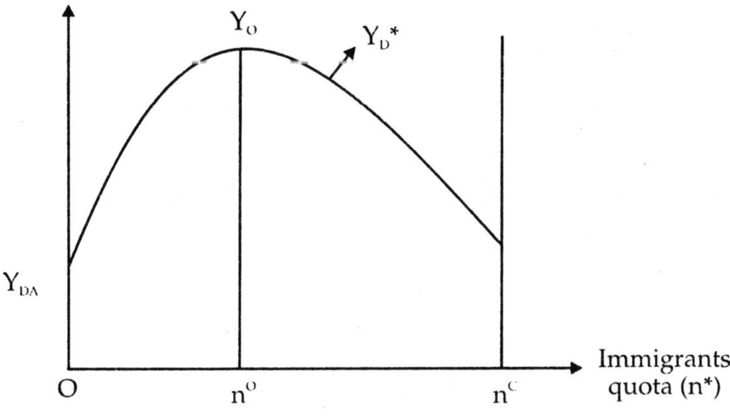

Let n^O be an optimum level of the immigration quota, at which $Y_D{}^*$ is maximised. $dY_D{}^*/dn^*$ can be expressed as,

$$dY_D{}^*/dn^* = I^* Q_{II} [F_n - F_{LO}][I_D{}^*/I^* - e] + n^*\{d W_I{}^*/dn^*)$$

(where $e = -(P_I{}^*/I^*) dI^*/dP_I{}^* =$ equilibrium price elasticity of the intermediate input demand)

Let e^O be the equilibrium price elasticity of the intermediate input demand, when n^O be the level of the immigration quota.

At n^O, $dY_D{}^*/dn^* = 0$

$\Rightarrow e^O = (I_D{}^*I/I^*) + (n^*/I^*) (d W_I{}^*/dP_I{}^*)$

Let I^D be the demand curve of the intermediate input and I^S be the supply curve of the intermediate input at n^O. Here E^O be the equilibrium point of the intermediate input market at which price elasticity of the intermediate input demand is $e^O = (I_D{}^*/I^*) + (n^*/I^*) (d W_I{}^*/dP_I{}^*)$.

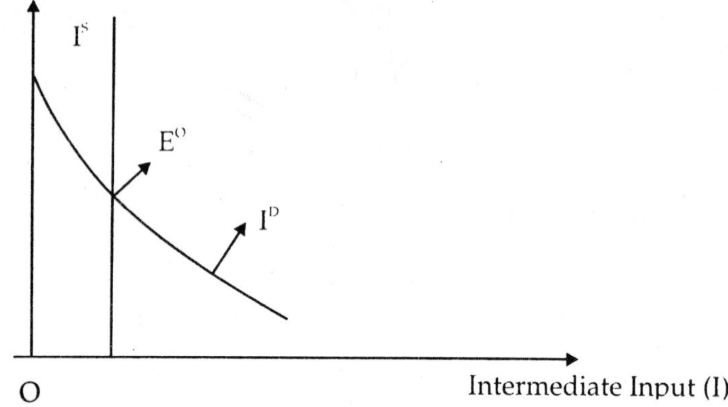

Foreign National Income (measured in terms of the final consumption good)

The foreign national income identity can be written as,

$Y_F{}^* = W_N{}^*. N_F + r_k{}^* K_F$

Foreign national income has two components—total

earning of the foreign labour and the total income of the foreign capital. An increase in the immigration quota increases the total earning of the foreign labour, but it may increase, reduce or may not change the second component, since $d\, r_k^*/dn^* \gtreqless 0$.

Equilibrium national income of the foreign country is,

$Y_F^* = W_N^*. N_F + P_I^* I_F^* - W_I^* n^*$

Differentiating both sides with respect to n* and after manipulating, we obtain.

$\Rightarrow dY_F^*/dn^* = -\, Q_{II}\, [F_n - F_{LO}][I_D^* + n^*\, F_n] - n^* Q_I\, F_{nn}$

Therefore in the region $(F_n - F_{LO}) > 0$, $dY_F^*/dn^* > 0$

Differentiating both sides with respect to n*, we obtain

$d^2\, Y_F^*/d\, n^{*2} = -Q_{II}\, [F_n - F_{LO}]^2 - [I_D^* + n^*\, F_n]\, Q_{II}\, [F_{nn} + F_{LOLO}]$
$-\, Q_I\, F_{nn} - 2n^*\, Q_{II} F_{nn} [F_n - F_{LO}]$

Now $d^2\, Y_F^*/d\, n^{*2} \gtreqless 0$, in the region $F_n > F_{LO}$.

At n^C level of immigration (at which $F_n = F_{LO}$), $dY_F^*/dn^* = -n^*(d\, WI^*/dn^*) > 0$ (since $(d\, W_I^*/dn^*) < 0$), and $d^2\, Y_F^*/d\, n^{*2} = -(d\, W_I^*/d\, n^*) > 0$. Therefore, Y_F^* is a positively sloped curve with a point of inflection at G point on Y_F^* curve. At $n^* = 0$, (that means, migration is completely restricted by the foreign government), $Y_F^* = W_N^*. N_F = OY_{FA}$. In this situation, foreign capital remains unemployed since no intermediate input is produced in the foreign country.

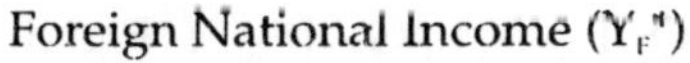

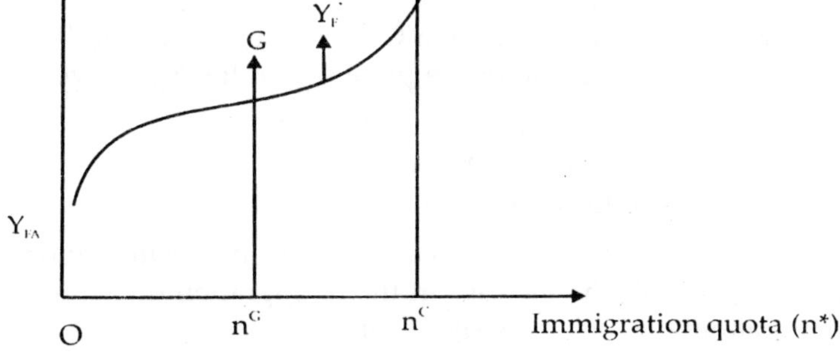

Combined Study about the Impact of an Increase in the Immigration Quota

Now we are combining Q^*, $Y_F{}^*$, and $Y_D{}^*$ curves in a single diagram. In this diagram, along upward moving vertical axis, the final consumption good Q^* and along downward moving vertical axis, the intermediate input (I) are plotted. Along the right side horizontal axis, immigration quota (n^*) and along the left side horizontal axis, price of the intermediate input (P_I) are measured.

Quadrant I

In the first quadrant, Q^*. $Y_F{}^*$, and $Y_D{}^*$ curves are drawn.

We know that $Q^* = Y_F{}^* + Y_D{}^*$. Therefore at every n^* level, Q^* is the vertical sum of $Y_F{}^*$ and $Y_D{}^*$.

At $n^* = 0$, (that means, migration is completely restricted by the foreign government), $Y_F{}^* = W_N{}^*. N_F = OY_{FA}$. In this situation, foreign capital remains unemployed since no intermediate input is produced in the foreign country. At $n^* = 0$, $Y_D{}^* = P_I{}^* I_A = OY_{DA}$. This OY_{FA} can be greater, or smaller than or same as OY_{DA}. Here we are assuming that $OY_{FA} > OY_{DA}$, since the foreign country is assumed as the developed country. At $n^* = 0$, $Q^* = P_I{}^* I_A + W_N{}^*. N_F \Rightarrow OA = OY_{FA} + OY_{DA}$.

Let, n^G be the immigration quota at the point of inflection G, at which $d^2\, YF^*/d\, n^*{}_2 = 0$.

$$\Rightarrow - Q_{II}\,[F_n - F_{LO}]^2 - [I_D{}^* + n^*\, F_n]\, Q_{II}\,[F_{nn} + F_{LOLO}] - Q_I\, F_{nn} - 2n^*\, Q_{II} F_{nn} [F_n - F_{LO}] = 0$$

$$\Rightarrow n^G = \{-Q_{II}\,[F_n - F_{LO}]^2 - Q_I\, F_{nn} - I_D{}^* Q_{II}\,[F_{nn} + F_{LOLO}]\} / \{2Q_{II} F_{nn} [F_n - F_{LO}] + F_n\, Q_{II}\,[F_{nn} + F_{LOLO}]\}$$

Now the point of inflection G on the $Y_F{}^*$ curve can be on the right side or left side of the point Y_O on the $Y_D{}^*$ curve.

At n^O, $dY_D{}^*/dn^* = 0$.
Therefore, $dQ^*/dn^* = dY_F{}^*/dn^*$
The slope of Q^* curve = The slope of $Y_F{}^*$ curve

From the picture it is clear that the domestic national income falls with the increase in the immigration quota, if the immigration level lies between n^O and n^C range.

Quadrant II

In the second quadrant I curve shows the relation between the intermediate input production and the level of the immigration quota.

$1 = I_D + I_F$

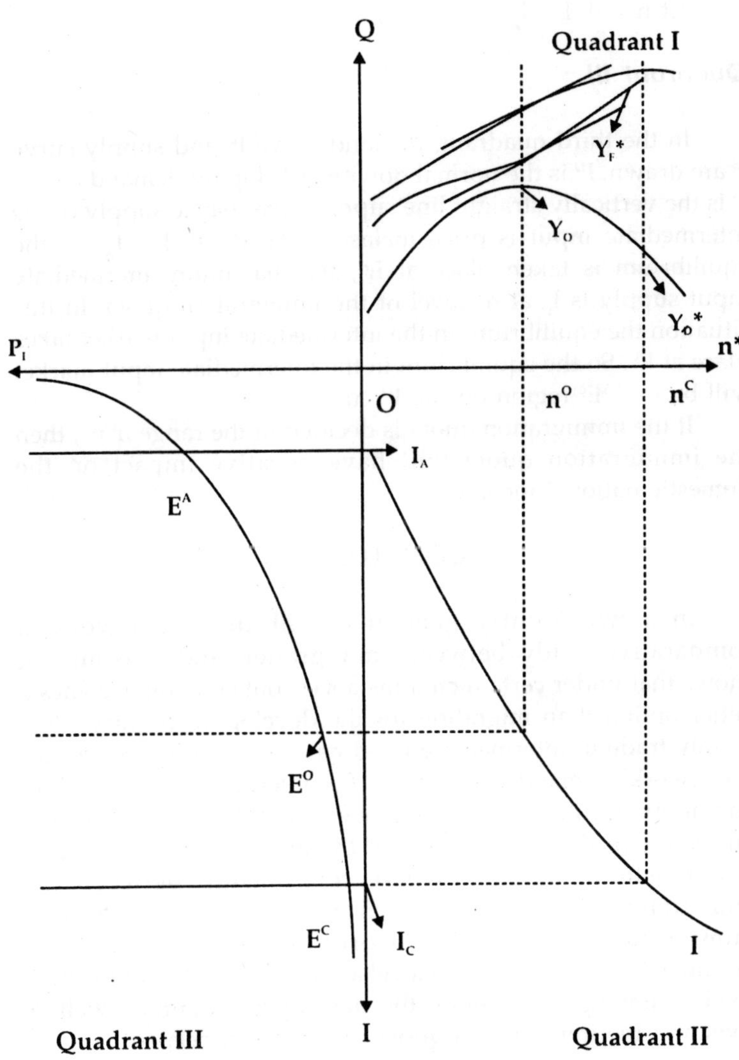

Differentiating both sides with respect to n* we obtain,

$dI/dn^* = F_n - F_{LO}$

In the region $F_n > F_{LO}$, $dI/dn^* > 0$.

Differentiating both sides with respect to n* we obtain,

$d^2I^*/d\,n^{*2} = [F_{nn} + F_{LOLO}] < 0$

At $n^* = 0$, $I = I_A$

Quadrant III

In the third quadrant, demand curve I^D and supply curve I^S are drawn. I^D is the normal downward sloping demand curve. I^S is the vertically straight line supply curve (since supply of the intermediate input is price inelastic). At $n^* = 0$, $I = I_A$, so the equilibrium is taken place at E^A, the maximum intermediate input supply is I_C at n^C level of the immigration quota. In this situation the equilibrium in the intermediate input market takes place at E^C. So the equilibrium in the intermediate input market will be in E^AE^c region on the I^D curve.

If the immigration quota is decided in the range n^On^C, then the immigration quota will have negative impact on the domestic national income.

4. CONCLUSIONS

In a two-country general equilibrium framework, a comparative study between immigration and outsourcing shows that under certain circumstances, outsourcing becomes a better option than migration for the developing country. Here mainly trade in intermediate good has been considered. In this framework, demand elasticity of the intermediate input plays an important role to determine the effect of the outsourcing and migration on the welfare level of the developing country. This paper established an inverse relationship between the immigration and outsourcing in a two-country framework. Immigration enhances the world welfare level and the developed country's welfare level at every stage. But at the high level of immigration quota, the developing country's welfare level and the immigration quota are inversely related.

From the above discussion it becomes clear that developing countries should frame their policy in such a way, which helps to obtain outsourcing contract and reduce the migration from the developing country, at a high level of migration. For the development of outsourcing sector, infrastructure (transportation, electricity, telecommunication, etc.) has to be improved. Improvement of infrastructure has dual impact. It may not help to expand outsourcing market, but it also provides the incentives to the domestic workers, who are planning to migrate to the foreign country. It will help to stop 'brain drain' also, though this paper does not consider the other social impact of the immigration.

This book is a part of my Ph.D. work. In this paper, I do not consider any technological differences in producing intermediate input, across the countries. Infact, the differences in the factor endowment of the countries are not given any importance in the model. My future research will be in these above mentioned areas.

References

Bandyopadhyay, Subhayu and Wall, Howard, J. (2005): 'Immigration and Outsourcing: A General Equilibrium Analysis'.

Chiang, Alpha C.: 'Fundamental Methods of Mathematical Economics': Third Edition.

Dueby, Rajeev (2003): 'Global Outsourcing; The India Story So Far': *Business World*, 12 May, 2003, 30-44.

Henderson, James M. and Quandt, R.: 'Microeconomic Theory: A Mathematical Approach'.

Jones, Ronald W. (1965): 'The Structure of Simple General Equilibrium Models', *The Journal of Political Economy*, Vol. 73, No. 6, 557-72.

Jones, Ronald W (2005): 'Immigration *vs.* Outsourcing: Effects on Labor Market', *International Review of Economics and Finance*, 14 (2005), 105-114.

Marjit, Sugata and Acharyya, Rajat (2002): 'International Trade, Wage Inequality and the Developing Economy: A General Equilibrium Approach': Physica-Verlag.

Ramaswami, V.K. (1968): 'International Factor Movement and National Advantage': *Econometrica*, Vol. 35, No. 139, 309-10.

Wiermann, Christian (2006): 'Labour Heterogeneity and Trade Liberalization', *Journal of Economic Integration*, 21 (1), 181-97.

SECTION II

DEVELOPMENT ISSUES

9

Capability Based Approach and India's Poverty

SUBRATA MAJUMDAR

1. INTRODUCTION

Hundreds of millions of Indians are poor by national and international standard. Indian policy-making and policies are dominated by discussion of poverty, and measure of poverty rightly attracted a great deal of attention in this debate. If poverty is declined as the inability to attain the minimum standard of life then the basic query centers around the definition of "standard of life" itself. The minimum calorie requirement for mere physical survival would undoubtedly dominate the fundamental poverty measure. However, the question is whether one should stop there or would extend the provision of other basic amenities (like shelter, clothing, etc.) in the definition to guarantee a minimum standard or living or not. Initially the measurement was solely dealing with income poverty, i.e. the minimum required income to ensure the minimum (decent) standard of living and later the importance of incorporation of non-income dimensions of poverty was gradually appreciated. Consequently, the concept of human poverty emerged. The transition from income to human poverty was greatly influenced the concept of "capability". It was recognized that not only the assurance of physical survival but the guarantee of minimum social dignity and status is what need to be protected. This approach eventually treats poverty as not merely a denial of human right at a personal level but an incidence of a serious social failure.

There is no disagreement over the position that poverty is a social shame and should be immediately eradicated, however, problem is faced in identifying the poor in terms of precise quantitative measures. While income poverty defines a clear cut poverty line (in terms of minimum required annual income per person) that works as a benchmark to demarcate the poor from the non-poor, the human poverty can only come up with an assessment of the proportion of deprived population in any particular region. For all practical purposes one has to come up with a comprehensive income measure that should incorporate both the personal and the regional dimensions of deprivation. A first step towards that would be the incorporation of other dimensions of food consumption in the definition of poverty line itself. In this paper an attempt is made to assess the inter-state variations in Indian poverty scenario in terms of one such comprehensive measure known as *capability measure.*

2. ORGANIZATION OF THE PAPER

This paper concentrates on the estimation of state-level poverty for ten selected states of India using capability-based approach. The steps adopted for this purpose may be described as follows:

- Estimation of India's poverty line (rural and urban separately) with capability-based approach using nutritional intake data of NSSO for the year 1999-2000;
- Calculation of the extent, incidence and rank of rural and urban poverty for ten major states of India using

both capability-based poverty line and other standard income poverty indices;
- Estimation and ranking of overall state level poverty using population weighted average of rural and urban poverty levels; and
- Finally, the calculation of rank correlation between capability-based poverty indices and traditional income poverty indices for these states to understand the commonness.

3. CAPABILITY APPROACH : THE CONCEPT

The traditional methodology of making poverty line is very simple. It considers only the cost of minimum caloric intake of a person. This means a person, whose income or per capita daily consumption expenditure is not enough to meet a certain minimum requirement of calorie intake, will be considered as a poor. This was the basic concept of income-based poverty line. However, under the new concept of poverty a person is considered as poor if he is incapable to achieve the minimum necessities of life. That means only caloric insufficiency is not the ideal demarcation point of poor and non-poor, the other dimensions of incapability should allow playing their role. These associated dimensions include needs like shelter, clothing, care services, etc. For sake of analytical simplicity these other capability-dimensions are assumed to be ideally consumed in an equiproportional way with caloric consumption. That means a minimum capability set contains two basic elements: one is nutritional attainment and other capability, consumed in a fixed proportion.[1] That means if a person wants to achieve higher living standard through capability set he must raise his expenditure on both nutritional intake others capabilities in a fixed proportion. Therefore, in a capability space the minimum required achievement set is an L-shaped contour [*Reddy, S., Visaria, S. and Asali, M. (2006)*].

Unlike calorie intake the other capability is difficult to quantify. Hence, one concentrates on more directly measurable characteristics like food energy, fats, protein, fiber-micro-nutrients and so on which the capability depends. This shifts our concentration from capability space to characteristic space.

The characteristic space considers the two major elements one is food energy and another is other characteristic. *The first element* is measured in terms of caloric intake from cereals consumption and *other characteristic* is measured from total consumption other than food such as protein, fat, micronutrients and fiber. When the threshold level of calorie intake is guaranteed to improve the overall quality of being substitution is allowed among different components of the characteristic set. However, below this threshold level no such substitution is allowed (see panel-1).

Panel 1

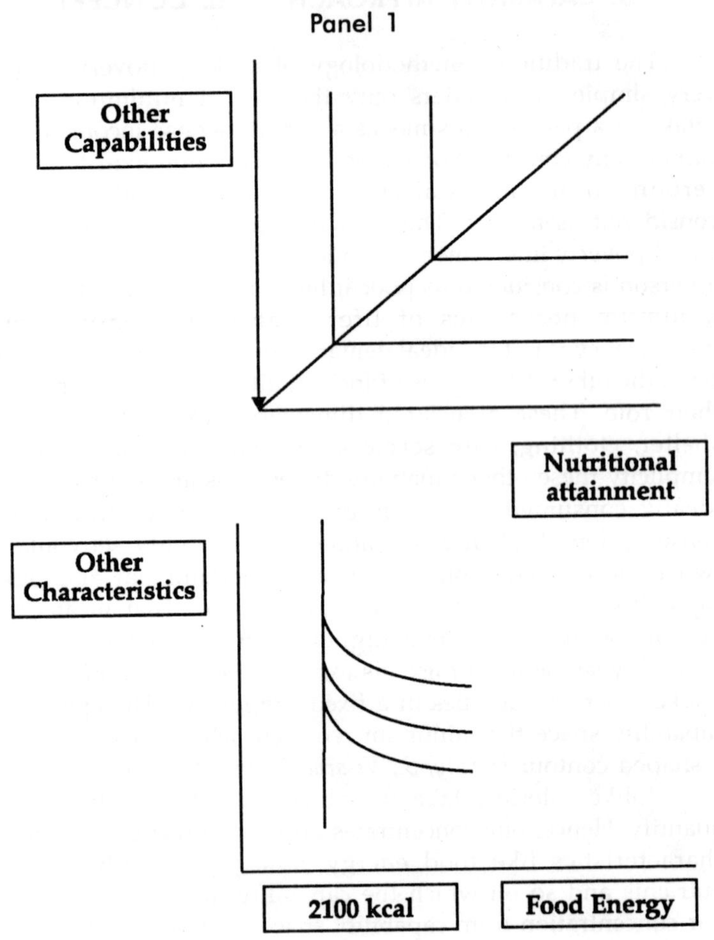

To overcome this problem the researchers have tried to focus on the food energy intake of individuals to anchor poverty line to a caloric adequacy threshold. This threshold is defined as 2100 kilocalorie (kcl) per day. A person with caloric intake larger than 2100 kcl enjoys a trade-off between the food energy and other characteristics to maintain the same contour level of adequacy set. However, if he has less than 2100 kcl then the substitution is not possible within the characteristic space. Therefore 2100 kcl consumption per day is assumed to ensure that the relevant person is enjoying not only the minimum required food energy but the other characteristic as well. That means if a persons is not able to attain 2100 kcl food energy he is considered unable to attain other non-rood characteristics or incapable to enjoy the basic needs of human life.

To estimate the poverty line with this approach it is required to divide the per capita consumption expenditure of entire population in different quintile. Now take that specific quintile where average per capita per day food energy intake is 2100 kcl. Name this quintile class as norm quintile class. Considerer the previous quintile class as a reference quintile class of the norm quintile class. Then calculate the average per capita per day caloric intake of that reference class. Suppose the per capita per day caloric intake of this class is x percent less than the norm class. Calculate the extra income required to lift up this reference classes from its original position to norm class. The equip-proportional assumption told us that the x percent extra expenditure is required for acquiring the food energy and also x percent extra non-food expenditure for accruing the non-food characteristics to reach the norm class. That means a linear scaling up is required not only for food expenditure but for non-food expenditure as well. Adding and aggregating the extra amount of food expenditure with original food expenditure and the non-food expenditure with extra amount of non-food expenditure of reference class we will get the countries poverty line. This amount of expenditure shows the minimum cost of achieving the minimum level of food expenditure along with the minimum level of non-food consumption. Therefore, this poverty line is called the aggregate poverty line or capability-based poverty line and shows the minimum requirement of persons to acquire the basic necessity of life. The example of the construction of poverty line in Vietnam will give a concrete picture of this methodology. This approach is useful because we do not have sufficient information to estimate directly the cost of achieving non-food capabilities considered essential for an individual's survival.

4. POVERTY LINE IN INDIA USING CAPABILITY MEASURE

This section describes poverty line on the basis of capability-based approach in Indian context considering the methodology of Vietnam VLSS. To make the Indian capability-based poverty line we have used the most usable secondary NSSO (National Sample Survey Organization) data of Nutritional Intake of period July 1999-June 2000. Here we have made some adjustment to the original Vietnam technique to build Indian capability-based poverty line. First of all due to the wide disparity in cost of living of rural and urban India and due to the unavailability of suitable regional price indices we have constructed two separate poverty lines with the basis of rural and urban nutritional intake data in India and called them rural and urban capability-based poverty lines. The second change that we have introduced is an equip-propotional change on the basis of caloric expenditure shortfall data instead of caloric shortfall of reference class from the norm class. In our technique we have increased reference class food and non-food expenditure on that proportion which is exactly the shortfall of caloric expenditure of reference class from the norm class. We have introduced some minor differences in assessment-technique for making it consistent with our available data structure. The third change that we have made which is the consideration of different norm calorie instead of 2100 kcl in different regions (rural and urban) due to unavailability of exact expenditure data of 2100 kcl. In Vietnam the VLSS data was used at unit level and our secondary NSSO Nutritional Intake data were utilized in a size-classed format. Now, we would like to describe the technique of derivation of rural and urban poverty line to clarify the differences and adjustments.

Methodology of Rural Poverty Line Setting in India using NSSO (1999-2000) Data

NSSO reports the data on MPCE class (Rs.), percentage of food expenditure of total expenditure, per capita per diem intake of calorie (kcl) and the average monthly per capita expenditure (Rs.). According to the capability approach the norm intake of calorie is 2100 kcl. But due to the non-availability of particular data I have considered 2054 kcl as the norm caloric intake for rural India. Therefore, sixth MPCE class is considered as the norm class of rural India. In this group the expenditure share for food consumption is 64%. Now the average monthly per capita expenditure of this group is Rs. 399.90. Therefore, the daily per capita expenditure is Rs. (399.90/30) = Rs. 13.33. So the daily expenditure on food of this group is Rs. (13.33 * 0.64) = Rs. 8.53. Now I have considered the fifth MPCE class which is the previous class of the norm class. Applying the same technique I have seen that the daily per capita expenditure of this class is Rs. 12.03. The daily per capita expenditure for food is Rs. (12.03 * 0.65) = Rs. 7.82. So the daily non-food expenditure is Rs. (12.03-7.82) = Rs. 4.21. Therefore, the amount of the expenditure of the food of this class is {(8.53-7.82)/7.82} = 0.091 times less than norm group. Therefore, according to the capability-based approach the fifth class needs 0.091 times more expenditure for food consumption and also 0.091 times more expenditure for non-food consumption (due to the assumption of same proportion complementarities between food and non-food items) to reach the minimum attainable capability. To attain the minimum capability the required per capita per day expenditure is Rs. [7.80 + (7.82*0.091) + 4.21 + (4.21*0.091)] = 13.12. So in terns of 30 days it will be Rs. (13.12 * 30) = Rs. 393.60. *So the calculated rural poverty line in India is Rs. 393.60 per capita per month.*

Methodology or Urban Poverty Line Setting in India using NSSO (1999-2000) Data

NSSO reports data on MPCE class (Rs), percentage of food expenditure of total expenditure, per capita per diem intake of calorie (kcl) and the average monthly per capita expenditure

(Rs). According to the capability approach the norm intake of calorie is 2100 kcl. But due to the non-availability of particular data I have considered 2091 kcl is the norm caloric intake in urban India. Therefore, sixth MPCE class is considered as the norm class of urban India. In this group the expenditure share for food consumption is 56%. Now the average monthly per capita expenditure of this group is Rs. 618.61. Therefore, the daily per capita expenditure is Rs. (618.61/30) = Rs. 20.62. So the daily expenditure on food of this group is Rs. (20.62 * 0.56) = Rs. 11.54. Now I have considered the fifth MPCE class which is the previous class of the norm class. Applying the same technique I have seen that the daily per capita expenditure of this class is Rs. 17.91. The daily per capita expenditure for food is Rs. (17.91 * 0.58) = Rs. 10.39. So the daily non-food expenditure is Rs. (17.91-10.39) = 7.52. Therefore, the amount of the expenditure of the food of this class is {(11.54-10.39)/10.39} = 0.111 times less than norm group. Therefore, according to the capability-based approach the fifth class needs 0.111 times more expenditure for food consumption and also 0.111 times more expenditure for non-food consumption (due to the assumption of same proportion complementarities between food and non-food items) to reach the minimum attainable capability. To attain the minimum capability the required per capita per day expenditure is Rs. [17.91 + (17.91 * 0.111) + 7.52 + (7.52 * 0.111)] = Rs. 28.25. So in terms of 30 days it will be Rs. (28.25 * 30) = Rs. 847.50. *So the calculated urban poverty line in India is Rs. 847.50 per capita per month.*

The striking feature of this estimate is that the urban poverty line is almost double valued than the rural poverty line. The ratio between the urban and rural poverty line in case of capability-based approach is 2.15. However, according to the traditional methodology the state by state urban and rural poverty line calculated independently without consideration of the implicit urban to rural price differential, the average ratio of urban to rural poverty line is around 1.4 and varies widely across stales. In the NSSO 50th Round (1993/94) it is more than 1.7 in Andhra Pradesh and nearly as much in Maharashtra, Madhya Pradesh and Karnataka, but less than unity in Assam (*Deaton & Kozel, 2005*). One plausible explanation for the disproportionate increase in urban poverty line in case of capability measure may lie in the fact that other non-food items are more costly in urban areas accounting for the higher cost of living.

5. POVERTY ESTIMATES AND NSSO DATA

Here we have estimated Head Count Ratio (H_R), Normalized Poverty Gap (NPG), Gini Index of Poor (Gp), Sen Index of Poverty (Ps), FGT Measures of Poverty and Squared Poverty Gap (SPG) separately for rural and urban areas in each state. Then we have considered the population weighted average of rural and urban indices to measure the state poverty level. The estimation procedure is illustrated taking the state of West Bengal as an example.

Estimation of Poverty in West Bengal

Here we have discussed how we estimate the level of poverty in West Bengal using capability-based measure with Nutritional Intake Data (1999/2000) of NSSO. First we have estimated rural poverty then urban poverty in West Bengal and finally considered the population weighted average of each sectors poverty level to estimate the state level poverty.

Estimation of Rural Poverty in West Bengal

To estimate rural poverty in West Bengal using our available data, the following steps are followed:

The Estimation of Average Monthly Expenditure of Various MPCE Classes in Rural West Bengal from Nutritional Intake Data (1999/2000)

Majumder (2006) has shown that Rs. 8.53 is required for consuming 2054 kcl. Rs. 0.00415 is the amount of required expenditure for getting 1 kcl in rural India.

Considering the first MPCE classes of Table IR (from NSSO 55th Round Nutritional intake In India) we will get the caloric consumption of the class is 1309 kcl. So the amount of expenditure of this class for caloric consumption is Rs. (0.00415*

1309) = Rs. 5.43235. This amount of expenditure is only 71% of total average per capita per day expenditure of this class. So the total average per capita per day expenditure of this class is Rs. (5.43235/0.71) = Rs. 7.651197183. Therefore, the average monthly total pre capita expenditure of this class in rural West Bengal is Rs. (7.651197183 * 30) = 229.5359115 = 229.54. Applying this methodology, Table 9.1 estimates all classes' average monthly per capita expenditure in rural West Bengal.

Estimation of Number of Persons Belonging to Different MPCE Classes in Rural West Bengal

Considering Table 5R (from NSSO 55th Round Nutritional Intake in India) we can estimate the sample proportion of people living in different MPCE classes in rural West Bengal. If we assume the sample to be representative then sample proportions will be the best estimates of the population proportions. Then the population strength of different MPCE class can be obtained by multiplying the sample proportion with total no. of rural population in West Bengal. According to the census 2001 the total number of rural population in West Bengal is 57748946. In Table 9.1 column 6 shows the number of population for each class.

Estimation of Urban Poverty in West Bengal

To estimate urban poverty in West Bengal using our available data, the following steps are followed:

The Estimation of Average Monthly Expenditure of Various MPCE Classes in Urban West Bengal from Nutritional Intake Data (1999/2000)

From Majumder (*op. cit.*) we have seen that Rs. 11.54 is required for consuming 2091 kcl. Rs. 0.00552 is the amount of required expenditure for getting 1 kcl in rural India. Considering the first MPCE classes of Table 1U (from NSSO 55th Round Nutritional Intake in India) we will get the caloric consumption of the class is 1352 kcl. So the amount of expenditure of this class for caloric consumption is Rs. (0.00552*

TABLE 9.1
Estimation of Average Per-Capita Expenditure from Nutritional Intake Data (Rural)

MPCE Classes (Rs.)	*% of food expenditure of total expenditure*	*Per capita per diem caloric intake (kcl)*	*MPCE= [{(0.00415) (col.-3)}/(col. 2/100)]* 30*	*Proportion of the people*	*Total No. of people= (57748946)* (col.-5)*
(col.-1)	*(col.-2)*	*(col.-3)*	*(col.-4)*	*(col.-5)*	*(col.-6)*
0-225	71	1309	229.54	0.04	2274779.82 (P)
225-255	72	1535	265.43	0.04	2404977.80 (P)
255-300	72	1641	283.76	0.08	4699410.15 (P)
300-340	71	1837	322.12	0.09	5247224.29 (P)
340-380	70	1935	344.15	0.10	5905583.89 (P)
380-420	68	1994	365.08	0.10	5903127.33 (P)
420-470	68	2160	395.47	0.11	6477963.70
470-525	67	2325	432.03	0.10	5824517.23
525-615	66	2379	448.77	0.11	6561486.93
615-775	64	2648	515.12	0.11	6109478.85
775-950	60	2821	585.36	0.05	3134577.81
950-more	48	3285	852.05	0.06	3205818.21
All	—	—	—	1	57748946

Source : Calculated From NSSO Nutritional Intake In India: 1999-2000.
(P): Poor class.

1352) = Rs. 7.46304. This amount of expenditure is only 68% of total average per capita per day expenditure of this class. So the total average per capita per day expenditure of this class is Rs. (7.46304/0.68) = Rs. 10.97506. Therefore, the average monthly total per capita expenditure of this class in rural West Bengal is Rs. (10.97506 * 30) = Rs. 329.2518 = Rs. 329.25. Applying this methodology, Table 9.2 estimates all classes' average monthly per capita expenditure in urban West Bengal.

Estimation of Number of Persons in Different MPCE Classes in Urban West Bengal

Considering the Table 5U (from NSSO 55th Round

TABLE 9.2
Estimation of Average Per-Capita Expenditure from Nutritional Intake Data (Urban)

MPCE Classes (Rs.)	*% of food expenditure of total expenditure*	*Per capita per diem caloric intake (kcl)*	*MPCE= [{(0.00552) (col.-3)}/(col. 2/100)]* 30*	*Proportion of the people*	*Total No. of people= (22427251)* (col.-5)*
(col.-1)	*(col.-2)*	*(col.-3)*	*(col.-4)*	*(col.-5)*	*(col.-6)*
0-300	68	1352	329.25	0.03	784738.46 (P)
300-350	69	1553	372.72	0.04	824613.38 (P)
350-425	66	1771	444.36	0.09	2051165.98 (P)
425-500	65	1954	497.82	0.12	2596654.91 (P)
500-575	60	1918	529.37	0.10	2245755.59 (P)
575-665	59	2103	590.27	010	2197905.69 (P)
665-775	57	2067	600.52	0.10	2221830.64 (P)
775-915	56	2220	656.49	0.10	2264895.56 (P)
915-1120	52	2270	722.91	0.11	2376545.34 (P)
1120-1500	49	2434	822.59	0.11	2520095.06 (P)
1500-1925	43	2604	1002.84	0.06	1291947.47
1925-more	40	3478	1439.89	0.05	1051102.94
All	—	—	—	1	22427251

Nutritional Intake in India) we can estimate the sample proportion of people live different MPCE classes in urban West Bengal. If we assume the sample to be representative then sample proportions will be the best estimates of the population proportions. Then the population strength of different MPCE class can be obtained by multiplying the sample proportion with total number of urban population in West Bengal. According to the census 2001 the total number of urban population in West Bengal is 22427251. In Table 9.2 column 6 shows the number of population of each class.

Table 9.3 present the poverty estimates for West Bengal as a whole.

TABLE 9.3
Estimate of Poverty in West Bengal

Indices	*Rural Proportion*	*Urban Proportion*	*Rural Poverty*	*Urban Poverty*	*State Poverty [(col. 2) (col. 4)+ (col. 3) (col. 5)]*
(col. 1)	*(col. 2)*	*(col. 3)*	*(col. 4)*	*(col. 5)*	*(col. 6)*
HR	0.72	0.28	45.77	89.55	58.02
NPG	0.72	0.28	23.35	34.32	26.42
Gp	0.72	0.28	8.77	14.95	10.50
Ps	0.72	0.28	13.76	39.53	20.97
FGT	0.72	0.28	3.43	12.3	5.91
SPG	0.72	0.28	5.45	11.78	7.22

Note :

$$H_R = \frac{\text{Number of people below poverty line (H)}}{\text{Total population (N)}}$$

$$TPG = \sum_{i=1}^{H} (Y_p - Y_i); \; Y_p = \text{income poverty line.}$$

$$Y_i = \text{income of i-th poor individual.}$$

$$NPG = \frac{APG}{Y_p} = \sum_{i=1}^{H} \frac{(Y_p - Y_i)}{HY_p}$$

$$G_p = \frac{1}{2H^2 \bar{Y}_\pi} \sum_{i=1}^{H} \sum_{j=1}^{H} |Y_i - Y_j|; \quad Y_\pi = \text{mean income of poor}$$

$$Y_i = \text{ith poor income}$$
$$Y_j = \text{jth poor income}$$

$$P_s = H_R \left[(NPG) + (1 - NPG) G_p \right]$$

$$FGT = P_2 = \frac{1}{N} \sum_{i=1}^{H} \left\{ \frac{(Y_p - Y_i)}{Y_p} \right\}^2$$

$$= H_R \left\lfloor (NPG)^2 + (1 - NPG)^2 (CV_p)^2 \right\rfloor$$

To estimate the state level poverty we have considered the population proportion weighted average of all poverty indices (rural and urban)[2] that we have estimated. According to the census 2001 the population proportion of rural and urban West Bengal is 72% and 28%.

Source : Calculated from NSSO Nutritional Intake in India 1999-2000.

6. Assessment of Poverty of Ten Major States in India by Capability Measure

In this section the methodology explained for the state of West Bengal has been applied in the context of nine other major Indian states where data were available separately for both rural and urban areas. Two major states like Assam and Gujarat could not be incorporated as data on urban areas were missing there. The included states are Andhra Pradesh (AP), Bihar (BIH), Karnataka (KAR), Madhya Pradesh (MP), Maharashtra (MAH), Orissa (ORI), Rajasthan (RAJ), Tamil Nadu (TN) and Uttar Pradesh (UP).

Tables 9.4 and 9.5 present the estimated values and ranks of state-level poverty for all ten selected states and India as a whole. Here the state-level HPI (obtained from Shariff, 1999) is

TABLE 9.4
Poverty of Ten Major States in India Using Capability Based Method

States	H_R (%)	*NPG* (%)	*Gp* (%)	*Ps* (%)	*FGT* (%)	*SPG* (%)	*HPI* (%)
AP	62.23	26.86	10.90	23.49	7.25	8.46	3978
BIH	58.96	19.29	9.23	16.16	2.71	3.84	5234
KAR	5276	27.32	10.49	19.74	6.30	7.93	32.10
MP	51.21	19.93	8.07	14.75	2.91	4.34	43.47
MAH	56.37	23.16	9.26	19.35	5.54	5.99	29.25
ORI	52.24	18.96	7.87	13.80	2.25	3.71	49.85
RAJ	25.93	19.67	6.91	8.90	2.88	4.45	46.67
TN	67.44	30.74	12.02	26.95	8.82	10.12	29.28
UP	30.96	18.24	5.38	11.08	2.27	3.79	48.27
WB	58.02	26.42	10.50	20.97	5.91	7.22	40.48
AI	43.08	21.55	9.19	13.96	3.95	5.04	39.36

Source : Calculated from NSSO 55th Round Data.

TABLE 9.5

Rank of Ten Major States According Poverty in India Using Capability Based Methods

States	H_R	*NPG*	*Gp*	*Ps*	*FGT*	*SPG*	*HPI*
AP	9	8	9	9	9	9	4
BIH	8	3	5	5	3	3	10
KAR	5	9	7	7	8	8	3
MP	3	5	4	4	5	4	6
MAH	6	6	6	6	6	6	1
ORI	4	2	3	3	1	1	9
RAJ	1	4	2	1	4	5	7
TN	10	10	10	10	10	10	2
UP	2	1	1	2	2	2	8
WB	7	7	8	8	7	7	5
AI	—	—	—	—	—	—	—

Source : Calculated from Table 9.4.

also reported to facilitate comparison. A few interesting observations are in order: (a) though in Rural WB there was a significant difference in the H_R-based poverty rank and the FGT based rank in all- WB level this difference is almost absent. Similar is the story for TN where in urban area the H_R-based rank differed substantially from the FGT-based rank. This apparent paradox can be resolved in terms of smoothing through aggregation procedure.

(b) The ranks of the states in terms of HPI are not in general similar to those in terms of H_R or FGT. A plausible explanation may be extended as follows: weak rank correlation between H_R and FGT suggests a wide variation in the intra-poor distribution of income. Now, intra-poor distribution can vary provided there are some occupational variations. These occupational variations may take place depending on the availability of infrastructural provisions. Since, HPI is sensitive to infrastructural provisions, hence, a weak correlation between FGT and HPI may not be unexpected. The figures in Table 9.6 confirms our hunch.

TABLE 9.6
Rank Correlation between Capability-based and Multidimensional Indices

	H_R	*NPG*	*Gp*	*Ps*	*FGT*	*SPG*	*HPI*
H_R	1	*	*	*	*	*	*
NPG	0.633	1	*	*	*	*	*
Gp	0.891	0.930	1	*	*	*	*
Ps	0.903	0.867	0.988	1	*	*	*
FGT	0.661	0.976	0.903	0.879	1	*	*
SPG	0.633	0.964	0.879	0.843	0.988	1	*
HPI	-0.406	-0.830	-0685	-0.673	-0.830	-0.818	1

Source : Calculated from Table 9.5.

As expected the poverty estimates obtained on the basis of Capability Measures are generally higher than those suggested by both the Planning Commission Expert Group and the NCAER studies based on standard money metric approach. The following section of this chapter will present a comparison of these alternative estimates.

7. COMPARATIVE ANALYSIS

In this section we have made a comparative analysis of our poverty measures and the traditionally calculated measures based on standard money metric approach reported in Table 9.7 following NCAER study (1999). If we compare Table 9.6 and Table 9.7 then a few interesting observations come up.

Though the state of AP enjoys the best status in terms of conventional poverty measures the rank changes to 9 out of 10 when the poverty line is re-defined following the capability approach. The opposite happens in case of ORI and UP. These sharp but diametrically opposite responses in rank following the inclusion of other characteristics in the specification of poverty line call for an intent attention. Using the NSSO 55th Round data on rural West Bengal it has been shown by Coondoo (2004) that the inter-decile differences in the consumption of Protein and Fat are more unequal compared to that of Calorie.

TABLE 9.7
Rank Correlation between NCAER Poverty Measures and Capability-based Poverty Measures

Indices	*Rank Correlation*
H_R	-0.297
NPG	-0.357
Gp	-0.418
Ps	-0.430
FGT	-0.606
SPG	-0.418

Source : Calculated from NHDR (2001), IHDR (1990) and NSS 55th Round.

So, the inclusion of these other nutrients in the calculation of poverty level would affect the incidence level of poverty substantially.

Table 9.7 shows negative rank correlation among all the measures or Poverty estimated by following two alternative definitions of poverty line. The absolute value of the correlation is the lowest for H_R and the highest for FGT. This indicates the increasing sensitivity of the measures with respect to the line change as the comprehensiveness of the measure increases.

8. CONCLUSION

Estimation of India's poverty line in terms of capability approach showed Rs. 393.60 per capita per month in Rural India at 1999-2000 prices and the corresponding estimate for Urban India is Rs. 847.50. Thus, the urban minimum requirement is more than doubly expensive than its rural counterpart. This is not only because the urban price index is higher than the rural but the minimum requirement in urban itself is very much different from the rural one. When the line is defined in terms of the standard money-metric approach then the range of variation between rural and urban areas across Indian states lies between 0.5 to 1.7. However, the incorporation of other food consumption like fat, protein, etc. caused aggravation of this difference and the incidence of poverty increased consequently.

Though now the base is higher with capability approach, the relative spread is lower, and, therefore, the Gini for poor under capability approach is consistently lower than that of the standard money metric approach. Analysis of rank correlation among all the poverty measures shows that the rank correlations between FGT and all other poverty measures for both rural and urban India are comparatively strong, the exception being H_R where it is abysmally low. This low correlation with H_R suggests the wide variation in the pattern of intra-poor income distribution across states.

Regarding the comparison of standard poverty measures and HPI a few interesting observations are in order: (a) though in Rural WB there was a significant difference in the H_R-based poverty rank and the FGT-based rank in all-WB level this difference is almost absent. Similar is the story for TN where in Urban area the H_R-based rank differed substantially from the FGT-based rank. This apparent paradox can be resolved in terms of smoothing through aggregation procedure. (b) The ranks of the states in terms of HPI are not in general similar to those in terms of HR or FGT. A plausible explanation may be extended as follows: weak rank correlation between H_R and FGT suggests a wide variation in the intra-poor distribution of income. Now, intra-poor distribution can vary provided there are some occupational variations. These occupational variations may take place depending on the availability of infrastructural provisions. Since, HPI is sensitive to infrastructural provisions, hence, a weak correlation between FGT and HPI may not be unexpected.

As expected the poverty estimates obtained on the basis of Capability Measures are generally higher than those suggested by both the Planning Commission Expert Group and the NCAER studies based on standard money metric approach.

Notes

1. Even within a country the minimum capability set varies from persons to persons according to age-sex composition. But for the sake of simplicity it will be conformable to fix up a uniform capability norm rather considering the different set of capabilities within a single country for different groups.
2. Basically Headcount and FGT measures hold the decomposable property, i.e., only for these two formulae total poverty can be decomposed

between rural and urban poverty, or, by implication rural and urban poverty can be combined to assess the total poverty of the state. However, to estimate state level poverty here we have implicitly assumed that this property holds in case of all poverty indices (see Bhattacharya and Coondoo).

REFERENCES

Coondoo, D., 'Distributional Inequality of Nutrition Intake in Rural West Bengal, 1999-2000: An Illustrative Study", Additional Reading of Economic Development and Welfare: Some Measurement Issues, 2004, Indian Statistical Institute, Kolkata.

Deaton, A. and Kozel, V. (eds.), The Great Indian Poverty Debate, 2005, Macmillan India Limited.

Planning Commission, Government of India, National Human Development Report, March 2002, Oxford University Press (New Delhi).

Reddy, S., Visaria S. and Asali, M., "Inter-Country Comparison of Poverty Based on a Capability Approach: An Empirical Exercise", International Poverty Centre—United Nations Development Programme (2006). (Working Papers are available online at <hltp:/www.undp.org/poverlycentre>).

Shariff, A., India Human Development Report, *National Council of Applied Economic Research*, 1999, Oxford University Press (New Delhi).

10

Gender Disparity in India : An Inter-State Analysis

JAYA MUKHERJEE

1. INTRODUCTION

It has often been argued that poverty, undernourishment, morbidity and mortality strike men as well as women. Hence, in any study of social deprivation, the focus should be on deprivation of entire families and there is no need for a separate gender-based analysis. Yet, in most societies of the world, one observes the existence of systematic inequality in the opportunities and predicaments of men and women. Women and men share many aspects of living together, collaborate with each other in many ways, and yet often end up with very different rewards and deprivations.

"Gender refers to socially constructed roles and socially learned behaviours and expectations associated with females and males" (World Bank, 2001). Women and men are different biologically. But all cultures translate these innate biological differences into a set of social expectations about what behaviours and activities are appropriate for women and men, and what rights, resources and powers they should possess. While these expectations vary considerably across societies, there are also some striking similarities. For example, in almost every society, the male child is ascribed the role of "protector" and "breadwinner" of the family while the primary responsibility of household and child care lies with women. Like race, ethnicity and class, gender is a social category that greatly influences one's opportunities in life and participation in the society and the economy. In fact, some societies do not have racial and ethnic divides, but almost all societies exhibit gender-based inequalities. Differences exist in access to and control of resources, economic opportunities, legal rights, social status and political voice. The direct costs of these gender-based inequalities are, of course, borne by women; but the indirect costs have to be borne by the entire society since the well-being of both present and future generations depends, to a large extent, on the well-being of women. Thus, "gender equality" is a core development issue.

The term "gender equality" has been defined in a variety of ways in the context of development. World Bank (2001) has defined it in terms of "equality under the law, equality of opportunity (including equality of rewards for work and equality in access to human capital and other productive resources that enable opportunity), and equality of voice (the ability to influence and contribute to the development process)". Robeyns (2006) has proposed the following fourteen capabilities as being crucial for the conceptualization of gender inequality in developed countries—(i) Life and physical health, (ii) Mental well-being, (iii) Bodily integrity and safety, (iv) Social relations, (v) Political empowerment, (vi) Education and knowledge, (vii) Domestic work and non-market care, (viii) Paid work and other projects, (ix) Shelter and environment, (x) Mobility, (xi) Leisure activities, (xii) Time-autonomy, (xiii) Respect, and (xiv) Religion. Although the capabilities have been defined for developed countries, most of these apply to developing countries as well. From the above list, Robeyns (2006) has identified two capabilities "education and knowledge" and "domestic work and non-market care"—to be of vital importance for the conceptualization of gender inequality and argued that in case of aggregation, greater weight should be given to them.

In this paper, we try to assess the extent of gender disparity in 15 major states of India. The states are Andhra Pradesh (AP), Assam (ASM), Bihar (BIH), Gujarat (GUJ), Haryana (HAR), Karnataka (KAR), Kerala (KER), Madhya Pradesh (MP), Maharashtra (MAH), Orissa (ORS), Punjab (PUN), Rajasthan (RAJ), Tamil Nadu (TN), Uttar Pradesh (UP) and West Bengal (WB). These states together accounted for more than 90% of the total population and more than 85% of the total geographical area of India in 2001.

The paper is organized as follows. Section II takes a look at inter-state differences in gender disparity and female deprivation as reflected by some important socio-economic indicators. Section III focuses exclusively on gender differences in time-use pattern of men and women. In section IV, we construct suitable composite indices for studying inter-state disparity in gender discrimination. Section V concludes the paper.

2. GENDER INEQUALITY IN INDIA

In this section, we take a quick look at gender inequality in 15 major states of India as reflected by some important socio-economic indicators. The indicators are shown in Table 10.1.

A very important indicator of gender inequality is "sex ratio". It shows the number of females per thousand males. According to Dreze and Sen (1989), in the absence of any discrimination, there should be more females than males in the population as are found in most parts of the developed world. However, sex ratios are female-adverse in all parts of India, except Kerala (refer to Table 10.1). They are more adverse in northern parts of India compared to southern parts. It is noteworthy that two of India's most agriculturally prosperous states, Punjab and Haryana, have very low sex ratios. Sex ratio is also very low in Uttar Pradesh. Dreze and Sen (1989) have argued that female-adverse sex ratios are the outcome of an anti-female bias in intra-household allocation of resources. Several socio-economic and cultural factors are believed to be

TABLE 10.1
Some Important Indicators of Gender Disparity and Female Deprivation

States	Sex Ratio (2001)	IMR (2005)		TFR (2005)	Women with Anaemia (%) 1998-99	MMR (1998)	FLR (15-49 yrs.) 2005	GDLR (2001)	GER (I-VIII) (2003-04)		LFPR (%) 1999-2000	
		M	F						Boys	Girls	M	F
(1)	(2)	(3)	(4)	(5)	(6)	(7)	(8)	(9)	(10)	(11)	(12)	(13)
AP	978	56	58	2.0	49.8	159	56.0	0.202	79.80	78.58	85.1	54.2
ASM	932	66	69	2.9	69.7	409	71.5	0.159	80.10	78.32	83.4	24.0
BIH	921	60	62	4.3	63.4	452	38.6	0.331	62.37	48.50	85.2	26.3
GUJ	921	52	55	2.8	46.3	28	62.2	0.211	104.19	89.36	84.9	44.6
HAR	861	51	70	2.8	47.0	103	64.2	0.224	71.53	71.49	77.4	27.4
KAR	964	48	51	2.2	42.4	195	62.5	0.184	97.95	93.76	85.0	45.4
KER	1058	14	15	1.7	22.7	198	97.5	0.056	96.61	94.51	80.8	35.3
MP	920	72	79	3.6	54.3	498	49.7	0.270	96.89	83.43	84.6	50.7
MAH	922	34	37	2.2	48.5	135	75.3	0.172	100.71	98.31	82.1	46.3
ORS	972	74	77	2.6	63.0	367	56.6	0.253	93.28	85.86	84.1	40.6
PUN	874	41	48	2.1	41.4	199	70.9	0.116	66.52	70.26	82.2	33.9
RAJ	922	64	72	3.7	48.5	670	40.1	0.337	103.65	87.19	82.6	50.2
TN	986	35	39	1.7	56.5	79	81.2	0.167	111.57	108.88	83.6	47.6
UP	898	71	75	4.2	48.7	707	47.9	0.297	81.09	74.86	83.3	29.1
WB	934	38	39	2.1	62.7	266	67.7	0.167	91.57	90.20	84.6	22.2
India	933	56	61	2.9	51 8	407	60.3	0.216	88.02	81.51	83.5	38.5

Sources : (1) Planning Commission (2002), Govt. of India, "National Human Development Report 2001".
(2) Council for Social Development (2006), "India: Social Development Report", OUP.
(3) Sample Registration System, 2005-06. (4) Economic Survey, 2003-04.

responsible for the existence of such gender bias. According to Agarwal (1997), one reason for relatively more adverse sex ratio in northern parts of India might be that the girl child is considered more of an economic burden in northern India (especially the north-west) than in the south. The paper cites three important reasons in support of this argument. Firstly, female labour force participation rates are much lower in the north-west than elsewhere in the country. Secondly, female/male marriage costs are higher in northern India because of the greater incidence and amount of dowry in the north relative to the south. Thirdly, there is a taboo on Hindu parents (especially among the upper castes) in northern India seeking any kind of material support from married daughters, while it is socially permissible for parents in south India to seek such support during any kind of crisis. We, thus, observe that just in terms of absolute numbers, women are at a disadvantage compared to men.

Discrimination against women begins from birth and continues throughout their life. This is evident from the fact that female Infant Mortality Rate (IMR) is higher than male IMR in all the 15 states and also at the all-India level (Table 10.1). This female disadvantage exists despite the fact that girls have a biological advantage in survival at birth over boys. Gender gap in IMR is most pronounced in the state of Haryana. It is not, therefore, surprising that Haryana has the lowest sex ratio among the 15 states.

Gender bias is also reflected in women-specific indicators like Total Fertility Rate (TFR), Maternal Mortality Rate (MMR), percentage of women suffering from anaemia, etc. TFR is considered to be an important indicator for studying female disadvantage. The greater the number of children women bear during their reproductive years, the less time and energy they will have for income-generating work. It also adversely affects their lifespan. Reduction in TFR is generally taken as an indicator of women's relative autonomy in decision-making within the household. Like sex ratio, TFR also shows a distinct regional pattern (refer Table 10.1). Southern states have relatively lower levels of TFR while it is high in states like Rajasthan, Uttar Pradesh, Bihar and Madhya Pradesh. Gender discrimination in resource allocation within the household and high levels of TFR result in high percentage of malnourished women. Percentage of women suffering from anaemia is quite high in the states of Assam, Bihar, Orissa and West Bengal. This factor assumes greater importance in case of pregnant women with adverse effect both on the mother and the child. These factors often interact with each other and result in high rates of maternal mortality. From Table 10.1, we observe that the states of Rajasthan, Uttar Pradesh, Bihar and Madhya Pradesh not only have high levels of TFR, but have high levels of MMR too. MMR is also high in Assam and Orissa—states with high percentage of anemic women. In fact, the state of Bihar shows poor performance in terms of all the three indicators.

Women's education is considered to be crucial in the study of gender disparity as education enhances a person's capability and reduces deprivation. Table 10.1 shows three educational indicators—Female Literacy Rate (FLR) in the age-group 15-49 years, Gender Disparity in Literacy Rates and Gender Disparity in Gross Enrolment Ratio (GER) for classes I-VIII. FLR is high in the states of Kerala, Tamil Nadu and Maharashtra while is very low in the states of Rajasthan, Uttar Pradesh, Bihar and Madhya Pradesh. Bihar and Rajasthan also have high gender disparity in literacy rates and GER.

A very important indicator of women's autonomy is female Labour Force Participation Rate (LFPR). Female LFPR is much lower that male LFPR in all the 15 states though it is relatively high in the states of Andhra Pradesh, Madhya Pradesh and Rajasthan. This is mainly because of the fact that men are generally expected to participate in market-based economic activities and become the breadwinners of the family while women are entrusted with the sacred duty of looking after and providing care to members of the household. As a result, women spend a major part of their time in household activities and are counted as not in the labour force. This feature often plays a very crucial role in explaining gender differences in intra-household resource allocation which in turn affects other outcomes of men and women.

Keeping this in mind, in the next section, we try to study in a little more detail gender difference in time-use patterns of men and women which is expected to provide useful insights for further analysis of gender discrimination.

3. GENDER INEQUALITY IN TIME-USE PATTERN

Conventional statistics on labour force and national income are expected to provide information on productive time-use by people (in economic activities) and the output produced by them, both of which present a basis for economic policy and planning. Since the market is viewed as the core of economic activity, participation in the labour force as well as the inclusion of production into national income accounts has been defined in relation to their connection to the market or to the performance of some "work for payor profit" (as defined by the International Conference on Labour Force Statistics, ILO, 1954). However, in almost every country (more so in underdeveloped countries), many productive activities are carried out outside the domain of the market. A major part of these activities is accounted for by the goods and services produced within the household, mainly for self-consumption. Women, all over the world, produce different goods and services for their household members. However, since these activities fall outside the purview of the market, they are considered as not having any economic value. Therefore, in all countries, these non-market "household care products" are not included in the domain of economic activity. But these unpaid household activities have definite opportunity costs and, therefore, economic worth. By ignoring the value of household work, our official statistics fail to capture the total production of the country and ignore the production efforts of a substantial portion of the population (mainly women and girls) whose production of non-market goods and services enable the conventional economy of the country to function effectively. Hence, a proper estimate of the country's economic activities would be possible only if imputed value of these activities are assessed and incorporated in the national income of the country. Moreover, it has to be remembered that human development comes about not only through greater incomes, better health and education and a better environment, but also through care. In fact, *care labour*—the work of providing care not only for the sick, the elderly and infirm, but just as much for each other, ones' dependents including children—is crucial for the quality and sustainability of *economic labour.* Most adults and children need care for emotional, physical and mental development as well as to maintain the capabilities acquired. A major part of this work is provided within the household by women and girls (often at the cost of schooling) with no remuneration. However, when it comes to benefits, they do not share equally.

Another feature to be noted is that, as social transformation takes place in the process of development, the same work can shift from non-market to market (e.g. food-processing, cooking and geriatric care in developing economies) and from market to non-market (e.g. house cleaning, laundry, etc. in developed economies). This is completely missed out by official statistical systems which focus primarily on market work resulting in wrong conclusions about increase or decrease in national incomes. Time-use data have greater potential for capturing aspects of social transformation. We, thus, observe that, apart from feminist perspectives, time-use surveys give more complete labour statistics and better capture the process of social transformation. It also makes explicit the work of children.

A fair amount of literature is now available on the evaluation of household services in the developed countries. The issue is slowly gaining importance in the developing world too. In its 50th round survey operations (July 1993 to June 1994), the National Sample Survey Organization (NSSO) paid attention to the issue of women's participation in housework. In this round, data was collected on participation of women in household work and other specified household activities which resulted in economic benefits to their households, for preparing an estimate of persons engaged in such activities at all-India and state level. The results have been published in Report No. 416 ("Participation of Indian Women in Household Work and Other Specified Activities, 1993-94"). In April 2000, the Central Statistical Organization (CSO) published a report based on a time-use survey conducted in six states of India. The time-use survey was conducted in 18,591 households spread over the states of Haryana, Madhya Pradesh, Gujarat, Orissa, Tamil Nadu and Meghalaya. The main objective of the survey was to collect data to properly quantify the economic contribution of women in the national economy and to study the degree of inherent gender discrimination in household activities. The field work of the survey was done during July 1998 to June 1999. A new activity classification has been used in this survey. All the activities were grouped into the following nine categories:

I. Primary production activities
II. Secondary activities
III. Trade, business and services
IV. Household maintenance, management and shopping for own household
V. Care for children, the sick, elderly and disabled of own household
VI. Community services and help to other households
VII. Learning
VIII. Social and cultural activities, mass media, etc.
IX. Personal care and self-maintenance

Categories I, II and III are directly identified as SNA (System of National Accounts) activities while categories IV, V and VI are grouped as extended-SNA activities. Finally, categories VII, VIII and IX are grouped as non-SNA activities. The time-use survey reports the weekly average time spent on these three broad groups of activities by sex (male/female) and place of residence (rural/urban). It also gives a detailed report of the household characteristics of the surveyed population as well as the respondents' background characteristics. Table 10.2 shows gender inequality in time-use pattern as observed from the survey.

A few interesting observations came up from the analysis of time spent on different broad activity groups at the all-state combined level. Total number of hours available in a week is 168 including the hours for sleep and rest. The direct (or explicit) economic activities are reported in SNA category whereas the implicit economic activities are reported in extended-SNA category. The non-SNA group basically reports the residual value. The survey reveals that out of 168 hours in a week, on an average, men spend about 42 hours in SNA activities as compared to about 19 hours by women. However, the situation completely changes when we consider the extended-SNA activities. In these activities, men spend only about 3.65 hours as compared to 34.63 hours spent by women.

TABLE 10.2

Gender Differences in Weekly Average Time (in hrs.) Spent on SNA, Extended-SNA and Non-SNA Activities

States	*SNA Activities*			*Extended-SNA Activities*			*Non-SNA Activities*		
	M	*F*	*M-F*	*M*	*F*	*M-F*	*M*	*F*	*M-F*
(1)	*(2)*	*(3)*	*(4)*	*(5)*	*(6)*	*(7)*	*(8)*	*(9)*	*(10)*
Haryana	37.72	21.26	16.46	1.99	31.06	-29.07	128.23	115.67	12.56
Madhya Pradesh	42.07	19.85	22.22	4.43	35.79	-31.36	121.47	112.38	9.09
Gujarat	43.63	17.60	26.03	3.19	39.08	-35.89	121.12	111.36	9.76
Orissa	40.12	17.07	23.05	4.47	35.70	-31.23	123.45	115.20	8.25
Tamil Nadu	42.54	18.93	23.61	3.19	30.46	-27.27	122.27	118.61	3.66
Meghalaya	45.94	26.34	19.6	7.16	34.52	-27.36	114.78	107.15	7.63
Combined	41.96	18.72	23.24	3.65	34.63	-30.98	122.42	114.58	7.84

Note : Gender gap = M-F.

Source : Central Statistical Organization (2000), "Time-use Survey".

We can see that the total average working time of men (45.6 hrs.) is less than that of women (53.6 hrs.). Moreover, we find that males spend 92.11% of their total working time on direct or explicit economic activities and 7.89% on implicit economic activities. The explicit-implicit break-up of this percentage for women is 35.45% and 64.55%. The explicit-implicit break-up for females reveals a dominance of implicit activities. The pattern is more or less the same in all the six states. Thus, on an average, females spend more time on economic activities (explicit and implicit combined). However, this effort being mostly non-marketed in nature passes unnoticed.

TABLE 10.3

Rural-Urban Gap in Weekly Average Time (in hours) Spent on Extended-SNA Activities

States	*Rural*		*Urban*	
	Male	*Female*	*Male*	*Female*
Haryana	1.74	30.67	3.11	32.74
Madhya Pradesh	4.42	35.47	4.43	36.99
Gujarat	3.25	37.55	3.09	41.57
Orissa	4.34	35.28	5.00	37.61
Tamil Nadu	3.51	29.52	2.70	32.08
Meghalaya	7.02	34.55	7.96	34.39
Combined	3.74	33.95	3.44	36.44

The survey also shows that there is not much difference in the time allocated to extended SNA activities among the rural and urban areas (Table 10.3). But urban men and women seem to devote slightly more time to these activities. This may be due to the fact that the urban system is more impersonal and market-oriented. Hence, even when an activity is unpaid in nature its recognition as a potential economic contribution is more likely in urban compared to rural areas.

However, when we look at the rural-urban break-up, significant variations have been observed in time-use pattern over the states. Maximum time spent in extended-SNA activities for rural males is observed in Meghalaya (7.02 hrs.) followed by

Madhya Pradesh (4.42 hrs.) and Orissa (4.34 hrs.). Minimum is observed in Haryana (1.74 hrs.). Here, it should be noted that empirical studies have shown that bias towards the malechild is greater in northern India compared to the other parts. This might be the reason behind the very low participation of males in housework in Haryana. In case of rural females, maximum time spent on housework is observed in Gujarat (37.55 hrs.) followed by M.P. (35.47 hrs.) and Orissa (35.28 hrs.). Minimum time is observed in Tamil Nadu (29.52 hrs.). The trend is somewhat similar in the urban areas. The survey also found that time spent on extended-SNA activities by currently married and widowed females was higher than that of never married and divorced. No significant impact of educational level was found in such activities.

The time-use survey provides for the first time data on some of the important activities which generally fall in the domain of women's lives. It reveals the extent of productive activities carried out by women within the domains of the household, but which are not considered as economic activity by our official statistics. In the next section, we turn our attention towards the construction of composite indices for the analysis of gender discrimination and female deprivation.

4. CONSTRUCTION OF COMPOSITE INDICES

In Section II, we looked at inter-state differences in gender-based inequality and women's deprivation as reflected by a few important indicators. However, we observe that in many cases, a state may have good performance with respect to one indicator but relatively poorer performance with respect to another. Therefore, in order to make overall comparison of the states, we construct two composite indices—Index of Gender Disparity (IGD) and Index of Female Deprivation (IFD). The indices have been computed for 15 major states of India for the year 2001. The indicators used for the construction of the two indices are shown in Table 10.4. The indicators have been chosen so as to reflect different dimensions of women's life like health and nutrition, education and participation in economic activity. In case of IGD, all the indicators denote some kind of male-female gap while the indicators of IFD are specific to women.

For constructing the composite indices, we first compute a deprivation index for each indicator. The deprivation index has been calculated by using the UNDP formula:

$$Z_{ij} = (\text{max. } X_i - X_{ij})/(\text{max. } X_i - \text{min. } X_i)$$

where Z_{ij} denotes the deprivation index for the jth region with respect to the ith indicator (X_i) and X_{ij} denotes the actual value of the ith indicator for the jth region. Since Z_{ij} is a deprivation index, lower the value of the index, lower is the level of deprivation denoted by it. However, in case of those indicators for which a higher value denotes a higher level of deprivation, the deprivation index has been computed as $(I - Z_{ij})$.

TABLE 10.4
Indicators Used in the Construction of the Composite Indices

Indicators used for constructing IGD	*Indicators used for constructing IFD*
Sex Ratio, Gender Disparity in Literacy Rates, Gender	Female Literacy Rate, Total Fertility Rate.
Disparity in Dropout Rate (Class I-X), Gender Disparity in	Proportion of Women with Anaemia.
Labour Force Participation Rate, Gender Disparity in Gross Enrolment Ratio (6-14 yrs.), Gender Disparity in Life	Female Life Expectancy at Birth. Female Labour Force Participation Rate
Expectancy at Birth	

Note : "Gender Disparity in Literacy Rates" has been computed as (Female Literacy Rate/Male Literacy Rate) * 100 following CSO (2007). The other disparity indicators have been computed in a similar manner.

Table 10.5 shows the values of IGD and IFD for the year 2001 along with the corresponding ranks of the states. From the table we observe that, on the basis of IGD, KER occupies the top position while UP occupies the bottom position. That is, among the 15 states gender disparity is lowest in KER (0.101) and highest in UP (0.872). It is to be noted that the range of deprivation is quite large. Moreover, all the southern states show relatively less gender disparity compared to others.

When IGD is compared with IFD, we find a very high correlation between the two indices (0.939). That is, states with high levels of female deprivation also exhibit high gender disparity. However, there are exceptions. For example, ASM occupies 9th rank with respect to IGD and 13th with respect to IFD while it is just the opposite in case of HAR. Again, MAH occupies the 2nd position with respect to IFD and 5th with respect to IGD while RAJ occupies 8th position with respect to IFD and 11th with respect to IGD.

TABLE 10.5
IGD and IFD for the Year 2001

States	*IGD*		*IFD*	
	Value	*Rank*	*Value*	*Rank*
AP	0.335	3	0.398	5
ASM	0.592	9	0.780	13
BIH	0.842	14	0.911	15
GUJ	0.489	7	0.481	7
HAR	0.652	13	0.593	9
KAR	0.372	4	0.396	4
KER	0.101	I	0.118	I
MP	0.607	10	0.642	11
MAH	0.432	5	0.360	2
ORS	0.619	11	0.648	12
PUN	0.483	6	0.400	6
RAJ	0.651	12	0.593	8
TN	0.324	2	0.378	3
UP	0.872	15	0.814	14
WB	0.582	8	0.625	10

Data Sources: (1) Planning Commission (2002), Government of India, "National Human Development Report, 2001".
(2) Economic Survey, 2003-04.
(3) Sample Registration System, 2005-06.

When the states are classified into certain range of values of IGD and IFD as shown in Table 10.6, it is observed that the states of AP, GUJ, KAR, KER, MAH, PUN and TN have absolute value of indices less than 0.5 for both IGD and IFD. That is, these states show relatively good performance with respect to both indicators. However, 8 states have values of IGD and IFD greater that 0.5.

TABLE 10.6
Classification of States on the basis of IGD and IFD for the year 2001

Value of the index	*IGD*	*IFD*
≤ 0.5	AP, GUJ, KAR, KER, MAH, PUN, TN	AP, GUJ, KAR, KER, MAH, PUN, TN
> 0.5 to ≤ 0.7	ASM, HAR, MP, ORS, RAJ, WB	HAR, MP, ORS, RAJ, WB
> 0.7	BIH, UP	ASM, BIH, UP

Therefore, it is observed that there exist considerable variations across the states both in terms of female deprivation and gender disparity.

5. CONCLUSION

This paper has tried to assess the extent of gender disparity in 15 major states of India. An attempt has been made to study both levels of female deprivation and gender disparity in some important dimensions of human life. The analysis has been done on the basis of important socio-economic indicators as well as on the basis of suitable composite indices. Attention has also been drawn towards gender differences in time-use pattern of men and women which often plays a very crucial role in determining intra-household resource allocation.

The study of time-use pattern of men and women reveals the extent of productive activities carried out by women within the domains of the household. In fact, women, on an average, spend more time on productive activities compared to men. However, most of the work that women do is non-marketed and unpaid in nature. Hence, it very often escapes the notice of society. This adversely affects their position and share of resources within the household. As a result, women lag behind men in every sphere of life.

The paper finds the existence of considerable variations across the states both in terms of female deprivation and gender disparity. Among the 15 major states, AP, GUJ, KAR, KER, MAH, PUN and TN show relatively good performance with respect to both female deprivation as well as gender disparity. Here it should be noted that in addition to regional variations, considerable rural-urban differences also exist. The paper also finds that gender disparity is highly correlated with female literacy rate but not so strongly correlated with per capita income or female labour force participation rate. This seems to indicate that female education can play a very crucial role in narrowing the existing gender gap. Education enhances women's capability and helps them to fight oppression. It makes them aware of their rights and privileges and improves their decision-making power within the household. Thus, from a policy angle, female education should be given utmost priority if we are to move towards the goal of gender equality.

References

Agarwal, Bina (1997), "Gender, Environment and Poverty Interlinks: Regional Variations and Temporal Shifts in Rural India, 1971-91", *World Development*, Vol. 25, No. I, pp. 23-52.

Aslaksen, lulie and Koren, Charlotte, "Unpaid Household Work and the Distribution of Extended Income: The Norwegian Experience", *Feminist Economics*, Vol. 2, No. 3, Fall 1996. Central Statistical Organization (2000), "Time-use Survey".

Central Statistical Organization (2007), "Proceedings of the National Seminar on Gender Statistics and Data Gaps, 5th Feb., 2004".

Dreze, Jean and Sen, Amartya (1989), "Hunger and Public Action", Clarendon Press, Oxford.

Hamid, Shamim, "Non-Market Work and National Income: The Case of Bangladesh", *The Bangladesh Development Studies*, Vol. XXII, June-September, 1994, Numbers 2 & 3.

Ironmonger, Duncan, "Counting Outputs, Capital Inputs and Caring Labour: Estimating Gross Household Product", *Feminist Economics*, Vol. 2, No. 3, Fall 1996.

Krishnaraj, Maithreyi and Chanana, Kamna ed., "Gender and the Household Domain: Social and Cultural Dimensions".

NSSO, Report No. 416 ("Participation of Indian Women in Household Work and Other Specified Activities, 1993-94").

Parikh, Kirit S. and Radhakrishna, R. ed. "India Development Report, 2004-05", IGIDR. Planning Commission (2002), National Human Development Report, India.

Robeyns, Ingrid (2006), "Sen's Capability Approach and Gender Inequality: Selecting Relevant Capabilities" in Agarwal, Bina, Humphries, Jane and Robeyns, Ingrid (2006) ed. "Capabilities, Freedom and Equality: Amartya Sen's work from a Gender Perspective", OUP.

Wages and Employment in India : The Post-Reform Dynamics

DIPA MUKHERJEE

1. INTRODUCTION

One of the major objectives of the economic planners in a labour surplus economy is to utilise its human resource up to the fullest extent. Apart from utilising available manpower optimally, this also helps in uplifting living standards of its citizen through provisioning of remunerative jobs. As a result, employment creation and wage security are primary goals of developing countries. This is true for India too, and since the Sixth Five Year Plan, wages and employment have been the thrust areas in our planning process. It was accepted at an early stage that mere creation of employment opportunities would not be enough for a populous country like us, and the nature of the jobs would also be important. Given the highly skewed nature of distribution of productive assets in our country, the likelihood of workers being exploited by employers is substantial. While being gainfully employed or not creates a primary divide in the economy, a secondary divide is created along high or low wages and permanency or otherwise of the job. And such divides by no means can be ignored.

Thus growth of employment, especially wage employment; nature of such employment growth and associated trends in wages are factors that are important both from the context of resource utilisation and that of poverty and inequality. In this paper we explore these issues in India.

We use NSSO data on Employment and Unemployment from the 50th and 55th Round surveys of NSSO pertaining to the years 1993-94 and 1999-2000 and in few cases those available from the latest NSSO Report for the 61st Round. This paper includes seven sections. In the next section a brief survey of recent works on related issues are mentioned. In the third section we provide an overview of the trends in employment and wages in India in the post-reform Period. The employment-wage linkage is discussed in the fourth section and the dynamics of the wage-employment process in the fifth. Factors affecting wage levels are explored in the sixth section and the seventh section sums up the study.

2. WAGE AND EMPLOYMENT—A BRIEF SURVEY

There have been several explorations of the issues related to wages and employment, at the theoretical level and in the Indian context.

It is often argued that low wage rate is not beneficial to economic development. Past records show that wage pressure often provides the inducement to technological innovation and also better working conditions (*Banerjee, 2005*). Though employment elasticity with respect to real wage is found to be negative, it does not necessarily mean that lowering of real wage leads to expansion of employment. Moreover, lowering real wage beyond a certain level may accentuate the problem of poverty (*Bhattacharya and Shaktivel, 2005*). Even the overall rise in real wage may result from substantial rise in wage level for one group of workers only, thereby leading to rising inequality.

Several studies have been put forward to analyse the kind of transformation that the wage structure is undergoing in the post-reform Period in India—both at aggregate level and across gender, sector, region, and different educational levels. Vasudeva Dutta (2005) has found rising wage inequality among regular workers and declining wage inequality among casual workers during 1983-99 for the adult male workers. Shareef and Gumber (2005) found that the reforms programme has helped the urban workers only, while benefits to the rural workforce are limited, targeted mainly towards the highly educated segment. They have also found that there has been a substantial increase in both real wages and gender gap in wages in rural areas. Considerable gender inequality in wages has also been observed by Rastogi (2005). Duraiswamy & Duraiswamy (2005) analysed returns to education in terms of wage premia and concluded that lowest wage premia per year of education is available for Primary education and highest to Secondary education.

Against this backdrop we would analyse the dynamics of employment and wages in India in the post-reform period. The interaction between them is proceeded by a brief overview of trends in employment and wages. Subsequently we also try to determine the factors that affect wage rates.

3. TRENDS IN EMPLOYMENT AND WAGES

1. Employment Trends

Total employment in India has increased from 300 million in 1993 to 340 million in 1999 (Tables 11.1(a) and (b)). During this period population increased from 778 million to 920 million, and the active workforce from 311 million to 355 million. Thus growth in labour-force lagged behind population growth rate during 1993-99 leading to a drop in Work Participation Rate from 40 per cent to 38.5 per cent. However, employment has grown further slowly and employment rate (as percentage of workforce) has declined from 96.4 per cent to 95.8 per cent during this period. However, during 1999-2004 period there has been a reversal of trend as regards labour market participation and WPR increased to 41 per cent. But

TABLE 11.1(a)
Total and Wage Employment in India—1993-99 by States

(in Millions)

State	Total Employment			Wage Employment			Share of Wage Employment (%)		
	1993	1999	2004	1993	1999	2004	1993	1999	2004
(1)	(2)	(3)	(4)	(5)	(6)	(7)	(8)	(9)	(10)
Andhra Pradesh	29.54	32.76	33.70	14.83	16.70	17.80	50.2	51.0	52.8
Arunachal Pradesh	0.30	0.27	0.36	0.06	0.05	0.07	21.0	18.4	20.3
Assam	6.65	7.21	8.74	2.83	2.98	2.75	42.6	41.3	31.5
Bihar	22.49	28.82	29.61	10.37	12.17	11.19	46.1	42.2	37.8
Goa	0.32	0.39	0.34	0.19	0.26	0.21	61.2	66.9	63.0
Gujarat	15.95	18.78	21.27	8.22	8.99	10.56	51.5	47.9	49.6
Haryana	5.68	6.17	8.14	2.11	2.24	2.98	37.1	36.3	36.6
Himachal Pradesh	2.43	2.51	2.86	0.47	0.58	0.77	19.2	23.1	27.0
J & K	0.88	2.59	2.38	0.24	0.60	0.64	27.0	23.3	27.0
Karnataka	18.12	20.97	22.67	8.49	10.22	11.90	46.9	48.7	52.5
Kerala	8.23	9.12	10.65	4.59	5.33	5.92	55.8	58.4	55.6
Madhya Pradesh	25.77	29.60	23.34	9.80	11.45	9.71	38.0	38.7	41.6
Maharashtra	30.05	36.03	39.46	15.72	19.70	21.05	52.3	54.7	53.4
Manipur	0.55	0.57	0.75	0.19	0.14	0.14	35.5	24.0	19.0
Meghalaya	0.76	0.75	1.02	0.18	0.19	0.26	23.9	25.3	25.4
Mizoram	0.22	0.24	0.33	0.06	0.05	0.06	29.2	22.5	19.4

(Contd.)

TABLE 11.1(a) (Contd.)

(1)	(2)	(3)	(4)	(5)	(6)	(7)	(8)	(9)	(10)
Nagaland	0.16	0.27	0.35	0.05	0.08	0.06	31.0	28.9	17.8
Orissa	11.84	12.61	13.66	4.93	5.76	5.90	41.6	45.6	43.2
Punjab	6.81	8.16	9.61	2.68	3.04	3.96	39.3	37.3	41.2
Rajasthan	16.76	17.50	21.92	4.08	4.29	5.88	24.3	24.5	26.8
Sikkim	0.13	0.17	0.21	0.05	0.07	0.07	41.6	39.9	34.9
Tamil Nadu	25.29	25.45	26.08	14.65	15.57	15.20	57.9	61.2	58.3
Tripura	0.81	0.82	1.02	0.42	0.42	0.50	51.1	51.6	48.8
Uttar Pradesh	44.58	50.38	57.98	11.55	13.20	15.45	25.9	26.2	26.7
West Bengal	22.31	23.48	28.24	10.68	10.58	13.32	47.9	45.1	47.2
Andamans	0.11	0.11	0.11	0.06	0.05	0.06	56.3	48.2	56.4
Chandigarh	0.22	0.31	0.30	0.17	0.20	0.21	76.5	64.9	68.6
Dadra & NH	0.06	0.07	0.09	0.03	0.03	0.05	57.1	47.9	57.8
Daman	0.03	0.05	0.05	0.02	0.03	0.03	55.0	59.7	62.0
Delhi	2.87	3.93	3.85	1.66	2.10	2.53	58.0	53.4	65.8
Lakshadweep	0.01	0.01	0.02	0.01	0.01	0.01	66.9	58.4	72.8
Pondicherry	0.23	0.28	0.30	0.15	0.20	0.20	65.4	70.9	67.0
LIG States[a]	183.07	207.64	218.02	70.16	78.60	82.40	38.3	37.9	37.8
HIG States[a]	117.11	132.73	151.34	59.41	68.66	77.07	50.7	51.7	50.9
All India	300.18	340.37	378.57	129.57	147.26	163.60	43.2	43.3	43.2

Note : a—Low Income and High Income states are as defined in text.
Source : Author's calculations based on NSSO (1995), NSSO (2001), and NSSO (2006).

TABLE 11.1(b)
Growth in Total and Wage Employment in India—1993-2004 by States

States	1993-99		1999-04		States	1993-99		1999-04	
	Total	Wage	Total	Wage		Total	Wage	Total	Wage
(1)	(2)	(3)	(4)	(5)	(6)	(7)	(8)	(9)	(10)
Andhra Pradesh	1.7	2.0	0.6	1.3	Nagaland	9.1	8.2	5.3	-4.9
Arunachal Pradesh	-1.7	-4.1	5.9	8.1	Orissa	1.1	2.6	1.6	0.5
Assam	1.4	0.9	3.9	-1.6	Punjab	3.1	2.1	3.3	5.4
Bihar	4.2	2.7	0.5	-1.7	Rajasthan	0.7	0.8	4.6	6.5
Goa	3.4	5.2	-2.7	-4.0	Sikkim	4.6	3.1	4.3	0.9
Gujarat	2.8	1.5	2.5	3.3	Tamil Nadu	0.1	1.0	0.5	-0.5
Haryana	1.4	1.0	5.7	5.9	Tripura	0.2	0.2	4.5	3.4
Himachal Pradesh	0.5	3.7	2.6	5.9	Uttar Pradesh	2.1	2.3	2.8	3.2
J & K	19.7	16.7	-1.7	1.3	West Bengal	0.9	-0.2	3.8	4.7
Karnataka	2.5	3.1	1.6	3.1	Andamans	0.0	-2.3	0.0	3.8
Kerala	1.7	2.5	3.2	2.1	Chandigarh	5.9	2.9	-0.7	0.7
Madhya Pradesh	2.3	2.6	-4.6	-3.2	Dadra & Nagar	2.6	0.1	5.2	12.3
Maharashtra	3.1	3.8	1.8	1.3	Daman	8.9	7.3	0.0	1.3
Manipur	0.6	-5.8	5.6	0.3	Delhi	5.4	3.9	-0.4	3.8
Meghalaya	-0.2	0.8	6.3	6.4	Lakshadweep	0.0	1.2	14.9	5.4
Mizoram	1.5	-3.0	6.6	4.9	Pondicherry	3.3	4.4	1.4	0.1
LIG States*	2.1	1.9	1.0	0.9	All India	2.1	2.2	2.2	2.1
BIG States*	2.1	2.4	2.7	2.3					

Note : a—Low Income and High Income states are as defined in text.
Source : Author's calculations based on NSSO (1995), NSSO (2001), and NSSO (2006).

employment has still lagged behind growth in labour force and employment rate has further declined to 95.7 per cent in 2004.

Against this backdrop, the share of wage employment in total employment has increased marginally from 43.2 to 43.3 per cent during 1993-99 and again declined to its earlier level during 1999-04. Substantial regional variation in share of wage employment exists, with wage employment being the predominant form in Chandigarh, Goa, Lakshadweep, Pondicherry, Delhi, Tamilnadu and Kerala. On the contrary, this share is significantly low in Himachal Pradesh, Arunachal Pradesh, Meghalaya and Uttar Pradesh in all the years. As expected, incidence of wage employment is significantly higher in the High Income Group (HIG) states compared to the Low Income Group (LIG) states and the gap between them has widened during 1993-2004.[1]

Concentrating on wage workers alone it is observed that during 1993-99 total wage employment has increased from 129 million to 147 million—growing at about 2.2 per cent per annum and to 163 million in 2004, growing at 2.1 per cent per annum. This growth, however, is not uniform—number of wage workers declining in Arunachal Pradesh, Manipur, Mizoram, West Bengal and the Andamans among the states, and in Production-related jobs among NOC groups during 1993-99.[2] Within this, growth has been faster for Regular workers (3.2 per cent per annum) compared to the Casual workers (1.6 per cent per annum) (Table 11.3).[3] Regular employment is predominant in occupations like Technical, Clerical and Administrative jobs; and naturally very low in Farming occupations. Due to these structural differences, the smaller states and UTs with predominant Tertiary sector have high share of regular workers. The share of regular workers is found to be increasing in almost all occupations except the farming sector where it is decreasing marginally. The rise in incidence of regular employment is most striking for the production-related sector. Juxtaposed with the decline in absolute number of workers in this sector, it is obvious that the brunt has been borne by the casual workers whose numbers in this sector have declined at 6.2 per cent per annum.

There is also a marked shift in the occupational distribution of wage workers from directly productive activities

Table 11.2
Total and Wage Employment in India—1993-2004 by Occupation

(*in Millions*)

Occupation Group	*Total Employment*			*Wage Employment*		*Share of Wage Employment (%)*		*Growth in Employment (% pa)*		
								Total		*Wage*
	1993	*1999*	*2004*	*1993*	*1999*	*1993*	*1999*	*1993-99*	*1999-04*	*1993-99*
(1)	*(2)*	*(3)*	*(4)*	*(5)*	*(6)*	*(7)*	*(8)*	*(9)*	*(10)*	*(11)*
Professionals	9.57	16.89	14.91	3.81	5.69	39.8	33.7	9.9	-10.2	6.9
Technical	7.22	8.60		5.45	6.36	75.5	73.9	3.0		2.6
Administrative	5.92	9.95	13.09	1.22	1.47	20.7	14.8	9.0	.5.6	3.1
Clerical	9.13	10.48	10.40	8.65	9.92	94.8	94.7	2.3	-0.1	2.3
Sales	21.17	23.12	30.76	2.95	3.81	13.9	16.5	1.5	5.9	4.4
Service	10.46	13.62	15.97	6.70	8.13	64.0	59.7	4.5	3.2	3.3
Farmers etc.	182.68	192.35	209.23	67.51	71.88	37.0	37.4	0.9	1.7	1.1
Production etc.	17.17	17.97	25.54	8.07	7.06	47.0	39.3	0.8	7.3	-2.2
Transport	12.31	13.94	19.91	6.72	8.12	54.6	58.3	2.1	7.4	3.2
Labourers nec.	24.54	33.45	35.52	18.48	24.81	75.3	74.2	5.3	1.2	5.0
All Occupations	300.18	340.37	378.57	129.57	147.26	43.2	43.3	2.1	2.1	2.2

Note : Occupational Classes are as in One-digit codes of National Classification of Occupations, 1968.
Source : Author's calculations based on NSSO (1995), NSSO (2001), and NSSO (2006).

TABLE 11.3
Regular and Casual Employment in India by Occupation

(in Millions)

Occupation Group	*Regular Employment*		*Casual Employment*		*Growth in Employment % per annum*	
	1993	*1999*	*1993*	*1999*	*Regular*	*Casual*
Professionals	2.39 (62.7)	3.49 (61.3)	1.48 (38.7)	2.21 (38.7)	6.5	6.9
Technical	5.32 (97.5)	6.24 (98.1)	0.19 (3.4)	0.12 (1.9)	2.7	-6.9
Administrative	1.08 (88.3)	1.42 (96.5)	0.15 (12.3)	0.05 (3.5)	4.7	-16.5
Clerical	8.47 (97.8)	9.60 (96.8)	0.24 (2.8)	0.32 (3.2)	2.1	5.0
Sales	2.11 (71.7)	3.05 (80.0)	0.84 (28.6)	0.76 (20.0)	6.3	-1.7
Service	5.00 (74.6)	6.10 (75.0)	1.74 (26.0)	2.03 (25.0)	3.4	2.6
Farmers etc.	3.09 (4.6)	3.08 (4.3)	64.45 (95.5)	68.80 (95.7)	-0.1	1.1
Production etc.	3.75 (46.5)	4.10 (58.1)	4.34 (53.8)	2.96 (41.9)	1.5	-6.2
Transport	4.24 (63.1)	5.40 (66.5)	2.50 (37.2)	2.72 (33.5)	4.1	1.4
Labourers nec.	5.27 (28.5)	6.79 (27.4)	13.28 (71.9)	18.02 (72.6)	4.3	5.2
All Occupations	40.71 (31.4)	49.28 (33.5)	89.21 (68.8)	97.98 (66.5)	3.2	1.6

Note : Figures in parenthesis are shares in total employment.
Source : Author's calculations.

(DPA—Farming and Production workers) to Tertiary occupations during 1993-99. But during 1999-04 period total employment declined substantially for Professionals and Technicals and increased for the Production group. How much of this is reflected in wage employment can be investigated only when further detailed database are available from NSSO. More of this dynamics will be discussed later.

TABLE 11.4
Average Wage Per Week by States

(in Rs. per worker)

States	*All*		*Regular*		*Casual*	
	1993	*1999*	*1993*	*1999*	*1993*	*1999*
Andhra Pradesh	251	353	592	765	156	207
Arunachal Pradesh	555	1164	632	1590	343	411
Assam	384	515	606	763	238	291
Bihar	271	343	815	1144	172	205
Goa	607	775	784	953	338	467
Gujarat	363	465	723	1000	201	246
Haryana	510	735	740	1040	308	370
Himachal Pradesh	661	890	943	1250	348	408
J & K	703	982	870	1277	343	492
Karnataka	346	424	825	965	177	225
Kerala	441	569	720	813	331	447
Madhya Pradesh	304	334	670	851	171	178
Maharashtra	425	502	819	944	165	203
Manipur	665	949	906	1303	471	345
Meghalaya	537	696	896	1239	265	337
Mizoram	611	1241	939	1597	364	452
Nagaland	934	1196	1004	1231	484	552
Orissa	264	313	665	936	150	163
Punjab	552	672	725	874	412	421
Rajasthan	497	642	796	1001	287	347
Sikkim	594	877	782	1094	279	286
Tamil Nadu	303	423	600	720	176	252
Tripura	461	522	800	972	312	318
Uttar Pradesh	390	496	746	886	212	240
West Bengal	410	479	727	973	214	244
Andamans	719	936	868	1167	342	485
Chandigarh	799	968	912	1014	450	432
Dadra & NH	272	571	612	832	185	360
Daman	638	698	688	794	580	340
Delhi	821	1405	892	1469	545	446
Lakshadweep	727	1002	837	1122	446	687
Pondicherry	394	446	575	664	194	273
LIG States[a]	334	418	707	908	188	218
HIG States[a]	401	523	753	939	209	260
All India	365	467	730	925	197	236

Note : a—Low Income and High Income states are as defined in text.
Source : Author's calculations.

2. Trends in Wages

In real terms average wage per worker per week has increased from Rs. 365 in 1993 to Rs. 467 in 1999, rising by about 4.2 per cent per annum (Table 11.4). Average wage for the casual workers has increased from Rs. 197 to Rs. 236 and that for the regular workers from Rs. 730 to Rs. 925 during this period. The regular workers are thus earning about four times per week compared to the casual workers. The average wage per manday for regular workers is twice that of casual workers, indicating that availability of jobs per week for the casual workers are almost half of that of the regular workers (Table 11.5). Average wage per manday in the aggregate has increased from Rs. 52 to Rs. 79, growing by 7.2 per cent per annum, i.e. at a faster rate than average wage per week. This hints at a declining availability of workday per week.

TABLE 11.5
Average Wage per Week by Occupation

(in Rs. per worker)

Occupation Group	*All*		*Regular*		*Casual*	
	1993	*1999*	*1993*	*1999*	*1993*	*1999*
Professionals	807	1045	1176	1557	188	235
Technical	975	1254	990	1270	425	434
Administrative	1672	2288	1830	2359	483	305
Clerical	873	1114	884	1129	351	650
Sales	399	482	428	523	323	319
Service	418	569	492	671	200	262
Farmers etc.	175	203	281	348	170	197
Production etc.	361	458	521	562	222	315
Transport	560	643	707	777	307	375
Labourers nec.	367	437	573	698	285	338
All Occupations	365	467	730	925	197	236

Note : Occupational Classes are as in One-digit Codes of National Classification of Occupations, 1968.

Source : Author's calculations.

There are however substantial disparities around these averages and while wage rates are considerably higher in Delhi, Chandigarh, the North-eastern states, Himachal Pradesh and most of the UTs, it is quite low in the lagging states like Orissa, Madhya Pradesh, Bihar and Tamilnadu. Administrative and Professional workers are highest paid workers, whereas wages in the Farming and Production-related jobs are the lowest (Tables 11.6 and 11.7). This hierarchy in wage structure is true for the subset of regular workers also. However, for the casual workers, the professionals are one of the lowest paid groups, perhaps because of a large part of them consists of 'professionals' of the lowest category, e.g. barbers, carpenters, cooks, blacksmiths, etc.

Table 11.6
Average Wage per Manday by Occupation

(in Rs. per worker)

Occupation Group	*All*		*Regular*		*Casual*	
	1993	*1999*	*1993*	*1999*	*1993*	*1999*
Professionals	115	174	168	241	27	44
Technical	139	196	141	198	61	79
Administrative	239	360	261	370	69	52
Clerical	125	173	126	175	50	107
Sales	57	75	61	80	46	54
Service	60	88	70	102	29	42
Farmers etc.	25	37	40	59	24	36
Production etc.	52	74	74	89	32	52
Transport	80	103	101	121	44	63
Labourers nec.	52	72	82	108	41	57
All Occupations	52	79	104	144	28	42

Note : Occupational Classes are as in one-digit Codes of National Classification of Occupations, 1968.

Source : Author's calculations based on NSSO (1995) and NSSO (2001).

TABLE 11.7
Average Wage per Manday by States

(in as per worker)

Occupation Group	*All*		*Regular*		*Casual*	
	1993	*1999*	*1993*	*1999*	*1993*	*1999*
Andhra Pradesh	36	60	85	115	22	37
Arunachal Pradesh	79	181	90	244	49	65
Assam	55	83	87	119	34	48
Bihar	39	59	116	169	25	36
Goa	87	130	112	159	48	80
Gujarat	52	81	103	158	29	45
Haryana	73	120	106	167	44	62
Himachal Pradesh	94	136	135	181	50	67
J & K	100	151	124	186	49	83
Karnataka	49	70	118	143	25	39
Kerala	63	108	103	137	47	91
Madhya Pradesh	43	54	96	129	24	30
Maharashtra	61	88	117	156	24	37
Manipur	95	148	129	196	67	57
Meghalaya	77	106	128	182	38	53
Mizoram	87	198	134	240	52	84
Nagaland	133	181	143	185	69	95
Orissa	38	54	95	139	21	29
Punjab	79	104	104	132	59	67
Rajasthan	71	97	114	146	41	54
Sikkim	85	133	112	158	40	50
Tamil Nadu	43	79	86	119	25	51
Tripura	66	79	114	142	45	49
Uttar Pradesh	56	81	107	131	30	42
West Bengal	59	81	104	146	31	44
Andamans	103	137	124	169	49	72
Chandigarh	114	154	130	162	64	67
Dadra and NH	39	97	87	135	26	63
Daman	91	115	98	129	83	59
Delhi	117	235	127	246	78	76
Lakshadweep	104	170	120	188	64	119
Pondicherry	56	87	82	117	28	58
LIG States[a]	101	69	48	136	27	38
HIG States[a]	108	91	57	152	30	48
All India	52	79	104	144	28	42

Note : a—Low Income and High Income states are as defined in text.
Source : Author's calculations.

4. EMPLOYMENT-WAGE LINKAGE

While both employment and average wage are increasing at the aggregate level, our main purpose is to examine the movement of employment across different wage classes. For that purpose, we have formed six wage classes corresponding to average wage per day of—Less than Rs. 20, 21-50, 51-100, 101-249, 250-499, and more than Rs. 500. Frequency distribution of wage earners among these classes indicate that in 1993, about 72 per cent of the workers were in the bottom two wage classes, 26 per cent in the middle two, and the remaining 2 per cent only in the top two wage classes (Table 11.8). The corresponding figures for 1999 are 51 per cent, 33 per cent, and 6 per cent respectively, indicating that there has occurred a consistent shift of workers from the bottom-most classes to the middle and higher wage classes.

Thus 1993-99 period has experienced not only rise in wage employment, but also remunerative job creation. Employment expansion during this period seems therefore not to be absolutely a distress a phenomenon as often apprehended. This trend is more prominent for regular workers, wherein proportions of workers have decreased for the middle wage classes also, and the top two wage classes exhibit strikingly high employment growth rates. For the casual workers, however, employment growth is highest for the middle wage classes.

Among the occupational classes, Farming sector workers are mostly in the bottom wage classes (95 per cent of them earning below Rs. 50 per day). Among others, employment is skewed among the top wage classes for the Administrative workers; towards middle wage classes for the Technical, Clerical, and Transport workers; and towards the bottom wage classes for the Production and Service workers.

The structure of workforce within the wage classes is also changing. While for the top and bottom wage classes, share of regular and casual workers has remained almost unchanged, in the middle wage class share of casual workers has increased from 24 per cent to 40 per cent (Table 11.9). Thus, though the hitherto casual worker dominated sectors (DPAs) are themselves shrinking, the downsizing being more prominent for the casual workers leading to a decline in overall incidence of

TABLE 11.8
Wage Workers Distributed in Wage Classes

Daily Wage Class (in Rs.)	*All*		*Regular*		*Casual*	
	1993	*1999*	*1993*	*1999*	*1993*	*1999*
20 and below	30.9	11.9	8.9	4.7	41.0	15.5
21-50	41.4	49.4	23.1	20.6	49.8	63.9
51-100	13.5	19.9	24.9	24.4	8.2	17.6
101-249	12.5	13.4	37.7	34.2	0.9	3.0
250-499	1.6	4.6	5.0	13.5	0.0	0.1
500 and above	0.1	0.9	0.3	2.7	0.0	0.0
Bottom	72.4	61.3	32.0	25.2	90.8	79.4
Middle	25.9	33.3	62.7	58.6	9.1	20.5
Top	1.7	5.5	5.3	16.2	0.1	0.1

Note : Bottom, Middle, and Top Wage Classes are Lowest two, Middle two, and Highest two wage classes respectively.

Source : Author's calculations.

TABLE 11.9
Share of Regular and Casual Workers in Different Wage Classes

Daily Wage Class (in Rs.)	*1993*		*1999*	
	Regular	*Casual*	*Regular*	*Casual*
20 and below	9.0	91.0	13.1	86.9
21-50	17.6	82.4	13.9	86.1
51-100	58.1	41.9	41.2	58.8
101-249	95.1	4.9	85.3	14.7
250-499	98.1	1.9	99.1	0.9
500 and above	96.7	3.3	98.6	1.4
Bottom	13.9	86.1	13.8	86.2
Middle	75.9	24.1	58.9	41.1
Top	98.0	2.0	99.0	1.0
All Wage Class	31.4	68.6	33.5	66.5
Wage Inequality (Gini Coefficient)	42.1	35.6	44.7	29.4

Note : Bottom, Middle, and Top Wage Classes are Lowest two, Middle two, and Highest two wage classes respectively.

Source : Author's calculations. Gini Coefficients are estimated using World Bank's free poverty software POVCAL, available from http://www.worldbank.org/sms/tools/povcal/index.h1m

casual employment, there is also a marked shift of workers from middle level regular jobs to middle level casual jobs. The comparatively higher growth of regular workers is concentrated in the top level jobs with significant casualisation in the middle and bottom level jobs. Added to this trend is the fact that growth rate of mandays of jobs lag far behind the growth rate of workers even for the regular workers. This indicates a decline in mandays available per worker for regular workers and seems to be a bit unnatural.

5. DYNAMICS OF WAGE EMPLOYMENT PROCESS

The wage employment scenario in the post-reform period is therefore marked by a substantial increase in wage employment, especially regular wage employment. However, incidence of casualisation has increased in the middle and bottom level jobs, along with a decline in mandays of work available per worker even among regular workers. So, there are clear indications of a shift from Full-time to Part-time jobs—a phenomenon which we may term *'Irregularisation'* of jobs. This trend is higher in the IDG states compared to the LIG states, and among DPAs and Administrative jobs compared to others. The rise in real average wage is partly because of an upliftment in the general wage structure and partly because of a change in composition of workforce—both across occupation and employment status. Shifts in employment structure from the low paying DPAs to the Tertiary sector activities enjoying higher average wage is raising the overall average. Moreover, the movement towards regular employment, especially for the top wage classes, is also contributing to the overall wage rise. Another interesting phenomenon that emerges is that earlier the casual workers were distributed among very few high paid professionals and large mass of low paid casual workers, mostly in DPAs. However, in recent past, casual employment is characterised by phenomenal growth of middle wage jobs. On the other hand, regular employment is being biased towards top wage classes. This is leading to polarisation of wage structure and rising inequality among regular workers along with lowering of inequality among casual workers, as measured by Gini Coefficient of daily wage earnings (Table 11.9). This, together with Tertiarisation of workforce, and Irregularisation of employment scenario are the three most important features of Wage-Employment dynamics in India in the post-reform period.

6. DETERMINANTS OF WAGE EARNINGS

We have already examined the dynamics of wage and employment in India in the recent past. It is observed that there is a moderate growth in wage employment along with a rise in average wages during the 1993-99 period. But still, the average earning of workers are quite low. More than 61 percent of the workers receive a daily wage lower than legislative minimum wage rate. Under such situation it is pertinent to identify the influence of different factors on the wage rate so that proper policies for wage upliftment can be framed. For that purpose we use the unit level records and regress log of daily wage rates earned by the workers on a number of independent variables. The objective is to examine how workers' characteristics like Gender, Residential location, Educational level, Social status, Age class affect their daily wage earning. Therefore, our explanatory variables are qualitative in nature and require the use of Dummy variables. Only intercept dummies without interaction are used to keep the model simple. Our control individual is therefore backward class illiterate female below fifteen years of age residing in rural areas of LIG states. The model estimates are provided in Table 11.10.

It is observed that as expected observable characteristics are important factors in determining wages with males earning significantly higher than females, the educated earning significantly higher than illiterates, and backward classes earning significantly lower than the advance classes. Moreover, daily wage rates are significantly higher in HIG states compared to LIG states and in urban areas compared to rural areas. Thus location also plays an important role in determining wages. Workers in the higher age groups (more than 30) earn significantly higher than both child and young workers. This perhaps is because of lack of skill and experience of the young workers, thereby reducing their bargaining power, and partly sums being paid to the child workers. This is a clear reflection of exploitation of child workers and the new entrants to the job

TABLE 11.10
Regression Coefficients—Daily Wage as Dependent—Log-linear Model

Variables	*All*		*Regular*		*Casual*	
	1993	*1999*	*1993*	*1999*	*1993*	*1999*
(Constant)	2.135**	2.670**	2.319**	2.652**	2.223**	2.765**
Gender	0.455**	0.369**	0.328**	0.305**	0.486**	0.410**
Sector	0.360**	0.271**	0.158**	0.121**	0.252**	0.199**
State Group	0.043**	0.137**	0.055**	0.112**	0.074**	0.198**
Literates	0.183**	0.192**	0.237**	0.206**	0.070**	0.105**
Primary and Mid.	0.389**	0.364**	0.403**	0.390**	0.150**	0.159**
Sec. and HS	1.013**	0.879**	0.839**	0.834**	0.295**	0.196**
Graduates	1.452**	1.410**	1.207**	1.265**	0.380**	0.360**
Social Class	0.028**	0.077**		0.038**		0.046**
Young Age	0.423**	0.330**	0.666**	0.521**	0.446**	0.377**
Middle Age	0.745**	0.689**	1.167**	1.104**	0.550**	0.480**
Advanced Age	0.785**	0.816**	1.327**	1.342**	0.464**	0.429**
Adj R Square	0.43	0.53	0.15	0.17	0.31	0.43

Note : Dependent variable is Natural log of Daily Wage.
** Denotes significance at 1% level. Coefficients having p-value exceeding 0.50 are omitted. The Control groups for the Dummy variables are as follows: Gender—Females; Sector—Rural; State Group—LIG; Social Class—Non-general.
Source : Author's calculations.

market because of their vulnerability. Most significant difference however is caused by education with completion of high school enabling an average worker to earn about twice of his illiterate counterpart. If we differentiate between regular and casual workers similar results are obtained. The only difference is that for the casual workers the age effect is significantly higher for the young workers also indicating higher exploitation of child labour among the casual workers. Moreover, this age impact is highest for the middle age category in case of casual workers and for the late age category for the regular workers. Such a result indicates the importance of experience among regular workers and youthful vigour and physical capabilities for the casual workers.

Comparing between LIG and HIG states it is observed that the rural-urban wage gap and the social gap are comparatively higher in LIG states while effects of education are higher in HIG states. Thus traditional forces are more powerful in the backward areas in determining wage rates whereas education and skill have been found to be the main determinants in the advanced regions. For the casual workers however, all these impacts are higher in the HIG states. There are some notable differences across occupational classes also. The most important feature is that the effects of various determinants are substantially low for the Farming occupations indicating somewhat flat wage rates offered in this sector. Among the others Gender-gap is highest among Production and Service workers and lowest among Clerical workers. Rural-Urban wage gap is highest for the Professional, Administrative, and Sales workers, and least for the Technical workers. Educational effect naturally is highest among Professional and Administrative workers, while the impact of middle age is highest for Sales, Transport and Production workers. The result confirms the general characteristics and capability requirement of the different occupations.

The wage equations when estimated separately for each of the states are not much different except a few notable characteristics. Gender gap in wages is significantly low in the North-eastern states and union territories while it is substantially high in Maharashtra, Kerala, Haryana, Andhra Pradesh, Tamil Nadu, Uttar Pradesh and West Bengal. Rural-Urban wage differential is significantly low in Haryana, Punjab, and Kerala where substantial agricultural development and rural development programmes have narrowed down the gap between the countryside and the towns. Compared to this, rural-urban differential is quite high in Bihar, Maharashtra, Karnataka, Madhya Pradesh, Orissa, Uttar Pradesh, West Bengal and north-eastern states (except Mizoram). Wage differential among social groups is significantly high in Gujarat, Orissa, Haryana, Jammu & Kashmir, Mizoram, Nagaland, Orissa. Uttar Pradesh, and Maharashtra. The impact of education is similar across all states indicating the universal importance of it in determining earning gaps.

These results are true for both the 1993 and 1999 period. However, there is a marked rise in the magnitude of the' coefficients over time for regional effect and social status effect. While the wage differentials attributable to preliminary educational attainment like literacy and primary schooling are declining, effects due to higher schooling and graduation etc. are increasing substantially for the regular workers. For the casual workers however, impact of elementary education is increasing.

7. CONCLUSION

Summarising the findings of this paper, it may be commented that the expansion of wage employment in India in the post-reform period has emerged as a growth-oriented phenomenon. Rise in employment has been associated with increasing share of regular workers, rise in average wage levels and an overall upward shift of the workforce structure across wage classes. Interestingly, for the middle wage level jobs there has occurred a substantial shift from regular workers to casual workers while for the top wage classes, share of regular workers has increased. This has resulted in rising wage inequality among regular workers and declining wage inequality among casual workers. In addition, there has occurred a shift of structure from directly productive activities to tertiary sector-related activities. More important however is the bias towards part time jobs among regular workers also leading to a significant decline in per week work availability. This regularisation of even the regular jobs emerges as a major area of concern in recent times, especially in the advanced states. Wage rates are observed to be affected by embodied human resource like education, age and gender on one hand and structural factors like location, social status and regional economic condition on the other. The impacts of these determinants are observed to have become more powerful over time. The rising importance of higher education among regular workers and elementary education among casual workers are clear indications of growing importance of skill formation in determining wages in the post-reform period. Moreover, since these attainments are skewedly distributed across gender and social status, importance of the latter factors are also rising.

Thus, Tertiarisation and Irregularisation of workforce, Casualisation of even the middle level jobs, Growing regional, social and interpersonal inequality in wage earnings, and Increasing importance of skill formation in determining wage rates have been the main features of wage employment dynamics in post-reform India. Our employment policies should naturally be framed accordingly. It is evident that the employment structure is moving from full-time regular jobs towards part-time, and in some cases casual jobs. The focus should therefore be not only on creating more jobs but creating more mandays of work. Enabling skill formation through attainment of at least middle levels of schooling will help in raising earning levels of the workers. Gender and social bias in educational attainment are reinforcing traditional skewness in wages against females and backward classes. Hence, bringing these marginalized groups to school should be an important agenda in new India.

NOTES AND REFERENCES

1. The states have been divided into Low Income Group (LIG) and High Income Group (HIG) accordingly as their Per Capita Net State Domestic Product are lower or higher than All India Per Capita Net Domestic Product respectively. The states belonging to LIG in both 1993 and 1999 are Assam, Bihar, Jammu & Kashmir, Madhya Pradesh, Manipur, Meghalaya, Orissa, Rajasthan, Tripura, and Uttar Pradesh, RIG states in both the years have been Andaman & Nicobar, Chandigarh, Delhi, Goa, Gujarat, Haryana, Himachal Pradesh, Karnataka, Kerala, Maharashtra, Mizoram, Pondicherry, Punjab, Tamil Nadu. Andhra Pradesh, Sikkim, and West Bengal were in LIG in 1993 but came up to BIG in 1999. On the other hand, Arunachal Pradesh and Nagaland were in BIG in 1993 but went down to LIG in 1999.
2. Occupational Classifications are according to the One-digit codes of National Classification of Occupations (1968). The Ten classes are Professionals; Technical and related workers; Administrative workers; Executive and Managerial workers; Clerical and related workers; Sales workers; Service workers; Farmers, Fishers, Hunters and Loggers; Production and related workers; Transport Equipment operators; and, Labourers not elsewhere classified.
3. Subsequent sections deal with 1993 and 1999 data only as detailed data for 2004 are yet not available from NSSO.

References

Shariff, Abusaleh and Gumber, Anil (1999), "Employment and Wages in India: Pre- and Post-Reform Scenario", *The Indian Journal of Labour Economics*, Vol. 42, No. 2.

Banerjee, Debdas (2005), "Trends of Factor Income Distribution in Indian Factories", *The Indian Journal of Labour Economics*, Vol. 48, No. 2.

Bhattacharya, B.B. and Shaktivel, S. (2005), "Employment, Wage and Output Relationship in India: A Comparison of Pre- and Post-Reform Behaviour", *The Indian Journal of Labour Economics*, Vol. 48, No. 2.

Vasudeva Dutta, Puja (2005), "Accounting for Wage Inequality in India", *The Indian Journal of Labour Economics*, Vol. 48, No. 2.

Rustogi, Preet (2005), "Understanding Gender Inequalities in Wages and Income in India", *The Indian Journal of Labour Economics*, Vol. 48, No. 2.

Duraisamy, P. and Duraisamy, Malathy (2005), "Regional Differences in Wage Premia and Returns to Education by Gender in India", *The Indian Journal of Labour Economics*, Vol. 48, No. 2.

NSSO (2000), *Unit Level Records on Sixth Quinquennial Survey on Employment and Unemployment in India, 1999-2000*, NSS 55th Round—July 1999-June 2000, National Sample Survey Organisation, Government of India.

NSSO (19%), *Unit Level Records on Sixth Quinquennial Survey on Employment and Unemployment in India, 1993-1994*, NSS Fiftieth Round—July 1993-June 1994, National Sample Survey Organisation, Government of India.

Websites: www.mospi.nic.in, www.planningcommission.nic.in

12

Sustainable Industrialization : A Case Study of Impact on Income and Employment

INDRAJIT BAIRAGYA

1. INTRODUCTION

Since the emergence of Capitalism industrialization has been considered as the essential ingredient of 'growth and development'. Industrialization has been assigned the key role for transformation of the traditional pre-capitalistic economy into capitalistic ones. Similarly, modernisation of whole of the economy in less developed countries is also supposed to be guided by the progress of the modern industrial sector. Early researchers working on the issue of economic development suggested a similar path of transformation of the traditional economies into modern industrialised ones. Such a structural transformation was considered to mitigate the problems of unemployment and poverty.

The pioneers of Indian planning also relied on such a course of development for Indian economy after independence. However, very soon it was understood that for the overall progress of the Indian economy balancing of industrial growth with that of agriculture was needed to avoid the problems of spiralling inflation and to maintain the essential process of domestic capital accumulation in modern industry. The modernisation of the traditional economy and thus the balance between agriculture and industry was advocated to mitigate the 'wage-good constraint' on one hand and to expand the 'home market' on the other for the industrial sector.

The doctrine of balanced growth ruled the policy domain as well. However, recently there is again a shift back to the idea of unbalanced growth with specific bias in favour of industry in general. The difference between the traditional path of industrialisation and present one is that, while the former was largely guided by the state the latter is significantly influenced by the private capital.

Thus, the dominance of industry on agriculture is re-established. This process, in fact, has become a national phenomenon in India. However, due to variations of geographical conditions, input supply and legal setup across the country there is found to be divergence between the regional/ state specific courses of industrialisation. Here, variations in regulatory framework across states have induced significantly such a diversified industrial structure.

Consequently, the state of West Bengal is also experiencing a particular type of industrial development. As a part of this process Sponge Iron industry, because of its various advantages have come up in a big way in different districts of West Bengal. This particular industrial expansion has created specific debates across the polity and society of the State. The issues that have come up for intense debate are 'land conversion' and the question of food security on one hand and environmental degradation and resource depletion on the other. Development of the Sponge Iron industry is a case in the sense that while on one hand it induces income and employment growth and thereby ensures social benefits, it brings in a significant way the issues involving economic and social costs on the other.

Through our case study we have tried to capture this particular debate hovering around the issues related to land conversion, food security and environmental as well as resource degradation. We have tried to bring out through our case study an implicit trade-off in the context of the process of development of sponge iron industry in West Bengal. Thus making the implicit trade-off explicit and quantifiable is the target of this paper.

2. AN OVERVIEW OF SPONGE IRON INDUSTRY IN INDIA

1. Steel industries have played a major role in industrialisation in all developed countries. In India also we are experiencing expansion of this sector. In last few years the demand for Indian steel has been increasing at the national and international market. In 1992, India's domestic consumption, export quantity and export value of steel were Rs. 16626.8* crore, 309456* tonnes and Rs. 373.4* crore respectively. But in 2005, these have increased to Rs. 87531.2* crore, 4857613* tonnes and Rs. 6315.5* crore respectively. Few years ago pig iron's aggregate demand was more than other competitive inputs of steel. But at present sponge iron's demand is fast expanding and it is much greater than pig iron. The production of sponge iron increases from 830* thousand tonnes in 1991 to 9942* thousand tonnes in 2005, while the production of pig iron increases from 1504* thousand tonnes in 1991 to 4310* thousand tonnes in 2005. Though the production of both sponge iron and pig iron increases, the rate of increase of sponge iron is much higher than that of pig iron. The comparative analysis of year-wise production change of sponge iron and pig iron can be shown with the help of the Table 12.1 and Graph 12.1.

Domestic consumption market size and total sale of sponge iron are continuously increasing*. Export quantity also increases at a remarkable rate. At present Indian share of sponge iron production is (approx.) 15%† of world production. At present the rate of growth of export quantity of pig iron is

* Data collected from CMIE.

† Report form Nagarik Mancha.

TABLE 12.1
Year-wise Percentage Change in Total Production of Sponge Iron and Pig Iron

	Dec. 1992	Dec. 1993	Dec. 1994	Dec. 1995	Dec. 1996	Dec. 1997	Dec. 1998	Dec. 1999	Dec. 2000	Dec. 2001	Dec. 2002	Dec. 2003	Dec. 2004	Dec. 2005
(1)	(2)	(3)	(4)	(5)	(6)	(7)	(8)	(9)	(10)	(11)	(12)	(13)	(14)	(15)
Sponge Iron	54.34	17.41	60.9	40.17	30.98	13.59	5.47	-0.63	0.02	3.18	1.79	14.32	18.83	31.7
Pig iron	6.78	14.82	23.41	23.33	2.36	15	3.81	-0.7	-4.61	-4.43	25.15	30.29	2.65	17.07

GRAPH 12.1
Year-wise % Change in Total Production of Sponge Iron and Pig Iron

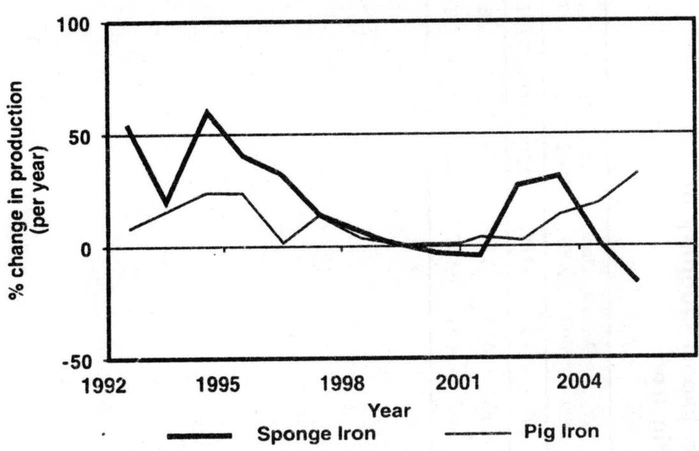

negative. The comparative analysis of rate of growth of export quantity of sponge iron and pig iron can be shown with the help of the Table 12.2 and Graph 12.2.

GRAPH 12.2
Year-wise % Growth in Export Quantity of Sponge Iron and Pig Iron

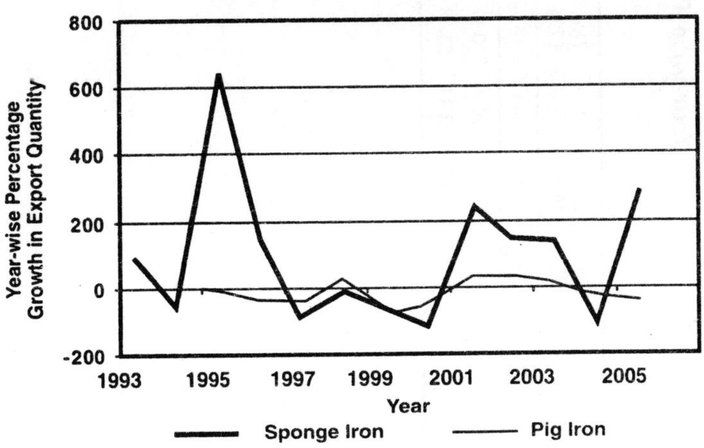

TABLE 12.2
Year-wise Percentage Change in Export Quantity of Sponge Iron and Pig Iron

	Dec. 1992	Dec. 1993	Dec. 1994	Dec. 1995	Dec. 1996	Dec. 1997	Dec. 1998	Dec. 1999	Dec. 2000	Dec. 2001	Dec. 2002	Dec. 2003	Dec. 2004	Dec. 2005
(1)	(2)	(3)	(4)	(5)	(6)	(7)	(8)	(9)	(10)	(11)	(12)	(13)	(14)	(15)
Sponge Iron	54.34	17.41	60.9	40.17	30.98	13.59	5.47	-0.63	0.02	3.18	1.79	14.32	18.83	31.7
Pig iron	6.78	14.82	23.41	23.33	2.36	15	3.81	-0.7	-4.61	-4.43	25.15	30.29	2.65	17.07

Production takes place in sponge iron factories in this area because labour is comparatively cheap. Suitable geographical conditions also act as an incentive. Labour is cheap because there is excess supply of labour. Excess supply as there is no other job opportunity. Furthermore, labour law is not fully maintained. Thus, labour cost could be reduced to the minimum in absence of regulation and excess supply of labour. The sponge iron units escape the regulation of the government of West Bengal by reducing the hours of operation for the pollution regulation devices. For availability of cheap labour, cost of production is also low. For the low cost of production more and more producers are attracted to invest. So there is a rise in the level of production.

Our case study reveals that while on one hand industrialisation is benefiting the local economy through employment and through other demand and supply side linkages, on the other hand, because of high pollution content these industries are affecting adversely on agricultural productivity and hence creating loss of employment and income. Thus there is a trade-off involving employment generation in industry and that of agriculture. A deeper enquiry might reveal deterioration of quality of life.

3. PLAN OF WORK

Industrialisation is thought to be the key solution for the perennial problem of unemplovment in our country. However, there is a trade-off involved in such a process. On one hand, industrialisation means employment generation, on the other hand, it causes resource reallocation, resource degradation and environmental damage. The latter in turn may adversely affect long run employment potentials. To understand the impact of industrialisation social cost benefit analysis seems to be highly relevant. We propose to undertake a detail cost benefit analysis involving such multidimensional problems using three sponge iron factories in Bankura district of West Bengal as our case study. However, from this case study we would try to derive certain general implications.

Several benefits are generated through the following processes:

(1) Employment is created as people are engaged in these sponge iron factories.
(2) As other factories come up through the exploitation of linkage effects arising from the growth of sponge iron factories, more employment will be generated.
(3) There are other positive spill-over effects in the region's economy as the region becomes more and more industrialised. These spill-overs may operate through demand side as well as supply-side linkages. Hence, we have to identify these linkage effects.

However, there are several social costs present in the process of growth in the sponge iron industries which may adversely affect the long run sustainability. The sponge iron industries cause environmental damage by the act of emitting smoke and resource degradation by depleting water reserves. Social costs of these industries arise in the following ways:

1. There is also loss of employment due to land conversion from agriculture to industry.
2. Water reserve depletion and air pollution causes loss of agricultural productivity creating the demand-side problem of employment generation.
3. Environmental pollution and resource depletion cause health hazards. Many problems may arise from such health hazards. This may result in loss of productivity of the labourers engaged in these industries as well as in other industries and in agriculture leading to the long run supply-side problem of employability.

So our next problem would be to estimate the cost of long run labour productivity loss and also to estimates the multidimensional costs of environmental and resource damage.

Hence the social cost benefit analysis seems to be highly relevant to understand the impact of growth of sponge iron industries.

4. METHODOLOGY AND SOURCES OF DATA

A study of cost-benefit analysis requires adequate

qualitative and quantitative data. CMIE data are used, but are not sufficient for our purpose. Because of the limitation of secondary data, we have undertaken a detailed primary survey.

Bankura districts of West Bengal is purposively selected because there are quite a large numbers of sponge-iron factories. The analysis is based on the field survey conducted in the year 2006 in five villages near to the three sponge-iron factories purposively chosen from Barjora block of Bankura District. Our survey covers 72 land owning households whose land is near to these sponge-iron factories. The total area covered in this way is 790.5 bigha. The sample of land is constructed considering the distances of different plots from the factories. Our sample covers different size class of land holding. From our sample survey we came to the conclusion that these three factories do not affect the land which is 3 kilometres or farther from the factories. We draw a circle of 3 kilometre radius putting the production unit at the centre. We can consider the impact of the production unit within the area of that circle. With increase in distance, we found, there is a distinct reduction in the impact. We construct four imaginary concentric circles within the stipulated area having in total 3 kilometre radius. The concentric circles are so designed that we get the following zones in terms of the distance between the respective zones and the production unit. The zones are : (1) 0-0.5 km; (2) 0.5-1 km (3) 1-2 km; and (4) 2-3 km.

Our survey also covers more than 80% households whose land was converted to construct the factories.

Valuation is done within the framework of cost-benefit analysis. In the process, a number of methodological issues in environmental analysis have been dealt with. The costs of environmental degradation have been calculated with the help of Contingent Valuation Method (CVM). For CVM (Davis, 1963) a hypothetical market is set-up. Then individuals are asked to state their minimum willingness to accept (WTA) for meeting up the extra costs arises for sponge-iron factories. In this process we· have used an open-ended referendum. We have started from a very high price and asked the individuals whether he would be satisfied with this amount or not. If yes, we have lowered the bid and repeat this process until the first no comes. If no was the initial position then we have kept on increasing the bid until the first yes comes. The average of WTA is calculated by arithmetic mean. At last we multiply the data with the total number of households.

5. DESCRIPTION OF THE SURVEY RESULTS

In our case study we have taken three sponge-iron factories, M.B. Ispat Corporation Ltd. and Rishav Sponge Pvt. Ltd. of Barjora Mouza and Govinda Impex (Pvt.) Ltd. of Sahebdihi Mouza in Barjora Block, Bankura District, West Bengal. Borjora is 8 kilometres away from Durgapur, a well-known industrial zone in West Bengal. M.B. Ispat Corporation Ltd. and Rishav Sponge Pvt. Ltd. are located on the two different sides of the main road half kilometre away from Borjora bus stand. Govinda Impex (Pvt.). Ltd. is situated on the same side of M.B. Ispat Corporation Ltd.

These three factories were established in 2003. Three factories are situated in close proximity and hence it is very difficult to dissociate the impacts of each factory on the surroundings. That is why we have to consider the three factories as one unit of production.

These three factories create some social benefits as well as social costs. At first we consider the social costs of these three factories.

1. Cost of Land-conversion

There is some loss of agricultural production, income and employment as agricultural land is converted to industry. Among the three factories Govinda Impex is established on the vested land. Our survey covers more than 80% of the land converted to construct other two sponge-iron factories. M.B. Ispat is situated on 21.82 acres of land. Out of this area 51% (approx. 11.444 acres or 33.43 bighas) was agricultural land. On the other hand, Rishav Sponge is situated on 23 acres of land area on which 17.39% (approx. 4 acres or 12 bighas) was agricultural land. Altogether 45.43 bigha of agricultural land was converted to construct these two sponge iron factories.

As agricultural land was converted to industry there is obvious loss of agricultural output, income along with employment. Both the farmers and the agricultural labourers have been suffering due to this loss.

(a) Loss of Income of the Cultivators Due to Conversion

Mainly paddy was produced there once in a year. But some portion of the converted land was double cropped. On the double cropped land wheat, mustard and some vegetables were produced after the harvest of paddy. The whole of the double cropped land has been converted to construct M.B. Ispat. The loss of income of the cultivators due to conversion can be shown with the help of following Table 12.3.

TABLE 12.3
Loss of Paddy Production Per Year due to Conversion

House-holds	*Area of Converted Land (bigha)*	*Area of Agricultural Land (bigha)*	*Name of the Factory*	*Per Bigha Production Loss (Kg.)*	*Wt. Average of per bigha Production Loss (Kg.)*
1.	13	3	Rishav Sponge	690	
2.	13	3	Do	690	
3.	42	6	Do	660	
4.	I	0	Do	0	
5.	10	6	M.B. Ispat	570	644.21
6.	9	4	Do	600	
7.	8	4	Do	600	
8.	9	4	Do	600	
9.	10	5	Do	720	
10.	5	3	Do	720	

Given the weighted average of per bigha production loss of paddy (644.21 kg.) and given the amount of agricultural land converted (45.43 bigha) we find that total production loss per year is 29266.46 kg.

The whole of the double cropped land was converted to construct the M.B. Ispat Pvt. Ltd. And 33.43 bigha of

TABLE 12.4
Loss of Production of Other Crops (Per year)

Product	*Amount of Land (bigha)*	*Per bigha production loss (Kg)*
Wheat	2	250
Mustard	3	300
Vegetables	2	190.5

agricultural land was converted to construct the M.B. Ispat. But survey covers 26 bigha of agricultural land among 33.43 bigha. So we have to reframe Table 12.2 in terms of total agricultural land which is used to construct M.B. Ispat Pvt Ltd.

We consider current market price of different crops in West Bengal. By reframing Tables 12.1 and 12.2 and also by considering price of different products corresponding revenue loss of the cultivators can be shown. To find the net loss of aggregate income of the cultivators we need to subtract cost of production of different crops from the corresponding revenue. We also consider the current wage rate of labourer in that area, i.e., Rs. 70 per day.

TABLE 12.5
Cost of Production of Different Products (Per Bigha)

Product	*Man-days required*	*Labour Cost (Rs.)*	*Cost of fertilizers (Rs.)*	*Cost of seeds (Rs.)*	*Cost of Pesticides (Rs.)*	*Other cost* (Rs.)*	*Total cost (Rs.)*
Paddy	20	1400	316.20	120	200	480	2516.20
Wheat	10	700	200	100	—	100	1100
Mustard	8	560	150	200	90	—	1000
Vegetables	12	840	50	50	60	—	1000

*Costs of tractor, spray machine, husking machine, etc.

(b) *Loss of Income of the Worker due to Conversion*

From Table 12.3 we know that the amount of man-days needs for per bigha cultivation of different crops and from

TABLE 12.6

Per Year Income Loss of the Workers

Product	*Amt. of Land (bighs)*	*Per bigha prod. loss (Kg.)*	*Total Prod. loss (Kg.)*	*Market price per kg (Rs.)*	*Total revenue loss (Rs.)*	*Per bigha cost of prod. (Rs.)*	*Total Cost of prod. (Rs.)*	*Net income loss (Rs.)*
(1)	*(2)*	*(3)*	*(4)*	*(5)*	*(6)*	*(7)*	*(8)*	*(9)*
Paddy	45.43	644.21	29266.46	6.20	181452.05	2516.20	114310.96	67141.09
Wheat	2.57	250	642.50	7.10	4561.75	1100	2827	1734.75
Mustard	3.86	300	1158	14	16212	1000	3860	12352
Vegetables	2.57	190.5	489.585	10	4895.85	1000	2570	2325.85

Table 12.4 we know that the amount of land which was used to produce different crops. The ongoing wage rate of the labourer is Rs. 70 per day. Considering these data the loss of income of the workers can be shown with the help of the following table:

TABLE 12.7

Per Year Income Loss of the Workers

Product	*Amount of Land (bigha)*	*Man-days required (per bigha)*	*Total man-days required*	*Total wage bill (Rs.)*
Paddy	45.43	20	908.6	63602
Wheat	2.57	10	25.7	1799
Mustard	3.86	8	30.88	2161.60
Vegetables	2.57	12	30.84	2158.80
Total			996.02	69721.40

Thus we get total income loss of the workers is Rs. 69721.40 with the loss of income for both cultivators and workers the total is Rs. 153275.09.

TABLE 12.8

Loss of Income, Employment and Agricultural Productivity (per year) Due to Conversion

Loss of Income (Rs.)	153275.09
Loss in Employment (Man-days)	996.02
Loss in productivity (Kg.)	
Paddy	29266.46
Wheat	642.5
Mustard	1158
Vegetables	489.585

2. Cost of Conversion of Water Bodies

It has been found that there is some loss in income, employment and agricultural output due to conversion of (three) water bodies with total surface area of 7.75 bigha. The income loss due to the conversion of water bodies can be determined by adding total fixed cost (TFC) and total variable cost (TVC) plus income loss of cultivators and income loss of workers. TFC is calculated by the loss of capital value of 7.75 bigha land plus principal amount of loan equivalent needed to dig 7.75 bigha water bodies divided by the life span of pond. TVC is equal to the per year interest cost on loan equivalent needed to dig 7.75 bigha water bodies. Per year income loss of the farmers due to conversion of water bodies is measured by adding TFC and TVC.

Farmers have used some agricultural land to dig another water bodies for the substitute of the previous. So the employment loss due to conversion of water bodies can be measured by the number of work generated per year of 7.75 bigha agricultural land. Production loss is also measured by the amount of total production (per year) of different crops in 7.75 bigha agricultural land.

Here we take into account per bigha capital value is Rs. 33333.33 (equal to sale price) and the life span of pond is 20 years. Interest rate of loan is 13% (equal to interest of bank loan).

TABLE 12.9

Loss in Income and Employment (per year) due to Conversion of Water Bodies

Loss in income (Rs.)	
(TVC+TFC)	66568.37
Cultivators	35332.66
Workers	11893.7
Total income loss	113794.73
Loss in employment (man-days)	169.91
Loss in production (kg.)	
Paddy	4992.63
Wheat	109.6
Mustard	197.5
Vegetables	83.52

3. Cost of Environmental Damage

These three factories caused environmental damage by the act of emitting smoke. We want to enquire, how the air pollution create problems for the people who are living near these industries. The problems arise in the following ways:

1. Air pollution causes loss of agricultural productivity. This creates the demand side problem of employment generation. Air pollution causes loss in income both in terms of quantity and quality.
2. Environmental pollution caused health hazard. This result in loss of productivity of the labourers engaged in these units, other industries, agriculture and also the households who are living near to these factories leading to the long run supply side problem employability.
3. There are some other effects on the surroundings such as adverse impact on milk production, animal husbandry, etc.

(a) As a consequence of air pollution the leaves of the new born crops are getting covered with thick layer of coal dust. As a result of this there is loss of income due to loss of productivity and quantity of output. This creates the demand side problem of employment generation.

Now we have to find out the area under different zones following the process that have already been discussed in Section 3.

The area under different zones can be shown with the help of following table.

TABLE 12.10
Area Under Different Zones

Different zones (km.)	*Area under different zones (bigha)*
0-0.5	713.036
0.5-1	2139.107
1-2	8556.428
2-3	14260.715

Now we have to find out the loss of production of different crops in different zones. This can be shown with the help of the Table 12.11.

TABLE 12.11
Loss of Production (per year) of different Crops in different Zones under the Area of Survey

Different zones (Km.)	*Survey covers (bigha)*	*Production loss of paddy (Kg.)*	*Production loss of wheat (Kg.)*	*Production loss of mustard (Kg.)*	*Production loss of vegetables (Kg.)*
0-0.5	329.25	77085	11300	3000	2800
0.5-1	95.00	19980	1100	200	—
1-2	161.5	38700	—	300	5585
2-3	117.75	6550	—	—	—

TABLE 12.12
Loss of Total Production of different in different Zones

Different zones (km.)	*Area under consideration (bigha)*	*Total production loss of puddy (Kg.)*	*Total production loss of wheat (Kg.)*	*Total production loss of mustard (Kg.)*	*Total production loss of vegetables (Kg.)*
0-0.5	713.036	166938.12	24471.7	6496.91	6063.78
0.5-1	2139.107	449887.95	24768.6	4503.38	—
1-2	8556.428	2050363.8	—	15894.29	295898.76
2-3	14260.715	793271.18	—	—	—
Total	25669.286	3460460.9	49240.3	26894.6	301962.54

It has been found that there is obvious reduction in productivity of surrounding land due to the pollution generated by sponge-iron factories. Farmers were compelled to stop production of wheat, mustard and vegetables in some areas. The area of cultivated land used to produce remains the same but the productivity of land is reduced and the cost of production remains the same as before. So there is some loss in income of the cultivators due to sponge-iron factories. Areas where the production is totally stopped the cost incurred in production is accordingly reduced along with the loss of the whole of the potential employment. Subtracting this amount of cost from the total income loss we get the net income loss for different crops and from that we can calculate the total income loss.

Net income and employment loss can be shown with the help of the Table 12.13.

TABLE 12.13
Net Loss in Income and Employment and Total Production

Different crops	*Total production loss (Rs.)*	*Total income loss (Rs.)*	*Decrease in cost (Rs.)*	*Loss in employment (mandays)*	*Net loss in income (Rs.)*
Paddy	3460460.9	21454858	—	—	21454857
Wheat	49240.3	349606.1	16250	147.5	333356.1
Mustard	26894.6	376524.4	1000	8	375524.4
Vegetables	301962.54	3019625.4	27500	330	2992125.4
Total				485.5	25155864

(b) There is not only the loss in quantity of the product, quality of the product also decreases. As a result of the decrease in quality price of the product is always less than the ongoing market price of other regions. Survey reveals that the amount of reduction of market price is (approx.) Rs. 20 per sacks (60 kg.). Loss of income due to decrease in product quality is Rs. 1279519.3.

(c) Survey reveals that environmental degradation causes health hazards of both workers (mainly on unskilled) and neighbouring households. Majority of the unskilled labourers are local. So the cost of health hazard is calculated by estimating the increased medical cost (per year) of the households (including life stock of animal). The average loss in income due to health hazard is Rs. 2668.48. The total loss in income due to health hazard is Rs. 6238906.20.

(d) Animal husbandry, milk production are also severely affected by air pollution. However, we can not represent the exact data because some observations are missing.

TABLE 12.14

Total Loss in Income, Employment and Agricultural Output Incurred as Direct Effects

Loss in income (Rs.)	32941359.32
Loss in employment (man-days)	1651.43
Loss in agricultural output (kg.)	
Paddy	3494719.99
Wheat	49992.4
Mustard	28250.1
Vegetables	302535.645

4. Cost of Resource Degradation

The sponge-iron factories requires large amount of water. SWID (State Water Investigation Department) of West Bengal has earmarked the Barjora zones as drought prone area. If the water is supplied in agriculture instead of these factories then agricultural output as well as income and employment will increase.

TABLE 12.15

Loss of Income, Employment and Agricultural Output due to Water Reserve Depletion

Loss in income (Rs.)	
Cultivators	2472530
Workers	2342200
Total	4814730
Loss in employment (man-days)	33460
Loss in production (kg.)	
Paddy	1077763.3

5. With the help of the 'consumption multiplier' we can calculate another income loss. As aggregate agricultural income falls, there will be loss of income through the operation of a negative multiplier process. Here we take into account the average mpc on local products consumption for our multiplier calculation. In fact, as agricultural income falls demand for locally produced and consumed goods and services falls as well that generates the negative spiral squeezing down the local economy. MPC on local products consumption is calculated on the basis of the per capita land holding of the households. Households are divided into three groups in terms of per capita land holding.

This can be seen with the help of Table 12.16

TABLE 12.16
Average mpc on Local Product Consumption

Per capita land-holding (higha)	*No. of households among survey*	*MPC on local product consumption (veg.)*	*Average of MPC*
<I	17	0.11	
1 <Land<2	35	0.19	0.193
>2	20	0.27	

With the help of employment multiplier we can calculate another employment gain arises through linkages. For

TABLE 12.17
Total Loss of Income, Agricultural Production and Employment

Loss in income (Rs.)	46727215
Loss in employment (man-days)	41782.6
Loss in production (kg.)	
Paddy	4572483.2
Wheat	49992.4
Mustard	28250.1
Vegetables	302535.6

calculating employment multiplier we consider all India average employment elasticity 0.16.

By taking into account the linkage effect we can calculate total loss in Income, employment and agricultural output.

The value of environmental degradation can also be calculated with the help of CVM. Following this process we get the average of minimum WTA is Rs. 13288 per household. Our survey covers 72 land owning households. In this process survey covers 790.5 bigha land. But the total area under consideration is 25669.286 bigha. Total (approx.) 2338 number of households holds the total land. Total loss of income through calculated by CVM is Rs. 31067344. The costs which have calculated directly arise through sponge-iron industries is Rs. 32941359.32. Two results are very close to each other.

6. BENEFITS DUE TO SPONGE IRON FACTORIES

We get several benefits through the following processes:

As production takes place there is obvious gain in income of the owners of these factories. Income is also gained in terms of wages earned by the labour force, rental earned on land, profits earned on man-made capital. Concentration will be given on income gain of local economy, so we do not bother about the income gain of the owner of factories. Here we consider the gain in income of local economy through supplying different inputs into these factories.

1. Benefits of Workers who are Engaged with these Sponge-Iron Factories

Employment is created as people are engaged in these sponge-iron factories. The engagement of labourers is classified into different types depending upon their technical knowledge. Different types of employment can be shown with the help of Table 12.18.

From the Table 12.18 we get 6422 man-days of work is generated by these sponge iron factories and total income gain of the workers is Rs. 631894.

TABLE 12.18
Different Types of Employment in the Sponge-Iron Factories (per year)

Class of labourer	*Number of labourers*	*Working days required (per month)*	*Average Wage rate (per day) (Rs.)*	*Total man-days required*
Skilled	38	26	218.37	988
Semi-skilled	16	26	91.35	416
Un-skilled				
Contractual	85	26	72	2210
Regular	108	26	78	2808
Total	247	—	—	6422

2. Benefits of the Cultivators due to Land Conversion

The farmers whose land was converted to construct these sponge-iron factories earn some income. The farmers sold their land in exchange of an amount of money. Many of them have spent that money for consumption, such as, construction of new houses, repairing of old houses or spent for marriage. Some had used the amount of money in business purpose.

So we observe that the money has been used either in consumption or in investment purpose. The income of the cultivators who have used the money in consumption purpose is calculated by TFC and TVC. Here TFC = Principal amount of loan divided by time period to refund the loan. TVC = The imputed interest cost (per year) of the loan. On the other hand the income of the cultivators who have used the money for investment purpose is calculated by the income generated from that investment.

Those who have invested the money for business purpose have also created some employment.

The income gain of the cultivators due land conversion can be shown with the help of the Table 12.19.

Survey covers 120 bigha land but total area of converted land is 134.46 bigha. By taking into the total converted land total

TABLE 12.19
Income Gain Per Annum of the Cultivators due to Land Conversion

House-holds	*Land sold (bigha)*	*Price per bigha (Rs.)*	*Total Price (Rs.)*	*Purpose of Money used*	*Interest cost per annum (Rs.)*	*Employment generated (mandays)*
1.	13	33333.33	433333.29	Consumption	56333.29	—
2.	13	33333.33	433333.29	Do	56333.29	—
3.	42	33333.33	1399999.8	Investment	108000	312
4.	1	20000	20000	Consumption	2600	—
5.	10	40000	400000	Do	52000	—
6.	9	40000	360000	Do	46800	—
7.	8	20000	160000	Do	20800	—
8.	9	20000	180000	Do	23400	—
9.	10	40000	400000	Do	52000	—
10.	5	40000	200000	Do	26000	—
Total			3986666.3		397466.58	—

income and employment gain of the cultivators can be calculated.

Here TFC = 4467059.5/20 = 223352.97 and TVC = 397466.58.

Total income gain of the cultivators due to conversion is Rs. 620819.55. The employment gain is 350 man-days.

TABLE 12.20
Gain of Owners of Converted Land and from that Employment Generation and Income Gain of Workers

Income gain (Rs.)	
Owners of converted land	620819.5
Workers	24500
Total	645319.5
Employment gain (man-days)	350

3. Benefits of the Producers of the Factors

TABLE 12.21
Gain in Income of the Producers of the Factories Sponge-Iron Factories

Income Gain (Rs.)	14,06,15,292***

*** The factories are not interested to provide any data. We have put the data by extrapolating from annual report 2005-06 of Steel Iron India Limited (SIIL).

Water is supplied with the help of Panchayat Samiti and Industrial Officer of Barjora Block in exchange of Rs. 7.50/KL. M.B. Ispat, Rishav Sponge and Govinda Impex requires 360 KL, 180 KL and 120 KL water per day respectively.

TABLE 12.22
Net benefits of the Panchayet Samiti by Supplying Water to the Factories and the Income Gain of Workers

Net income gain of Panchayet Samiti	–57,670
Income gain of workers	4,64,420
Total income gain	406750
Employment gain	3069

TABLE 12.23
Total Direct Gain of Income and Employment for the three Factories

Direct Income Gain (Rs.)	
Without Producers' Income	1683963.5
With producers' Income	142299256
Direct Employment Gain (man-days)	9841

5. Benefits through Linkages

There are some positive spill-overs in the region's economy

as the region becomes industrialised. As production takes place in the sponge-iron factories, some employment is created so purchasing power increases of that people. So demand for other goods will increase. As a result, other industry will develop and create more employment. Side by side engagement in business will also be increased.

With the help of the multiplier analysis we can calculate another income and employment gain which will arise through the different linkages with the total income gain. Here we take into account the average mpc on local products (0.193) as consumption multiplier and 0.16 (all India average) as employment multiplier.

By taking into account the above income and employment gain we can calculate total gain in income and employment due to sponge iron factories. This can be shown with the help of the Table 12.24.

TABLE 12.24

Total Gain in Income and Employment Including Linkage Effects

Total gain in income (Rs.)	
Without producers' Income	2086430.8
Total gain in Employment (Man-days)	11710.8

Here consumption multiplier is calculated through mpc on local products (mainly on food). Investors mpc on local products (mainly on food) is very low. So Investors' income doses not affect region's economy through linkages.

From the Table 12.25 we see that due to expansion of the sponge-iron factories there is some gain in employment but loss in income and agricultural output is very high.

Net Present Value Benefit per year (NPVB) = TB–TC.
NPVB (With Investors' surplus) = –4,47,31,119.2
NPVB (With Investors' surplus) = 9,58,84,173

Survey reveals there is 14953261.3 kg. loss of agricultural production and 45.43 bigha agricultural land is converted. From

TABLE 12.25
The Cost Benefit Analysis of Our Case Study can be Shown with the help of the Following Table

	Gain	*Loss*
Income (Rs.)		4,68,17,550
Without Investors' Income	20,86,430.8	
With Investors' Income	14,27,01,723	
Employment (man-days)	11710.8	41782.6
Agricultural output (kg.):		
Paddy		4572483.2
wheat		49992.4
Mustard		28250.1
Vegetables		302535.6

our case study we can interpret that the problem of micro food security may arise. From a case study of three sponge iron factory it has been seen that 4953261.3 kg agricultural production loss. Agricultural production reduces much higher due to sponge iron than other industries because sponge iron industries are highly polluting. If this process continues it may generate micro food security problem in future.

7. MACRO ANALYSIS OF OUR PROBLEM

In Lewis Ranis-Fei framework agriculture industry is analysed from the perspective of industrialisation. It is shown how through supply side agriculture helps the process of industrialisation in less developed countries. Agriculture supplies food, raw-material and labour to industry. Cheap and abundant supply of these inputs helps the process of capital accumulation in industry to go unhindered. It is shown that without an appropriate growth of agriculture the process of industrial accumulation can not be sustained for long. However, in our study we find a reverse impact of industrialisation on agricultural productivity. This reverse negative impact can be captured through simple modification of the Ranis-Fei framework. It could be shown that the reverse impact will have a reaction on the process of industrialisation as well.

If we consider all the industries together we can say that undoubtedly there is a huge fall in agricultural productivity due to land conversion, environmental degradation and resource depletion. All these three effects affecting negatively agricultural productivity may put a check on industrialisation initiating in classical 'Ricardian profit squeeze' inhibiting the process of accumulation and growth in industrial sector as a whole.

In the traditional agricultural sector there is disguised unemployment, perhaps even a core of surplus labour, and the wage rate is given by income sharing. Here another factor land is also taken into account. In the traditional agricultural sector there is some unutilised or barren land. Let us assume that the cost of preparing a unit of land for agricultural activities is also given.

Here we consider that there is a composite factor (T) including both labour and land.

$$T = \lambda_1 l_1 + \lambda_2 l_2$$

where l_1 = amount of land and l_2 = the corresponding amount of labour. λ_1 and λ_2 are two different constant. $0 < \lambda_1, \lambda_2 < 1$.

The agricultural production function is a function of the composite input.

$$\text{i.e. } Q = f(T)$$

Figure 12.1 (the basic idea taken from D. Ray, Development Economics, OUP 1998) provides schematic description of how the composite factor and the corresponding agricultural surplus are transferred in the process of development through industrialisation. As in Ranis-Fei model here also Diagram 12.1 depicts the industrial sector and Diagrams 12.2 and 12.3 the agricultural sector. In Figure 12.1 agricultural composite factor is considered from right to left while the industrial composite factor is considered from left to right. Let us assume that the total composite factor in the economy is OA. Out of which OB amount of surplus composite factor is present in the agricultural sector. In Diagram 12.3, the total product curve with respect to the composite factor is represented by AED. The cost for the composite factor is given at C^*.

$$C^*=W^*+L^*$$

where W^* is cost for labour and L^* is the cost of land to ready for agricultural production.

The composite factor C^* is proportional to the angle OAD. In Figure 12.1B, C*GFH represents the average agricultural supply curve. And in Figure 12.1A, *ss* is the supply curve of composite factor of the industry and *dd* is the value of marginal productivity curve of industrial composite factor. On the one hand supply of composite factor helps the process of capital accumulation in industry. So *dd* curve shift right. But on the other hand, (i) Industrial pollution => Decrease in agricultural production => Increase in price of food => Money wage increase => Profit decrease.

(ii) Industrial pollution => Health hazards => Decrease in labours productivity => Marginal productivity of composite factor decreases => *dd* curve shift to the left.

On one hand *dd* curve shifts to the right. On the other hand *dd* curve shift to the left. So shift of the *dd* curve is dependent on the relative strength of the two shifts.

Average agricultural surplus remains the same up to the transformation of OC amount of composite factor from agriculture to industry. But the transformation of composite factor OC reduces the average agricultural surplus. As a result of decrease in average agricultural surplus, price of agricultural output will increase. To maintain the same real wage rate as before money wage rate would have to be increased.[2] Hence, the composite input supply curve becomes upward rising. This raises the cost of production in industry restricting accumulation.

As a consequence of environmental degradation the total product curve of agricultural output shifts downward. And average agricultural surplus curve as in Figure 12.2B will also shift in downward directions. But extent of shift will be different depending on marginal pollution and marginal pollution effect. Two different situations may arise.

Fig. 12.1(A)

Fig. 12.1(B)

Fig. 12.1(C)

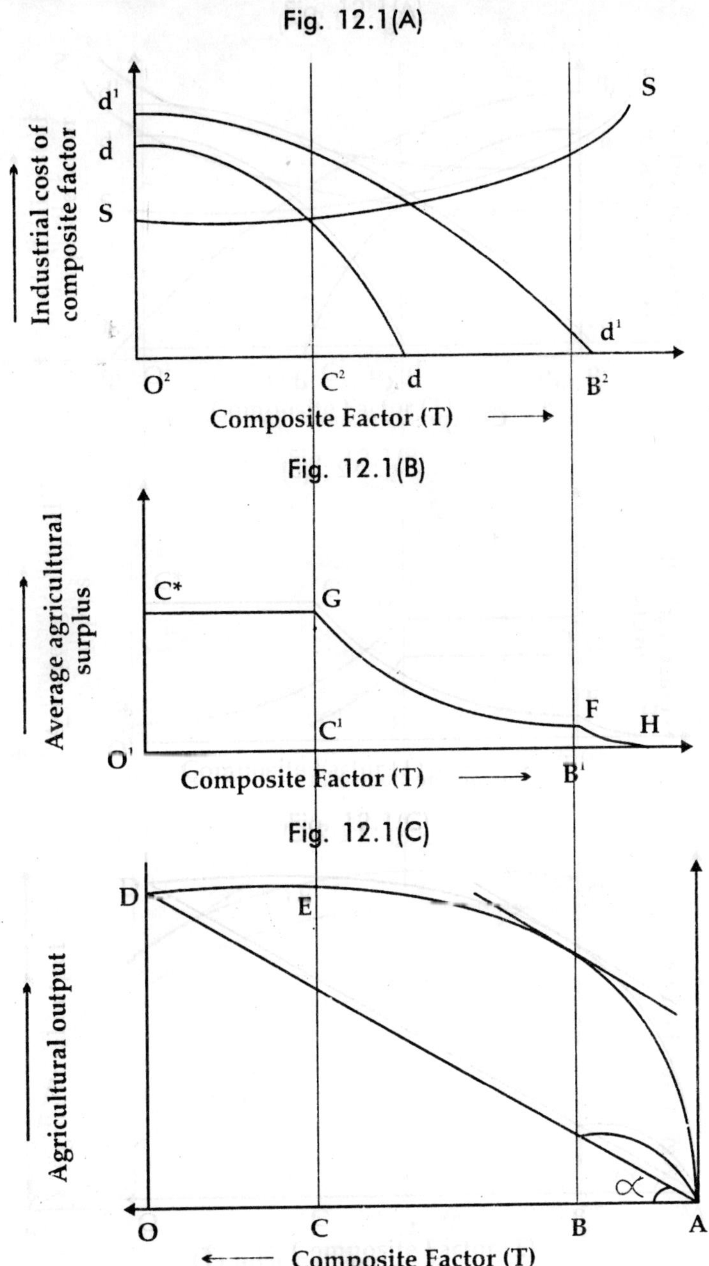

Fig. 12.2(A)

Fig. 12.2(B)

Fig. 12.2(C)

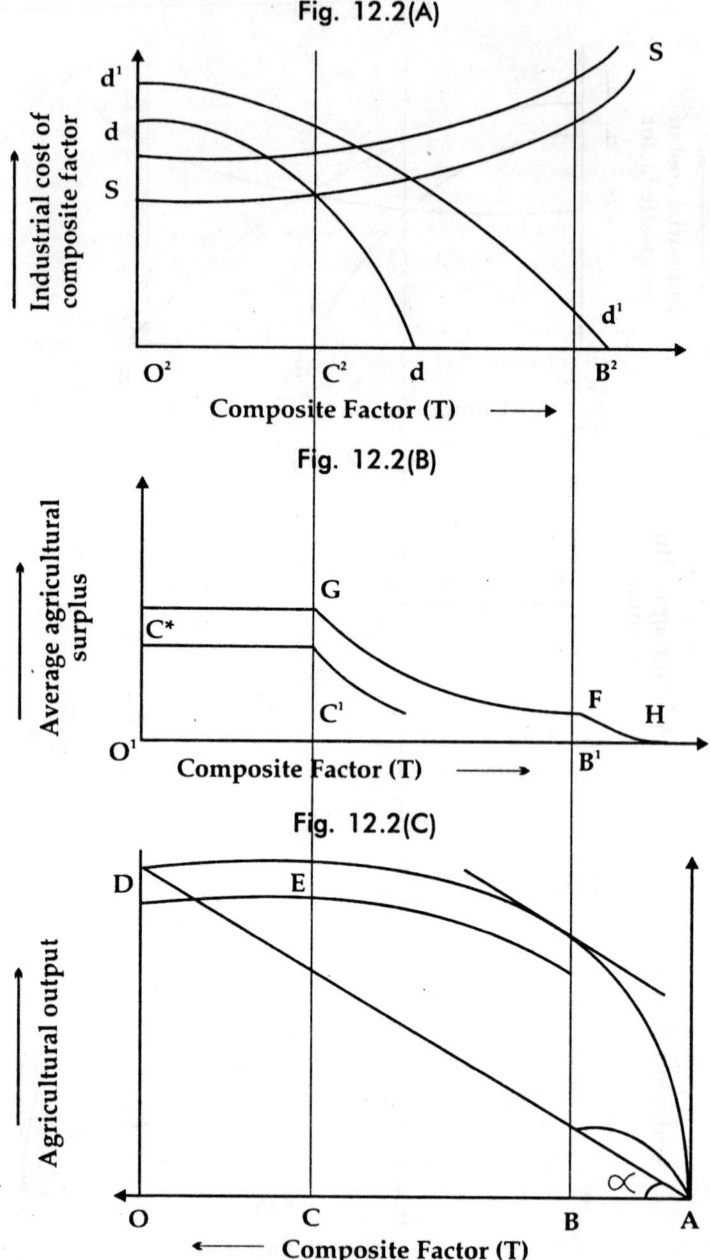

Fig. 12.3(A)

Fig. 12.3(B)

Fig. 12.3(C)

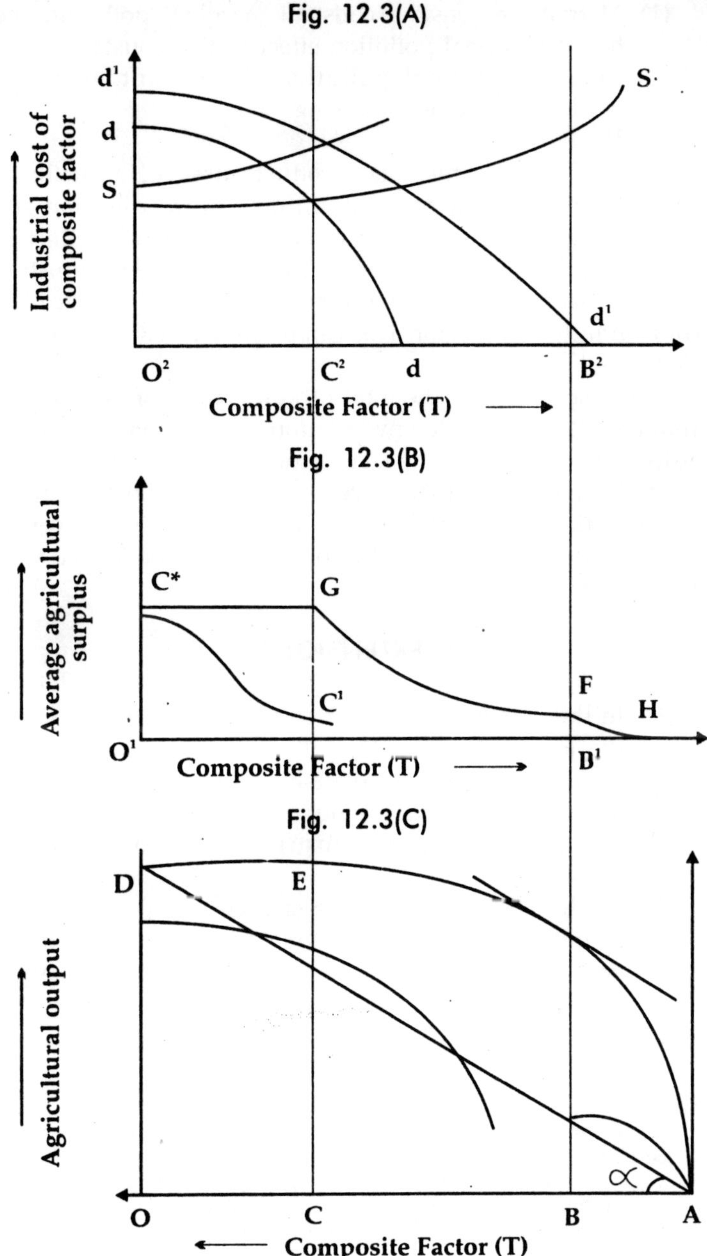

(1) At first we consider constant marginal pollution and hence marginal pollution effect is also constant.
(2) Even if marginal pollution is constant, marginal pollution effect is increasing.

In the first case the total product curve of agricultural output (AED) will shift parallelly in downward direction and hence average agricultural surplus curve will also shift in downward parallelly. As a result 'ss' curve in the industrial sector will shift in leftward directions. This will reduce the surplus in industrial sector. This can be shown with the help of Figure 12.2.

In the second case the total product curve of agricultural output (AED) will shift downward more rapidly than before. As transformation of composite factor from agriculture to industry increases, the total product curve, average agricultural surplus curve and the industrial labour supply curves and diverges more and more from the original one. This can be shown with the help of Figure 12.3.

8. EXTENSIONS

1. In this paper we consider cost-benefit analysis only in the local economy. We will consider the cost-benefit analysis in a broader scale in our further paper.
2. More detail analysis about the regional development that arises through industrialisation could also be considered.
3. Health costs can also be measured in a proper way.
4. In our further study we will consider in more detail analysis about several stages of demand and supply side linkage effects of industrialisation.

NOTES

1. Report from Nagarik Mancha.
2. Cost of composite input to industry increases due to the increase in wage-cost. It may have a spill-over effect on land cost as well for industry, but no direct impact of food price on land cost as such. Still due to increase in food price, as wage-cost rises total cost rises in industry.

References

Bhattacharya, R.N. (ed.) 2001. Environmental Economics—An Indian Perspective, New Delhi: Oxford University Press.

Hanley, Nick, J. Shogren, and Ben White (1999), Environmental Economics, New Delhi: Macmillan.

Lewis, A. (May 1954), "Economic Development with Unlimited Supply of Labour", The Manchester School, 22, 139-92.

Murty, M.N. and Surender Kumar (Feb., 2001), "Environmental and Economic Accounting for Indian Industry", *IEG Working Paper.*

Murty, M.N., Surender Kumar and Mahua Paul (Feb., 2001), "Environmental Regulation, Productive Efficiency and Cost of Pollution Abatement: A Case Study of Sugar Industry in India", *IEG Working Paper.*

Pamquist, R.B. , Leon E. Danielson (Feb. 1989), "A Hedonic Study of the Effects of Erosion Control and Drainage on Farmland Value", *American Journal of Agri. Eco.*, Vol. 71, No. 1, pp. 55-62.

Ranis, G. and J.C. Fei (September 1961), "A Theory of Economics Development", *American Economic Review*, Vol. 51, pp. 533-58.

Ranis, G. and J.C. Fei (June 1963), "The Ranis-Fei Model of Economic Development: Reply", *American Economic Review*, Vol. 53, pp. 452-54.

Ray, Debraj, Development Economics (2001), New Delhi: Oxford University Press.

Sankar, U. (ed) 2001, Environmental Economics: Oxford University Press.

Santakumar, V. and A. Chakraborty (Nov., 2000), "Environmental Valuation and its Implications on the Costs and Benefits of a Hydroelectric Project in Kerala, India", *Working Paper No. 309*, CDS, Thiruvananthapuram.

Sikder, Saumyen, Contemporary in Globalisation, Oxford University Press.

Reports

Survey of Indian Sponge-Iron Industry (2005) : Prepared by Joint Plant Committee.

Majumder, Sarajit, and Sarmishtha Sen, Durgapur Silpha Dushan, Nagarik Mancha.

Action against sponge-iron units (9 March 2006): *The Statesman.*

A report on *Anandabazar Patrika* (5 April 2006).

13

River and Government : A Case Study of Narmada[1]

Raj Kumar Sen and Somnath Hazra

I. INTRODUCTION

Rivers are much older than human civilization and it is a long story how rivers influenced the lives of living world all through this span barring the last 250 years or so. The rivers helped human beings like their mother nourishing them for all sorts of requirements. People used to depend on the rivers and history shows that the large cities usually grew on the banks of rivers. From the ancient times India regarded some of her mighty rivers not only sacred but also used to worship them. Narmada is one of such seven sacred rivers of India originating at Amarkantak where pilgrims visit to pay their tribute to the Goddess Narmada. India's heritage regards *parikrama* along the banks of Narmada a religious ritual from time immemorial. Governments were there and they also used the rivers in the same manner as the people used to do. However in present times its role has changed and in this paper we like to devote in the following sections how this role in modern times have interacted with the rivers in general and Narmada in particular. For this purpose we are concentrating on the modern period only and specially for India since 1950s with a focus on the Narmada Valley Project to demonstrate the interaction between first the governments and rivers and then the government of India and the Indian river system and finally the government of India and the governments of MP, Gujarat, Maharashtra and Rajasthan and the river Narmada.

II. GOVERNMENT AND INDIAN RIVERS

In 1776 when the industrial revolution started in England, human beings began to exploit the natural resources without any consideration for their protection and preservation. The plethora of scientific inventions and new discoveries made the people think that they will be the ultimate ruler of this world and be able to conquer the natural system including the rivers which once upon a time they used to treat with awe and admiration. The ever increasing demand for water required for industrialization led the governments to help the industries to store more water in the form of reservoirs by building dams on different rivers. Requirement of dams enhanced over time with the increase in such requirements for the purpose of agriculture and also to protect them from the different vagaries of nature like flood, erosion of banks, increasing urbanization, etc. Invention of electricity in the 20th century made human beings to search for its source through hydro-electric power generation. This again requires a continuous flow of water for which dams became important. Thus the government and the society started to interact with river in a new way to have more water, more electricity and to avoid floods and droughts.

When India became independent the concept of welfare society gained ground throughout the world with the gradual spread of the various communication systems like radio, telegraph, airways and the print media. People became aware that India belongs to the low income group of countries and naturally she wanted to grow fast to catch up the high income countries as early as possible. The example of Soviet Russia was at hand to follow a centralized planning strategy so that the long process of capitalistic development may be shortened. This led to the adoption of centralized five year planning when emphasis was given in the first plan to control of floods, growth of food production and generation of power among others. To achieve these targets India started her multipurpose river valley projects which required the construction of large number of dams over the numerous rivers of India. Such was the euphoria for these projects that the first prime minister of India while inaugurating the Bhakra Nangal Project in Punjab called it a modern temple of new India. This comment however he had to withdraw in 1962 before his death but that is a different story. This project was built in the model of Tenessy Valley Project of USA and it was followed over the subsequent five year plans almost every where and India became a country of big dams in the developing world.

However, the utility and popularity of the big dams gradually declined throughout the world due to their high cost in terms of money, displacement of large number of people, destruction of nature in the form of submergence and low benefits in terms of less than expected amounts of flood control, irrigation and electricity generation. One of the associates in such big dam projects had been the World Bank through its loans for such grandiose schemes. The concern of environment and displaced people gradually found voice in different corners of the world. It was found alternatives to such big dams exist and viable too in the form of minor and medium dams and reservoir and alternative source of energy so that the disequilibrium in the nature and in the society may be minimized. The sanctioning of such big dam projects were gradually reduced during the subsequent plans considering the unsatisfactory performance of many of them but not before the sanctioning of Narmada Valley Project which was the only one sanctioned in the Seventh Five Year Plan in April 1987. It should be remembered in this context that all sorts of development will lead to disequilibrium in the nature. But the nature has a tendency to restore the equilibrium over time but if the disequilibrium is carried too far it will not be possible for nature even to restore the equilibrium and heal the damages over time.

This Project has been termed as not only the largest river project in the world (*Alvares and Billory 1987*) but also as the world's largest planned ecological disaster. It is a colossal project which involved the setting up of the large number of dams in the valley through which the mighty and scared river Narmada flowed majestically sustaining then about 20 million of people in the heart of India. Of these two biggest dams, namely the Narmada Sagar in Madhya Pradesh and the Sardar Sarovar in Gujarat together hold more water than any other dam in the country. This has been publicized by the authority as one of the most ambitiously conceived projects in human history. On the other hand, the destructive economic potential and the disaster that it has brought to the lives of nearly a million people who are evacuated from their traditional habitat because of the submergence of extensive areas due to the construction of these dams, have prompted environmentalists all over the country and abroad to label it in the negative way and to them the initiation of the project was nothing but the pronouncement of the death sentence of the river Narmada.

However not only for Narmada but also for all types of projects commissioned in the name of economic development of India have resulted in eviction of people from the project sites and invariably in all cases they did not receive proper rehabilitation and adequate compensation. Thus the present phase of relationship between the government and the river since independence has led to the intervention of the courses of a large number of rivers for developmental purposes. Thus throughout the Indian history when the government had always taken the help of the rivers for the daily use of the citizens literally from their cradles to graves, is now playing a role which is really destructive for the rivers in the name of the process of economic development primarily aimed at upgrading the level of living of the population.

III. GOVERNMENT AND NARMADA

The original objectives of construction of mega dams on Narmada was to supply water to drought prone areas and make arrangement for irrigation in all the four states affected by it. The negative impacts of this project are both environmental in the form of submergence of huge areas which included forests, cropland, historical sites and societal due to loss of habitat for large number of people in this area, mostly tribals and certainly economic in the form of unfavourable benefit-cost ratio. We also find how the government in the interest of the population of one area has neglected the human rights and livelihood of the depressed people in another flouting all norms of environmental protection in this process. For instance in case of the Narmada Sagar project which is now renamed as Indira Sagar Pariyojana, the current estimated cost of the irrigation component is nearly Rs. 591 crores at the 1990 price level while the power component was Rs. 1575 crores. The unofficial estimate put these figures at a much higher level with a value of Rs. 3528 crores for the power component.

In this context we may refer to the Report of the Independent People's Commission (2004) which gives the vivid report of the State accountability in the context of the Indira Sagar Dam. It may be pointed out that on the basis of their visit in the project affected villages and areas facing full or partial submergence, the Commission has prepared their report which is really crucial in the context of relationship between the Government and the river so far as the displacement of the people is concerned. As this dam has resulted in the complete submergence of the Harsud town and the process of forcible dispossession of approximately 130 odd villages during 2000-04, these displaced people subsist scattered among undeveloped sites, forest and slums, living under inhuman conditions while the rising dam waters submerged their lands. The State machinery had been diligent in the precise execution of forcible displacement during this period and the Commission observed from their interview of more than 1400 affected persons, the distracting testimonials about the extent of state repression before this displacement. Public dissent was suppressed through the constant presence of police forces which intimidated the citizens into submission.

On 1st July 2004, the seven hundred year old town Harsud, the habitat of 22 thousand people was razed to the ground; though this acquisition was declared exactly two decades ago the resettlement site for the new Harsud town at Chanera, 17 kilometers from Harsud, no arrangement was undertaken for the resettlement infrastructure which commenced only in March 2004. In the true sense the new rehabilitation sites were not habitable at the time when the citizens of Harsud were forcibly relocated there. When the Commission visited this new site at Chanera in 2004 there were no provision for water, electricity, drains, roads, transport, sewers, markets, healthcare or crematoriums. The resettlement site was haphazardly assembled and was not a planned township. The oustees were forced to live in an extremely unhealthy condition with insufficient water and sanitary facilities leading to the spread of chronic gastrointestinal diseases. The original residents of Chanera also did not welcome the new neighbours who were labeled as villagers who received everything as free *(Phokatvada)*. The relatively affluent people among the displaced left for nearby towns leaving the unfortunate ones who were compelled to stay there consisting of mainly economically marginalized lower caste and *Adivasi* people and facing the discriminatory behaviour of the authorities. The mistreatment by the state also faced little organized resistance barring a few pockets of resentment due to the lack of any organized efforts to mobilize the people to protest against the ongoing injustices.

Thus it is observed in this context by the Commission that while official administration charged with the responsibility of forcibly displacing people leading to utter human suffering, they are ethically and legally obligated to act with integrity so that the displaced people are adequately informed of and accorded their rights and received requisite resettlement and rehabilitation without harassment and without being subject to extortions and violence. As this did not happen, there are human rights failure in the Indira Sagar Dam which raises fundamental questions about the nature and structure of state sponsored large scale development including the viability of mega dams. In this context we can relate the implementation of such projects which leads to the issues of the failure of state responsibility to afford people's right to give or withhold consent to state intervention that affects their lives, to information, decision-making and to their life, livelihood and cultural survival. Due to such failure of the state to ensure this right, we find emergence of civic and political discontent. The Commission observed people's experience of disposition and disenfranchisements connected with the Indira Sagar Dam which was escalated due to deliberate abandonment of their rights and their mistreatment on the part of all authorities working in this project.

IV. CONCLUSION

All these heart breaking descriptions of the Indira Sagar Dam leads to the conclusion that when the people in power try to follow a policy to subjugate the natural forces without following the policy of coexistence with them, this also leads to negative reactions which do not remain confined within the particular region only but spread in a hydra-headed manner to other areas also. The example of Narmada Valley Project clearly demonstrates the unsustainable nature of present policy of overall exploitation of environmental and ecological resources to which we referred earlier as our mother. The state trying to build up an unjustified and unsustainable relationship with the rivers have led to a violent conflict with all who were dependent on her. In this process the state has trampled not only human rights of the people whom they are supposed to protect but also has out stepped from its jurisdiction to gain its control which is both unethical and unjustified. What we said at the very beginning, it is extremely important to follow and enforce the principle of live and let live effectively in all sectors of human life and its relationship with living and non-living environment. Of course the current development paradigm based on the western principles of consumerism, utility and profit maximization without paying any heed to values and morality requires to be changed. Let us hope that the people become aware of this truth before it is too late. Otherwise the nature is bound to take revenge, the symptoms of which are becoming evident in the form of the impending doom of global warming and other forms of climate change, the magnitude and destructive power of which are beyond the imagination of human beings.

Note

1. Paper presented in the International River Festival during 23-25 February 2008 at Bandrabhan organized by Narmada Samagra.

References

Bahuguna, S. (1990): Dams and Disaster: There are Alternatives. *The Hindu,* 22 July.

Baba Amte (1990): *The Case Against the Narmada Sagar Project and the Alternative Perspective,* Anandwan.

CAISA (1988) : *In Sorrow and Anger the Victims Speak,* Bhopal.

CCPAL (1988): Review and Rescheduling of the Implementation Programme. Sardar Sarobar Narmada Project, *Final Report,* July.

Morse, B., T.R. Berger: (1992): *Sardar Sarovar: The Report of the Independent Review.* Resource Futures International, Inc. Canada.

Report of the Independent People's Commission (2004): *Without Land or Livelihood.* The Indira Sagar Dam: State Accountability and Rehabilitation Issues.

Roy, K.C. (1991): Environment and Culture in Economic Development. K.C. Roy *et. al.* (eds.) *Economic Development of Poor Countries.* IIDS. World Press, Calcutta.

Sen, Raj Kumar (1989): An Approach Towards the Eighth Five Year Plan. *The Economic Studies.* Vol. 28, No. 1, Calcutta.

Sen, Raj Kumar (1992, 1995 (p)): Environment *versus* Development: The Indian Experiences of Narmada and Baliapal, Roy, K.C. *et. al.* (eds.): *Economic Development and Environment: A Case Study of India.* Oxford University Press, New Delhi.

14

Role of Micro Finance in Empowering Rural Poor in West Bengal—A Case Study

ABDUL MOTIN AND HIRON KUMAR BANERJEE

In the developing countries, the rural poor consist (without exception) mainly of the landless, the marginal farmers and agricultural labourers who have practically no asset and depend only on their physical labour. One cause of poverty in these countries may be the poor peoples' lack of access to productive capital (Coleman 1999).[1] In these countries, local moneylenders are the principal source of credit to poor households, who often charge exorbitantly high rate of interest (100 percent or more than 100 percent per annum). Commercial banks, who charge interest rate generally in the range of 10 percent to 20 percent do not cater to the needs of the rural poor who require only small loans. The fundamental disadvantages faced by the formal lending institutions such as commercial banks and government lending agencies are the costliness of screening loan applicants, monitoring borrowers, and writing and enforcing contracts owing to imperfections in the Judicial system, backward infrastructure (e.g. transport and communication), and low level of literacy (Besley, 1995).[2] The village moneylender, on the other hand-holds all necessary information regarding his clients and can monitor their activities much more easily and cheaply than their potential competitors including the commercial banks. But the high cost of borrowing from the informal credit market precludes undertaking of many potentially profitable projects. This inefficiency may have a greater impact on poor women and children under their care than on men because women generally have even less access than men to formal credit markets.[3] Hence delivering sustainable, low cost credit to the poor, especially to poor women, should lead to increase in efficiency and equity by increasing their income and expenditure on children. Then our problem is to develop a system in which everybody (especially the poorest of the poor) can have access to credit, of course, with a regular repayment.

Micro credit through the Self-Help Groups (SHGs) has been claimed to be a solution to most of the problems that originated out of the efforts to alleviate poverty using the instrument of credit. The basic objective of a micro credit programme in the rural areas in any country is to reduce poverty of the rural poor through giving them small loan for income generating activity. 'Micro credit' symbolizes small loans extended to the poor for undertaking self-employment projects that would generate income and enable them to sustain themselves and their families. Generally, these loans are offered without any collateral. A distinguishing feature of peer group lending (Micro Credit through SHG) programmes is the aspect of joint liability which makes each group member mutually liable for the entire group's repayment obligations: each member of the group is held in default unless all loan repayments are made. This is a common feature in most cases of group loan contracts including the SHG system.

Micro finance as a tool to fight world poverty has created a debate in recent years over the nature and scope of potential tradeoffs between outreach,[4] impact[5] and sustainability[6] in micro finance lending (J. Conning).[7] Question arises whether joint liability lending or for that matter any type of micro finance really helps the poor.

As a matter of fact, the Grameen Bank in Bangladesh could function very well in terms of repayment rates but had little impact on poverty. Pitt and Khandker (1998) find, using data from three programmes in rural Bangladesh that borrowing from group lending schemes increased consumption of poor households. However, Murduch (1998b) has argued that Pitt and Khandker's result reflects programme selection effects rather than effect of borrowing *per se*. However, Coleman (1999) studies the question of programme impact in Northeast Thailand. He finds, "Impact is insignificant on physical assets, savings, production, sales, productive expenses, labour time, and most measures of expenditure, on health and education. On the other hand, impact is significant and negative on expenditure for men's health care. Perhaps more importantly, impact is significant and positive on women's high-interest debt because a number of members had fallen into a vicious circle of debt from moneylenders in order to repay their village bank loans. And impact is significant and positive on women's lending out with interest because some members engaged in arbitrage, borrowing from the village bank at its relatively low interest rate and then lending the money at a mark-up. There is no evidence in these results that village bank loans are being directly invested in productive activities with a positive return." And he concluded, "the poor are poor because of reasons other than lack of access to credit".[8]

The Swarnajayanti Gram Swarojgar Yojana (SGSY) was launched on first April, 1999 by restructuring the Integrated Rural Development Programme (IRDP), Training of Rural Youth for Self-Employment (TRYSEM), Development of Women and Children in Rural Area (DWCRA), Supply of Inputs and Tools in Rural Area (SITRA), Ganga Kalyan Yojana (GKY), and Million Wells Scheme (MWS) which were in operation in India for alleviation of poverty. The objective of the SGSY is to bring the poor families above the poverty line within a period of time. This objective is to be achieved by organizing the rural poor into Self-Help Groups through the process of social mobilization, training and capacity building and provision of income generating assets.

This paper seeks to evaluate the success of the SHG system in the district of Bankura in West Bengal. The exercise has been done not from the lender's point of view (lender's cost, profits, and loan recovery rates), but from the borrowers' viewpoint (empowerment of borrowers through alleviation of poverty).

STUDY AREA

Since inception a total number of 7266 Self-Help Groups (SHGs) have been formed up to June 2006 in the Bankura district of which 5023 (69.95 percent) groups are women groups. Out of the total number of groups formed, 4701 (64.70 percent) groups have been able to pass Grade-I during the same period, i.e. up to June 2006.

Our study has been conducted in two gram Panchayats, namely, Saltora and Amradanga under Taldangra block. Altogether 14 SHGs have been studied covering 205 members (households). In the Taldangra Block, our study area, 280 groups are operating at present. Most of these groups had been started in the year 2003 or after 2003. Before 2003, there were only a very small number of groups. Actually, when the Swarna Jayanti Swarojgar Yojana (SGSY) was launched in April 1999, it was wholly a Government programme. The concept of Self-Help specially of Self-help Group in the context of poverty alleviation was not comprehensible even to the educated community. District Rural Development Cell (DRDC) of the district headquarters somehow got the idea and they tried to disseminate that through the District Magistrates or the Collectors. From the district magistrates, it came down to the bottom level functionaries of the government, the Panchayat.[9] Some government officers like District Magistrates (DMs), Sub-Divisional Officers (SDOs), Block Development Officers (BDOs), and Child Development Project Officers (CDPOs) also took personal interest in the formation of Self-Help Groups. SGSY started in this background in the district of Bankura.

METHODOLOGY

The study is based mainly on primary data collected on the basis of a questionnaire prepared beforehand. The data were collected in two parts: the first set of questions takes into account the personal status personal status of the respondents such as number of members in the family, educational status, occupation, income, expenditure, etc. while the second set of questions deals with the question of empowerment of the respondent.

The question prepared beforehand were put to the members of the group orally both in the group and individually, and the answers were examined and cross-checked with the responses of fellow members in the presence of the people of the locality. A participatory and interactive approach has been used to gauge their sense of self-esteem and economic and social ability to face the reality. The data/information thus gathered have been analysed by the use of simple statistical techniques like average Standard Deviation, coefficient of variation, Skewness, Correlation and Regression.

ANALYSIS OF DATA

Out of the fourteen groups that we have surveyed, eight groups were promoted by Integrated Child Development Scheme (ICDS) workers, four groups by Gram Panchayat and the rest two by social workers. Through our interaction with the groups during survey it was revealed that there is at least one ICDS worker in each group. On query, it was learnt that each and every such worker was threatened by her superior officer to be discharged from service in case she fails to promote at least one group under her care. And being thus frightened, they were compelled to promote groups. Panchayats were also told to form groups and they in turn requested locally acceptable social workers for their help in promoting groups. It was also told that if some persons, belonging to the BPL[10] category form Self- Help groups, they will be entitled to have some financial help from the government in the form of subsidy. At last the journey began without knowing where to go.

Structure of the Groups

The SHGs surveyed under this study were formed by the people belonging to the socio-economically backward sections of the society. Altogether 14 SHGs have been studied covering 205 members (households). Of these 14 groups, four groups consist of members from Tribal families (one Santal and three Adibasis), two groups consist of Muslim women, four of Scheduled Caste people and other four groups consist of members from General Caste. Among the groups surveyed, two groups (14.28 percent) consist only of male members and the rest twelve groups (85.72 percent) consist only of female members. Out of the total 205 respondents, fourteen members belonged to the APL[11] category and the rest 191 members were BPL at the time of formation of groups.

Group members are well known to each other and have social relationship with each other. Membership of the group varies from 11 to 18 average being 15. Male and female groups operate separately. One male group, however, included one widow after her husband's death. But she remained totally inactive with respect to the activities of the group.

Family Size

Average family size of the sample households is round about five (5) with three adult and two children. Skewness for number of male children and number of female children are 0.6 and 1.2 respectively, which indicate that most of the families have higher number of male children compared to the number of female children. However, overall male female ratio is 51:49.

Literacy

Nearly one-third (66 in total) of the total members were literate and two-third is (139 in total) were illiterate at the time of forming the groups. After formation of Self-Help Groups most of the members had been made literate, at least functionally literate[12] either through peer learning method or through Mass Literacy Campaign (MLC). Regarding education level, most of the members of one particular group were educated up to Madhyamik level. It is to be noted here that most of the Muslim female members in the group (total 35) had education only up to Primary level. 18 members still remained illiterate.

Meetings

Group meeting was held regularly, once or twice in a month. Fifty percent of the groups were very much particular in recording the resolutions of the meeting in minutes book. Two male groups were found to be self-dependent in this regard. But others depend badly on the promoter/motivator of the particular group for noting down the proceedings of the meeting in their minute-book. Many minute-books were found incomplete during survey. However, there was no doubt that the meetings were held regularly. Presence of members in the group meeting was quite satisfactory in the sense that almost all the members of the group concerned remained present in the group meeting and put their signature in the minute-book.

In the group meetings, members initially discussed savings and money matters only. But as time passed, any issue that concerned the interest of members was discussed in the meetings. These could be family problems like a woman's husband coming home drunk and beating her, health problems in the family and of the neighbours, education of children particularly of girls, immunization of mother and child, family planning, prevention of early marriage of girls, drinking water problem, roads in the locality, want of attendance in the Gram Samsad Meeting and so on depending upon the socio-economic and political environment of the locality.

Land Holding

The members of the groups were very poor in the true sense of the term. Forty-three respondents had neither any land of their own nor they could hire any land for cultivation. Seven respondents owned three decimal of land and others owned 76 decimal of land on average. But the lands they possessed were Patta and Khas lands distributed by the government in their favour during Land Reforms in their area. Most of these lands are monocropping lands. Generally paddy and vegetables are grown, when and where water/irrigation is available.

Thrift Fund

The group members were found to save regularly. At the time of joining the groups, members of 13 groups would save only Rs. 10 per month. Recently that has been increased to Rs. 20-Rs. 30 per month. Members of only one group were found to have saved larger amount, Rs. 100 per month. Generally these savings were collected in the monthly meeting by the group leader who may be the chairperson or the secretary of the group. All the groups had opened savings account with the Mallabhum Gramin Bank, Sabrakone, in Taldangra block. The accounts were operated by the group leader, Sabhapati/Sabhanetri and the cashier.

Average own fund per group was Rs. 15923 with a minimum of Rs. 7012 and a maximum of Rs. 31300 and with a standard deviation of Rs. 7422. Members were given short term and medium-term loan both for consumption (in case of loss of crop, ill-health, and ceremonial expenditure) and production purposes. In spite of maintaining Pass Book for each and every member, a Register for thrift fund was maintained. Accounts were placed and discussed in the monthly or fortnightly meetings of the group with full transparency. The savings had become an inspiration to most of the female members because they had realized that the money solely belongs to them which they could use to meet unforeseen expenditures in the family. It had also been noticed that some of the group members were capable of saving more than Rs. 10 or Rs. 20 monthly but they had not yet changed it formally. All the sample groups charged Rs. 2 per month per Rs. 100 as interest on loan from own fund and the interest so earned was added to the Group's own fund.

Loans

All the groups covered by this study had received a Revolving Fund of Rs. 25000. But the concept of SHG-bank linkage was not clear to the group members. This could be clear from the following facts.

(a) The loan amount received from the bank by the groups carried from Rs. 15000 to Rs. 55000. Most of the groups had taken loan only once amounting to Rs. 15000 only of which Rs. 10000 is subsidy. This indicates the low credit absorption rate of the group. No effort on behalf of the groups in this regard was noticed during our interaction with the groups.

(b) The revolving fund was divided equally among the members where group members do not carry on group activity/activities as if it was their own money. Thus 'need' received less attention while disbursing the loan among members. This does not suit with the purposes of forming self-help groups.

(c) Almost all the group members except the group leaders told that they joined the group because they were told that they would receive a handsome amount of money, Rs. 125000, in the form of subsidy. Years rolled on but the said amount of subsidy was still beyond their reach. This made the group members frustrated. Being disappointed, some members left the group. In spite of that most of the members remained in the groups realizing that at least something was being saved in her/his account. Now the mind-set of the group members has changed. They are not hankering for subsidy. Each and every member expressed their willingness to run the groups even if subsidy is not granted to them. The only thing they need is a big loan. This is no doubt a positive sign in favour of sustenance of the groups.

(d) The SHG members had taken up income generating activity with a small amount of loan amounting to Rs. 800 to Rs. 1500 per head. But instalments for repayment of loan were not fixed though repayment was a regular one. Generally, repayment is made after harvesting or as and when earning is high because of change in demand or due to seasonal variations. Three members were found to be partially defaulter.[13] But as a whole each and every group was very particular in repayment of loan. But payment of instalment amount was very low which indicates the low loan absorption capacity of the members.

In some cases, the group members availed themselves of loans also from group's own funds.

But the process of internal lending of savings (loan from own fund) among members was very slow.

ASSETS HOLDINGS

Barring the APL households, other households in the sample do not possess any asset as such. The only mentionworthy asset they possess is Kancha or Semi Pucca house the average value of which stands at Rs. 12929. In most cases the house has been constructed by themselves. Asset in the form of livestock is worth not more than Rs. 8588. Only two groups own pump sets, threshers, and carts with joint ownership. No other group owns such type of assets. The households possess another type of asset in the form of durable consumption goods the value of which stands at Rs. 3887 per family. Durable consumption goods consist mainly of bicycles, wall clock or table clock or wrist watch, in some cases a radio and in some others gold ornaments. However, on an average a family's asset holding, excluding the value of land they possess stands at Rs. 25990.

One should note that only land, livestock and machineries are important from the point of view of production. No group member has purchased any land. They have got it from the government when it distributed the ceiling surplus land as a part of Land Reform policy. But it is interesting to note that before the group members joined the group they used to rear livestock on 'Bhag' (share). Generally big farmers, those who have small work force, give their goats or cows to the poor to rear them. They take their kids and the calves when they are ready for sale. The poor are paid Rs. 100 to Rs. 150 per goat and some more per cow at the time of selling out their kids and calves.[14] After joining the group, they have their own livestock. It is revealed that group formation played a positive role in favour of building productive assets worth around Rs. 10000 per family on an average. Regression analysis shows that assets in the form of livestock has a positive impact on SHG income of the members at the 0 percent level of significance whereas all other assets including land have no/insignificant impact on SHG income.

Revolving Fund (RF)

Those groups, which have proved their viability or sustainability, are entitled to receive revolving fund (RF). RF consists of two parts, namely, bank loan and government subsidy provided through the DRDA. This RF is kept in a special type of account named Cash Credit Account (CCA). The special feature of CCA account is that it is not a loan granted once for all. Subject to an upper limit a group can withdraw from that account any amount within the limit it wants as loan. It appears from the collected data that each Grade-I passed group has been granted a RF of Rs. 25000 only. Average loan taken till January, 2006 is around Rs. 36000[15] per group with a Median value (= Modal value) of Rs. 25000. The minimum and the maximum amount of loan taken by the groups are Rs. 15000 and Rs. 75000 respectively. Subsidy granted to the groups varies from Rs. 5000 to Rs. 10000 with a Median (and Mode) of Rs. 10000.[16]

It appears from the data collected that the contribution of bank in the loan to the SHGs is very insignificant and sometimes it is nil. The maximum amount of loan granted by the bank at a time is Rs. 25000. But in most cases SHG's own fund together with the subsidy given by the DRDA exceeds the loan advanced by the bank to the SHGs. For instance, for the lowest saving group in the sample, subsidy and own fund together stands at Rs. 12012 (Rs. 5000 as subsidy plus Rs. 7012 as own fund). In this case loan advanced by the bank is Rs. 15000 only. In the case of highest saving group in the sample, subsidy and own fund together stands at Rs. 41300 (Rs. 10000 as subsidy plus Rs. 31300 as own fund) but the amount of loan advanced by the bank is only Rs. 25000.

Activities Adopted

It has been observed that the members do not necessarily follow a common activity or group activity. Members of the two male groups work together as a group. But in their cases also no single activity has been adopted. They have adopted various activities relating to agriculture. In other cases, it has been observed that members carry out individual activities of their own choice. These activities include dairy, rearing of goats, babui grass rope-making, poultry, making plates from Sal leaves, trade in agricultural crops and in some cases cultivation of vegetables. In the selection of activities, previous knowledge of the members played a vital role. Income generating activities which get priorities are livestock schemes like dairy and Goatery (67 percent), Poultry and duck rearing (8 percent), Babui grass rope making (18 percent), agriculture (5 percent), paddy husking (1 percent) and making plates of Sal leaves (1 percent). However, income from SHG activities is not sufficient to support their family expenditure for 67 percent sample households. This income is an additional source of income. Their main source of income is labour on agriculture.

Chart 14.1
Pie Diagram Showing Activities Adopted by Sample Households

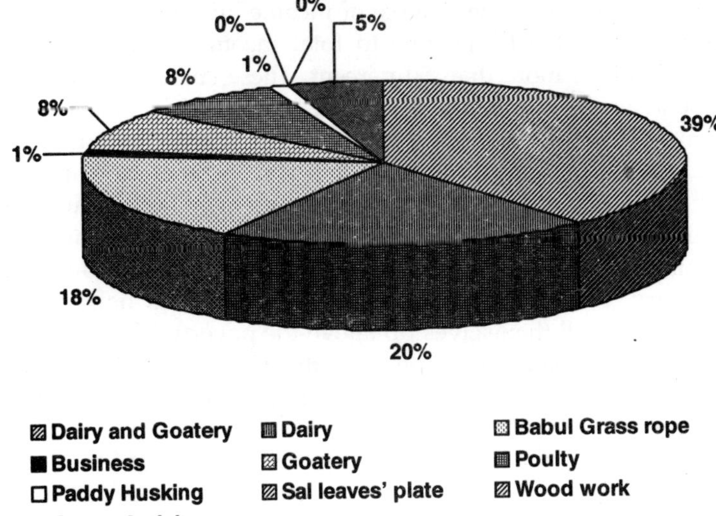

Sample size n = 205.

Three groups have received training for rearing of goats organized by the District Rural Development Agency (DRDA). They had helped them also in building goat-shed for rearing of goats free of costs. It should be noted here that the training they received proved quite insufficient in times of epidemic.[17]

Income

Average annual income of the surveyed group members is found to be Rs. 27533. Contribution of SHG loan run enterprise to the total income is Rs. 5632 on an average. The difference between Mean (Rs. 27533) and Median (Rs. 22000) coupled with positive skewness 6.56 implies that households having relatively low annual income are more in number than those having relatively high annual income. Percentage wise, 21 percent of total income comes from SHG loan-run activities and 79 percent from other source, mainly from wage. Average per capita income per month for the group members stands at Rs. 472. The Median value and modal value are Rs. 390 and Rs. 500 respectively with standard deviation of Rs. 409 and skewness 5.6. If we look into the data in more detail we see that one household has no other source of income but SHG income and contribution of SHO income to total income for another five households is more than 50 percent. These six families mainly depend on SHG income. The Modal value of income earned from SHG activity is Rs. 6000 per year with a minimum of Rs. 1800 and a maximum Rs. 18000. This income has helped in supplementing the income of the group members. If income from the SHG loan-run activities is not included in the total income, 110 families out of 205 families will fall under BPL category. So we see that group formation has helped 183 families to pull themselves up above the poverty line of Rs. 302 per capita consumption[18] per month—a success rate of 89.26 percent. This signifies the importance of forming Self Help Groups.

Regarding the factors on which the income from SHG loan-run enterprise depends, we selected six factors such as family size, assets other than land, land holding, income from other source, type of activities adopted and level of education. Family size was again classified according to the number of adult

Table 14.1
Regression of SHG Income on Explanatory Variables in Bankura

Summary Output						
			Numeraire = Paddy Husking			
Regression Statistics						
Multiple R	0.485601179					
R Square	0.235808505					
Adjusted R Square	0.175158386					
Standard Error	3213.348779					
Observations	205					
ANOVA						
	df	*SS*	*MS*	*F*	*Significance F*	
Regression	15	602191750.8	40146116.72	3.888013904	4.62325E-06	
Residual	189	1951540361	10325610.38			
Total	204	2553732112				
	Coefficients	Standard Error	t Stat	P-value	Lower 95%	Upper 95%
Intercept	2259.522891	1253.099321	1.803147486	0.072957866	-212.3332656	4731.379047
Education	725.8507486	180.6772728	4.017388227	8.48719E-05	369.4478509	1082.253646
No of adult members in the family	336.9333069	186.3618573	1.807952077	0.072203742	-30.68296786	704.5495816

(*Contd.*)

Table 14.1 (Contd.)

Assets in land	2.226869193	2.885002768	0.771877663	0.441150934	-3.464069853	7.917808239
Asset in the form of Livestock	0.091767556	0.03427286	2.677557614	0.00806876	0.02416112	0.159373992
Other Assets	-0.000970147	0.008024811	-0.120893438	0.903903867	-0.016799841	0.014859547
Income from other Source	-0.036549004	0.010949215	-3.338047839	0.001016096	-0.058147359	0.014950648
D2 D&G	1205.19607	1176.523722	1.024370395	0.306969674	-1115.607523	3525.999663
D3 Goatery	1133.854358	1178.679724	0.96196985	0.337293864	-1191.202151	3458.910868
D4 DRY	79.03710806	1267.044363	0.062379117	0.950326844	-2420.326953	2578.40117
D5 BGR	1732.923481	1280.64872	1.353160671	0.177620618	-793.2764535	4259.123416
D6 Sal plate	104.7075315	3407.754147	0.030726258	0.975520273	-6617.407728	6826.822791
D7 PLTRY	-755.5072836	1959.584857	-0.385544561	0.700267584	-4620.972545	3109.957977
D8 BUSI	1342.944232	3421.909268	0.392454658	0.695164538	-5407.093336	8092.981799
Agriculture and Dry	2470.833698	1428.350613	1.729850973	0.08528941	-346.7220993	5288.389496
D1 AGR	729.9979102	1225.089574	0.59587309	0.551972929	-1686.606389	3146.602209

members and child members in the family. Assets other than land were classified into four groups, namely, house, livestock, machinery/tools and durable consumption goods. It may be assumed that the family size, land holding size and assets holding as well as income from other sources will have a positive correlation with the income from SHG run enterprise. However, data analysis on the above factors shows a variety of interesting results. The impact of land holding as well as of asset on the income from SHG loan run enterprise is insignificant. Only asset in the form of livestock has a positive though moderate impact on the SHG income. As regards the size of the family, not the family size as such but the number of adult members in the family has a direct relationship with the income from SHG loan-run enterprise (Regression coefficient is 336.93, significant at 7% level of significance). This is obvious because an extra adult member means an extra earning unit. But things do not go the same as stated above. This is due to the problem of child labour from which every BPL families suffer. In every BPL family children are in some form or other engaged in work to augment their family income. And so there exists a positive correlation between family income and family size. When family income is correlated with the number of adult members only, this implies that children in those families are not employed/engaged in income earning activities. What do they do then? Most probable answer is that they go to school. This will be clear if we examine the relationship between the level of education and income from SHG run enterprise. The level of education is highly correlated positively with SHG income (Regression coefficient is 725.85, significant at less than 1% level of significance). This implies that members have become interested in sending their wards to school.

So far as income from activities carried on by the SHG members is concerned, among the nine activities such as Paddy Husking, Agriculture, Dairy, Goatery, House Poultry, Babui Grass Rope-making, Sal leaves plate-making, Business, Dairy with agriculture—SHG income from paddy husking is Rs. 2260. This income is statistically significant at 7 percent level. This has been taken as numeraire. SHG income for Dairy with agriculture is Rs. 4730 (Rs. 2260+Rs. 2470). This income is significantly greater than that from paddy husking at 8 percent level of significance (see regression table). For Agriculture, Dairy, Goatery, House Poultry, Salleaves plate-making, Babui Grass Rope-making, and Business, SHG income is not significantly different from that of paddy husking. Babui Grass Rope-making appears to be the next best gainful activity adopted by the group members with regression coefficient Rs. 3993 (Rs. 1733 + Rs. 2260) but not significant at 5 percent level. Business also appears to be a gainful activity adopted by the group members. But engagement with business requires at least some level of education. This again justifies the willingness of the SHG members to educate their children. However, all the activities adopted by the SHG members as income generating activity have positive impact on their income as it appears from the above regression table.

Data analysis shows a negative correlation between the income from SHG loan-run enterprise and the income earned from other source (Regression coefficient is –0.036549, significant at less than 1 percent level). General experience suggests that income of a family from any source may be helpful in increasing income from an enterprise run by the same family. Because whatever the source may be, it forms a strong economic base for the family. But this was not found to be true in this case. Rather the opposite was true. The logic may be that the poorest of the poor who have negligible income from sources other than SHG, grab this opportunity whole heartedly. In that case SHG business becomes the main source of their livelihood. And those who earn a sizeable income from alternative sources find little interest in SHG business. This explains the negative relationship between income earned from SHG loan-run enterprise and the income from other sources. A policy implication may follow from this:

> Self-Help Groups formed with the poorest of the poor may show better performance than better off poor to increase their income through SHG activity.

Expenditure Pattern

Average per capita expenditure per month of the sample households has been estimated to be Rs. 354 with a minimum of

Rs. 213 and maximum of Rs. 1000. The difference between Mean (Rs. 354) and Median (Rs. 315) coupled with positive skewness (2.68) implies that the number of families having low per capita monthly expenditure is more than those with relatively high per capita, monthly expenditure. However, monthly per capita expenditure worth Rs. 354 indicates that the households incurring that expenditure are well above BPL (Rs. 302). Fourteen members of the sample households were above poverty line at the time of joining the group. The rest 191 members were BPL. The sample groups were formed in between the year 2000 to 2002. So we can reasonably accept the estimate of poverty level of the census 2001. Population census 2001 measured the poverty line by per capita expenditure per month which was estimated to Rs. 272. However, Department of Panchayat and Rural Development Government of West Bengal, estimated Rs. 302 per capita per month expenditure as the poverty line for West Bengal. According to this estimate those people are poor whose consumption per month is below Rs. 302. So we see that group formation has helped the poor families to pull themselves up above the poverty line of Rs. 302

Chart 14.2
Expenditure Patterns of Sample Households

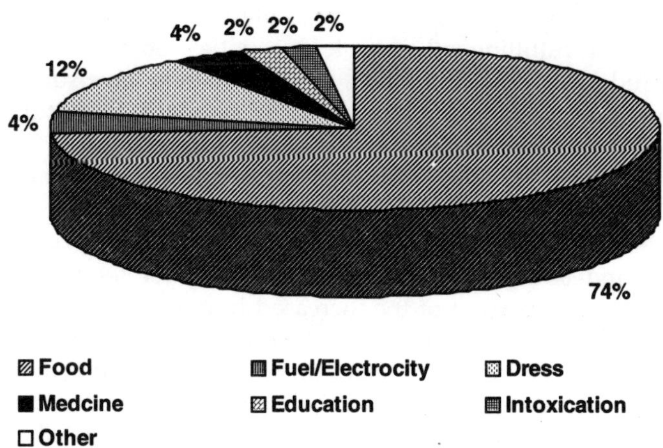

Sample size n = 205.

per capita consumption per month. But if we look at the break-up of total expenditure, we see that share of expenditure on food items is 73 percent of total expenditure followed by dress 10 percent, Medicine 5 percent, fuel/electricity 4 percent, education 2 percent and intoxicative items (like beetle leaf, bidi, cigar, tobacco, Guraku, liquor, etc.) 4 percent. This reveals that 98 percent of income is spent on the bare necessities of life needed for survival. The food items include cereals 57.13 percent, edible oil 8.42 percent, vegetables 11.25 percent, meat/fish 6.02 percent, grossaries 14.54 percent and sugar 2.64 percent. The expenditure pattern of the sample households proves that they are still in the initial phase of development. Because, when a person crosses the line of starvation (poverty line), with every increase in his income he will spend more income for food, for more food and better food. When and only when he reaches a certain desired level, he will think of allocation of increased income for purchasing goods other than food items. During interaction with group members surveyed, some of them responded saying that they did not buy fish/meat and even vegetables. They eat fish/meat as and when they get enough time for catching it. This generally occurs during the slack agricultural season when wage employment for them is rarely possible. Same thing can be said regarding consumption of milk, egg, fruits, etc. Members of the three fourth of the SHGs surveyed, carry on House Dairy, Goatery and/or Poultry. They sell it for fulfilling other basic necessities. So we can safely conclude that though the BPL group members have succeeded in attaining a minimum level of living standard, they still have to progress more to attain a decent living standard. This is proved from the Engel elasticities calculated from the data collected from the surveyed group members. The Engel elasticity for food is 0.947 followed by medicine 0.919, dress 1.697 and education 1.342. Engel elasticity for food indicates that about 95 percent of the increased income is spent on food.

One thing should be noted here. It is seen that only 2 percent of total income is spent on education. But this does not necessarily mean that they are not willing to have education for their wards. The fact is that they are very much interested in this regard which is observed from the Engel elasticity of education. The Engel elasticity of education for the surveyed households is

TABLE 14.2

Engel Elasticities in Respect of Sample Households in Bankura

Item	*Food*	*Dress*	*Medicine*	*Education*	*Intoxication*	*Others*
(1)	*(2)*	*(3)*	*(4)*	*(5)*	*(6)*	*(7)*
P-value	1.8292E-111	1.87991 E-39	8.51978E-12	0.036632967	0.067125036	0.41778
Engel elasticity	0.947264731	1.169733197	0.919148487	1.342011508	1.178102678	0.07460
Adjusted R Square	0.917217728	0.57348241	0.201808785	0.016515304	0.011571299	0.01077
F	2250.21585	273.9475454	52.57785677	4.425698558	3.388179282	3.21188
Significance F	1.8292E-111	1.87991E-39	8.51978E-12	0.036632967	0.067125036	0.07460

estimated to be 1.342 which is rather elastic. Moreover, the average age of group members being 30-35 years, age of most of their wards are below 14 years. Almost all children go to school but the parents do not have to incur any expenditure on education except for buying writing materials and for engaging private tutors although free education is provided by government up to the Higher Secondary level. There are schools also for tribal students where arrangements for keeping children for the whole day are there with the provision of meal. All the nearby tribal families avail of that opportunity which has made that area drop out free.

Empowerment

The meaning of empowerment is 'having authority'. The most important is the sense of having it. The acknowledgement of the existence of an individual along with her/his views, ideas and intelligence is the main thing. Empowerment makes a person self-confident. Only a self-confident individual can take decision, give suggestion and even control her/his own life. However, it is a very tough and long process to empower oneself. Empowerment process is tougher in rural areas because the lives of poor women in our country appear in one way or another to be affected by a number of institutional factors. The most important among these institutional factors is social taboos, which make poor women lose their self-confidence and control over their own income and even control over their own lives. Even when a woman is economically empowered, social taboos act as the most powerful impediment to her empowerment. Women's access to education and information along with control over their own income as well as social exposure and property rights can facilitate their empowerment process. All these, in turn, can influence the economic growth of the country and thereby eliminate poverty.

Considerable emphasis has been placed in the literature on primary education being the key to the success of women's empowerment process. Education is an entitlement that enables a woman to use her skill and knowledge to increase her capabilities. *Proper education will help to reduce the family size, which is considered to be one of the basic causes of poverty in most developing countries*. Experts agree that education of girls and women is associated with reduced fertility. The most important link between female education and reduced fertility is the effect of education on the age at marriage. But to have a strong impact on fertility a girl must have completed primary school and also have secondary school education. Delayed marriage delays the first pregnancy and reduces the fertility span in a woman's life. Education improves a woman's awareness of her own worth and the worth of her children and through interactions with a wider world she becomes aware of opportunities open to her beyond motherhood. Education leads to aspirations for better qualified children. The number of children, especially, the number of sons which women consider desirable, decreases with increase in education. Education brings in status and prestige for women through social and economic autonomy and self-reliance. Besides education, survival rate of female children, female labour participation rate, proportion of unmarried female in the age group of 15-19 and the involvement of women as clients (Bank) with direct access to financial services are some other important factors by which the degree of empowerment can be judged.

We have used correlation matrix to judge the correlations among different qualitative aspects of the programme measured by some score variables suitable for the purpose. Significance of the correlation is also tested by using the conventional t-statistics such that $t^2 = \frac{r^2 \times \text{degree of freedom}}{1-r^2}$, where r is the correlation coefficient.

With 205 observations the degree of freedom is 203. Thus with 1 percent level of significance t is greater than 2.576 for all values of r greater than 0.19.

Aspiration Level

Data analysis shows that the perception of the SHG members regarding the impact of their activities on income/ economic condition is very high. 96 percent group members (184 out of 191 BPL members) admit that group formation and adoption of activities through provision of loan by the group

Table 14.3

Degree of Linear Association among the SHG Income and Aspiration Related Factors in Bankura

Aspiration Level	*Income from SHG run enterprise*	*Improvement of economic condition*	*Poverty alleviation*	*Women's position in the family*	*Willingness to educate children*	*Future prospects of wards*
(1)	(2)	(3)	(4)	(5)	(6)	(7)
Income from SHG run enterprise	1					
Improvement of economic condition	0.169829	1				
Poverty alleviation	0.166235	0.77095314**	1			
Women's position in the family	0.167809	0.60359394**	0.614194**	1		
Willingness to educate children	0.093316	0.1 7679401	0.208741 **	0.289405**	1	
Future prospects of Wards	0.098727	-0.0694369	-0.033920	-0.0711095	0.074281	1

have helped them in increasing their family income. 3.5 percent members were not confident enough in telling whether SHG activity affected their income positively. It seems in those cases incomes have not increased significantly. Only 0.5 percent members responded with a negative answer saying that their incomes have not changed at all. Obviously, they are the unsuccessful members. However, 91 percent members opine that by this way (with the help of the group) they can get rid of their poverty. Similarly, 89 percent of the female members admitted that their position/status within their family has improved. 94 percent members expressed their willingness to educate their children/wards. The rest 6 percent members were silent on this particular point because they did not have any son/daughter below the age of 14. In that sense, each and every member is keen on getting education for their wards. Their aspiration level about the future of their wards goes up to the level of Doctor (one respondent), Engineer (two respondent), Teacher, Service, etc. 33 percent members could not make out what they want to see in their wards in future. All the above variables namely perception about the improvement of economic condition, poverty alleviation, position of the female members in the family, education of children and future prospect of their wards are positively correlated with the income from SHG loan-run enterprise. Correlation coefficients in all the above cases are positive.

Awareness Test

Regarding opportunities availed of by the members themselves, members of organizations other than SHG appear to be well informed and are in a better position to utilize the opportunities available to them. Correlation coefficient between the membership of other organization and information on credit facilities provided by the government is 0.71. Again, availability of government assistance for housing for the poor depends on the relation with the Panchayat. Correlation coefficient between consciousness about Government Planning on housing for the poor and regular contact with Panchayat is 0.38. Whereas consciousness on family planning is related to the relation with social worker or institution (correlation coefficient is 0.45) and

Table 14.4

Degree of Linear Association among the SHG Income and Awareness Related Factors in Bankura

	Income from SHG run enterprise	*Member of any other organisation*	*Consci-ousness of credit facilities*	*Conci-ousness on housing (IAY)*	*Consci-ousness on education*	*Consci-ousness on medical and health facilities*	*Consci-ousness on family planning*	*Relation with social worker*	*Reads news and/or listen to Radio*	*Relation with Pan-chayat*	*Aware-ness of local problems*
(1)	(2)	(3)	(4)	(5)	(6)	(7)	(8)	(9)	(10)	(11)	(12)
Income from SHG run enterprise	1										
Member of any other organisation	-0.190**	1.000									
Consciousness of credit facilities	-0.132	0.710	1.000								
Consciousness on housing (IAY)	0.008	0.187**	0.182	1.000							

Consciousness on education	-0.070	0.336**	0.280**	0.418**	1.000						
Consciousness on medical and health facilities	-0.200**	-0.126	-0.053	-0.011	0.259**	1.000					
Consciousness on family planning	-0.047	-0.088	-0.092	0.101	0.000	0.269**	1.000				
Relation with social worker or institution	0.033	-0.017	-0.023	0.114	0.138	0.031	0.450**	1.000			
Reads news and/or listen to Radio or T.V.	-0.091	0.365**	0.359**	0.061	-0.040	0.097	0.079	0.176**	1.000		
Relation with Panchayat	-0.116	0.085	0.083	0.381**	0.173	0.053	0.323**	0.128	0.079	1.000	
Awareness of local problems	-0.067	0.049	0.048	0.219**	0.099	0.154	0.575**	0.259**	0.046	0.575**	1

with the awareness of local problems (correlation coefficient is 0.51). A high correlation coefficient between awareness of local problems and relation with the Panchayat for information implies that those who keep close contact with the Panchayat know much better about the locality as well as about the various facilities provided by the Government for the poor.

Building Leadership

SHG is very much helpful in building leadership quality among its members. During interaction with the respondents, 93 percent members admitted that they are able and willing to take the charge of running their group if they are asked to do so. Only 7 percent members expressed their inability and unwillingness for taking over the charge of the group. This is undoubtedly an important indicator of self-confidence. But so far as female member's participation in the decision-making process is concerned they are still in an adverse position in exercising their decision making powers (correlation coefficient between exercising of voting power and SHG income is –0.352).

Social Security

Strong correlation is observed between better sanitation and better health for the family and for the neighbours (correlation coefficient is 0.899). But only 37 percent members own privy in their home. The members are, however, well aware of that problem and they have deposited their shares for Sulava Souchagar (Low Cost Privy) to the local authority, i.e. local Panchayat.

Empowerment of Women and Poor People

Formation of SHG, it is assumed and found to be true, will help the group members to improve their economic condition. It will also empower the poor, especially the women. 96 percent group members (184 out of 191 BPL members) admitted that group formation and adoption of activities through provision of loan by the group had helped them in increasing their family income. 89 percent of the female members admitted that their

TABLE 14.5
Degree of Linear Association among the SHG Income and Leadership Related Factors in Bankura

Building Leadership and Democratic Organisation	*Income from SHG run Enterprise*	*Want to take the leadership*	*Helps others in the locality*	*Seeks regular help from promoter*	*Operates passbook himself*	*Attend Gram Samsad meeting*	*Who take the decision of voting?*	*Who takes the decision of marriage?*
(1)	(2)	(3)	(4)	(5)	(6)	(7)	(8)	(9)
Income from SHG run enterprise	1							
Want to take the leadership	0.008	1						
Helps others in the locality	-0.08	0.190**	1					
Seeks regular help from promoter	0.092	-0.03	-0.09	1				
Operates passbook himself	0.2	-0.1	-0.02	0.121	1			
Altend Gram Samsad meeting	0.207**	-0.04	-0.04	0.112	-0.02	1		
Who takes the decision of voting?	-0.35**	0.108	-0	-0.25**	-0.1	-0.17	1	
Who takes the decision of marriage?	-0.04	0.017	-0.18	-0.19**	0.007	0.015	0.134	1

TABLE 14.6

Degree cf Linear Association among the SHG Income and Social Security Related Factors in Bankura

Enhancement of Social Security	*Income from SHG run enterpris*	*Care for belter health*	*Care for belter education for the children*	*Whether care for better sanitation*	*Whether owns a privy*	*Care for better nutrition*	*Conscious of local problems*	*Participates in TL/ PY campaign*
(1)	*(2)*	*(3)*	*(4)*	*(5)*	*(6)*	*(7)*	*(8)*	*(9)*
Care for better health	-0.17	1						
Care for belter education for the children	-0.1	0.388**	1					
Whether care for belter sanitation	-0.19**	0.899**	0.412**	1				
Whether owns a privy	0.07	-0.33**	0.111	-0.31**	1			
Care for belter nutrition	0.001	0.071	0.042	0.073	0.006	1		
Conscious of local problems	-0.1	0.696**	-0.14	0.679**	-0.6**	0.049	1	
Participates in TLC/PYC	0.166	0.08	-0.05	0.076	-0.06	0.017	0.145	1

position/status within their family have improved. Correlation between willingness to educate male children and that for female children is also very high (0.9173). This implies/indicates that those who want to educate their male children also want to educate their female children. This also indicates that even in the BPL families gender discrimination in the field of education is becoming narrow. There is also a positive correlation between eagerness for educating their children and improvement of women's position in the family (Correlation coefficient is 0.30). From this one can conclude that improvement of women's position in the family will lead to a qualitative transformation of the family through education for both male and female. Joining SHG has improved the employment opportunities of the member households. In the pre-SHG situation they would remain idle in the lean seasons and hence approach moneylenders for consumption loan at exorbitantly high rates of interest. The scope for gainful employment has gone up among the sample households through the loan-run enterprises. Women participation rate as principal worker in the sample has been estimated to be 90 percent. This has helped in reducing poverty of the members and their dependence on moneylenders for consumption loans. Again, the number of unmarried female in the family is positively correlated with the number of earning female member in the family (correlation coefficient is 0.585) which implies that in those families where opportunity of employment for women is lower, greater is the chance of getting them married early. A probable reason may be that the guardians of unmarried women want to shift the burden of their daughters to in-laws as early as possible where there are little chances of employment. This is true especially in cases of the poor families who can hardly afford to look after their families including the unmarried girls properly. They have a natural tendency to avail of the first chance of getting their daughters/sisters married irrespective of their age of maturity. So early marriage of girls can be stopped or at least be reduced through creation of opportunities for their gainful employment. SHG can play and are playing a vital role in this respect.

Infant mortality rate below the age of 5 (q_5) for our sample households is fairly lower than the national average (74). Infant mortality rate below the age of 5 has been estimated at 57 and

TABLE 14.7

Degree of Linear Association among the SHG Income and Empowerment Related Factors in Bankura

Empowerment of women and poor people	*Income from SHG run enterprise*	*Women's position on in the family*	*Conscio- usness on family planning*	*Female child below 5 years died*	*Male child below 5 years died*	*Want to educate female child*	*Want to educate male child*	*Owns a pass book in the bank*	*No. of female engaged in wor*	*No. of unmarried female in 15-1*	*Want to take the leaders hip*	*Operates pass nook him- self*
(1)	(2)	(3)	(4)	(5)	(6)	(7)	(8)	(9)	(10)	(11)	(12)	(13)
Income from SHG run enterprise	1											
Women's position in the family	0.168	1										
Consciousness on family planning	-0.047	-0.039	1									
Female child below 5 died	-0.032	0.195**	0.026	1								
Male child below 5 died	-0.006	-0.116	0.028	0.173	1							
Want to educate female child	4E-04	0.058	-0.037	-0.061	0.068	1						

Want to educate male child	0.013	0.011	-0.039	-0.051	0.072	0.917**	1					
Owns a pass book in the bank	0.205**	0.067	0.052	-0.092	-0.097	-0.019	-0.005	1				
No. of female engaged in work	-0.016	0.014	-0.062	-0.097	0.193**	0.053	0.02	-0.18	1			
No. of unmarried female in 15-19	-0.004	-0.014	-0.007	0.053	0.096	0.223**	0.225**	0.398**	0.585**	1		
Want to take the leadership	0.008	0.239**	-0.026	-0.190**	-0.062	-0.065	0.008	0.092	0.028	-0.11	1	
Operates passbook himself	0.2**	-0.026	-0.01	0.017	0.018	-0.045	-0.026	-0.121	0.196**	-0.167	-0.096	1

46 respectively for males and females. The more important thing is that the q_5 for females is lower than that of males. Correlation analysis of the collected data shows that mortality rates among children is negatively correlated with SHG income, number of females engaged in work and improvement of women's position in the family. This is highly important because mortality rates among children have a strong influence on the reproductive behaviour of couples and thus on fertility rates.

All these discussion lead us to conclude that SHGs have helped the participating rural poor in their gaining empowerment.

6. Social Development Programme

Members are also engaged in various programmes for social development, a few of which are mentioned below:

(a) Members of the 11 groups are also members of Astasol-Rajpur Joint Forest Management Committee and are in charge of Restoration and Protection of 200 acres of forest area.

(b) Women members of 4 tribal groups are also active members of Mata Sikshsa Committee (Mother Education Committee) in tribal areas. Besides, they are members of Village Education Committee (VEC), which consists of male and female members in equal proportions.

(c) Most of the women members of the surveyed groups act as member of Swasthabidhan Committee (Health Committee at the village level), formed by the Panchayat. They normally participate in various vaccination programmes for both child and mother, and campaign against Cholera, Diarrhoea, Malaria, Leprosy and other diseases under the guidance of the Panchayat.

(d) Group members are now the facilitators and motivators of school drop-out students. A few members are engaged in teaching neo-literates of adult literacy programme.

(e) They are fighting against addiction to liquor and trying to make the people within and outside the family understand the adverse effects of intoxicating articles/ items on health as well as on the economic condition of the family.

(f) They have started a move towards making the locality a Nirmal one (clean village) under the Yojana 'Nirmal Gram' (Clean Village) and as already mentioned, have deposited their shares for Sulava Souchagar to Panchayat.

To conclude, it is not that forming groups and running them successfully have made the group members rich. However, they are now able enough to earn their livelihood. More importantly, they have become able to overcome their vulnerability and mental poverty (lack of voice, power and representation).

NOTES

1. Brett E. Coleman, JOE, 1999.
2. M. Ghatak, JOE, 1999.
3. Brett E. Coleman, JOE, 1999.
4. Outreach: The term outreach is typically used to refer to the effort by NGOs to extend loans and financial services to an ever-wider audience (breadth of outreach) and especially toward poorest of the poor (depth of outreach.
5. Impact: Impact refers to the extent to which the incomes and welfare of those so reached is raised.
6. Sustainability: refers, in most discussions, to full cost recovery or profit-making, and is associated with the aim of building micro finance institution that can last into the future without continued reliance on government subsidy or donor funds.
7. J. Conning, JOE, 1999, pp. 51-77.
8. Brett E. Coleman, JDE, 1999.
9. Panchayat: Elected Council at the Village Level, the lowest tier of the three-tier Panchayati Raj System.
10. BPL (Below Poverty Line) people mean poor people whose level of consumption expenditure is below a composite measure of total household consumption per member or below a nationally defined level of consumption expenditure. Generally it is measured in terms of calorie intake (2100 calorie a day in rural area and 2400 calorie in urban area per capita). The Census of India 2001, estimated Rs. 272 per capita expenditure per month as the poverty line. National Sample Survey Organisation (NSSO) estimated the poverty line at Rs. 211.30 (Rs. 454.11)

for the year 1999-2000 in the rural area (Figure in the brackets indicate the poverty line for the urban area). However, we have used Rs. 302 (as fixed by Panchayat and rural Development Department) as the poverty line for West Bengal.

11. APL means above poverty line.
12. Functional literacy refers to the ability of the members in signing their names and keeping simple accounts of the SHG (deposits and loans).
13. Partial/Semi Defaulter: means those persons/members who repay their loans but instalments are not paid in due time.
14. SHG members were originally very poor and lacked capital necessary for buying livestock (goats or cows, etc.). But they had sufficient idle hours in their possession as they found no job, particularly in the slack season. So they used to take goats or cows from big farmers on share. The goat or the cow thus given to poor farmers for rearing is not meant for sale. Only their kids or calves obtained in future when they are matured will be sold in the market by the owner and the relevant poor farmer will get a paltry sum out of that. Generally, it takes roughly one year for a goat since its birth to be ready for sale at a price of Rs. 800 to Rs. 1000. But the poor used to get Rs. 100 to Rs. 150 only as her/his share. In case of cows it takes 2.5 years to 3 years to be ready for giving milk. The general practice is that the Bhagidar (poor shareholder) is entitled to get the calf of the first birth. In lieu of that, the owner will get the milk. If it is a female calf, the Bhagidar would rear it for herself/himself. Otherwise (male calf), it is sold again to the owner of the cows at a price decided by both the parties (owner and the Bhagidar). But in fixing the price low bargaining power of the Bhagidar usually results in fixing low price of the male calf. In this way, the poor are exploited.
15. Grade-I passed group is entitled to withdraw Rs. 25000 as loan at a time. The groups have taken loan to the extent of Rs. 36000 on an average implies that they have withdrawn cash several times as credit from CCA.
16. A special feature of the district of Bankura is that the amount of subsidy has been decided on the basis of own fund of the group with a minimum of Rs. 5000 (when own fund of the group is less than or equal to Rs. 5000) and a maximum of Rs. 10000 (when own fund is equal to or more than Rs. 10000).
17. The state of West Bengal provides services in the field of animal health through a well organized network. At present there are 110 state level and 341 block level veterinary hospital and 3247 primary veterinary health centre at Gram Panchayat level. There are also 45 Animal Development Pathological Laboratory, 2 Veterinary Poly Clinic, 2 Rabies Prevention Centre, one Regional Diseases Diagnostic Centre, and one Disease Monitoring and Surveillance System. Beyond that, Institute of Animal Health and Veterinary Biological, Belgachhia, Kolkata is always at service by producing animal vaccine for the State and for the country as a whole. However, no veterinary surgeon is available at the gram Panchayat level animal health centre. Actually these are run by the so called 'Pranibandhu', a group of personnel, trained specially for artificial breeding and helping the rural people in the treatment of some common animal diseases.

One veterinary Poly Clinic has been set up in Berhampore (Murshidabad) in 2004-05. Another three Poly Clinics at Barasat (North 24-Parganas), Suri (Birbhum), and Malda (Malda District) have been proposed to be set-up.

The State Government encourages the formation of SHG/co-operatives to take up animal husbandry schemes through the provision of 20 percent subsidy (maximum Rs. 10000), 70 percent margin money loan (6 percent rate of interest) and 10 percent of owner's share. Under this programme from 2002-03 to 2004-05, 240 Swarojgaries in 24 SHG/cooperatives have been assisted.

18. For the poor we can reasonably assume that their income = expenditure.

REFERENCES

Amendments in the Guidelines of SGSY, Ministry of Rural Development, Government of India, Krishi Bhavan, New Delhi.

Beartriz Armenda'riz de Aghion. On the design of a credit agreement with peer monitoring, JOE, 1999, Vol. 60 (1999) 79-104.

Brett E. Coleman, The impact of group lending in Northeast Thailand, JOE, 1999, Vol. 60 (1999) 105-41.

Dilip K. Ghosh: Poverty Alleviation Programmes in West Bengal, An Overview, Vidyasagar University, *Journal of Economics*, Vol. VIII, 2002.

East India Human Development Report, 2004.

Ghatak, M., 1999. Group Lending, Local Information and Peer Selection, JOE, Vol. 60, 27-50

Harper, M., 2003. Self-help groups and Grameen bank groups: What are the differences? Beyond Micro Credit, Vistaar Publication, New Delhi, 169-98.

Mira Seth, 2001: Women and Development, the Indian Experience. Sage Publications, New Delhi.

Sakuntala Narasingham, 1999: Empowering Women, an Alternative Strategy from Rural India. Sage Publications, New Delhi.

SGSY Guidelines, Ministry of Rural Development, Government of India, New Delhi

Thomas Fisher, M.S. Sriram, 2002: Beyond Micro Credit—Putting Development Back into Micro Finance, Vistaar Publication, New Delhi.

Vijay Mahajan, From Micro Credit to Livelihood Finance, *EPW*, Vol. XL, No. 41, October 8-14, 2005.

15

Progress, Problems and Impact of Self-Help Groups in West Bengal : A Comparative Study

SUBRATA KUMAR RAY

I. INTRODUCTION

Generation of self-employment for the poor in rural areas is one of the most important components of anti-poverty and rural development programmes in India. Swarnajayanti Gram Swarozgar Yojana (SGSY) which came into being on 1st April, 1999 after merging the erstwhile Integrated Rural Development Programme (IRDP). Training of Rural Youth for Self-Employment (TRYSEM), Development of Women and Children in Rural Areas (DWCRA), Supply of Improved Toolkits to Rural Artisans (SITRA), Ganga Kalyan Yojana (GKY) and Million Well Scheme (MWS) is the major on going programme for self-employment generation for marginalised sections of rural communities. This programme is entirely different from erstwhile programmes of self-employment in terms of strategy envisaged for its implementation in the earlier version of self-employment programmes was their concentration on the inputs rather than output (finished products) and their marketing. To rectify this situation, SGSY provides avenues for promotion of marketing of the goods produced by the swarozgaries by way of involvement and participation of them in exhibitions/melas at "international, national, state and sub-state levels (Pal, 2002). The SGSY focuses on group approach by organizing the poor into self-help groups (SHGs) through social mobilization. This is a single cell self-employment programme for rural poor aimed at establishment of large number of micro-enterprises. The policy expectation is to ensure that the group members or swarozgaris (self-employed) come out of poverty clutches through incremental income. The group approach stems from the underlying assumption that the poor will help themselves, their own organisation will help them by taking steps for their upliftment. The SHG is the surer way in reaching the poor and assisting them in terms of credit, technology, market, etc. Building capacity to manage own resources (as well as subsequent external credit), developing saving habit and community orientation, the members will have economic emancipation, self-identify and assertiveness (Mandal, 2005). The failure of the formal credit institutions in effectively meeting requirements of rural poor has been the major reason for innovations in micro finance. The SHG-Bank Linkage Programme, launched by NABARD in 1992, is a landmark in the field of micro-financing in India. On the basis of their saving pattern, SHGs are given the bank loans to fulfil the loan requirements of its members ((Naithani, 2001). Independent studies of micro credit programmes show that providing easy and affordable access to credit and other financial services to poor families can have a host of positive impacts on their livelihoods (Yunus, 2004). In this context, the present paper makes a comparative study of panchayat-led and non-governmental organization (NGO)-SHGs for highlighting the progress, problems and impact in West Bengal (W.B.) with special reference to Purba and Paschim Medinipur district.

II. REVIEW OF EXISTING LITERATURE

In this section we shall make a brief review of existing literature on SHGs. Dasgupta (2001) has examined the different aspects of micro financing through informal groups like SHGs. Dutta and Raman (2001) have examined the co-existence of heterogeneity and social cohesion in SHGs and also the impact of SHGs and also the impact of SHGs on income level of members in Andhra Pradesh. Namboodiri and Shiyani (2001) have examined the potential role of SHGs in term of reach, linkage with banks for savings and credit for the weaker sections of rural households in Gujarat. Satish (2001) has made a study relating to some issues in the formation of SHGs in the states like Karnataka, Maharashtra and Uttar Pradesh, Madheswaran and Dharamadhikary (2001) have highlighted the aspect of empowering rural women through SHGs in Maharashtra, Gurumoorthy (2000) has also discussed about the empowerment of rural women through SHGs. Ojha (2001) has highlighted the role of SHGs in rural employment generation. Mandal (2005) has made an assessment of SHSY and SHGs in India. Thakuria (2005) has highlighted about the growing mission of self-helping, Das (2003) has concluded that the micro-credit-SHGs model has got tremendous attention in recent years and micro-credit SHGs integration could be the way out for overall rural development *vis-a-vis* poverty alleviation. There also exists a large number of studies on SHGs, viz. Kulshresth and Gupta (2001, 2002) Tripathy (2003). Singh (2003) Sarangi (2003), Chattergee (2003, 2002), Dogra (2002) Chowdhury (2005), Rao (2005) Dadhichi (2001), Malhotra (2005), etc.

From this brief review of existing literature on SHGs it may be said that there is a scope to conduct a comparative study of panchayat-led and NGO-led SHGs for analysing the progress, problems and impact of SHG activities in W.B. with special reference to Purba and Paschim Medinipur district.

III. OBJECTIVES OF THE STUDY

The objectives of the present study are:

1. To examine the progress of different aspects of SHGs in India by states. W.B. by districts, blocks of Purba and Paschim Medinipur and Gram Panchayats (GPs) of Sahid Matangini block in Purba Medinipur.
2. To conduct a comparative study of Panchayat-led and NGO-led SHGs for analyzing the impact and problems of SHG activities in Sahid Matangini block in Purba Medinipur district.

IV. DATA BASE AND METHDOLOGY

The secondary data used for this study has been collected from various government sources, viz. Economic survey of Government of India (GOI), Statistical Abstract of Government of W.B., Economic Review of Government of W.B. Office of Paschim and Purba Midnapore Zilla Parishad, Office of Sahid Matangini Block. The progress of SHGs activities using secondary data has been observed for India by states, W.B. by districts, blocks of Purba and Paschim Medinipur, GPs of Sahid Matangini Block. The field level data for different variables relating of SHGs activities has been collected from 20 SHGs (12 SHGs led by Panchayats and 8 SHGs led by NGOs) in Sahid Matangini block. The simple statistical techniques like percentages, growth rate, rank, mean, standard deviation (S.D.), etc. have been used for this study. For measuring the progress of SHGs activities using secondary data we have studied the factors like number of SHGs formed, credit-saving ratio, saving per SHG, cash credit per SHG % of grade-I or grade-II passed, etc. Again, the field level study has considered the factors like income and employment generated from SHG activities, condition of women members engaged in SHG activities, etc., for measuring performance, activities and also made a comparison between Panchayat-led and BGO-led SHGs.

V. PROGRESS OF SHGs IN INDIA BY STATES AND W.B. BY DISTRICTS

In this section we shall highlight the progress of SHGs in India and districts of W.B. there is a positive growth rate of SHGs in states but in terms of growth of SHGs there is a wide variation among states. Linkages of Banks with SHGs are found impossible Banks with SHGs are found impossible for this variation. States such as Andaman and Nicobar, Gujarat, Karnataka, Kerala, Orissa and Uttar Pradesh have comparatively lower growth whereas other states have higher growth of SHGs. The states with lower growth rates might have begun their SHG-bank linkage programme at an earlier stage so that it may already have sufficient linkages and further linking is quite difficult. Most of the states with lower growth rate will have a lower number of SHGs linked in the recent years compared to states that have a high growth rate (Soundarapandian, 2006). There are vast credit variations among the states and among the regions. Among the regions, southern region is the best region in financing SHGs, next that the performance of central region, eastern region and western region is moderate. The northern and north-east regions are comparatively poor. While considering the number of groups the southern region, central region, eastern region have enrolled more SHGs. Other regions enrolled less SHGs. Among the regions southern region distributed more credit and per capital credit per SHGs are very high. While considering the states among the region Pondicherry and Tamil Nadu states are performing well and have distributed more credit. In central region Chhattisgarh state distributed more credit and per capita credit. In western region Goa State's per capita credit is high and in northern region Haryana and Punjab states per capita credit is very high. Eastern region and north eastern region's per capita credit per SHGs are up to the level and Mizoram, the only state in north eastern region, recorded 101428.5 rupees per capita distributed of the SHGs. It could be clear that the level of credit is increased and one can find a sigh of development of SHGs and involved more economic activities (Loganathan and Asokan, 2006). As per GOI own information total SHGs formed in all India upto July 2006 has been 19,60,883 (Table 15.1). Andhra Pradesh has ranked first either in case of total SHGs or in case of women SHGs. But Assam and Lakshadeep have ranked first and second respectively in case of % of women SHGs formed. It is found that 14. 29% SHGs be women SHGs in India as a whole. On the other hand, 11.58% and 5.74% SHGs in all India have passed grade-I and II respectively. Assam and

TABLE 15.1

State/U.T. Wise Formation and Performances of SHGs (upto July 2006) in India

(Rs. in million)

Sl. No.	State/U.T.	Total SHG Formed	No. of SHG Passed Grade-I	No. of SHG Passed Grade-II	Women SHG Formed	No. of SHG % Taken Eco. Activities	% of group formation	% of Grade-I passed	% of Grade-II passed	% of Women SHG	% of SHG taken Eco Activities	Per Capita Credit per SHG (as on 31st March 2005)
	(1)	(2)	(3)	(4)	(5)	(6)	(7)	(8)	(9)	(10)	(11)	(12)
1.	Andhra Pradesh	618603(1	48278	25115	137124	6347	31.55	7.8	4.06	22.17	1.03	55709.9
2.	Arunachal Pradesh	357(25)	35	32	29	56	0.02	9.8	8.96	8.12	15.39	4275
3.	Assam	21373(15	7895	8514	11347	5146	1.09	83.73	39.84	53.09	24.08	
4.	Bihar	21622(14	0101	4916	7805	2625	1.1	46.72	22.74	361	12.14	24339.1
5.	Goa	795(24)	164	80	90	80	0.04	20.63	10.06	11.32	10.06	7468.6
6.	Gujarat	62567(8)	6010	1383	822	1596	3.9	4.81	2.21	1.31	2.55	2777.5
7.	Haryana	9429(18)	472	1158	873	1128	0.48	15.61	12.28	9.26	11.96	59871.6
8.	Himachal Pradesh	6482(21)	654	797	324	790	0.33	10.09	123	5	12.19	31746.8
9.	Jammu and Kashmir	9320(19)	463	164	289	244	0.47	4.97	1.76	3.1	2.62	34353.38
10.	Karnataka	41240(11	5533	5443	4359	3636	2.1	13.42	13.2	10.57	8.82	33710.7
11.	Kerala	57109(9)	5999	3452	5358	1598	2.91	10.5	60.4	9.38	28	41038.8
12.	Madhya Pradesh	223981(2	2188	5946	4702	4896	11.42	5.44	2.65	2.1	2.19	24626.3

(Contd.)

TABLE 15.1 (Contd.)

(1)		(2)	(3)	(4)	(5)	(6)	(7)	(8)	(9)	(10)	(11)	(12)
13.	Maharashtra	161288(4)	7472	8670	16,57	6448	8.23	10.83	5.38	10.39	4	31401.7
14.	Meghalaya	6611(20)	632	156	435	75	0.34	9.56	2.36	6.58	1.13	31244.9
15.	Orissa	153667(5)	22659	9274	20225	5226	7.84	14.75	6.04	13.16	3.4	20428.5
16.	Punjab	6322(22)	485	225	556	313	0.32	7.67	3.56	8.79	4.95	47156.2
17.	Rajasthan	26656(12)	2924	1293	882	1083	1.36	10.97	4.85	3.31	4.06	23564.9
18.	Sikkim	1149(23)	141	116	223	116	0.06	12.27	10.1	19.41	1.01	32142.8
19.	Tamil Nadu	162517(3)	19893	6314	24220	4726	8.29	12.24	3.89	14.9	2.91	76026.9
20.	Tripura	17891(16)	3003	1007	1952	1794	0.91	16.78	563	10.91	10.03	12587.4
21.	Uttar Pradesh	115210(7)	20289	16945	4729	19416	5.88	17.61	14.71	40.1	16.85	26375.6
22.	West Bengal	151953(6)	26690	7586	31475	2241	7.75	17.56	4.99	20.71	1.47	13622.4
23.	Lakshadweep	2(26)	0	0	1	0	0	0	0	50	0	
24.	Uttaranchal	13007(17)	1462	1409	883	1249	0.66	11.24	10.83	6.79	9.6	41020.4
25.	Chhattisgarh	46988(10)	2548	1294	941	1063	2.4	5.42	2.75	2	2.26	92605.7
26.	Jharkhand	24744(13)	3127	1207	0.3902	1554	1.26	12.64	4.88	15.77	6.28	33195.3
	Total	1960883	227117	112496	280303	73446	100	11.58	5.74	14.29	3.75	1236338.7

Note : Figures in brackets indicate ranks.
Source : Ministry of Rural Development, GOI.

TABLE 15.2

District-wise Formation and Performances of SHGs in West Bengal by Districts

Districts	*Total No. of SHGs Formed*			*R'04*	*R'06*	*G.R.(%) (No. of SHGs)*		*No. of Women SHGs*			*R.W.SHGs*		*G.R (%) Women SHGs*	
	2002 (upto Dec.)	*2004 (upto (Dec.)*	*2006 (upto July)*			*2002-06*	*2004-06*	*2002 (upto Dec.)*	*2004 (upto (Dec.)*	*2006 (upto July)*	*2004 (upto Dec.)*	*2006 (upto July)*	*2002-06*	*2004-06*
(1)	*(2)*	*(3)*	*(4)*	*(5)*	*(6)*	*(7)*	*(8)*	*(9)*	*(10)*	*(11)*	*(12)*	*(13)*	*(14)*	*(15)*
24 Parganas (N)	1824	9261	11270	3	5	517.87	21.693	1044	8301	2899	3	4	177.68	-65.076
24 Parganas (S)	7365	8619	8937	4	9	21.34	3.6895	4640	5386	48	6	18	-98.97	-99.109
Bankura	1206	4514	6940	11	12	475.46	53.744	764	3194	801	10	13	4.8429	-74.922
Birbhum	835	2909	8173	14	10	878.80	180.96	475	1527	1488	16	7	213.26	-2.554
Burdwan	3016	5923	10514	7	6	248.61	77.511	1307	3381	2341	9	5	79.112	-30.76
Cooch Behar	1807	6170	9130	6	7	405.26	47.974	1699	5978	3782	4	3	122.6	-36.735
Darjeeling	0	1814	1460	1.7	18	#DIV/01	-19.51	0	901	129	18	17	#DIV/01	-85.683
Hooghly	1925	5017	3312	9	15	72.05	-33.98	15	2799	444	11	16	2860	-84.137
Howrah	1142	2323	3243	15	16	183.98	39.604	1127	2246	595	14	15	-47.2	-73.508
Jalpaiguri	1327	7171	14044	5	2	958.33	95.844	1313	5856	6158	5	1	369	5.1571
Malda	1222	3947	9053	12	8	640.83	129.36	1199	2483	2302	12	6	91.993	-7.2896

(Contd.)

Table 15.2 (Contd.)

(1)	(2)	(3)	(4)	(5)	(6)	(7)	(8)	(9)	(10)	(11)	(12)	(13)	(14)	(15)
Murshidabad	2586	4760	7900	10	11	205.49	65.966	202	3999	208	8	9	498.02	-69.792
Nadia	981	3288	6664	13	13	579.31	102.68	695	2413	038	13	11	49.353	-56.983
Uttar Dinajpur	421	1633	4612	18	14	995.49	18242	133	1114	1462	17	8	999.25	31.239
Purulia	991	5551	11331	8	4	1043.39	10413	55	4376	3869	7	2	6934.5	-11.586
Dakshin Dinajpur	1389	1897	3009	15	17	116.63	58619	1134	1824	976	15	12	-1393	-46.491
East Midnapore	10547	1283	12572	2	3	19.20	11.424	8223	9469	728	2	14	-9115	-92.312
West Midnapore	13644	6771	18695	1	1	37.02	11.472	9957	12503	1170	1	10	-8825	-90.642
Siliguri	656	887	1094	19	19	66.77	23.337	255	758	46	19	19	-82.64	-93.931
Total	52884	103738	151953			187.33	46.478	3427	785.08	34475			-8.094	-59.909

(Contd.)

TABLE 15.2 (Contd.)

Districts	% of W.R. SHG 2006	% of SHG	Gr. I Passed		GR (%) of Gr. (2004-06)	% Gr.I 2006	R % of Gr. I 2006	Gr. II Passed		GR (%) of Gr. II (2004-06)	% of Gr. II 2006	R % of Gr. II 2006	SHGs taken eco. activities (2006)	
			2006	2006				2004	2006				No.	%
(1)	(16)	(17)	(18)	(19)	(20)	(21)	(22)	(23)	(24)	(25)	(26)	(27)	(28)	(29)
24 Parganas (N)	25.7232	6	4806	3629	-24.5	32.2005	1	675	452	-33.037	401	10	132	1.1713
24 Parganas (S)	0.53709	19	6345	1696	-73.3	18.9773	8	180	218	21.111	244	13	38	0.4252
Bankura	11.5418	14	1454	1210	-16.8	174352	9	129	78	-39.535	1.12	17	11	0.1585
Birbhum	18.2063	10	1902	1151	-39.5	14083	13	439	155	-64.692	1.9	15	160	1.9577
Burdwan	22.2656	8	3533	2015	-43	191649	7	884	692	-21.719	658	6	173	1.6454
Cooch Behar	41.4239	2	3623	2506	-30.8	27448	4	3623	654	-81.949	7.16	5	180	1.9715
Darjeeling	8.83562	15	717	344	-52	23.5616	5	94	191	103.19	13.1	2	207	14 178
Hooghly	13.4058	13	3188	387	-879	1168.48	14	1380	304	-77.971	918	3	128	3.8647
Howrah	18.3472	9	1481	256	-82.7	7.89393	17	861	256	-70.267	1.89	4	347	107
Jalpaiguri	43.8479	1	3012	2815	-654	20.0441	6	41	73	78.49	052	18	25	0 178
Malda	25.428	7	1353	939	-306	103723	16	211	170	-19.431	1.88	16	7	0.0773
Murshidabad	15.2911	12	2522	1144	-54.6	14481	12	510	264	-48.235	334	12	114	1 443
Nadia	15.5762	11	1762	992	-43.7	14.886	11	531	247	-53.484	3.71	11	333	4997

(Contd.)

Table 15.2 (Contd.)

(1)	(16)	(17)	(18)	(19)	(20)	(21)	(22)	(23)	(24)	(25)	(26)	(27)	(28)	(29)
Uttar Dinajpur	31.6999	5	502	725	44.4	15.7199	10	82	11	35.366	2.41	14	2	0.0434
Purulia	34.1453	3	1565	3225	106	28.4617	3	471	0	-100	0	19	0	0
Dakshin Dinajpur	32.436	4	1205	868	-28	28.8468	2	243	163	-32.922	5.42	8	136	4.5198
East Midnapore	5.79065	17	7876	621	-921	4.93955	19	2987	2499	-16337	19.9	1	214	1.7022
West Midnapore	6.25836	16	898	2093	-76.7	11.1955	15	863	999	15.759	53.4	9	8	00428
Siliguri	4.20475	18	417	74	-823	6.76417	18	161	60	-62.733	5.48	7	26	2.3766
Total	20.7136		56243	###	-52.5	17.5646		11397	7583	-33.439	4.99		2241	1.4748

Notes: GR = Growth Rate, R = Rank, W = Nomen. Gr = Grade.
Source : Govt. of West Benge.

Bihar have ranked first and second respectively either in case of % of grade-I passed or in case of % of grade-II passed. The percentage of SHGs taken economic activities has been highest for Assam.

Let us examine the different aspects of SHGs in the districts of W.B. It is observed that the total number of SHGs formed in W.B. has increased from 52.884 to 151963 during 2002-06 (Table 15.2). The growth rate of total number of SHGs formed has been 187.33% for W.B. In 2006, Paschim Midnapore has ranked first in case of total number of SHGs formed. On the other hand, Jalpaiguri has randed first in case of women SHGs formed. In July 2006 the percentage of women SHGs formed in W.B. has been 20.71. It has been maximum for Purilia. The number of SHGs passed grade-I or II has declined over years during 2004-6 for the districts. In W.B. 18% and 5% SHGs have passed grade-I and II respectively. The percentage of grade-I passed has been maximum for North 24-Parganas and that of grade-II passed become maximum for Purba Medinipur. On the other hand, 1.47% SHGs in W.B. has taken economic activities. This percentage share has become largest for Howrah.

VI. PROGRESS OF SHGs IN BLOCKS OF PURBA AND PASCHIM MEDINIPUR

In this section, we shall highlight the different aspects of SHGs in blocks Purba and Paschim Medinipur.

(A) Purba Medinipur

In Purba Medinipur, there exists 25 blocks. The total number of SHGs formed in Purba Medinipur has increased from 2109 to 12572 during 2001-06 (Table 15.3). The growth rate of number of SHGs formed has been 496.11%. 45.47% and 74.07% SHGs in Purba Medinipur have passed grade-I respectively in March 2001 and March 2006. On the other hand, the % of grade-II passed has increased from zero to 27.74% during 2001 to 2006. The block level analysis shows that in case of number of SHGs formed Nandigram-III and Moyna have ranked first respectively in March 2001 and March 2006. Side by side, the % of grade-I passed has been highest for Haldia in

Table 15.3
Purba Midnapore Block-wise Position on SHG of March 2001 and March 2006

(Amount in Rs. Lakh)

Blocks	Total No. of SHGs		G.R. of No. of SHGs	Grade I passed		% of Grade I passed	
	2001 March	2006 March		2001 March	2006 March	2001 March	2006 March
(1)	(2)	(3)	(4)	(5)	(6)	(7)	(8)
Tamluk	184(2)	683(4)	271.20	131	542	71.19(5)	79.36(8)
Sahid Matangini	52(17)	406(14)	680.77	21	313	40.38(15)	77.09(10)
Panskura-I	153(3)	637(7)	316.34	9	500	5.9(21)	78.5(9)
Panskura-II	23(24)	399(15)	1634.78	8	253	34.78(18)	6341(19)
Mayna	49(18.5)	847(1)	1628.57	37	541	75.51(4)	6387(18)
Nandakumar-I	57(1(3)	2(6)	1043.86	48	51	84.21(2)	84.51(5)
Sutahata	95(10)	369(21)	288.42	0	190	0(24)	51.49(22)
Haldia	18(5)	334(24)	183.05	117	287	99.15(1)	85.63(3)
Nandigram-I	83(13)	717(2)	763.86	66	294	79.52(3)	4100(24)
Nandigram-II	103(7)	375(20)	264.08	63	303	61.16(7)	80.8(7)
Mahisadal	93(11)	387(16)	316.13	40	251	43.01(13)	6486(17)
Contai-I	49(18.5)	573(10)	1069.39	16	417	32.65(19)	72.77(13)

Contai-II	39(19)	383(18)	882.05	21	270	53 85(9)	705(14)
Contai-III	77(14)	654(5)	749.35	32	586	41.56(14)	89.60(22)
Ramnagar-I	114(6)	451(12)	295.61	57	291	50(10)	11.10(25)
Ramnagar-II	131(4)	612(9)	367.18	64	563	4825(11)	92(1)
Bhagabanpur-I	100(8)	384(17)	284.00	4	287	422)	74374(11)
Bhagabanpur-I	92(12)	506(11)	450.00	57	341	6196(6)	674(15)
Pataspur-I	26(22)	363(22.5)	1296.15	15	225	57.7(8)	61.98(20)
Pataspur-II	41(19)	363(225)	785.37	20	206	48.78(12)	56.75(21)
Khajuri-I	25(22)	378(19)	1412.00	0	254	0(24)	67.2(16)
Khajuri-II	29(21)	441(13)	1420.69	0	378	0(24)	8571(4)
Egra-I	99(9)	617(8)	523.23	30	507	30.30(20)	82.17(6)
Egra-II	67(15)	348(23)	419.40	25	177	37.21 (16)	50.86(23)
Nandigram-III	210(1)	693(3)	230.00	18	515	37.14(17)	74.31(12)
Total	2109	12512	496 11	959	9312	45.47	74.07

(Contd.)

TABLE 15.3 (Contd.)

Blocks	Grade II passed 2001 March	Grade II passed 2006 March	% Gr-II 2006 March	GR of Gr-I (%)	S/SHG 2006	CC/SHG 2006	CSR 2006
(1)	(9)	(10)	(11)	(12)	(13)	(14)	(15)
Tamluk	0	232(16)	34.55(7)	313.74	0.07	0.18	2.8
Sahid Matangini	0	145(10)	35.71(6)	1390.48	0.02	0.13	6.41
Panskura-I	0	73(17.5)	1146(22)	5455.56	0.02	0.11	5.86
Panskura-II	0	64(19)	16.04(19)	3062.50	0.02	0.11	5.54
Mayna	0	267(4)	31.52(9)	1362.16	0.07	0.12	1.7
Nandakumar-I	0	20(2)	47.4(3)	1047.92	0.04	0.2	4.88
Sutahata	0	48(10)	13.01(21)	0.00	0.05	7.3	154.6
Haldia	0	88(10)	2635(14)	145.30	0.04	0.09	2.09
Nandigram-I	0	242(5)	33.75(8)	345..45	0.03	0.1	3.9
Nandigram-II	0	70(8)	45.33(4)	380.95	0.06	0.15	2.42
Mahisadal	0	4(23)	3.62(24)	527.50	0.09	0.09	1.05
Contai-I	0	273(3)	47.64(2)	2506.25	0.1	0.2	1.9
Contai-II	0	65(18)	16.97(18)	1185.71	0.09	0.33	3.86
Contai-III	0	273(1)	57(1)	1731..25	0.1	0.11	1.13
Ramnagar-I	0	44(22)	9.76(23)	410.53	0.09	0.14	1.5

Ramnagar-II	0	130(13)	2124(16)	77969	0.04	0.09	2.31
Bhagabanpur-I	0	450(9)	39.06(5)	7075.00	0.02	0.1	4.64
Bhagabanpur-I	0	142(11)	28.06(13)	49825	0.07	0.13	1.86
Pataspur-I	0	52(20)	14.33(20)	1400.00	0.04	0.16	3.98
Pataspur-II	0	101(14)	30.58(10)	930.00	0.09	0.2	2.1
Khajuri-I	0	197(15)	23.31(12)	0.00	0.01	0.09	6.25
Khajuri-II	0	133(12)	3016(11)	0.00	0.09	0.16	1.75
Egra-I	0	6(24)	9(25)	1590.00	0.03	0.1	3.13
Egra-II	0	73(17.5)	20.98(17)	608 00	0.07	0.12	1.73
Nandigram-III	0	177(1)	25.54(15)	560.26	0.08	0.14	1.66
Total		3488	27.74	871.01	0.06	0.13	2.25

Note : CC = cash credit, GR = growth rate, Gr = grade, S = saving, CSR = credit saving ratio.
Source : Purba Medinipur Zilla Parishad.

March 2001 and for Ramnagar-II in March 2006. The % of grade-II passed has been maximum for containing III in March 2006. Again, the growth rate of grade-I passed in Purba Medinipur has been 871.01% during 2001-06. It has been highest for Panskura-I block. In Purba Medinipur the saving per SHG and cash credit per SHG has been Rs. 6000.00 and Rs. 13,000.00 respectively in March 2006. Again, the credit-saving ratio in the district as a whole has been 2.25. It has been highest for Sutahata block.

(B) Paschim Medinipur

In Paschim Medinipur there exists 29 blocks. The number of SHGs formed in Paschim Medinipur has increased from 11,689 to 18441 during 2002-06 (Table 15.4). The growth rate has been 66.32%. 76.3% SHGs in Paschim Medinipur be women SHGs in March 2006. The growth rate of grade-I passed in Paschim Medinipur has been 83.30% during 2002-06. The % of grade-I passed has risen from 51.50% to 60% in the district as a whole. The number of SHGs formed has been highest for Garbeta-I in March 2002 and for Debra in February 2006. The growth rate of both the numbers of SHGs formed and grade-I passed is highest for Debra block during 2002-06. The % of grade-I passed has been highest for Keshpur in March 2002 and for Kharagpur-II in February 2006. On the other hand, 9.92% SHGs has passed grade-II in the districts as a whole during February 2006. The % of SHGs passed grade-II has been maximum for debra block. In 2006 the credit saving ratio, saving per SHG have been 1.58, Rs. 0.06 million, Rs. 0.09 million respectively for the district as a whole. The credit-saving ratio has been highest for Garbeta-III block.

VII. PROGRESS OF SHGs IN G.P.s OF SAHID MATANGINI BLOCK

In Sahid Matangini block, the total number of SHGs formed has increased from 293 to 402 during 2002-06 (Table 15.5). The % of women SHGs has also risen from 75.08 to 96.77%. Khakadra G.P. has ranked first in case of either total

TABLE 15.4
Paschim Midnapore Block-wise Position on SHG of April 2002 and February 2006

(*Amount in Rs. Lakh*)

Blocks	*SHG formed*				*Growth rate (%)*	*Women SHG*		*Passed Grade - I*		*Growth rate (%)*
	March 2002		*Feb. 2006*			*Feb. 2006*	*%*	*Mach 2002*	*Feb. 2006*	
(1)	*(2)*	*(3)*	*(4)*	*(5)*	*(6)*	*(7)*	*(8)*	*(9)*	*(10)*	*(11)*
Grabeta-I	756	(1)	985	(4)	30.30	362.00	36.80	477(1)	693	45.3
Garbeta-II	396	(15)	619	(17)	51.30	325.00	52.50	255(9)	395	54.9
Garbeta-III	510	(8)	559	(18)	9.60	417.00	74.60	278(8)	393	41.4
Keshpur	524	(7)	1019	(2)	94.5.0	604.00	59.30	460(2)	747	62.4
Midnapore	430	(12)	691	(12)	60.70	232.90	33.60	302(6)	394	30.5
Salboni	461	(11)	701	(10)	53.50	595.00	98.30	179(16)	296	65.4
Dantan-I	246	(26)	388	(26)	57.70	388.00	100.00	117(21)	161	37.6
Dantan-II	253	(25)	409	(23)	61.70	407.00	99.40	175(17)	321	83.4
Debra	352	(18)	1058	(1)	200.60	1050.00	99.70	65(26)	775	1092
Keshiary	262	(24)	784	(8)	199.20	781.00	100.00	181(15)	470	159
Khargpur-I	627	(3)	555	(13)	5.50	655.00	100.00	3404)	426	25.3
Khargpur-II	298	(21)	367	(27)	85.40	367.00	100.00	214(2)	347	62.1
Mohanpur	280	(22)	332	(28)	18.50	332.00	100.00	165(8)	203	22.3

(*Contd.*)

TABLE 15.4 (Contd.)

(1)	(2)	(3)	(4)	(5)	(6)	(7)	(8)	(9)	(10)	(11)
Narayangarh	480	(10)	305	(7)	67.70	800.00	99.40	81(24)	456	463
Pingla	298	(21)	427	(22)	3.30	425.00	99.80	133(9)	213	60.2
Sabang	561	(5)	331	(16)	12.50	624.00	98.9^0	240(0)	442	84.2
Binpur-I	505	(9)	706	(11)	3980	98.00	13.90	189(4)	329	74.1
Binpur-II	404	(14)	922	(5)	128.20	832.00	90.20	230(1)	591	157
Gopiballavpur-I	119	(28)	482	(19)	305.00	206.00	42.70	74(25)	239	223
Gopiballavpur-II	182	(27)	404	(24)	122.00	206.00	51.00	129(20)	263	103.9
Camboni	290	(21)	318	(29)	9.70	105.00	33.00	57(27)	123	115.8
Chargram	679	(2)	‘010	(3)	48.70	514.00	50.10	3185)	596	87.4
Nayagram	278	(23)	74	(9)	18.40	393.00	50.80	40(28)	192	380
Sankrial	542	(6)	308	(6)	4910	788.00	97.50	198(14)	364	83.8
Chandrakona-I	369	(16)	435	(21)	17.90	435.00	100.00	201(13)	329	63.7
Chandrakona-II	355	(17)	399	(25)	12.4	384	962	91(23)	185	103
Daspur-I	417	(13)	33f	(14)	528	629	98.7	296(7)	414	39.9
Daspur-II	616	(4)	335	(15)	3.1	625	98.4	431(3)	494	14.6
Ghatal	301	(19)	75	(20)	578	341	718	100(22)	172	72
Total	11689		18441		14022	14022	76.3	60.7	11027	83.30

(Contd.)

TABLE 15.4 (Contd.)

(Amount in Rs. Lakh)

Blocks	Passed Grade-II		% of Grade-I		% of Gr. II	TS	CC	CSR	S/SHG	CR/SHG
	March 2002	Feb. 2006	March 2002	Feb. 2006	2006	2006	2006	2006	2006	2006
(1)	(12)	(13)	(14)	(15)	(16)	(17)	(18)	(19)	(20)	(21)
Grabeta-I	0	84	63.1(10)	70.35(7)	8.25	60.61	93.82	1.548	0.062	0.095
Garbeta-II	0	41	64.4(9)	63.8(14)	6.62	38.51	40.2	1.044	0.062	0.0652
Garbeta-III	0	109	54.51(14)	70.3(8)	19.5	26.83	93.4	3.481	0.048	0.167
Keshpur	0	80	87.8(1)	73.3(5)	7.85	67.98	157.75	2.321	0.067	0.155
Midnapore	0	36	70.2(5)	57(17)	5.2	32.12	64.57	2.010	0.046	0.093
Salboni	0	24	38.8(21)	41.4(26)	3.4	61.6	20.68	0.336	0.087	0.029
Dantan-I	0	24	476(17)	41.5(25)	6.2	18.44	28.02	1.520	0.048	0.072
Dantan-II	0	66	69.2(7)	78.5(2)	16.1	22.45	63	2.806	0.055	0.154
Debra	0	278	18.5(27)	73.2(6)	26.3	12.46	123.7	9.928	0.012	0.117
Keshiary	0	58	69(8)	56(19)	704	34.46	45.25	1.313	0.044	0.058
Kharqpur-I	0	84	54.2(16)	6(12)	12.8	48.23	76.5	1.586	0.074	0.117
Khargpur-II	0	62	71.81(2)	95(1)	16.9	27.5	32.3	1.175	0.075	0.088
Mohanpur	0	48	58.9(12)	61.1(15)	14.5	28.98	49.35	1.703	0.087	0.149
Narayangarh	0	75	17(28)	56.6(18)	9.3	38.6	46.9	1.215	0.048	0.058
Pingla	0	40	44.6(19)	50(20)	9.4	25.5	36	1.412	0.060	0.084

(Contd.)

TABLE 15.4 (Contd.)

(1)	(12)	(13)	(14)	(15)	(16)	(17)	(18)	(19)	(20)	(21)
Sabang	0	91	43(20)	70(9)	14.4	51.75	39.95	0.772	0.082	0.063
Binpur-I	0	28	37.4(22)	46.6(22)	3.4	19.16	34.96	1.825	0.027	0.050
Binpur-II	0	133	57(13)	64.1(14)	14.4	91.03	86.48	0.950	0.099	0.094
Gopiballavpur-I	0	11	62.2(11)	49.6(21)	2.3	5.67	12.15	2.143	0.012	0.025
Gopiballavpur-1	0	76	70.9(4)	65.1(10)	18.8	50.54	28.7	0.568	0.125	0.071
Jamboni	0	38	19.66(26)	387(27)	11.9	12.22	14.25	1.166	0.038	0.045
Jhargram	0	10	47(18)	59(16)	1	66.55	107	1.608	0.066	0.106
Nayagram	0	3	14.4(20)	24.8(29)	1.03	17.2	18.75	1.090	0.022	0.024
Sankrial	0	34	36.5(23)	45(24)	4.2	38.77	63.5	1.638	0.048	0.079
Chandrakona-I	0	54	54.5(15)	76(4)	12.4	23.08	50.4	2.184	0.053	0.116
Chandrakona-1	0	47	25.6(25)	46(23)	11.8	10.34	26.25	2.539	0.026	0.066
Daspur-I	0	63	70.98(3)	65.01(11)	9.9	53.14	73.65	1.386	0.083	0.116
Daspur-II	0	97	70.01(6)	77.8(3)	15.3	39.11	85.35	2.182	0.062	0.134
Ghatal	0	30	33.2(24)	36.2(28)	6.3	10.87	19.85	1.826	0.023	0.042
Total	0	1829	51.50%	60%	9.92	1033.7	1632.67	1.579	0.056	0.089

Note : CSR = Credit Saving Ratio, S/SHG = Saving/SHG, CR/SHG = Credit/SHG, TS = Total Saving, CC = Cash Credit.

Source : Paschim Medinipur Zilla Parishad.

Table 15.5
Progress Report of Sahid Matangini Block (GP-wise) on SGSY of April 2003 and January 2006

Sl. No.	GPs	SHG Formed		GR %	Women SHG formed		GR %
		April 2003	January 2006		April 2003	January 2006	
(1)		(2)	(3)	(4)	(5)	(6)	(7)
1.	Santipur-I	21(7)	24(7)	14.28(7)	18(6)((85.7))	24(8)((100))	33.33(10)
2.	Santipur-II	34(3.5)	56(3.5)	64.7(4)	34(2)((100))	56(3)((100))	64.7(6)
3.	Kharui-I	25(6)	19(8)	-40	9(9)((36))	19(9)((100))	111.11(4)
4.	Kharui-II	19(8)	33(5)	3.68(3)	12(8)((63.2))	33(6)((100))	175(1)
5.	Khakarda	48(1)	65(1)	37.5(5)	42(1)((87.5))	65(1)((98.5))	54.76(8)
6.	Balluk-I	15(9)	17(9)	13.33(8)	7(10)((46.71))	16(10)((94.1))	128.57(2)
7.	Balluk-II	33(4)	64(2)	93.9(2)	32(3)((97))	64(2)((100))	100(5)
8.	Raghunathpur-I	28(5)	56(3.5)	100(1)	23(5)((82.14))	50(4)((89.4))	117.39(3)
9.	Raghunathpur-II	36(2)	42(4)	16.66(6)	27(4)((75))	37(5)((88.1))	37.03(9)
10.	Dhalhara	34(3)	25(6)	-24.47	16(7)((47.1))	25(7)((100))	56.25(7)
	Total	293	402	37.2	220	389	76.83

(*Contd.*)

Table 15.5 (Contd.)

Sl. No.	GPs	Grade-I Passed		GR %	Grade-II Passed		GR %
		April 2003	January 2006		April 2003	January 2006	
(1)		(8)	(9)	(10)	(11)	(12)	(13)
1.	Santipur-I	16(6)((76.15))	20(8)((83.33))	25(9)	1((4.76))	5((20.8))	400.00
2.	Santipur-II	31(2)((91.17))	43(4)((76.8))	38.7(7)	0	15((26.8))	0.00
3.	Kharui-I	9((9)(36))	10(10)((52.6))	11.11(10)	0	0	0.00
4.	Kharui-II	10(8)((52.63))	27(6)((81.82))	170(1)	2((10.53))	10((20.3))	400.00
5.	Khakarda	33(1)((68.75))	56(1)((84.85))	69.69(4)	4((8.33))	35((53))	775.00
6.	Balluk-I	7(10)((40.67))	11(9)((64.71))	57.14(5)	30((20))	5((29.4))	33.33
7.	Balluk-II	30(3)((90.1))	53.(2)((82.81))	77.66(3)	3((9.1))	23((35.94))	666.66
8.	Raghunathpur-I	23(5)((82.14))	47(3)((83.93))	104.34(2)	5((17.86))	25((44.64))	400.00
9.	Raghunathpur-II	28(4)((17.78))	36.(5)((85.71))	28.57(8)	3((8.33))	21((50))	600.00
10.	Dhalhara	15(7)((14.12))	21(7)((84))	40(6)	5((14.71))	6((24))	20.0
	Total	202	324	60.4	26	145	457.69

(Contd.)

TABLE 15.5 (Contd.)

Sl. No.	GPs	Credit per SHG		Credit/Member		CSR			MSEA		GR(%)
		April 2003	January 2006	April 2003	January 2006	April 2003	April 2003-Jan. 2006	% of Recovery	April 2003	January 2006	
	(1)	(14)	(15)	(16)	(17)	(18)	(19)	(20)	(21)	(22)	(23)
1.	Santipur-I	6190.5(5)	1916.67(9)	722(2)	1917(1)	24.1(2)	6(2)	60	130	190	—
2.	Santipur-II	8823.5(1)	1598.2(10)	880(1)	1598(3)	28.3(1)	1.7(1)	50	300	370	23.33
3.	Kharui-I	2400(10)	7894.7(7)	577(9)	652(10)	19.2(9)	66910)	50	60	60	0.00
4.	Kharui-II	3157.9(9)	7272.7(8)	366(10)	741(9)	12.2(10)	0.87(6)	50	60	90	50.00
5.	Khakarda	6250(4)	18333.3(1)	664.6)	1721(2)	22.1(6)	1.3(4)	45	300	530	76.67
6.	Balluk-I	3333.3(8)	8529.5(6)	617(8)	792(8)	20.6(8)	0.86(7)	50	50	60	20.00
7.	Balluk-II	6969.7(2)	11953.1(4)	678(5)	1062(6)	22.6(5)	1.4(3)	50	230	320	39.13
8.	Raghunathpur-I	6071.4(6)	9553.6(5)	688(4)	937(7)	22.9(4)	0.8(9)	52	150	330	120.00
9.	Raghunathpur-II	6944.4(3)	16785.7(2)	661(7)	1183(5)	22.1(7)	1.1(5)	50	250	150	
10.	Dhalhara	3823.5(7)	13800(3)	703(3)	1228(4)	23.4(3)	0.85(8)	55	130	320	146.15
	Total	5733.8	13557.2	680	1236	23	1.17	61.2	1660	2420	45.78

Note : Figurs in ( ) indicate rank. WSEA = Women started economic activities. GR(%) = Growth rate (%)
MSEA = Members started economic activities. Figures in (( )) indicate percentage.

Source : Sahid Matangini Block Office.

SHGs formed or women SHGs formed during 2003-6. The growth rate of total SHGs formed has been highest for Raghunathpur-I. On the other hand, the growth rate of women SHGs formed has been maximum for Kharui-II. The percentage of Other grade-I or grade-II passed has increased over years for the district as a whole and highest for Khakarda G.P. The credit-saving ratio has been highest for Santipur-II. It is to note that the credit saving ratio has declined over years during 2003-06. In Jan. 2006, the credit per member and credit per SHG have been maximum for Santipur-I and Khakarda respectively.

VIII. IMPACT AND PROBLEMS OF SHGs: A MICRO LEVEL STUDY

In this section, a micro-level study has conducted among 20 SHGs (12 Panchayat-led and 8 NGO-led SHGs) having 200 members selected randomly for highlighting a cooperative analysis of impact and problems of Panchayat-led and NGO-led SHGs. The details regarding number of members from two types of SHGs are given in Tables 15.6 and 15.7. It is customary to present the demographic and social background of the group members as they exert tremendous influence on availing credit and its utilization.

TABLE 15.6
Details of SHG Led by Panchayat

Name of the led Panchayat	*Total No. of SHGs*	*Total No. of Members*		*Total*
		Male	*Female*	
Dhalhara	3	0	29	29
Khakarda	5	0	51	51
Santipur-I	1	0	14	14
Santipur-II	3	12	20	32
Total	12	12	114	126

Source : Field Survey.

TABLE 15.7
Details of NGO-led SHGs

Name of the led Panchayat	*Total No. of NGOs*	*Total No. of Members*		*Total*
		Male	*Female*	
Dhalhara	2	10	10	20
Khakarda	0	0	0	0
Santipur-I	4	10	25	35
Santipur-II	2		19	19
Total	8	20	54	74

Source : Field Survey.

(A) Age Profile

The details of age profile show that in case of panchayat-led SHGs 18% of the selected members belong to the age group 15-25 years and 72% of them to the age group 25-45 years. On the other hand, in case of NGO-led SHGs, 80% of the beneficiaries belong to the age group 15-45 years. This distribution reveals that 80-90% of the beneficiaries belongs to the economically active segment of the population.

(B) Social Status

The distribution of beneficiaries according to their social groups reveals that in case of Panchayat-led SHGs 40% of the beneficiaries belong to weaker sections, i.e. SCs, STs and OBCs. But 30% of the beneficiaries belong to weaker sections in case of NGOs-led SHGs.

(C) Literacy Status

It seems that the SHGs are giving equal importance to illiterate and literate people. These data shows that in case of Panchayat-led SHGs 70% of the members have educational level of Class I-VII and in case of NGO-led SHGs 60% of the members belong to educational level of Class I-VII, 30% and 40% of the members belong to educational level of class IV-XII respectively in case of Panchayat-led and NGO-led SHGs.

(D) Family Size

The average size of the member's family is 6 members for both types of SHGs.

(E) Land Holdings

No doubt the rural poor mostly belong to assetless groups or have marginal value of assets. An attempt is made in Table 15.8 to explain the land ownership of sampled members, as the primary asset in rural areas is agricultural land. The average size of the land holding is 0.26 acres for both types of SHGs (which shows that all the members are from marginal farmers' category).

Let us now examine the scenario of provision of loans, purpose of loan and repayment of loan. It is found that the loans have been provided for the purposes of cloth business, dairy, tailoring, grossary shop, rice processing, poultry, cultivation of paddy, flower, oilseeds, betel vine in case of both types of SHGs. In case of Panchayat-led SHGs the average amount of loans varies from Rs. 33,000.00 to Rs. 25,862.00. 60%, 30% and 10% of the members received loans respectively between Rs. 3,000.00 to Rs. 15,000.00 between Rs. 15,001.00 to Rs. 20,000.00 and Rs. 20,001.00 to Rs. 25,862.00. On the other hand, in case of NGO-led SHGs the average amount of loans varies between Rs. 2,000.00 to Rs. 15,000.00. 70% of the members received loans between Rs. 2;000.00 to Rs. 10,000.00. Thus the average amount of loans has been larger in case of Panchayat-led SHGs. Again, the repayment performance is better in case of NGO-led SHGs. We have also calculated the coefficient of variance (C.V.) for the distribution of loans across the sample households of either Panchayat-led SHGs or NGO-led SHGs. It is found that the values of C.V. are 20.32 and 23.26 respectively for Panchayat-led SHGs and NGO-led SHGs. These values indicate that more consistency is found for the distribution of loans among the households in case of Panchayat-led SHGs compared to NGO-led SHGs.

TABLE 15.8
Distribution of Operational Holdings (Acress)

Panchayat

Ownerhip of Land	*0-0.25*		*0.26-0.50*		*0.50 and above*		*total*		*average*
	HHs	*Land*	*HHs*	*Land*	*HHs*	*Land*	*HHs*	*Land*	
(1)	*(2)*	*(3)*	*(4)*	*(5)*	*(6)*	*(7)*	*(8)*	*(9)*	*(10)*
Own Land	80	18.5	12	5.5	5	3.1	94	28.1	0.3
Leased in	13	3.2	15	1.8	1	0.6	32	4.7	0.15
Leased out									
Total	93	21.7	27	7.3	6	3.7	126	32.8	0.26

NGO

Own Land	25	7.8	15	6	6	1.1	46	14.9	0.62
Leased in	17	3	10	0.5	1	0.9	28	4.4	0.16
Leased out									
Total	42	8.1	25	6.5	7	2	74	19.3	0.26

Source : Field Survey.

Impact on Income and employment

Let examine the impact of SHG activities on income and employment. It is observed from Table 15.9 that average income generated has been higher for Panchayat-led SHGs as compared to NGO-led SHGs. The share of income generated from the SHG Activities in total family income has been higher in case of Panchayat-led SHGs as compared to NGO-led SHGs. Again, the contribution of Panchayat-led SHGs in total family income has been substantial. Side by side, it is found that the C.V. for the distribution of income among the households be higher in case of Panchayat-led SHGs (18.61) as compared to NGO-led SHGs (15.61). It implies that more equal distribution of income among the sample households is observed in case of NGO-led SHGs. On the other hand, the Table 15.10 shows that the impact on

TABLE 15.9
Impact on Income Generation in the Year 2005

Panchayat

(Amount in Rs.)

Sl. No.	Financing activities	No. of HHs	IGFP	TFI	Average Ing	POIFP
1.	Cloth business	17	110000	153000	6470.588	71.90
2.	Dairing	20	14500	180000	7250	80.56
3.	Tailoring	18	85000	110000	4722.222	77.22
4.	Grossary	9	60000	75000	6666.667	80.00
5.	Rice processing	15	90000	120000	6000	75.00
6.	Poultry	8	5800	7500	7250	77.33
7.	Agriculture					
	(a) Paddy	12	50000	67000	4166.667	74.63
	(b) Flower	9	47000	62000	5222.222	75.81
	(c) Oil seeds	10	43000	57000	43000	75.44
	(d) Betel vine	8	44500	62000	5562.6	71.77
	Total	126	732500	961000	5813.492	76.22

(Contd.)

TABLE 15.9 (Contd.)

NGO

Sl. No.	Financing activities	No. of HHs	IGFP	TFI	Average Ing	POIFP
1.	Cloth Business	12	70000	180000	5833.33	38.89
2.	Dairing	8	42000	120000	5250.00	35.00
3.	Tailoring	5	30000	100000	6000.00	30.00
4.	Grossary	21	90000	230000	4285.71	39..13
5.	Rice processing	8	52000	100000	6500.00	52.00
6.	Poultry	2	12000	45000	6000.00	26.67
7.	Agriculture					
	(a) Paddy	7	28500	56000	4071.43	50.89
	(b) Flower	8	33500	76000	4187.50	44.08
	(c) Oil seeds	2	10000	50000	5000.00	20.00
	(d) Betel vine	1	4001	1800	4001.00	22.23
	Total	74	372001	975000	5027.04	38.15

Notes : 1. EGFP=Income generated from the project.
2. POIFP=% of income from the project.
3. TFI=total family income.

Source : Field Survey.

employment generation is better in case of Panchayat-led SHGs. It is seen that higher income and employment have generated in case of non-farm activities.

Problems of SHGs

Let us examine the Problems faced by SHGs:

(A) After joining in the SHG activities the burden of work on women has increased for both types of SHGs. They are working for 12-17 hours per day during the post-SHG period. They have to participate not only in domestic works but also in different economic activities. It has made in some cases, an adverse impact

TABLE 15.10
Impact on Employment Generation in the Year 2005

Panchayat

Sl. No.	Financing Activities	No. of HHs	Total employment generated	Average employment generated
1.	Cloth Business	17	1800	105.88
2.	Dairing	20	6000	300.00
3.	Tailoring	18	5960	331.11
4.	Grossary Shop	9	2250	250.00
5.	Rice Processing	15	1800	120.00
6.	Poultry	8	2560	320.00
7.	Agriculture			
	(a) Paddy	12	1080	90.00
	(b) Flower	9	1530	170.00
	(c) Oil Seeds	10	1200	120.00
	(d) Betel vine	8	2000	250.00
	Total	126	26180	207.78

NGO

Sl. No.	Financing Activities	No. of HHs	Total employment generated	Average employment generated
1.	Cloth Business	12	810	67.50
2.	Dairing	8	1840	230.00
3.	Tailoring	5	1170	234.00
4.	Grossary Shop	21	7350	350.00
5.	Rice Processing	8	708	88.50
6.	Poultry	2	440	220.00
7.	Agriculture			
	(a) Paddy	7	530	75.71
	(b) Flower	8	1040	130.00
	(c) Oil Seeds	2	200	100.00
	(d) Betel vine	1	200	200.00
	Total	4	14288	193.08

Source : Field Survey.

on vital domestic functions, e.g. child care etc., and health of women.

(B) It is seen that the meeting of sample SHGs are not held regularly. In some cases, the resolution books, etc., are not maintained properly. The factors behind these irregularities are lack of education/training (particularly in case of females), more responsibility for domestic functions in case of females, etc. As a result, the groups have become dependent on other persons having the required skill for completing these tasks.

(C) The main obstacle in the way of development of SHGs is the sale of their products. The theory behind the formation of SHGs is that there exists a large number of buyers and sellers in the product market, homogeneous product, full mobility of information, etc. but those characteristics do not seen in reality. Big companies have occupied almost the whole market. Products are not homogeneous. Perfect mobility of information is not found. Under these circumstances, it has become very difficult for weaker organizations like SHGs to compete in the market effective. So this may also explain why the SHGs do not start economic activities.

(D) The principle of profit maximization has become an indicator of success for banks in the post-liberalization era. As a result, the social responsibility of banks has decreased. The banks are imposing different conditions for passing grade-I or II. These have made difficult for SHGs to pass even Grade-I in some cases and lost the motivation of SHGs members. The factors like exorbitant service charge imposed by banks higher transaction costs, etc., are also the hindrances in the way of progress of SHGs.

(E) Similar mind of group members is a necessary element for the existence SHGs in the liberalized era. But it is not seen in reality. The members are more interested in individual enterprise as compared to group efforts. Thus individualism, lack of homogeneity, solidarity and cohesiveness, etc., are acting as hindrances in the way of progress of SHGs in a country like India. As a result, our sample NGOs have also started to finance some individual projects/enterprises (in lieu of group projects) for generating self-employment.

(F) In case of NGO-led SHGs it is seen that the members have to pay an extra-interest rate imposed by the groups (which is not found in case of panchayat-led SHGs) and this higher interest payment is a factor creating excess burden on the members and hence they are not able to borrow larger amount of loan. It creates an adverse effect on the expansion of activities of members of NGO-led SHGs.

(G) Since there is a provision for getting revolving fund/ credit linkage (i.e. subsidy) in case of panchayat-led SHGs, so the peoples, particularly people below poverty line (BPL) are more attracted to opt for the panchayat model as compared to NGO model. Again, since there are more opportunities to reach/motivate people through panchayat representatives and development programmes, hence there are greater scopes for forming SHGs led by panchayats as compared to SHGs led by NGOs. Side by side, since the panchayat is a mainstream or a part and parcel of the life of rural poor/people, so they make more trust upon panchayats as compared to NGOs. This factor may also act for more spread of panchayat-led SHGs in a country like India.

(H) The political problems often creates problems for the expansion of SHGs. The government rules and regulations sometimes do not able to include some peoples (who are not belonging to BPL category) to join in SHGs-led by panchayats. Under this circumstance, there is a scope to participate in SHG activities through NGO-led SHGs. In this case NGO model is better.

IX. CONCLUSIONS

In this section we shall first summarize the study and then give some policy prescriptions. It is observed that programme of micro finance through SHGs has been making rapid strides in both India and W.B. both Purba and Paschim Medinipur districts have played a significant role for spreading SHG activities in the districts of W.B. The block level/G.P.-wise analysis also shows almost an optimistic scenario of progress of different aspects of SHG activities.

The major findings from the field level study are as follows:

(1) The provision of loans is larger in case of panchayat-led SHGs and repayment performance is better in case of NGO-led SHGs. More consistency is seen for the distribution of loans among the households of panchayat-led SHGs.
(2) The impact on employment and income generation has been better in case of panchayat-led SHGs.
(3) The SHGs activities have created an excess burden on the women members. There exists irregularities in office procedures, problem of selling the product exorbitant service charge and higher transaction costs for getting loans, lack of homogeneity, individuals, etc. which are acting as hindrances in the way of progress of SHGs.
(4) The panchayat-led SHGs are more acceptable to rural poor as compared to NGO led SHGs. Thus, there is a more prospect for spread of panchayat-led SHGs in a country like India.

Despite the existence of many obstacles in the way of progress of SHGs, there is a good prospect for the progress of SHGs. The following measures may be taken for better functioning of SHGs:

(1) The greater emphasis should be given on (a) the unity responsibility, awareness, etc. among the members, (b) the utilization of local resources and the fulfilment of local demand for better progress of SHGs.
(2) More SHGs may be formed for the production of environment friendly products, which have a high domestic and foreign demand.

(3) The larger provision of cheap credit should be made not only for more progress of SHGs but also to bring poorest to the poor under SHG activities.

(4) The educational level and quality among members should be increased. The simplification of office procedure may be done for relieving the burden of work among the members (particularly women who find little time for rest).

(5) The SHG activities may be considered as a weapon for empowerment of women and social change in a country like India.

(6) Though it is observed from the micro-level study that panchayat-led SHGs are more suitable, but it is to be noted that the spread of both models be emphasized for accelerating both social and economic development in India. It is also to note that the least political interference is essential for the way of functioning of SHGs.

To conclude, the organizations like SHGs may be considered as a model for radical social transformation of less developed countries like India.

References

Annual Report, 2002-03, Ministry of Rural Development, GOI.

Antony, Valsamma (2006), 'Education and Empowerment—The Key to Women Empowerment', *Kurukshetra*, Vol. 54, No. 4, February.

Chavan, P. and R. Ramakumar (2002), 'Micro-Credit and Rural Poverty: An Analysis of Empirical, *Kurukshetra*, Vol. 53, No. 3, January.

Chatterjee, Dr. S. (2005). 'Networking SGSY, Banks and SHGs: Initiative in Uttar Pradesh'.

Dasgupta, R. (2001) 'An Informal Journey through Self-Help Groups', *Indian Journal of Agricultural Economic (I.J.A.E.)*, Vol. 56, No. 3, July-September.

Dutta, S.K. and M. Raman (2001), 'Can Heterogeneity and Social Cohesion Coexist in Self-Help Groups?', *Indian Journal of Agricultural Economic (I.J.A.E.)*, Vol. 56, No. 3, July-September.

Dadhichi, C.C. (2001), 'Micro Finance—A Panacea for Poverty Alleviation: A Case Study of Oriental Gramin Project in India', *I.J.A.E.*, Vol. 56, No. 3, July-September.

Das, S., (2003), 'Self-Help Groups and Micro Credit: Synergic Integration', *Kurukshetra*, Vol. 51, No. 10, August.

Dogra, V.M., (2002), 'Women Self-Help Groups: Profiles from Andhra Pradesh and Karnataka', *Kurukshetra*, Vol. 50, No. 6, April.

Economic Survey, 2003-04, GOI.

Gangaiah, C., B. Nagaraja, and C. Vasudevulu Naidu, (2006), 'Impact of Self-help Groups on Income and Employment: A Case Study, *Kurukshetra*, Vol. 54, No. 5, March.

Gurumoorthy, T.R. (2000), 'Self-Help-Groups Empower Rural Women', *Kurukshetra*, Vol. 48, No. 5, February.

Gupta, Dr. M.L and Namita Gupta (2006), 'Economic Empowerment of Women through SHGs', *Kurukshetra*, Vol. 54, No. 4, February.

Ghosh, M. (2006), 'Bursting Balloons', *The Sunday Statesman Magazine*, October 22.

Ghosh, M. (1983), 'Bank Project Resucitates Rural Bangladesh,' *The Sunday Statesman*, September 4.

Kulshrestha, Dr. L.R. and A. Gupta, (2001) 'Self-Help Group: Innovations in Financing the Poor', *Kurukshetra*, November.

Kulshrestha, Dr. L.R. and A. Gupta (2002), ' NGOs in Micro Financing: Partners in Rural Development', *Kurukshetra*, Vol. 53, No. 3, January.

Koutsoyannis, A. (1979), 'Theory of Econometrics,' 2nd edition.

Longnathan, Dr. P.R. Asokan, (2006), 'Inter-Regional Development of Self-Help Groups in India', *Kurukshetra*, Vol. 54, No. 11, September.

Malhotra, R. (2005), 'Imperative Need for Fine-tuning, The SGSY', *Kurukshetra*, Vol. 53, No. 8, June.

Mandal, A. (2005), 'Swarnajayanti Gram Swarozgar Yojana and Self-Help Group: An Assessment', *Kurukshetra*, Vol. 53, No. 3, January.

Madheswaran, S. and A. Dharmadhikary (2001) 'Improving Rural Women through Self-Help Groups: Lessens from Maharashtra Rural Credit Project, *I.J.A.E.*, Vol., 56, No. 3, July-September.

Haque, Mohammedul (2006), 'Dhubri Hatchery: Ray of Hope for Self-Help Groups', *Kurukshetra*, Vol. 54, No. 11, September.

Namboodiri, N.V. and R.L. Shiyani (2001), 'Potential Role of Self-Help Groups in Rural Financial Deepening', *I.J.A.E.*, Vol. 56, No. 3, July-September.

Naithani, P. (2001), 'Micro-Financing The Self-employment Activities Sea-Saw of Ideas', *Kurukshetra*, Vol. 49, No. 10, July.

Ojha, R.K. (2001), 'Self-Help Groups and Rural Employment', *Yojana*, Vol. 45, May.

Pal, Dr. M. (2002), 'Swarnajayanti Gram Swarozgar Yojana: Evolution Assessment and Future Prospect,' *Kurukshetra*.

Rath, N. (1985), 'Garibi Hatao—Can IRDP Do it', *EPW*, Vol. 20, No. 6, February 9.

Rao, R. (2005), 'Women's Groups Herold: A Wind of Change in Rural Uttaranchal', *Kurukshetra*, Vol. 53, No. 3, January.

Rao, V.M. (2002), 'Women's Self-Help Groups: Profiles from Andhra Pradesh and Karnataka,' *Kurukshetra*, Vol. 50, No. 6, April.

Rao, C.A. (2003), 'Women Empowerment through SHG and DWCRA—A Study in Andhra Pradesh,' *Indian Journal of Regional Science (I.J.R.S.)*, Vol. XXXV, No. 1.

Ray, S.K. and A. Das ((2005), 'Self-Help Groups in West Bengal with Special Reference to Purba Medinipur District: Some Issues', Published in Seminar volume on Self-Help Groups: A New Way of Rural Development, K.D. College of Commerce, Paschim Medinipur.

Sarangi, P. (2003), 'Self-Help Groups: An Experiment in Orissa', *Kurukshetra,* Vol. 51, No. 4, February.

Satish, P. (2001), Some Issues in the Formation of Self-Help Groups', *I.J.A.E.,* Vol. 56, No. 3, July-September.

Singh, Dr. O.R. (2003), 'Role of NGOs in Fostering Self-Help Groups: A Case Study of MYRA DA', Vol. 51, No. 4, February.

Sau, S. (2006), 'S. Asahayak Dal: Paschim Medinipur Zilla,' (in Bengali version), Aahawan (Paschim Medinipur).

Soundarapandian, Dr. M. (2006), 'Micro Finance for Rural Entrepreneurs : Issues and Strategies', *Kurukshetra,* Vol. 54, No. 11, September.

Sarkar, A. (2006), 'Arthnaitik Vikalpa Nai, Kintu Samaj Badaler Bara Astra', (in Bengali Version)', *Kurukshetra Patrika,* October 19.

Thoner, D.B., Kerblay and R.E.F. Smith (1966), 'Chayanov on the Theory of Peasant Economy', Homewood, Illinois, Richard D. Irwin.

Tenth Five Year Plan, 2002-07, GOI.

Thakuria, N. (2005); 'The Growing Mission of Self-Helping, *Kurukshetra,* Vol. 53, No. 3, January.

Tripathi, O.M. (2003) 'Making Insurance Everybody's Business : The SHG Way,' *Kurukshetra,* Vol. 51, No. 4, February.

Tripathy, K.K. (2006), 'Micro-Credit Invention and Poverty Alleviation', *Kurukshetra,* Vol. 54, No. 11, September.

Yunus, M. (2004), 'Grameen Bank, Micro-Credit and Millennium Development Goals', *EPW,* Vol. XXXIX, No. 36, September 4.

———, (2000), 'Banker to the Poor : The Autobiography of Muhammad Yunus, Founder of the Grameen Bank', The University Press Ltd., Dhaka.

Yadav, S.S. (2006), 'Self-Help Group Movement in Rajasthan : Bright Prospects', *Kurukshetra,* Vol. 54, No. 11, September.

16

Reforms and Growth in India and East Asian Countries : A Comparative Analysis

PRANKRISHNA PAL

Economic Reforms in India have started on July 24, 1991 to correct the problem of macro-economic imbalances in the economy. The primary objective of the reforms was to put the economy on a sustainable high growth path by establishing an incentive framework that helps movement towards the best possible allocation of factors of production across various sectors in the economy and the most efficient input combination within a production sector. Since 1991 a period of 15 years has passed and the economy has witnessed changes in different economic sectors.

Here East Asia consists of several countries. The major countries are: Combodia, China, Indonesia, Korea, Malaysia, Mongolia, Myanmar, Philippines, Thailand and Vietnam. Among them, China is the prime country. India is a low-income country in South Asia while China is a lower middle-income country in East Asia, according to the size of the economy. At present China and India are not the Asia's "sick men". The growth rate of GDP in China is 10% and in India 6-7%. Per capita income of these two countries are $ 1290 and $ 620 respectively (WDR, 2006). Thus these two countries are rising rapidly. In China, economic reforms have started in 1978 and India has undertaken economic reforms in 1991. In both the countries structural changes have occurred. China has advantage in manufacturing while India in services. Thus China and India are complimentary to each other.

In this paper we are to examine the impact of economic reforms on the growth of output and the growth of merchandise exports and imports in India and East Asia with special reference to China during 1990-2004.

ECONOMIC REFORMS POLICY IN INDIA AND CHINA

The first Generation of Economic Reforms in India was started on July 1991 with the introduction of short-term stabilization programme, structural adjustment and high growth. These policies can be grouped into three broad heads: (i) a new industrial policy based on liberalization and "market-friendly" economy, (ii) public sector reforms and exit policy, and (iii) trade policy reforms with liberalization of the exchange rate system. The Industrial Policy of July 1991 has three important facets. The first deals with deregulation, delicensing, decontrol and debureaucratization. The second aspect focuses on profit maximization and makes competitive efficiency the kingpin for future industrial growth. Quality improvement and efficiency optimization become the main keys for achieving success. The third facet highlights the urgent necessity of opening up of the Indian economy and specially emphasizes the necessity for globalization and internationalization of our economy to make the strategy of export-led growth a success (Ghosh, 1994).

After achieving some degree of stabilization and structural balance in our economy, we have introduced the Second Generation of Economic Reforms during BJP Government's regime. The Second Generation Reforms have ushered in the opening of the insurance sector, relaxation of the controls on foreign entry of capital and entry of private sector in the banking arena with better innovation and greater freedom. The extra dose of liberalization with globalization landed the Government in troubled spot. Public borrowing could not be kept under disciple and fiscal deficit appeared to be out of control. To overcome this crisis, the Government instead of depending on an overdose of deficit financing, boldly has undertaken recourse to "the disinvestment policy". (Ghosh, 2003). This is all about a brief discussion of the Reforms Policy in India.

Like India China is also going through the process of economic reforms. China has started the reforms in 1978. The reforms have come under the phases:

(i) *Rural and agricultural reform (1978-83)* : The economy of China has depended on rural industrialization. Household Responsibility System/Agricultural Responsibility System (HRS/ARS) in agriculture was introduced and farm households were allowed to lease land from the state and sell their output to official procurement agencies at State determined prices. Also, Township and Village Enterprises (TVEs) in industry was established for the production and sale of industrial commodities outside the Central plan.

(ii) *Reform of urban sector (1984-91)* : It has started in 1984-85. It aimed at giving greater autonomy for industrial units, including greater freedom to determine contract prices and select input and outputs.

(iii) *Globalisation and internationalization* : It has started in the early eighties. The initial market opening began in 1979 with the devaluation of highly over-valued exchange rate. Trade liberalization has progressed throughout the 1980's. Exporting firms were permitted to hold a large portion of foreign exchange. Special Economic Zones were set-up in the coastal regions of Jiangsu, Zhejiang and Guangdon. As a result, foreign direct investment in China has increased significantly. In fact, China has proved the superiority of "Gradualism and Experimentation" to rapid "Top-Down Reform" based on a "Big-bang" policy.

The Chinese miracle is not based on a "shock therapy" but rather on a "gradual therapy". The reforms in China were gradual, incremental and often experimental. Economic liberalization programme can click even without political liberalization.

With this background of the reform policies of India and China, we now examine the impact of reform policies on the growth of the Indian economy and East Asia with special reference to China during 1990-2004.

Structure of Output

Structure of output has been changing over time in the world economy during the globalization period. Generally total output (Gross Domestic Product, GDP) of any country generates from three main sectors: agriculture, industry and services. Estimates (Table 16.1) reveal that composition of GDP has been changing in East Asian Countries and India during the

TABLE 16.1
Percentage Distribution of GDP in East Asian Countries and India during 1990-2004

Countries	*Agriculture (%)*		*Industry (%)*		*Services (%)*	
	1990	*2004*	*1990*	*2004*	*1990*	*2004*
Cambodia	—	33	—	29	—	38
China	27	13	42	46	31	41
Indonesia	19	15	39	44	42	41
Korea	9	4	42	41	50	56
Malaysia	15	10	42	50	43	40
Mongolia	17	21	30	30	52	59
Myanmar	—	—	—	—	—	—
Philippines	22	14	35	32	44	54
Thailand	13	10	37	44	50	46
Vietnam	39	22	23	40	39	38
East Asia	25	13	40	45	35	42
India	31	21	28	27	41	52

Source : World Development Indicators, 2006, World Bank.

globalization period of 1990-2004. The share of agriculture has declined in all the East Asian countries and India during 1990-2004. On the other hand, the share of services has significantly increased in almost all the East Asian countries and India excepting Indonesia, Thailand and Vietnam. Among the countries, Mongolia has registered the highest (59%) followed by Korea (56%), Philippines (54%) and India (52%), etc. in 2004. Interestingly, we note that the contribution of service sector has significantly increased in India (41% to 52%) and China (31% to 41%) during this period. Thus compared to China, India has gained more service sector's income during the globalization period. This is due to the fact that from the mid of 1990s India's economy has been characterized by what World Bank (2004) calls "India's Services Revolution". During this period there has indeed occurred a qualitative change in India's sectoral composition (Rakhit, 2007). Also, the contribution of industry has increased in most of the East Asian States excepting Korea, Philippines and India during the reforms period. Here, among the Asian states, Malaysia (50%) is the leading country followed by China (46%), Thailand (44%) and Indonesia (44%), etc. in 2004. In India, the industry's share was 27% in 2004. However, compared to India, the industry's share in China has significantly increased from 42% in 1990 to 46% in 2004. This is due to the fact that the Chinese Government has undertaken different industrial policies during the reform periods. And as a result, industrial sector has developed, small-scale and cottage industries have expanded and various types of goods have produced at the cheapest costs. This is the impact of globalization on the Chinese economy.

Growth of Output

We have already said that the share of services has been increasing in almost all the East Asian countries specially China and India during the globalization periods of 1990-2004. Let us now examine the growth of output and its sector in the Asian countries and India during the globalization two sub-periods: 1990-2000 and 2000-04.

Estimates (Table 16.2) reveal that the GDP growth rate has displayed a downward trend in East Asia and its constituent

TABLE 16.2
Average Annual Growth Rate (%) of Output in East Asian Countries and India during 1990-2004

Countries	*1990-2000*				*2000-04*			
	GDP	*Agri.*	*Industry*	*Services*	*GDP*	*Agri.*	*Industry*	*Services*
Cambodia	7.1	3.9	14.3	7.1	6.3	2.8	14.2	3.9
China	10.6	4.1	13.7	10.2	9.4	3.4	10.6	9.8
Indonesia	4.2	2.1	5.3	4.0	4.6	3.9	3.8	5.7
Korea	5.8	1.6	6.0	5.6	4.7	-1.0	6.2	4.0
Malaysia	7.0	0.3	8.6	7.3	4.4	3.4	4.2	4.7
Mongolia	3.5	3.7	2.3	0.5	5.2	-3.3	8.4	6.9
Myanmar	7.0	5.7	10.5	7.2	—	—	—	—
Philippines	3.4	1.7	3.5	4.0	3.9	2.4	2.4	5.8
Thailand	4.2	1.0	5.7	3.8	504	3.2	6.9	4.3
Vietnam	7.9	4.3	11.9	7.5	7.2	3.6	10.1	6.6
East Asia	8.5	3.4	11.0	8.0	8.1	3.4	9.1	8.4
India	6.0	3.0	6.3	8.0	6.2	2.0	6.2	8.2

Source : World Development Indicators, 2006, World Bank.

states during 1990-04: East Asia (8.5% to 8.0%), Combodia (7.1% to 6.3%), China (10.6% to 9.4%), Korea (5.8% to 4.7%), Malaysia (7.0% to 4.4%) and Vietnam (7.9% to 7.2%). This deceleration of GDP growth of these East Asian countries has been attributed by the deceleration of agricultural growth in all the countries and the deceleration of industrial growth in most of the countries during the globalization period. Specifically, we like to mention that the declaration of GDP growth is due to that of agriculture, industry and services in the states of Combodia, China and Vietnam. On the other hand, the GDP growth has displayed an upward trend in the East Asian states of Indonesia (4.2% to 4.6%), Mongolia (3.5% to 5.2%), Philippines (3.4% to 3.9%) and Thailand (4.2% to 5.4%). Among these states, only in Thailand this upward trend growth rate has caused by the upward trend growth rates of the three components of agriculture, industry and services. Thus we see that among the East Asian countries, Combodia has displayed the prime position in industrial growth followed by China and Vietnam; China the leading position in services growth followed by Mongolia and Vietnam. This is the discussion of the growth of output in East Asian countries during the globalization period of 1990-2004.

Let us now discuss the India's growth of output. Its GDP growth rate has increased marginally from 6.0% during 1990-2000 to 6.2% during 2000-04. Only the service sector growth rate has increased from 8% to 8.2% while the agricultural and industrial growth rates have declined from 3% to 2% and 6.3% to 6.2% respectively. Thus we see that India's GDP growth rate has remarked by 'Service-led Growth'. This is due to the fact that increasing dominance of services' GDP has gone hand in hand with emergence of India as a major exporter of services, specially in IT and IT-enabled products (this will be discussed in later). Since the early 90s both merchandise and services exports of India have grown at a higher rate than GDP as well as world exports. However, growth of services' exports has been much more spectacular, specially from the mid-1990s. Performance of services was much more impressive. With an average growth of 17.05% the country's services exports as a proportion of world exports of services rose from 0.53% to 2.32% between 1992 and 2005. Thus during 1995-2005 growth of India's services exports (at 21.5%) was almost two times that of world exports (Rakhit, 2007).

Let us now make a comparison of growth of output in India and East Asia with special reference to China. Estimates (Table 16.2) reveal that the GDP and the sectoral growth rates of India have been lower than that of East Asia and also of China during the globalization period, though India's GDP growth rate has increased while GDP growth rates of East Asia and China has declined during this period.

Structure of Merchandise Exports and Imports

Let us now examine merchandise exports and imports of East Asian countries and India during 1990-2004. Here the items of exports and imports are food, agricultural raw material, fuel, ores and metals and manufacturing goods. Estimates (Table 16.3) reveal that the structure of merchandise exports

TABLE 16.3
Percentage Distribution of Merchandise Exports and Imports in East Asean Countries and India during 1990-2004

Countries	Exports										Imports									
	Food		Agri. Raw-materials		Fuel		Ores and Metals		Manuf.		Food		Agri. Raw material		Fuel		Ores and Metals		Manuf.	
	1990	2004	1990	2004	1990	2004	1990	2004	1990	2004	1990	2004	1990	2004	1990	2004	1990	2004	1990	2004
(1)	(2)	(3)	(4)	(5)	(6)	(7)	(8)	(9)	(10)	(11)	(12)	(13)	(14)	(15)	(16)	(17)	(18)	(19)	(20)	(21)
Cambodia	—	1	—	2	—	0	—	0	—	97	—	8	—	2	—	10	—	0	—	80
China	13	4	3	1	8	2	2	2	72	91	13	4	3	1	8	2	2	2	72	91
Indonesia	11	14	5	6	44	18	4	7	35	56	11	14	5	6	44	18	4	7	35	56
Korea	3	1	1	1	1	4	1	2	94	92	6	5	8	2	16	22	7	7	63	63
Malaysia	12	8	14	2	18	12	2	1	54	76	7	6	1	1	5	6	4	4	82	81
Mongolia	—	3	—	13	—	3	—	43	—	38	—	14	—	1	—	20	—	1	—	65
Myanmar	51	—	36	—	0	—	2	—	11	—	13	—	1	—	5	—	0	—	81	—
Philippines	19	6	2	1	2	1	8	2	38	55	10	6	2	1	15	11	3	2	53	79
Thailand	29	14	5	5	1	2	1	1	63	75	5	5	5	3	9	12	4	3	75	76
Vietnam	—	23	—	2	—	21	—	1	—	53	—	6	—	3	—	11	—	3	—	77
East Asia	15	6	6	2	13	6	3	2	60	80	8	5	5	3	5	9	3	6	77	77
India	16	10	4	1	3	9	5	7	70	73	3	4	4	3	27	35	8	5	51	53

Source : World Development Indicators, 2006, World Bank.

and imports in East Asian countries and India has changed during the globalization period of 1990-2004. Manufacturing goods of exports and imports have enjoyed the prime position in all the countries. In respect of merchandise exports its share has significantly increased in the countries of China (72% to 91%), Indonesia (35% to 56%), Malaysia (54% to 76%), Philippines (38% to 55%), Thailand (63% to 75%), East Asia (60% to 80%) and India (70% to 73%) during the period under study. But in respect of merchandise imports' its share has more or less constant. Also, we note that the shares of food, agricultural raw-material, fuel and ores and metals have declined in almost all the East Asian countries in respects of merchandise exports and imports. But in India the exports shares of food and agricultural raw-material have declined while that of full and ores and metals have increased during 1990-2004. Similarly, the imports shares of food and fuel have increased and that of agricultural raw material and ores and metals have decreased.

Compared to China, India has exported more food, fuel and ores and metals; and imported also more fuel and ores and metals during the globalization period due to her reforms policy. On the other hand, China has exported more manufacturing goods due to her reforms policy.

Let us now turn to the aspect of the distribution pattern of service (commercial) exports and imports of East Asian Countries and India during 1990-2004. Here we have four types of services: transport, travel, insurance and financial services and computer, information and communication (i.e. IT and IT-based). Estimates (Table 16.4) reveal that the share of transport services in India has deceased in respects of exports and imports during 1990-2004, but the import share has been greater than the export one. But in case of travel, exports share has decreased while imports share has increased. Also, insurance and financial services of exports and imports have increased. But in case of IT services both exports and imports share have increased, exports of IT services are greater than imports of that one due to revolution of IT industries during the globalization period.

In East Asia, the shares of transport, travel, insurance and financial services of exports have decreased and the share of IT services has increased. But the imports share of transport service

TABLE 16.4

Percentage Distribution of Service (Commercial) Exports and Imports in East Asian Countries and India during 1990-2004

Countries	*Exports*								*Imports*							
	Transport		*Travel*		*Ins. and Financial Services*		*Computer, Information and Communication*		*Transport*		*Travel*		*Ins. and Financial Services*		*Computer, Information and Communication*	
	1990	*2004*	*1990*	*2004*	*1990*	*2004*	*1990*	*2004*	*1990*	*2004*	*1990*	*2004*	*1990*	*2004*	*1990*	*2004*
(1)	*(2)*	*(3)*	*(4)*	*(5)*	*(6)*	*(7)*	*(8)*	*(9)*	*(10)*	*(11)*	*(12)*	*(13)*	*(14)*	*(15)*	*(16)*	*(17)*
Cambodia	—	13.7	—	79.5	—	—	—	6.8	24.5	62.8	—	10.3	—	5.0	75.5	22.0
China	47.1	19.5	30.2	41.5	4.0	0.8	18.7	38.3	78.9	34.3	11.4	26.7	2.3	8.8	·7.4	30.2
Indonesia	2.8	13.2	86.5	27.7	0.0	1.8	10.7	57.4	47.4	19.5	14.2	12.4	4.0	3.4	34.5	64.7
Korea	34.7	56.0	34.5	14.3	0.1	2.9	30.7	26.8	39.8	36.1	27.5	24.2	0.3	1.2	32.4	38.6
Malaysia	31.8	20.6	44.7	43.8	0.1	2.5	23.5	33.1	46.9	36.1	26.9	16.4	—	3.5	26.2	44.0
Mongolia	41.8	32.7	10.4	56.2	4.6	1.2	43.2	9.9	56.2	40.2	0.8	38.8	6.3	8.2	36.8	12.8
Myanmar	—	7.1	81.0	87.5	5.9	—	13.1	5.5	3.5.4	51.2	22.6	6.5	2.5	—	39.5	42.4
Philippines	8.5	27.3	16.1	49.1	0.5	1.4	74.9	22.2	56.9	48.1	6.5	25.9	3.4	5.5	33.2	22.5
Thailand	21.1	23.0	68.7	53.1	0.2	0.7	10.0	23.3	58.1	47.3	23.3	19.7	5.5	5.6	13.6	27.4
Vietnam	—	—	—	—	—	—	—	—	—	—	—	—	—	—	—	—
East Asia	32.3	19.9	43.5	42.2	2.0	1.0	22.2	37.0	65.5	36.8	15.8	23.9	2.6	7.4	16.2	32.0
India	20.8	13.3	33.8	16.8	2.7	3.5	42.7	66.4	57.5	36.7	6.6	13.8	5.8	6.5	·30.1	43.1

Source : World Development Indicators, 2006, World Bank.

has decreased and that of travel, insurance and financial services and IT services have increased during the globalization period. However, we observed that travel services of exports are the main export services of the East Asian countries of Combodia (80%), China (42%), Malaysia (44%), Mongolia (56%), Myanmar (88%), Philippines (49%) and Thailand (53%) in 2004. Indonesia and Korea are the prime in respects of IT services and transport services exports respectively. Similarly, on the import front, the transport service import is the prime share of China (34%), Mongolia (40%), Myanmar (51%), Philippines (48%), and Thailand (47%) while IT services import is the prime share of Indonesia (65%), Korea (39%) and Malaysia (44%) in 2004.

Let us now make a comparative study of services exports and imports between India and China during the globalization period. In China, the shares of transports, insurance services and IT services exports have decreased while travel services exports share has increased during 1990-2004. 'Travel services exports are the prime services exports. On the import front, the share of transport services had decreased and the shares of travel, insurance and IT services have increased during the globalization period. Here transports services are the main import services. But in India the exports and imports shares of IT services have increased, though the exports shares have significantly increased. This IT services are the prime position in respects of services exports and imports due to the implementations of the reforms policy during the period under study. Exports shares of transport and travel have decreased while that of insurance and financial services has increased during 1990-2004. Also, imports shares of transport have decreased while that of travel and insurance and financial services have increased during the globalization period.

Intensity and Openness of Trade

Intensity of trade (exports/imports) of a country is the ratio between trade value and GDP while openness of trade of a country is the ratio between exports plus imports and GDP. So we have two types of trade intensity : exports intensity and imports intensity. Trade intensity and openness of trade are thus two indicators of a country which reflect country's growth and development with respect to other countries. Trade intensity may be one-way traffic while openness of trade may be two-ways traffic. Thus in our study we have computed these two indices of Asian countries and India to examine the nature of trade (exports/imports) of these countries with respect to their GDP during the globalization period of 1990-2004.

Estimates (Table 16.5) reveal that due to implementation of reforms policies in India and East Asia particularly in China, exports and imports intensities of these countries have remarkably increased during 1990-2004. Exports intensity is more than imports intensity in the countries of China, Indonesia, Malaysia and East Asia while the reverse has happened in the countries of Combodia, Mongolia, Vietnam and India. Thus we see that China is an export-oriented country whose exports are more than imports during the globalization period. This is due to implementation of her reform policy. On the other hand, India is now an import-oriented country whose

TABLE 16.5

Intensity of Trade and Openness of Trade in East Asian Countries and India during 1990-2004

Countries	*Exports Intensity (%)*		*Imports Intensity (%)*		*Openness of Trade (%)*	
	1990	*2004*	*1990*	*2004*	*1990*	*2004*
Combodia	6	65	13	76	19	141
China	19	34	16	31	35	65
Indonesia	25	31	24	27	49	58
Korea	28	44	29	40	57	84
Malaysia	75	121	72	100	147	221
Mongolia	24	75	53	87	77	162
Phillipines	28	.52	33	51	61	103
Thailand	34	71	42	66	76	137
Vietnam	36	66	45	74	81	140
East Asia	24	43	23	40	47	83
India	7	19	9	23	16	42

Source : World Development Indicators, 2006, World Bank.

imports are more than exports. Now-a-days India moves towards the export-oriented country due to recent export-import policy implementation.

Openness of trade gives us the real position of the country in respect to her foreign trade. It has increased in all the East Asian countries and India during 1990-2004. This increase in trade openness is due to the reforms policy of the respective country during the globalization period. It indicates the growth of the country in respect of her foreign trade. Also, China has low trade openness compared to other East Asian countries. India has also low trade openness compared to China during 1990-2004.

CONCLUSIONS

Economic reforms in India have started on July 1991 while that in China in 1978. In both the countries structural changes have occurred. China has advantage in manufacturing while India in services. Thus these two countries are complimentary to each other during the globalization period of 1990-2004.

Compared to China, India has gained more service sector's income during 1990-2004. This is due to the fact that from the mid of 1990s India's economy has been characterized by what World Bank (2004) calls "India's Services Revolution". India's GDP growth rate has thus remarked by 'Service-led Growth'. On the other hand, the industry's share in China has significantly increased due to implementation of industrial policies during the reform periods. The GDP and the sectoral growth rates in India have been lower than that of East Asia and China, though India's GDP growth rate has increased while GDP growth rates of East Asia and China has decline during this period.

Compared to China, India has exported more food, fuel and ores and metals. China has exported more manufacturing goods. China is an export-oriented country while India is an import-oriented country. Also, openness of trade has increased in both China and India during 1990-2004, but India has low trade openness compared to China.

REFERENCES

Chen, J. and B. Hu (1993), "China's Rural Industrial Development and Surplus Labour Transfer", presented at the National Workshop on Rural Industrialization in Post-Reform China, Beijing, China.

Dutta, R. (1995), "New Economic Reform—Need for Some Rethinking", *The Indian Economic Journal*, Vol. 42, No. 3.

Gale Johnson, D. (1990), "The' People's Republic of China—1978-1990, International Centre for Economic Growth, San Francisco.

Ghosh, Alok (1994), "Economic Reforms in India and China and the Need for Revamping the Banking Sector", *Artha Beekshan*, Vol. 3, No. 2.

———, (2003), "Disinvestment and Economic Reforms in India", *Artha Beekshan*, Vol. 12, No. 3.

Jefirey Sachs and Wing Thye Woo (1994), "Structural Factors in the Economic Reforms in China and EEFSU", *Economic Policy*, April.

McMillan, J. and Naughton, B. (1992), "How to Reform a Planned Economy: Lessons from China", *Oxford Review of Economic Policy.*

Pal, P.K. (2007), "Economic Reforms, Growth and Employment in India" (Summary), *Artha Beekshan*, Vol. 15, No. 4.

Pal, P.K. (2006), "Pattern and Growth of India's Economy Since 1980s", *Occasional Papers*, Department of Economics, Rabindra Bharati University, Vol. XIV, 2006.

Rakshit, Mihir (2007) '"Services-led Growth: The Indian Experience", *Artha Beekshan*, Vol. 15, No. 4.

World Bank (2004), "Sustaining India's Services Revolution: Access to Foreign Markets", Domestic Reform and International Negotiation.

World Bank (2006), World Development Report.

World Development Indicators, 2006, World Bank.

Gravity Analysis of Indo ASEAN Trade Flows

AVIJIT MANDAL

INTRODUCTION

In the recent trend of globalization a country of India's size and aspirations has to look beyond its immediate neighborhood to seek economic opportunities. It is with this objective, India adopted *"Look East Policy"*[1] (LEP) to integrate with the Asian neighbours, particularly the member countries of Association of South-East Asian Nations[2] (ASEAN) in 1991. Indo-ASEAN relation got momentum only about a decade ago after the adoption of LEP by India in 1991. This relation has been reinforced by recognizing India as a member of Asian Regional Forum[3] (ARF) in 1996. India's renewed interest in closer economic and political relations with her South-East Asian neighbours was reciprocated by many of them who seemed to be pursuing an unstated "Look West" policy of increasing their interaction with India. Before the launch of LEP, India was really not interested in the East Asia. Its attitude towards the ASEAN during the early years of its birth was timid. It is only after the commencement of its LEP Indo-ASEAN nexus geared up from dialogue partnership in 1992 to a full dialogue partnership during the fifth ASEAN summit in Bangkok in 1995.

The Indo ASEAN partnership seeks to exploit mutual benefits in diverse areas of human capital, trade and investment, infrastructure development, science and technology and tourism. The intensification of the economic linkages with the ASEAN has led India into a second phase of its "LEP". Phase-I of the policy was characterized by trade and investment linkages. Phase-II is marked by arrangements for free trade areas and establishing institutional economic linkages between the countries of the region and India. The importance of common market and free trade agreement within Asia cannot be ignored. A trade bloc comprising India, China, South Korea and the ten ASEAN nations would represent a giant free trade zone. Indian economy has increasingly integrated with East Asian countries as important source of trade and investment.

The present paper is organised as follows. Section 2 deals with comparative pictures of the general economic indicators. In section 3 patterns of India's trade flows has been presented. Section 4 describes the gravity model as a tool to predict bilateral trade flows between India and ASEAN. In section 5 descriptions of data are presented. Section 6 deals with the estimation results. Section 7 presents the prediction of India's trade flows to ASEAN. Section 8 deals with conclusion.

2. COMPARATIVE PICTURE OF GENERAL ECONOMIC INDICATORS

Being the largest democracy in the world, India soon after independence acted as an inspiration for many newly independent nations in South-East Asia. At the same time, these countries in South-East Asia and India recognised the strategic importance of developing relations with one another to promote and facilitate their cooperation and utilization of greater business opportunities. Unfortunately, the relationship came under strain for the next three decades due to the differences of opinion in ideological outlook and security relationships during the Cold War. The adoption of the "Look East Policy" by India in 1991 and ASEAN's strong desire to forge closer ties with India has transformed the Indo-ASEAN relation in its original status. This transformation did not come easily. The financial crisis of 1997 and the developments in South Asia also affected the dialogue relations between ASEAN and India. However, ASEAN-India dialogue relations have overcome these challenges and are now on the upswing. This paved the way for both sides to enter into a new phase of a strategic relationship.

TABLE 17.1

Selected Economic Aggregates of India and ASEAN Countries (2004-05)

Country	*Population (In Million)*	*GDP at current market prices (US \$ Million)*	*Growth Rate of GDP (in %)*	*Per Capita GDP (US \$)*	*Interest Rate*[4]
India	1091	680287.40	6.90	623.50	10.25-10.75
Brunei	383.4	5181	2.90	13879	1.04
Cambodia	13,872	4864	7.70	358	4.68
Indonesia	219,142	258266	5.10	1193	6.71
Laos	5,904	2137	5.50	423	10.47
Malaysia	26.207	118318	7.10	4625	3.00
Myanmar	56,003	9081	5.00	166	9.50
Philippines	84,241	86106	6.00	1042	6.63
Singapore	4,296	106884	8.40	25207	0.41
Thailand	64,994	163547	6.10	2537	1.00
Vietnam	83,156	45402	7.70	554	6.60
ASEAN	55819.84	800087	6.10	1455	5.00
ASEAN 6[5]	66543.90	738302	5.90	8080.50	3.13

Source : ASEAN Statistical Year Book, 2005 and Reserve Bank of India Handbook of Statistics.

As compared to India's vast population of 1091 million, ASEAN's population (Please see Table 17.1) stands at a level of 549.8 million. The growth rate of population in India is 1.9% per year in comparison with 1.5% of ASEAN economies. As far as macro-economic indicators are concerned ASEAN's Gross Domestic Product (GDP) is almost 1.18% times India's GDP in 2004 (Please see Table 17.1). ASEAN 6 covers the 90% of the ASEAN's GDP. In tune with present growth trend the ASEAN economy will grow at an annual rate of 5-6% over the next few years. Last three decades have witnessed a period of high economic growth and improved human development for most of the ASEAN economies. Despite the economic crisis of 1997 in the region, ASEAN economies have moved to a path of phenomenal economic success. ASEAN economies are expected to continue with its encouraging growth. India is lagging in GDP per capita as compared to ASEAN countries. ASEAN's average per capita GDP is more than double the level of the India. But in case of growth rate of GDP, India is ahead of ASEAN countries. Over the past five years from 2000 to 2004 India has averaged an annual growth rate of 6% as compared to ASEAN's 5.2%. India is expected to grow at a higher rate in the years to come. In Purchasing Power Parity (PPP) India is the fourth largest economy in the world. The two important factors, e.g. population and GDP characterise the vastness of Indian economy as well as the domestic market. India is emerging economy of the world with a gross domestic product of $ US 680 billion and a consumer market of nearly 1.2 billion people.

The remarkable growth performance of the ASEAN economies hinges on the implementation of policies for macroeconomic stability, and export promotion. Greater emphasis has been given on human resource developments. In the post liberelisation period after 1990 India has adopted outward looking policy with a view to integrate the domestic economy with the world. Domestic as well as the foreign policies provide the strategy to establish the framework for globalization of India's trade and to promote productivity, modernisation and competitiveness of Indian industries and thereby to enhance its export capabilities.

3. INDO ASEAN TRADE PATTERNS

The hoary past of the India's relation with the South-East Asian countries dates back to the ancient period, contributing to the historical and civilization resemblances between them.

India's trade with this region was mainly on spices and textiles. Now the product basket changed quite a lot. India's exports to ASEAN mainly consists of oil meals, gems and jewellery, meat and meat preparations, cotton yarn, fabrics, machinery, rice, drugs and pharmaceuticals, chemicals, etc. ASEAN's exports to India include artificial resins, plastic material, natural rubber, wood and wood products, electronic goods, organic chemicals, edible oils, fertilizers, etc.

To accelerate the trade relation between them several initiatives have been taken both at regional and bilateral levels. Regional initiatives start with establishment of CSCAP (Council for Security Cooperation in Asia Pacific) in 1994 to contribute to the efforts towards regional confidence building and enhancing regional security. Second in the line is the creation of BIMSTEC (Bangladesh, India, Myanmar, Sri Lanka and Thailand Economic Cooperation) in 1997 to promote trade cooperation. Last one is the initiation of Mekong Ganga Cooperation (MGC) Project in 2000 by six nations, e.g. India, Myanmar, Thailand, Laos, Cambodia and Vietnam. This project aims to develop trade, tourism, communications and transport linkages between India and Mekong basin countries. At the bilateral level there are several agreements between India and individual members of ASEAN. Important agreements are trade agreement between India and Myanmar (2003), Indo-Thai Free Trade Agreement (2004) and Comprehensive Economic Cooperation Agreement (CECA) between India and Singapore (2005).

It is interesting to see that India's total trade with ASEAN has been increased from US $ 7.1 billion in 2000-01 to US $ 17.5 billion in 2004-05 (Please see Table 17.2). It shows the annual growth rate of 29%. ASEAN 6 covers more than 90% of the total trade with India. Among the members Singapore holds the maximum share and least share comes from Laos in total trade with India over the sample time period (See Table 1.1 in Appendix 1). Laos is the only country with which India's total trade declines over the time period. It is worth-mentioning that the shares of Cambodia, Myanmar, Philippines and Thailand in India's total trade with ASEAN have increased more than double in volume but their percentage shares have fallen during the reference period. It can be justified with the statement that India's total trade shows high annual average growth rates of

40%, 37% and 34% with Indonesia, Singapore and Vietnam respectively.

TABLE 17.2
India's Trade Flows with ASEAN

(In US $ Million)

Sl. No.	*Year*	*Export*	*Import*	*Total Trade*	*Trade Balance*
1.	2000	2913.76	4147.48	7061.22	-1233.7
2.	2001	3457.00	4387.22	7844.23	-930.22
3.	2002	4618.54	5150.17	9768.71	-531.63
4.	2003	5821.74	7433.16	13254.9	-1611.4
5.	2004	8425.88	9114.66	17540.54	-688.78

India's export to ASEAN is growing at the annual average rate of 38% and that of import is about 24% (Refer to Table 1.2 in Appendix 1). India's export to Singapore has increased more than three times with an annual average growth rate of 71%. The other significant ASEAN members for India's export destination are Indonesia, Vietnam, Cambodia and Philippines. As far as volume of trade is concerned India imports maximum amount from Singapore with six times increase from 2000 to 2004. But the annual average growth rate of import is highest for Vietnam (120%) followed by Brunei, Philippines, Indonesia and Thailand. Though the India's export is growing faster than import, trade balance continues to remain in favour of ASEAN over the whole period from 2000 to 2004 (See Table 1.3 in Appendix 1). However, the negative trade balance of India has been reduced by 44% during the years. India has trade surpluses with Brunei, Cambodia, Laos, Philippines, Thailand and Vietnam. It has trade deficit with the remaining members. India is having negative as well as increasing trade deficit with Indonesia and Malaysia. Singapore shows fluctuating trade balance over the whole period with India.

It is apparent form the above table that ASEAN has become a major trading partner for India. As compared to the other significant trading partners India's total trade is growing much faster with ASEAN (See Table 17.3). Growth rate of

TABLE 17.3

Growth Rate of India's Total Merchandise Trade with Major Trading Partners

Sl. No.	Major Trading Partners	Growth Rate (2000-04)
1.	ASEAN	29.7
2.	EU	14.9
3.	USA	13.7
4.	World	19.9

India's total trade is almost double for ASEAN as compared to other major trading partners. The data also shows that the India's trade with ASEAN is more than the growth rate of India's trade with the rest of the world throughout the sample period. So ASEAN has become important destination for India.

TABLE 17.4

Indo ASEAN Trade in Global Perspective (2000-04)

Sl. No.	Year	Indo-ASEAN Total Trade as a % of	
		ASEAN Trade with World	India's Trade with World
1.	2000	0.89	7.43
2.	2001	1.10	8.24
3.	2002	1.27	8.56
4.	2003	1.54	9.33
5.	2004	1.66	9.25

However, India is not turning out to be a significant trading partner for ASEAN. Indo ASEAN total trade as a percentage of India's total trade with world has improved from 7.43% to 9.25% (See Table 17.4). Whereas India accounts for 0.89% of ASEAN global trade in 2000. It has increased to 1.66% in 2004. An assessment of shares commanded by India and ASEAN in each other's global trade illustrates the asymmetry in market penetration. ASEAN enjoys a prominent position in India's import market, but India's share in ASEAN's global imports has always been modest. In particular, while Singapore,

Malaysia and Indonesia occupy fairly respectable share in India's total imports, the converse is not true. In the global perspective ASEAN is the fifth most important market in terms of Indian exports and fourth in terms of imports.

4. GRAVITY MODEL AS A TOOL TO PREDICT INDO ASEAN TRADE FLOWS

1. Theoretical Background of the Gravity Model

Gravity theory can be considered as a relational theory which describes the degree of spatial interaction between two or more points in a manner analogous to physical phenomena. Newton's gravity theory states that the gravitational force A_{ij} between two objects i and j is proportional to their respective masses m_i and m_j and inversely proportional to the squared distance d^2_{ij} between these objects. Therefore, this law can be formulated as:

$$A_{ij} = \frac{Fm_i m_j}{d_{ij}^2}$$

F is a gravitational constant. (1)

Several formal attempts have been made to show the presence of gravitational force in the social phenomena. J.Q. Steawart (1948) was among them to do so. With the help of gravitational force, he defines demographic force as constant times the product of two masses divided by the squared the distance separating the masses. Here mass has been measured by population. In empirical studies mass has been measured in number of ways. W. Isard and G. Freutel (1954) used income as a measure of mass and developed the concept of income potential. Gravity theory has proven to be useful in describing social phenomena in space such as population migration, flow of goods, money and information, traffic movement and tourist travel.

According to the gravity approach, trade between two countries is directly related to their income and inversely related to the distance between them. The antecedents for using the gravity approach to model international trade flow date back to

Tinbergen (1962), Poyhonen (1963) and Linnemann (1966). Trade is assumed to occur when domestic production is not equivalent to domestic demand. Essentially, certain fields of production have an advantage in certain regions or countries, which results in specialization of production and division of labour. In trade theory this specialization of production explains why trade occurs in terms of comparative advantage in production. Thus trade theory, as a rule explains why trade in different products but can not explain why some countries' trade links are stronger than others and why the level of trade between countries tend to increase. This indicates the limited applicability of trade theory in explaining the size of the trade flows. On the contrary, the gravity model allows more factors can be taken into account to explain the extent of trade as an aspect of international flows.

Gravity equation in its basic form can be formalized as:

$$T_{ij} = A\frac{GDP_i\ GDP_j}{D_{ij}} \tag{2}$$

where T_{ij} = Trade between country i and j,
A = A constant,
GDP_i/GDP_j = Incomes of the country i and j respectively,
D_{ij} = Distance between two countries

In spite of its empirical success at predicting bilateral trade, initially it lacks theoretical background. Linneman (1966), Leamer and Stern (1970) were the first to provide theoretical justification of the gravity model and many others have followed. Since Anderson (1979) it is no longer true that the gravity model lacks theoretical foundation. It has been showed that gravity equation can be derived from traditional and new theories of trade. There are several formal theoretical foundations for the gravity equation in international trade [Anderson (1979), Bergstrand (1985, 1989 and 1990), Helpman and Krugman (1985), Deardorff (1995)).

2. Estimation of the Gravity Model for Indo-ASEAN Trade

Despite its simplicity, the gravity model explains the pattern of bilateral trade flows extremely well. Its empirical success depends not only in its simplicity in explaining why countries trade in different products but also in its capability in explaining why some countries trade more extensively than others.

The gravity model simply states the volume of trade T_{ij} between countries should be positively related to the countries' income (GDPs) and negatively related to distance D_{ij} between them. Taking logarithm of equation 2 we get:

$$LnT_{ij} = \alpha + Ln(GDP_i) + Ln(GDP_j) - Ln(D_{ij}) + u_{ij} \quad (3)$$

where α = log A and u_{ij} = Disturbance term.

This equation shows the basic form of the gravity model. Here size of the trading partners is measured by GDP. Distance between the trading partners is used as a proxy for trade resistance variables in terms of transport and communication costs. This paper tries to analyse the bilateral trade flows between India and ASEAN members over time. So the data contains both the time series and cross-section parts. To explain the Indo-ASEAN trade the generalized form of the above gravity equation (1) is expressed as:

$$LnT_{ijt} = \alpha + \beta_1 Ln(GDP_{it}^*) + \beta_2 Ln(PCGDP_{it}^*) + \delta Ln(D_{ij}) + u_{ij} \quad (4)$$

i = 10 ASEAN Members and j = India

T_{ijt} = Export from the country of origin i to the trading partner j in export equation or Import from j to i in import equation.

GDP_{it} = Gross Domestic Product of ASEAN Members.

GDP_{jt} = Gross Domestic Product of India.

$PCGDP_{it}$ = Per capita GDP of ASEAN Members

$PCGDP_{jt}$ = Per capita GDP of India

Dis_{ijt} = Distance between India's capital and Foreign capital.

u_{ijt} = Disturbance term.

t = It is the time period varies from 2000 to 2004.

α, β_1, β_2 δ are the parameters which are to be estimated. Here GDP and PCGDP in the model are taken in multiplicative form in accordance with the most popular form of the gravity equation.

The most popular extension of the gravity equation is the inclusion of the dummy variables in the basic equation 4. Here we incorporate the common dummies that are considered in almost all the augmented gravity equation.

These dummies takes care the other factors that may influence trade volume. So the augmented form of the gravity equation can be written as:

$$LnT_{ijt} = \alpha + \beta_1 Ln(GDP_{ti}{}^{*} GDP_{ji}) + \beta_2 Ln(PCGDP_{jt}{}^{*}) + \delta Ln(D_{ij})$$

$$+\gamma_1 (BORDER) + \gamma_2 (BLTAGREE) + \gamma_3 (COLONY) + u_{ijt} \quad (5)$$

Here BORDER, BLTAGREE and COLONY are all dummy variables. γ_1, γ_2, and γ_3 are the coefficients of the dummy variables which are to be estimated in the study.

BORDER = 1, if any of the ASEAN members shares a *common border* with India; = *0*, otherwise.

BLTAGREE = 1, if India is *having any agreement* with any of the members of the ASEAN; = *0*, if not.

COLONY = 1, if any of the ASEAN members are the *colonies*[6] any time in history; = *0*, if not.

By adding the population and area variables into the above model we get the modified version of equation (5) as:

$$LnT_{ijt} = \alpha + \beta_1 Ln(GDP_{ti}{}^{*} GDP_{jt}) + \beta_2 Ln(PCGDP_{ti}{}^{*} PCGDP_{jt}) +$$
$$\beta_3 Ln(Pop_{it} * Pop_{jt}) + \beta_4 Ln(Ar_i * Ar_j) + \delta Ln(D_{ij}) + \gamma_1 (BORDER)$$
$$+\gamma_2 (BLTAGREE) + \gamma_3 (COLONY) + u_{ijt} \quad (6)$$

where Pop_i and Pop_j represents the population of ASEAN members and India respectively. Ar_i, Ar_j show the areas of ASEAN and India respectively.

Depending on the purpose of the study the models in 4, 5 and 6 may further be transformed for estimation.

5. DATA

Here in this paper Indo-ASEAN trade has been considered for the period from 2000 to 2004. The paper studies India's trade with the 10 ASEAN members. So the data pertains to the 10 trading partners with 50 observations.

This paper considers trade in all commodities (HS 2002 classification). Here we represent total merchandise trade which includes both export and import. India's export and import data with ASEAN members have been taken from Director General of Foreign Trade of India. Data for GDP is taken from RBI Handbook of Statistics and ASEAN Statistical Year Book 2005. We obtain PCGDP (Per capita GDP) by dividing GDP with population. Original data are expressed in US dollars. To facilitate comparison across countries and time we need data expressed in real values. To obtain real values the trade and GDP data have been divided with US consumer price index (US CPI). The US CPI data has been taken from US Bureau of Labour Statistics. Distances[7] are measured by great circle air distance between capital cities.

6. ESTIMATION OF THE GRAVITY MODEL FOR INDO ASEAN TRADE

In this paper we have pooled data to be estimated by the gravity model. The relationship between trade flows in one hand and the explanatory variables on the other hand is estimated by ordinary least square (OLS) method.

The gravity equation 4 introduced in the previous section is estimated to calculate the India's trade potential with ASEAN members. The estimated results are presented in the Appendix table. Looking at the regression results for exports (See Table 2.1 in the Appendix 2) it can be seen that the explanatory variables explain 95% variation in the dependent variable of India's export to ASEAN members. Thus the gravity equation fits the export data very well. Export flows from India to ASEAN members are positively correlated with GDP while distance between them is export reducing factor. However, distance is not statistically significant. This can be interpreted as the closeness of the ASEAN members with India. The coefficients of almost (except for the coefficient of the dummy for common border) all the dummies are significant at 1% level and all of them are of expected signs. The estimated coefficient of dummy for regional trading agreement is significant and its value is almost one. Thus it shows that any regional or bilateral trading agreements facilitate trade flows. It implies that India is expected to export more to the ASEAN members with which it is having bilateral or regional agreements. The dummy variable for colony is included in the gravity equation to capture the influence of the previously colonized ASEAN members in the trade flows. The estimated coefficient of this dummy is not only very highly significant but also is of reasonable magnitude. The regression result shows that the estimated coefficient for common border is positively correlated with the India's export to ASEAN members and is statistically significant. Thus the adjacency variable helps to increase bilateral trade flows between India and ASEAN members.

It is also clear from the regression results for import gravity equation that the gravity model fits the import data for India very well. Again GDP variable significantly influences India's import to ASEAN. But gravitational force of income is more important for imports than for exports. However, in both the export and import gravity equations distance is found to be insignificant variable because of the closeness of the ASEAN members with India. Another important difference between the two models is that coefficient of the dummy for common border is comparatively very high (5.58) in import equation than in the export (0.53) one. Furthermore, the coefficient of the dummy for common border is statistically highly significant in the import model. The coefficient of dummy for regional/bilateral trading agreements gives the lower value for import gravity equation. Thus it shows that for India being a part of the any regional or bilateral agreements is more significant for exports than for imports.

7. PREDICTION OF INDIA'S TRADE FLOWS

Now the above mentioned models are explained to predict average exports and imports of India to the ASEAN members and calculate the ratios between actual and predicted trade flows. So this section is devoted to the analysis of ratios between actual and predicted trade flows of India to the ASEAN members.

If the ratio between predicted and actual values for exports (imports) exceeds 1 then India is overtraded in exports (imports) with the corresponding ASEAN member, and if it is less than 1, then it is under traded.

1. India's Actual and Predicted Exports

As to the India's exports, considering trade with all ASEAN members, India's actual exports are more than the predicted, i.e. on the whole India is under traded (Refer to Table 3.1 in Appendix 3). Turning to the trade with different countries India is clearly overtraded with Cambodia, Malaysia, Myanmar, Singapore and Vietnam. But India still has strong trade potential with Brunei, Indonesia, Laos, Philippines and Thailand. India has highest export trade potential with Thailand followed by Laos and Indonesia. As far as India's export is concerned, due to high degree of India's openness to the international trade it is in total 1.14 times overtraded. It should be mentioned that India is overtraded with ASEAN 6 mainly due to intensive trade with Singapore. Actual export flows to Singapore is 3.2 times higher than the predicted. Conclusion about India's export trade potential with ASEAN 6 will change if Singapore is excluded.

2. India's Actual and Predicted Imports

India's import shows the mixed picture of trade potential with ASEAN members. India's actual import is 1.91 times higher than the predicted (See Table 3.1 in Appendix 3). Furthermore, the result suggests that India is overtraded with Brunei, Indonesia, Malaysia, Myanmar and Singapore. However, India is seriously undertraded with Thailand, Vietnam and Laos. In case of Cambodia, India's value of actual import does not differ much with the predicted one. India is overtraded with almost all the members of ASEAN 6 except Philippines and Thailand. But India's actual import from Thailand is seriously behind the predicted one. Due to extensive trade with Singapore, Indonesia and Malaysia India is over trade with ASEAN 6 as a whole.

8. CONCLUSION

The major issue of this paper is to find out the countries with which India is over or undertraded relative to the predicted trade flows by the gravity models and therefore where the trade potential for India can be found. As far as India's trade potential with ASEAN members are concerned the findings are summarized below:

1. India is overtraded both in exports as well as imports with all ASEAN members as a whole.
2. India's actual exports and imports are also higher than the predicted values for ASEAN 6.
3. In case of exports India is undertraded with Brunei, Indonesia, Laos, Philippines and Thailand. India has huge opportunity to expand its export potential with Thailand.
4. India's actual exports is less than the predicted values for Cambodia, Malaysia, Myanmar, Singapore and Vietnam.
5. Brunei, Indonesia, Malaysia, Myanmar and Singapore are the countries with which India is overtraded in case of imports.
6. The value of actual import from Thailand, Vietnam and Laos is far behind the predicted import flows.

Export and import gravity equations were run using India's trade data from the year 2000 to 2004. Both export and import gravity equation explains 90% of the variation in trade flows between India and ASEAN members. It was shown that India's international trade adjusts to the normal gravitational forces of income and is repelling effect of distance to trading partners. Thus India tends to have trade relations with rich countries, but the larger is the distance between India and ASEAN members the smaller is the trade flows between them. Colonial legacy plays an important role in determining Indo-ASEAN trade. India tends to have more trade with those ASEAN members which were colonies any time in history.

Notes

1. Look East Policy was launched by India in 1991 as a response to the end of cold war following the collapse of the Soviet Union. This political consensus has emerged to promote trade liberalization to participate in the new trend of globalization. It was more than a foreign policy for India as it provides a development alternative in the age of globalization.
2. Association of South-East Asian Nations was established on August 8, 1967 in Bangkok by the five original member countries, e.g. Indonesia, Malaysia, Singapore and Thailand. Brunei Darussalam joined on January 8, 1984, Vietnam on July 28, 1995, Laos and Myanmar on July 23, 1997, and Cambodia on April 30, 1999.
3. Asian Regional Forum aims to promote stable relationship between member countries. It can be viewed as useful complement to the bilateral alliances and dialogues between India and ASEAN member countries, which are at the heart of the region's security architecture.
4. The interest rate for India covers the prime lending rate of the five major Public Sector Banks. In case of ASEAN members the interest rate represents 3 months deposit rate.
5. ASEAN 6 consists of Brunei, Indonesia, Malaysia, Philippines, Singapore and Thailand.
6. Brunei, Malaysia, Singapore and Myanmar were the British colonies. Cambodia, Laos and Vietnam were occupied by French colonizers. Indonesia was Dutch colony and US occupied colony was Philippines.
7. Great circle distance is measured between any two longitude-latitude combinations, i.e. as crow flies between two cities. Distance data are taken from www.cepii.fr/anglaisgraph/bdd/distances.htm.

References

Agarwal, P. (2003): 'WTO Negotiations Towards Cancun: Implication on Indian Paper and Newsprint Industry', *Discussion Paper No. 57*, Research and Information System for Non-Aligned and Other Developing Countries (RIS), New Delhi.

ASEAN Secretariat (2005): ASEAN Statistical Year Book, ASEAN Statistical Database.

Asher, M.G., R. Sen and S. Srivastava (2003): 'ASEAN-India: Emerging Economic Opportunities in *Beyond the Rhetoric: The Economics of India's Look-East Policy*' edited by F. Grare and A. Mattoo, Manohar Publications, New Delhi, India, pp. 45-79.

———, (2003): 'India and the Asian Economic Community', *Discussion Paper No. 53*, Research and Information Systems for the Non-Aligned and Developing Countries (RIS), New Delhi, India.

Asher, M.G., Rahul Sen and Ramkishen S. Rajan (2004): 'ASEAN-India Economic Relations Current Status and Future Prospects', *Economic and Political Weekly*, pp. 3296-07.

Batra, Amit (2004): 'India's Global Trade Potential: The Gravity Model', Indian Council for Research on International Economic Relations, *Working Paper No. 151*, December.

Bhattacharya, B. and M. Ariff (2002): 'Study on AFTA-India Linkages for the Enhancement of Trade and Investment', A Report Submitted to the Government of India and the ASEAN Secretariat, May.

Bhattyacharya, S.K. (2004): 'Does Bangladesh Benefit from Preferential Trade with India? A Gravity Analysis', *Economic and Political Weekly*, pp. 5033-43.

Kumar, N (2003): 'India-ASEAN Partnership', *The Hindu*, October 7.

———, (2002): 'Towards an Asian Economic Community: The Relevance of India', *Discussion Paper No. 34*, Research and Information System for Non-Aligned and Other Developing Countries (RIS), New Delhi.

Young, O.K. (2005): 'Advancing the ASEAN-India Partnership in the New Millennium', *Discussion Paper No. 96*, Research and Information System for Non-Aligned and Other Developing Countries (RIS), New Delhi.

www.rbi.org.in, www.asean.org.

APPENDIX 1

TABLE 1.1
India's Total Trade with ASEAN

(in $ US million)

Sl. No.	Countries	2000	2001	2002	2003	2004
1.	BRUNEI	3.46 (0.05)	3.22 (0.04)	4.77 (0.05)	4.93 (0.04)	5.6 (0.03)
2.	CAMBODIA	9.18 (0.13)	12.41 (0.16)	20.45 (0.21)	18.88 (0.14)	18.37 (0.10)
3.	INDONESIA	1309.99 (18.55)	1570.52 (20.02)	2206.93 (22.59)	3249.29 (24.51)	3950.34 (22.52)
4.	LAO PD RP	6.24 (0.09)	3.2 (0.04)	1.73 (0.02)	0.56 (0.00)	2.7 (0.02)
5.	MALAYSIA	1784.95 (25.28)	1907.23 (24.31)	2214.79 (22.67)	2939.33 (22.18)	3383.07 (19.29)
6.	MYANMAR	234.4 (3.32)	435.32 (5.55)	411.11 (4.21)	498.65 (3.761	519.1 (2.96)
7.	PHILIPPINES	265.65 (3.76)	342.63 (5.55)	595.77 (6.101	443.64 (3.35)	599.62 (3.42)
8.	SINGAPORE	2341.02 (33.15)	2276.4 (29.02)	2856.39 (29.24)	4210.22 (31.76)	6652.01 (37.92)
9.	THAILAND	868.04 (12.29)	1056.22 (13.46)	1090.2 (11.16)	1440.75 (10.87)	1767.27 (10.08)
10.	VIETNAM SOC REP	238.29 (3.37)	237.08 (3.02)	366.57 (3.75)	448.65 (3.38)	642.46 (3.66)
11.	ASEAN Total	7061.22	7844.23	9768.71	13254.9	17540.54
12.	ASEAN 6	6573.11 (93.09)	7156.22 (91.23)	8968.85 (91.81)	12288.16 (92.71)	16357.91 (93.26)

Note : Figures in the parentheses are percentage share in total Indo-ASEAN Trade.

Source : ASEAN Statistical Yearbook, 2005; Director General of Foreign Trade, Ministry of Commerce and Industry, Government of India.

TABLE 1.2
India's Trade Relation with ASEAN

($ US Million)

Sl. No.	Countries	Exports					Imports				
		2000	2001	2002	2003	2004	2000	2001	2002	2003	2004
	(1)	(2)	(3)	(4)	(5)	(6)	(7)	(8)	(9)	(10)	(11)
1.	BRUNEI	3.31	2.86	4.45	4.59	5.06	0.15	0.36	0.32	0.34	0.54
2.	CAMBODIA	7.86	11.29	19.84	18.6	18.13	1.32	1.12	0.61	0.28	0.24
3.	INDONESIA	399.75	533.71	826.06	1,127.21	1,332.60	910.24	1,036.81	1,380.87	2,122.08	2,617.74
4.	LAO PD RP	6.24	3.16	1.58	0.43	2.65	0	0.04	0.15	0.13	0.05
5.	MALAYSIA	608.15	773.69	749.37	892.77	1,084.06	1,176.80	1,13;.3:54	1,465.42	2,046.56	2,299.01
6.	MYANMAR	52.71	60.89	75.07	89.64'	113.19	181.69	374.43	336.04	409.01	405.91
7.	PHILIPPINES	202 61	247.79	472	321.53	412.23	63.04	94.84	123.77	122.11	187.39
8.	SINGAPORE	877.11	972.31	1.421.58	2,124.84	4,000.61	1,463.91	1,304.09	1,434.81	2085.38	2,651.40
9.	THAILAND	530.12	633.13	711.2	831.69	901.39	337.92	423.09	379	609.06	865.88
10.	VIETNAM SOC REP	225.9	218.17	337.39	410.44	555.96	12.39	18.91	29.18	38.21	86.5
	Total	2,913.76	3,457.00	4,618.54	5,821.74	8,425.88	4,147.48	4,387.22	5,150.17	7,433.16	9,114.66

Source : ASEAN Statistical Yearbook, 2005; Director General of Foreign Trade, Ministry of Commerce and Industry, Government of India.

TABLE 1.3

India's Balance of Trade with ASEAN

(in $ US Million)

Sl. No.	*Countries*	*2000*	*2001*	*2002*	*2003*	*2004*
1.	BRUNEI	3.16	2.50	4.13	4.25	4.52
2.	CAMBODIA	6.54	10.17	19.23	18.32	17.89
3.	INDONESIA	-510.49	-503.10	-554.81	-994.87	-1285.14
4.	LAO PD RP	6.24	3.12	1.43	0.30	2.60
5.	MALAYSIA	-568.65	-359.85	-716.05	-1153.79	-1214.95
6.	MYANMAR	-128.98	-313.54	-260.97	-319.37	-292.72
7.	PHILIPPINES	139.57	152.95	348.23	199.42	224.84
8.	SINGAPORE	-586.80	-331.78	-13.23	39.46	1349.21
9.	THAILAND	192.20	210.04	332.20	222.63	35.51
10.	VIETNAM SOC REP	213.51	199.26	308.21	372.23	469.46
11.	ASEAN 6	-1331.01	-829.24	-599.53	-1682.90	-886.01
12.	Total	-1233.70	-930.23	-531.63	-1611.42	-688.78

Source : Director General of Foreign Trade of India, Ministry of Commerce and Trade.

APPENDIX 2

TABLE 2.1
Regression Results for Export Gravity Equation

(in $ US million)

Variables	*Coefficients*	*Values*
Intercept	$\bar{\alpha}$	-8.042 (-1.286)
GDP	$\bar{\beta}_1$	1.569** (27.464)
PCGDP	$\bar{\beta}_2$	0.123* (1.906)
Distance	$\bar{\delta}$	-1.054 (-1.336)
BLTAGREE	$\bar{\gamma}_1$	0.984** (3.617)
COLONY	$\bar{\gamma}_2$	1.474** (4.445)
BORDER	$\bar{\gamma}_3$	0.536 (1.519)

Note : ** and * denotes that the coefficients of the explanatory variables are significant at the 1% level and 5% level. R^2 = 0.96 and Adjusted R^2 = 0.95. Figures in the parentheses are t-values.

TABLE 2.2
Regression Results for Import Gravity Equation

(in $ US million)

Variables	*Coefficients*	*Values*
Intercept	$\bar{\alpha}$	-25.233 (-1.479)
GDP	$\bar{\beta}_1$	2.481** (15.923)
PCGDP	$\bar{\beta}_2$	0.388* (2.208)
Distance	$\bar{\delta}$	-0.565 (-0.263)
BLTAGREE	$\bar{\gamma}_1$	0.573 (0.772)
COLONY	$\bar{\gamma}_2$	1.456 (1.610)
BORDER	$\bar{\gamma}_3$	5.582** (5.803)

Note : ** and * denotes that the coefficients of the explanatory variables are significant at the 1% level and 5% level. R^2 = 0.90 and Adjusted R^2 = 0.88. Figures in the parentheses are t-values.

APPENDIX 3

Table 3.1
India's Trade Potential with ASEAN Members in Exports

ASEAN Members	*Potential (Ratio between actual and Predicted values)*
Brunei	0.66
Cambodia	1.61
Indonesia	0.63
Lao	0.62
Malaysia	1.13
Myanmar	1.35
Philippines	0.94
Singapore	3.24
Thailand	0.40
Vietnam	1.29
ASEAN 10	1.14
ASEAN 6	1.05

Note : Author's Estimation.

Table 3.1
India's Trade Potential with ASEAN Members in Exports

ASEAN Members	*Potential (Ratio between actual and Predicted values)*
Brunei	1.08
Cambodia	0.87
Indonesia	1.17
Lao	0.24
Malaysia	2.43
Myanmar	17.62
Philippines	0.65
Singapore	4.08
Thailand	0.15
Vietnam	0.21
ASEAN 10	1.91
ASEAN 6	1.85

Note : Author's Estimation.

FDI in BRIC Economies : How Important?

SUVRANSHU PAN

I. INTRODUCTION

BRIC—named after the economic co-operation among four important trading partners, namely Brazil, Russia, India and China who emerged as the trade giants in the twenty-first century. India, in particular, is more than another BRIC in the wall. It is interesting to know that the year 2006 marks the Indian economy's coming of age in a globalize world. Not only are Foreign Direct Investment (FDI) inflows and outflows at record highs, but also the latter has exceeded the former.

As we know that it is not possible to buy development so cheaply. The provision of foreign capital may yield a more adequate infrastructure but rarely by itself generates rapid development unless there are already large investment opportunities going a-begging. So much, then, for fears expressed in the 1990s over how multinationals would swallow up Indian Industry. FDI inflows during April-October in 2007 was $ 6.1 billion, against $ 2.6 billion in the corresponding period in 2006. They could cross $ 10 billion by March, far more than the inflows in any previous fiscal year. FDI outflows are set to exceed $10 billion this calendar year (2007-08), providing that Indian companies are taking on the world with this products, services and capital.

This paper particularly takes an initiative to find out the macro-economic performance of FDI in BRIC economies. We have analyzed the FDI's macro-role in the following manner. Section I gives some introductory remarks on BRIC economies. Section II analyzes the procedure of building BRIC and role of FDI in India in bridging the competitive gap, fortune of FDI and FDI in retail. Section III suggests the driven force of BRIC economies with macro-economic scenario and performance of FDI in these economies. Section IV emphasizes some suggestions for role of FDI in BRIC.

II. FDI IN INDIA : PROCEDURE OF BUILDING BRIC

If Indian companies are now able to snap up companies abroad, it is in large measure because the Government changed the policy environment. In 1978, a study by the Federation of Indian Chambers of Commerce and Industry (FICCI) notes, the Government used to see overseas investments by Indian companies as a means of promoting Indian exports, among other things. Accordingly, overseas investments were allowed only in the form of joint ventures, with the Indian partner holding a minority stake. The Government was then paranoid about running outs of foreign exchange reserves and did not allow companies to send cash for acquisitions abroad, except in rare cases.

In 1992, the Government allowed automatic clearance for investments of upto $ 2 million. Over the years the limit has been relaxed. Investment in unrelated businesses has also been allowed. However, India Incorporation isn't taking too much money out of the country for its shopping spree. Large companies with a global presence are using the money available with their subsidiaries abroad. Indian firms are also finding it easier to borrow money abroad (it's cheaper, anyway) as foreign lenders are more confident about lending to Indian companies, thanks to the Indian economy's good performance and the robust performance of Indian firms. The Boston Consulting Group's list of 100 global challengers includes 21 Indian companies. These include five Tata Companies (Tata Consultancy Services, Tata Motors, Tata Tea, Tata Steel, Videsh Sanchar Nigam Ltd.), Videocon, Bharat Forge, Cipla, Larsen and Toubro, the Reliance group, Hindalco, Infosys, Wipro, Ranbaxy and the State Owned Oil and Natural Gas Corporation. While China and India are over-represented in the list, China is still far ahead of India with 44 companies on the list. Brazil is far behind with only 12.

TABLE 18.1
Top 10 Deals of 2006

Date	*Foreign Company*	*Indian Company*	*(SM)*
17.10.06	Corus Group, UK	Tata Steel	10,512
14.08.06	Omimex de Columbia, Columbia	OVL/Sinopec	850
28.03.06	Daewoo Electronics, S. Korea	Videocon plus US equity fund	735
23.08.06	Energy Brands, US	Tata Tea	677
16.02.06	Betapharm Arzneimittel, Germany	Dr Reddy's Laboratories	
17.03.06	Eve Holding, Belgium	Suzlon	566
16.06.06	Sinvest, Norway	Aban Lloyd Chiles Offshore	446
29.03.06	Terapia, Romania	Ranbaxy Laboratories	324
04.06.06	Sabah Forest Industries, Malaysia	Ballarpur Ind. plus US equity fund	261
25.06.06	Eight O'Clock Coffee, U.S.	Tata Coffee	220

From Table 18.1, it is found that the deals have been coming swift and fast in 2006 and new records are constantly being set. If the $ 10 billion Corus deal goes through, the Tatas will, of course, leave everyone else in the shade. But other companies are also spending big bucks and moving strongly on foreign markets. So you have Videocon's bid to buy Daewoo Electricals which will cost an estimated $ 735 million. And there's Dr. Reddy's which sheeled out $ 571 million (Rs. 2,250 crore) to buy German pharmaceutical company Betasharm. Today, the tables have been turned, and while Sinar Mas ran into severe financial trouble after the Asian Crisis, Ballarpur has just bought Malaysian company Sabah Forest Industries for $ 261 million. The deal ensures a steady supply of raw material for Ballarpur, which has now become a muscular regional player.

Among the first Indian companies in the international arena were, of course, that fastmoving winners in sectors like software and pharmaceuticals where India has long had an edge of its own. Take a look at Ranbaxy's non-stop buying spree. This year Ranbaxy has bought six pharmaceutical companies--four in Europe, one in the US and another in South Africa. It dipped deep into its pockets and bought Ramanian Firm Terapia for $ 324 million and South African firm Be-Tabs Pharmaceuticals for $ 70 million. Also reviving up and racing into the international racetrack as auto companies like Tata Motors and Mahindra and Mahindra and components firms like Bharat Forge—even though they haven't made any big buys this year. Bharat Forge, particularly, has built its position internationally buying up distressed companies. It's now the world's second largest forging company.

If we look at the future of Indian industrial deal with MNCs with the help of FDI it is found that India has just started out on the acquisition trial and a two-way process is beginning. Two remarks can be made:

- Indians are looking at targets beyond Indian shores, and
- Foreigners are suddenly looking at Indians as potential buyers.

Tata Steel acquired Anglo-Dutch firm Corus for $ 8 billion; Videocon bought South Korea's Dalwoo Electronics for $ 572 million; Aban Lloyd bought Norwegian oil major Sinvest for $ 425 million and Suzlon Energy pocketed Belgium's Hansen Transmission for $ 565 million. A decade and a half of reforms have turned around India's mindset, from one that gleaned opportunities out of crises. In the mid-90s, the secretary general of a leading industry chamber, echoing the views of the Bombay Club, linkened MNC interest in India to a cowboy invasion. Swadeshi groups of the right and left said India would be reduced to an economic and financial banana republic. Where are they today?

FDI inflows of about $ 45 billion in 15 years, which is less than China's FDI in a single year, are more a trickle than a flood. Yet, it is remarkable how this capital infusion transformed India's telecom and financial services sectors in particular. The Indian entrepreneur, far from being steamrolled by competition, has emerged stronger. Those who expected India to be a tiny services engine and little else have been proved wrong. Manufacturing firms too straddle the global stage. According to a recent report by Boston Consulting Group, Brazilian, Russian, Indian and Chinese companies (BRIC economies) are set to impact industries and markets around the world. Of the 100 cutting-edge firms in these countries identified by BCG, a fifth are Indian companies. India opted for opening up the economy as a response to the balance of payments crisis of 1991—and it worked. No longer is it seen as a poor, exotic land of snakes, palaces and elephants. It is recognized, if not feared, for its economic and scientific potential. Having established it as a major emerging economy, its next task is to prove that it is more than another BRIC in the wall. The next year is expected to see a US-led downturn; India's chance lies in turning that into an opportunity. As per as the performance of FDI in India is concerned, India is more than another BRIC in the wall. So,

'Go West, Young Man'.

1. Bridge the Competitive Gap

The four emerging economies, namely India, Brazil, China and Russia are fast 'closing the gap' between themselves and the developed world. According to the IMD *World Competitive Yearbook (2007),* while the US still ranks No. 1 in the world in terms of competitiveness, 40 other economies are either increasing or maintaining their competitiveness. For the first time, the ranking indicates not only the competitive position of nations in 2007 but also their ability to catch up with the leader (the US). The International Institute of Management

Development (lMD) brings the rankings, which take into account factors such as economic performance, government efficiency and infrastructure, out once a year.

Over the years, India has shown a steady rise in its competitiveness. From No. 42 in 2003, India rose to No. 27 in 2006. Its ranking remains unchanged this year. While India has managed a decent performance in both business efficiency and economic performance, it lost out, however, on the infrastructure front. The increase in India's overall competitiveness can be attributed largely to economic performance in which the country ranked 10th, among 55 countries in the world. Infrastructure (50th rank) continues to be a major drag of India's march towards the top. India also scored particularly low on parameters such education and health and environment.

The IMD study also showed that there is room for improvements elsewhere. India has slipped in both economic performance and government efficiency. In economic performance, it lost three positions compared to 2006. In government efficiency, it feels from 30 in 2006 to 33 in 2007.

2. FDI Fortune for India

Bengal doesn't figure high up on the FDI totem pole among Indian states. Placed seventh among the states, its image as a desirable investment destination looks a bit ragged. The bitter truth is that it isn't among the hotspots for foreign investment. Kolkata, as the metropolis of the east, has been trailing behind Mumbai, Chennai, Delhi, Bangalore and even Hyderabad, which is developing at a frenetic pace. Delhi and its immediate neighbourhood of Gurgaon and Noida have emerged as the hottest FDI destination in the country with an inflow of Rs. 12,470 crore during the past three years. Among Indian states, Bengal comes behind the southern states and Gujarat, which has surprisingly fallen behind in the past two years, to the sixth spot. Table 18.2 shows the state-wise break-up for FDI inflows in India from January 2000 to March 2007.

The FDI flows into West Bengal have been down to piffle, just $ 336 million in the last six years from January 2000 to March 2007. This works out to a measly 1.21 per cent of the total

TABLE 18.2
State-wise Break-up for FDI Inflows (2000-07)

State or Region	Amount of FDI Rs. Crore	Amount of FDI $ Billion	Percentage of Total
Delhi & NCT	30,142	6.80	24.85
Maharashtra	26,386	5.80	20.80
Tamil Nadu	9,983	2.20	7.87
Karnataka	9,151	2.02	7.21
Andhra Pradesh	5,177	1.14	4.08
Gujarat	4,140	0.90	3.26
West Bengal	1,531	0.34	1.21

Source : *RBI Bulletin*, June 2007, Mumbai.

FDI flowing into the country. In contrast, the national capital region, including Delhi and adjoining area of Gurgaon and Noida, has succeeded in attracting FDI worth $ 6.8 billion during this period, which accounts for 24.85 per cent of the total inflow. A Rs. 342 crore proposal of Mitsubishi Chemicals for Calcutta figures among the major projects charred for the state during the financial year 2007-08. The Japanese company plans to expand its operations for manufacturing, marketing and distribution of Purified Terephthalic Acid (PTA). But let's be fair that Bengal has several FDI proposals that are in various stages of the approval process. Mitsubishi Chemicals has already announced that it intends to invest another Rs. 1,700 crore in a second plant at Haldia.

The Centre has just cleared Indonesia-based Salim Group's plan to invest $ 500 million (Rs. 2,250 crore) in a clutch of infrastructure projects in the state. But with the land acquisition posing problems in the state after the protests in Singur and Nandigram, senior commerce ministry officials expect the pace of FDI inflows to remain low. A break up of the FDI flows over the past three years show that the state was attracting relatively smaller amounts of FDI compared to the other leading states. At the bottom of the heap are eastern states like Bihar, which have not managed to attract any FDI equity at all. States like Manipur and Meghalaya are also fall in this category. Similarly, Assam, which had seen an FDI inflow of Rs. 19.94 crore during 2003-04, saw the figure drop to Rs. 13.39 crore in 2004-05 and then to nil during 2005-06. Orissa, which is now in line for big ticket investments such as Posco and Mittal Steel, did not see any FDI in the two year period between 2003-05 but managed to attract Rs. 351 crore during 2005-06. Likewise, Jharkhand is yet to open its account even as it is in talks with major players like Mittal Steel. Interestingly, FDI inflows into the national capital region have accelerated with over Rs. 2,064 crore coming in during the first two months of the current year which is nearly half as much as the Rs. 4,565 crore that it attracted during 2006-07. The following Table 18.3 gives details about state-wise inflows of FDI in recent years.

TABLE 18.3

FDI Inflows in Rs. Crore (April-May)

State	*2003-04*	*2004-05*	*2005-06*	*2006-07*
Delhi	2,123	3,718	4,565	2,064
Maharashtra	1,355	3,183	4,290	301
Karnataka	927	1,131	1,818	498
Tamil Nadu	604	358	1,190	1,468
Andhra Pradesh	353	748	1,057	336
Gujarat	610	686	269	2,463
West Bengal	85	467	408	136

Source : *SIA Newsletter*, July 2007, Government of India, New Delhi.

Maharashtra with a total FDI inflow of Rs. 9,130 crore has kept its second rank while adjoining Gujarat has been overtaken by Tamil Nadu and Andhra Pradesh in the last two years. Karnataka with its epicentre at Bangalore has kept its third position over the last three years. The RBI data made available to the ministry of commerce and industry is based on the FDI equity inflows and hence is a good indicator of the amount of productive investment that has flowed into the country. The combined investment for the entire country works out to Rs. 59,283 crore during the last three financial years apart from Rs. 5,416 crore that has come in during the first six months of

2007. The sectoral flows of the FDI equity show that industry-wise telecommunications has attracted the highest amount at Rs. 5,528 crore followed by the transportation industry with Rs. 3,533 crore, chemicals (other than fertiliser) have attracted Rs. 3,063 crore, drugs and pharmaceuticals account for Rs. 2,614 crore and cement and gypsum seeing an inflow of Rs. 2,016 crore. Interestingly, FDI in the services sector has crossed the Rs. 6,995 crore mark with as much as Rs. 1,089 crore coming in April and May of 2007. Consultancy services have accounted for Rs. 1,644 crore in this year.

3. FDI in Retail : Indian Scenario

Entry of FDI in retail, on the backburner since the current central government expressed concern over the fallout of entry of large chains like Wal-Mart on corner stores, might move forward with checks on retooling of cheap imports and monopoly formation—factors that can impact small shops adversely. The view in government is that entry of FDI as well as large domestic players in retail offering a range of goods can be considered afresh once specific measures to buffer "mom and pop" enterprises are put in place. The entry of retail chains has been delayed by political opposition and some manoeuvring within government but has not been shelved altogether.

There is a growing confidence that small shops are not threatened to the extent that has been made out. In fact, corner stores are seen as fairly resilient with their ability to provide "home service" not likely to diminish. While some small shops—ranging from shacks selling eggs, bread and cigarettes to larger commodity and grocery sellers—may have to wind up, most will continue supplying local communities, it is felt. The entry of food chains like McDonalds did not drive the *dhabas* or Indian fast food suppliers out of business. Similarly, small shops will adapt and survive. The government will ensure that large retailers do not deny local markets a fair playing field by supplying cheap imports sourced from countries with low manufacturing costs. This was a valid area of concern and it is suggested to prevent business practices that could deliver an unfair advantage to MNCs and other foreign entrants in retail trade.

Large retailers turning trade in their areas of operator into monopoly structures is another aspect that would be addressed. Steps could be considered to prevent or limit monopolies that could disadvantage suppliers by dictating purchase price. This would hurt suppliers like farmers even though elimination of middlemen is expected to boost their margins. Even as the politically sensitive argument of big chains gobbling small shops is being sorted out, the rapid emergence of mall cultures in cities is referred to as an indicator that big retailing has already arrived even though not yet in the form of chains like Wal-Mart or Asda. Malls offer a range of branded goods competitively priced and are often the preferred distention of shoppers.

There is fallout for business like individual garment sellers, but here again a certain reinvention as inevitable. With the growth of businesses like printing, branded food products, groceries and cosmetics, many kirana-type shops in the 1980s gave themselves a makeover with on degree of success and catered to the new demands of an emergent middle class in India. If we look at some monitoring afresh it is found that:

- Entry of FDI into retail is being monitored by PMO.
- Centre will ensure that large retailers do not supply cheap imports sourced from countries with low manufacturing costs.
- Steps will be considered to prevent or limit monopolies that could disadvantage suppliers by dictating purchase price.

III. BRIC TO DRIVE GROWTH

India, China, Russia and Brazil are emerging among the fastest growing markets, with two out of every seven people in the world will have a personal computer in 2015. The world will see more than two billion personal computers (PCs) in use by 2015 driven by a growing technology aware population as well as falling prices, global research firm Forrester analyzed. The technology research firm said there would be more than one billion PCs in use by the end of 2008, while a rapid growth in emerging markets and expansion into the untapped markets would take the numbers to over two billion by 2015.

The World Bank expects the world population to rise to seven billion by 2015 which simply means that on an average every two out of seven people would use a PC in the next eight years. The four emerging markets—Brazil, Russia, India and China—would account for more. According to Table 18.4 the number of PCs has already crossed 22 million marks at the end of 2007, suggesting one PC for approximately every 50 Indians.

TABLE 18.4
Hot Growth of PC's in BRIC

Year	*World Population (bn)*	*World PCs (no. of units)*	*India's Share*	*BRIC Share*
2007	6.5	1 Billion	22 Million	—
2015	7	2 Billion	—	775 Million

There is nothing more important to the long-term health of the technology industry—and personal technology in particular-than the ability to deliver relevant, accessible and affordable technology to the billions of people worldwide who have not been exposed to it.

1. Macro-economics within BRIC

Brazil

Among the Latin American countries, Brazil continue to benefit from her sound macro-economic policies and structural reforms. The favourable external environment continues to support economic activity, but it is now domestic demand that is leading growth, with private consumption and business investment growing briskly. Inflation, although remaining generally well contained, has picked up, while the current account recorded a surplus of 0.4 percent of GDP in 2006 (Table 18.5). Given the recent uptick in inflation, central bank of Brazil has appropriately tightened monetary policy, and has thereby enhanced the credibility of their relatively new

TABLE 18.5
Macro-Scenario in BRIC

Country	*Real GDP*				*Consumer Prices*				*Current Account Balance*			
	2003	2004	2005	2006	2003	2004	2005	2006	2003	2004	2005	2006
(1)	(2)	(3)	(4)	(5)	(6)	(7)	(8)	(9)	(10)	(11)	(12)	(13)
Brazil	0.5	5.2	3.7	3.5	14.8	6.6	6.5	4.6	0.8	1.9	1.1	0.4
Russia	7.3	7.1	6.0	5.5	13.7	10.9	11.8	9.7	8.2	10.2	11.4	8.7
India	7.5	7.3	6.7	6.4	3.8	3.8	4.0	3.6	1.2	0.3	-0.3	-0.3
China	9.3	9.5	8.5	8.0	1.2	3.9	3.0	2.5	3.2	4.2	4.2	4.0

Source : World Economic Outlook, 2007, April, IMF.

inflation—targeting framework. Exchange rate flexibility has played a key role in supporting this framework, as well as in helping to improve external sector performance and increasing the region's resilience to shocks. Inflow of FDI thus helps a vital role in Brazil in recent years. While the inflation-targeting framework do not preclude intervention in the foreign exchange market, intervention needs to be consistent with achieving the inflation objective in Brazil. Here government's adherence to sound macro-economic policies and its pursuit of structural reforms are paying-off.

Russia

GDP growth is as expected to moderate to more sustainable levels in 2007 in Russia. The outlook remains generally favourable; external and commodity price developments are expected to be generally supportive of activity, although capacity constraints and inadequate investment are beginning to limit the benefits that some economies can reap. Russia has made impressive progress on disinflation in recent years with sound monetary and fiscal policies in the context of a commodity price boom. GDP growth in Russia slowed in the second half in 2007, mainly owing to weakening oil production growth and a slowing of investment. Despite the slowdown, inflationary pressures remain strong with labour markets in high-growth regions particularly tight. With credit growth booming, heightened vigilance over banks' portfolios in desirable, accompanied by increased efforts to strengthen bank supervision.

India

In 2007, GDP growth in emerging Asia picked up to 7.8 percent of which real GDP grews at 7.5 percent in this period. India partly reflected by substantial oil price subsidies, reflected in a commensurate deterioration in the fiscal position. In recent years, GDP growth in India has slowed modestly, but is expected to remain robust, with the impact of uneven monsoons and higher oil prices being offset by buoyant industrial activity and strong investment. The RBI has raised interest rates and allowed somewhat more exchange rate flexibility, which eased liquidity conditions. Still short-run interest rate is low here. Agricultural reform, which is critical for poverty reduction, and trade, capital liberalization and FDI inflow exposed to interest rate risk given its large holding of government securities.

China

GDP growth in China has remained very strong. Recent real effective depreciation of the renminbi and continued strong productivity growth relative to trading partners would help mitigate possible adverse effects on employment. On the fiscal side, the deficit in recent past was considerably lower than budgeted primarily owing to surging revenues, maintaining a tight fiscal stance would help contain demand pressures, as well as help address medium-term expenditure pressures arising from potential bank restructuring and pension liabilities, and social and infrastructure needs. Further progress with bank and public enterprise reforms remains critical in China. Greater labour market flexibility in China would also help manage the challenges of a rapidly growing labour force.

2. Performance of FDI in BRIC

The ascent of multinational firms has played an important role in overall trade growth and in the changes in the composition of trade. FDI inflows and outflows are good indicators of increasingly international nature of firms in BRIC economies. With inflow and outflow of FDI, these four countries coming closure in recent times.

Table 18.6 gives the overall picture of capital flow worldwide. Total capital flows (net) moves from $ 157.3 billion in 1998 to $ 189.6 billion in 2007. Here we have found that net official flows shown some negative trend in recent years though net private flows grew from $ 107.5 billion in 1998 to $ 212.1 billion in 2007. The flow of net foreign direct investment showed some ups and downs picture. It increased in 2001 with $ 177.2 billion from $ 159.5 billion in 1998 but decreased to $ 167.3 billion and again increased to $ 203.5 billion in 2004 and 2007 respectively.

TABLE 18.6
Capital Flows World-wide

(US $ bn.)

Capital Flows	*1998*	*2001*	*2004*	*2007*
Total Capital Flows, net	157.3	88.7	159.3	189.6
(a) Net Official Flows	56.3	13.5	-48.3	-49.9
(b) Net Private Flows	107.5	74.9	192.4	212.1
(i) Net Direct Investment	159.5	177.2	167.3	203.5
(ii) Private Portfolio Investment (net)	22.6	-49.4	52.7	44.6
(iii) Other Private Flows (net)	-74.7	-52.9	-27.6	-36.0

Sources : (i) World Economic Outlook, 2007, IMF.
(ii) Statistical Outline of India, TATA, 2008.

In Table 18.7 we have placed the inflow of FDI in BRIC economies. India improved marginally in this matter but Brazil shown an impressive growth in inflaming FDI. China and Russia rather maintain a static rate of inflow in recent past. The table also shows that inflow of FDI in the world also moved very vast from $ 127.5 billion in 1990 to $ 1449.8 billion in 2005

TABLE 18.7
Inflow of FDI in BRIC Economies

(US $ bn.)

Country	*1990*	*1995*	*2000*	*2005*	*2007*
India	0.2	2.1	2.3	5.7	7.2
China	3.5	35.8	40.8	44.2	48.4
Brazil	0.9	5.5	30.7	32.8	22.6
Russia	5.4	54.5	62.5	81.3	88.5
Developing Countries	20.3	106.2	240.2	248.5	231.4
Developed Countries	100.6	208.4	1005.2	1241.5	531.8
World	127.5	328.9	1270.8	1489.8	1129.2

Sources : (i) Statistical Outline of India, TATA, Various Issues.
(ii) RBI Bulletin, January 2008.

but decreased to $ 1129.2 in 2007. Industries also showed some imbalances in the requirements of FDI. Inflow of FDI in developed countries moved to $ 1241.5 billion in 2005 from $ 100.6 billion in 1990 and decreased to $ 531.8 billion in 2007. The case is also same for the developing countries where inflow of FDI moved a high of $ 248.5 billion in 2005 from $ 20.3 billion in 1990 but sliced down to $ 231.4 billion in 2007. The smallest receiver of FDI from BRIC economies is remains India with $ 0.2 billion in 1990 and $ 7.2 billion in 2007. This inflow moved gradually for China and Russia as both countries accepted lots of FDI in recent past. The figure for China is $ 3.5 billion in 1990 to $ 48.4 billion in 2007 and for Russia it is $ 5.4 billion in 1990 to $ 88.5 billion in 2007. For Brazil the inflow is not increased properly as it increased from $ 0.9 billion in 1990 to $ 32.8 billion in 2005 but down to $ 22.6 billion in 2007.

Table 18.8 shows some discrepancies in global FDI capital flows in recent past. BRIC economies also faced the same

TABLE 18.8
Discrepancies in Global FDI Capital Flows

(US $ bn.)

	1990	*1995*	*2000*	*2005*	*2007*
Total					
Abroad	-224.3	-333.8	-442.5	-1375.5	-620.9
In Reporting Economy	197.7	327.9	461.4	1489.8	729.2
Discrepancy	-26.6	-5.9	18.9	114.3	108.3
Equity Capital					
Abroad	—	-183.1	-237.5	-993.6	-349.7
In Reporting Economy	—	230.0	274.9	975.7	442.5
Discrepancy	—	46.9	37.4	-17.9	92.8
Reinvested Earnings					
Abroad	-46.7	-97.2	-123.1	-185.7	-145.1
In Reporting Economy	1.2	38.4	65.1	119.7	62.3
Discrepancy	-46.5	-58.8	-58.0	-66.0	-82.8
Other Capital					
Abroad	—	-53.5	-81.9	-196.2	-126.1
In Reporting Economy	—	59.5	121.4	394.4	224.4
Discrepancy	—	6.0	39.5	198.2	98.3

Source : IMF, BOPSY, Various Issues.

problem in FDI inflow. Table 18.9 shows the discrepancies in global FDI investment income flows. The case is also same for the BRIC economies. To maintain a solid trade partnership for these four member countries, the strong bond of FDI inflow and outflow is must among these nations. For macro-economic development and better performance in the balance of payment, the gaps of saving-investment and trade gap are duly removed with proper balances of FDI inflows and outflows.

TABLE 18.9

Discrepancies in Global FDI Investment Income Flows

(US $ bn.)

	1990	*1995*	*2000*	*2005*	*2007*
Total					
Credit	130.4	206.5	267.8	375.5	341.7
Debit	83.4	161.9	203.4	336.7	290.4
Discrepancy	47.0	44.6	64.4	38.8	51.3
Dividends and Distributed Branch Profits					
Credit	—	100.7	126.1	157.9	156.7
Debit	—	101.8	110.2	163.1	165.5
Discrepancy	—	-1.1	15.9	-5.2	-8.8
Reinvested Earnings					
Credit	46.7	97.2	123.1	185.7	145.1
Debit	1.2	38.4	65.1	119.7	62.3
Discrepancy	45.5	58.8	58.0	66.0	82.8
Interest					
Credit	—	8.6	18.6	31.9	39.9
Debit	—	21.7	28.1	53.9	62.6
Discrepancy	—	-13.1	-9.5	-22.0	-22.7

Source : IMF, BOPSY, Various Issues.

6. CONCLUDING REMARKS

Since 2005, BRIC economies came closure and formed a strong union, which is not in the same leagues of ASEAN, WTO,

SAFTA and SAARC. The member countries of BRIC set-up an unbroken agenda on co-operation in social, economic, financial, external and infrastructure matters by which these economies establish this institution. Foreign direct investment is a proven beneficial for these economies. Since the economic reforms in mid-eighties, India has opened her economy to foreign economies. China and Brazil opened their economies first after the Indian reformation was taken place though Russia was an old customer in the business.

It is just the beginning for all the four member countries to sit together, act together and benefited accordingly. Russia, member of the G-8 economies, can resemble this relationship with strong bonding with the other three nations. Hope these BRIC nations will share the maximum percentage in world trade with inflow of FDI and policy-makers do achieve the initiatives taken by them. From the growing importance of India, Brazil and China in world market, it is hopeful that BRIC economies would be the leader of world with their performances in respective fields. Like bricks of a solid wall, BRIC countries also be able to build up a concrete upstairs in the world market soon.

References

Ananda Bazar Patrika, 2007, 'Briddhir Adhar', Vol. 85, No. 293, January 2, Tuesday, Kolkata.

Balakrishnan, Paran, 2006, 'The Great Shopping Spree', *The Telegraph*, Sunday, December 17, Kolkata.

Deshpande, Rajew, 2007, 'Retail FDI Back on Agenda', *The Times of India*, July 24, New Delhi.

Forrester, 2007, *Worldwide PC Adoption Forecast, 2007 to 2015*, New Delhi.

IMD, 2007, World Competitive Yearbook, Institute of Management Development, Laussane, Switzerland.

IMF, 2006, World Economic Outlook, World Economic and Financial Surveys.

Mahajan, Nilima, 2007, 'BRIC Builders Bridge the Competitive Gap', *The Times of India*, Friday, May II, Kolkata.

Pan, S. and R.K. Sen, 2007, Foreign Direct Investment and Trade in India, Deep and Deep Publications, New Delhi.

Pan, S., 2005, Globalization, Foreign Direct Investment and Indian Economy, *RBU Occasional Papers*, Vol. XII, pp. 29-35, February, Kolkata.

Pan, S., 2004, Foreign Direct Investment and Indian Economy Since 1991, Ph.D. Thesis (Unpublished), R.B.U., Kolkata.

Pan, S., 2007, West Bengal as a Destination of Foreign Direct Investment, in Sen and Dasgupta (eds.) : *West Bengal Today—25 Years of Economic Development*, pp. 255-79, Deep and Deep Publications, New Delhi.

RBI, *Reserve Bank of India Bulletin*, Various Issues, New Delhi.

Summers, Lawrence, 2006, 'Go West, Young Man', *The Times of India*, Tuesday, December 26, Kolkata.

TATA, *Statistical Outline of India*, Various Issues, Mumbai.

UNCTAD, 2001, *World Investment Report: Promoting Linkages*, UN.